MW01011505

The Vegetable Book
A Texans Guide to Gardening

The VEGETABLE BOOK

A Texan's guide to gardening

by Dr. Sam Cotner

Editor:
Rita Miller

Book Design:
Don Mulkey

Illustrations:
Mike Lee
Don Mulkey

Photographs:
Used by permission of:
Art Abbott
William D. Adams
Chris S. Corby
Sam Cotner
Jerry Parsons
Betsy Ritz
Mary Gail Rundell
Texas Gardener Magazine

TG Press
P.O. Box 9005
Waco, Texas 76714

Library of Congress Catalog Card Number: 85-62379.
ISBN: 0-914641-01-8
Printed in Japan by Dai Nippon Printing Co. Ltd. through DNP (America), Inc.

To my wife Ann, and children Kelli and Steven for their patience and understanding; to my friends and co-workers for sharing their knowledge and expertise; and especially to my parents for encouraging my interest in the wonderful world of horticulture.

TABLE OF CONTENTS

APPENDICES

INTRODUCTION

No where but Texas are vegetable gardeners faced with so many bugs, blights and soil maladies, not to mention drought and other weather related problems.

To be successful, a Texas gardener needs access to accurate, relevant information pertaining to Texas conditions. Nothing makes a Texan madder than to have someone from Connecticut or Illionis tell him how to garden, or to plant varieties touted for northern climes and have them fail miserably in Texas. What a Texan really needs is information designed to help him or her garden successfully right here in Texas.

Just as TEXAS GARDENER magazine strives to meet these needs on an ongoing basis, this book is intended to be a comprehensive source of information written specifically for gardeners in the Lone Star State. It represents a compilation of over 30 years of practical hands-on experience by Dr. Sam Cotner, an avid home gardener and one of the state's most respected professional horticulturists.

We've organized the book by specific crops. So if it's time to plant beans, just flip to the chapter on beans and you will find everything you need to know about growing them, from soil preparation to variety selection to disease control. You don't have to wade through chapter, after chapter to pick out the information you need for a specific crop.

We've spared no detail in covering 31 major Texas crops ranging from asparagus to watermelons. In lesser detail, we've also covered 15 minor crops such as horseradish, chives and endive. Also included are appendices intended to compliment each chapter by providing information common to all crops.

This book is no substitute for hard work or good weather, but it can help you overcome our tough growing conditions and have the most productive vegetable garden ever.

Chris S. Corby
Editor/Publisher
TEXAS GARDENER

ASPARAGUS

Scientific Name: *Asparagus officinalis*
Family: *Liliaceae*
Perennial
Cool Season
Varieties: UC 157, Jersey Giant
Expected Harvest: 8 to 12 spears per crown per year

ASPARAGUS

Asparagus has been around almost since the beginning of recorded history. The Egyptians, Greeks and Romans all treasured it as a culinary delicacy to be enjoyed primarily by the elite of their societies. With the fall of the Roman Empire, its availability and popularity declined, but not for long. Asparagus soon graced the tables of Europe and spread to England by the 1650s. Early settlers brought it to the United States where it has grown continually in popularity—and price!

In fact, if you were going to categorize any one vegetable as sophisticated, it probably would be asparagus. It's one of the *classy* foods that's year round, pound for pound, one of the most expensive vegetables available in supermarkets across Texas. As a result, asparagus, or grass as it's called in the produce trade, is considered by most of us Texans to be a luxury at the dinner table—unless you either have an oil well or, more likely, you grow your own!

Asparagus can grow anywhere in Texas, but how well it does and how well satisfied you will be with it depends on two factors—where it's grown and your greed at harvesttime.

Generally, the farther north you garden in Texas, the better luck you will have with asparagus. The reason for this is fairly complex, but worth explaining. The root system of the asparagus plant consists of a combination of feeder roots, rhizomes and, most importantly, fleshy storage roots. The shoots (spears) produced in the early spring come from buds on the rhizomes, which are actually underground stems and not roots. The materials stored in the storage roots and used for spear production are the result of the photosynthetic activities of the plant during the growing season. Photosynthesis is the process carried out in the leaves of plants to manufacture the carbohydrates needed for growth and development. Bright warm days, along with cool or cold nights, cause the plants to manufacture more carbohydrates than is needed for asparagus plants to grow and the excess is accumulated in the fleshy storage roots.

Conversely, year-round temperate growing conditions and warm nights inhibit this excessive carbohydrate production and its accumulation in the storage roots. Therefore, the warm days and nights so common in South Texas most of the year cause asparagus plants to use most of their photosynthetic products for current growth, with little excess accumulated in the storage roots for next year's crop of spears. The results should be obvious: declining production of fewer and smaller spears.

If you garden in the area south of San Antonio, you will experience the problem of declining production. However, you can minimize the effects of the warm temperatures by reducing the length of the harvest period, which should not be longer than about four weeks. This will allow the plants, or ferns, to develop earlier and have a longer period to manufacture and accumulate carbohydrates in their storage roots for next year's crop of spears. This is especially true during the first two or three harvest periods.

More on harvesting later! However, it's important to remember that it's the foliage of the asparagus plant that produces next year's harvest. So curb your appetite and avoid harvesting for too long of a period in the spring.

Preparing Your Asparagus Bed

Asparagus is a perennial crop and hopefully will occupy space in your garden for a number of years. Therefore, considerable thought and effort should go into deciding where to locate your asparagus bed and into getting the ground ready for planting.

Full-size asparagus plants can grow to a height of 5 feet or more so it's a good idea to plant them on the north side of your garden to avoid shading low-growing crops. Also, you should not plant anything else within 4 feet of your asparagus bed to allow for easy harvesting and to prevent root damage when you're preparing the soil for other garden crops.

I've intentionally used the term "bed" several times to describe an asparagus planting area simply because the term is very descriptive and accurate. A bed, in the minds of most folks, instantly is associated with comfort and enjoyment. Similarly, every effort should be made to properly make up the bed, because the comfort provided the asparagus plants will reward you with lots of enjoyment come harvesttime!

It's absolutely imperative that your asparagus bed be well-drained. If your soil is heavy and tight, the addition of liberal amounts of organic matter will help greatly. If you think poor soil drainage still might be a

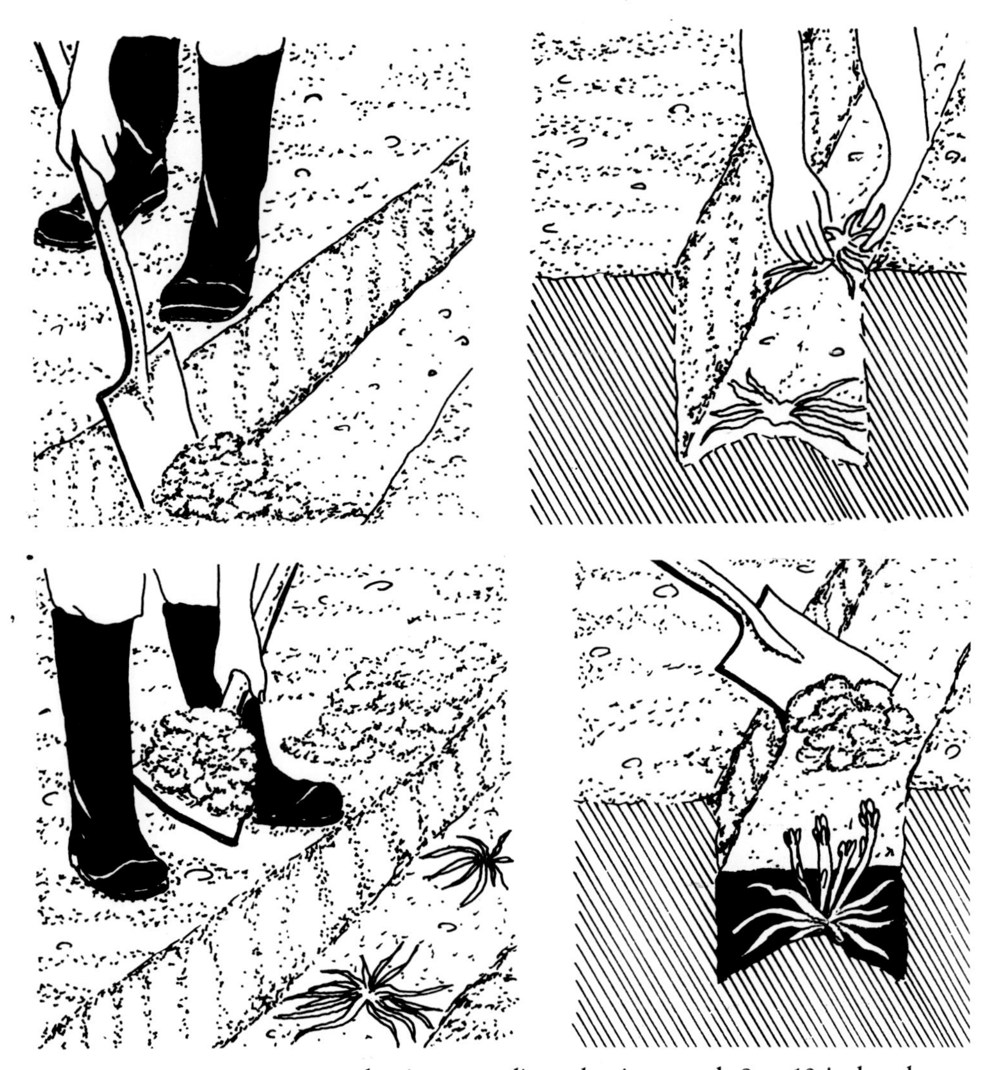

To prepare your asparagus planting area, dig a planting trench 8 to 10 inches deep. Place the crowns in the trench and cover with soil. As plants grow, gradually fill the trench with soil.

problem, consider building an elevated bed using railroad ties, cinder blocks or a similar material.

An ideal asparagus bed is 3½ to 4 feet wide and can be as long as your appetite is big. Spade or till the area for your future bed at least 10 to 12 inches deep—the deeper the better. Afterwards, spread 3 to 4 inches of organic matter, such as well-decomposed leaves, grass clippings or hay, over the area. Also add aged barnyard fertilizer at the rate of about ½ pound per square foot. In addition, the plants usually will benefit from the use of a complete fertilizer, such as 10-20-10, applied at the rate of ½ pound per 100 square feet of bed area.

If you are gardening in acid soils that have a pH of less than 6.0, which is common in some areas of East Texas, lime should be added. The amount of lime needed will vary greatly, depending on your soil type and its degree of acidity. Generally, about 2 to 6 pounds of agricultural limestone per 100 square feet of bed will correct any pH problem. Use the lower rate if your soil is sandy and the higher rate for heavy soils. (For more information on adjusting your soil's pH, see page 394.) After you have applied all the necessary "ingredients," thoroughly mix them into the soil. At last, after much effort, your bed finally is ready for planting!

The bed preparation just described can occur at any time of year, regardless of where you live in Texas. However, since newly planted crowns can be damaged if exposed to extremely cold temperatures, planting should occur only in late winter or early spring, depending on your location.

Planting Of The Crown

Crowns are the root system of the asparagus plant. Asparagus can be grown from seed or transplants, but the ideal situation is to plant 1- to 2-year-old crowns that have a healthy, vigorous and well-developed mass of roots. When buying your crowns, avoid those that appear old, woody and dried out. Occasionally, nurseries and garden centers offer 3-year-old crowns, but don't purchase them because they generally lack vigor and will do poorly.

After you get the crowns, plant as soon as possible. However, if planting is delayed, keep them from drying out by placing them in a plastic bag in your refrigerator where they will keep for about a week.

A properly prepared asparagus bed easily can accommodate two rows of asparagus spaced 2½ to 3 feet apart. Use a shovel or heavy hoe to dig planting furrows or trenches. If your soil is sandy, dig the furrows about 10 inches deep. If your soil is heavy, they should be only about 8 inches deep. The furrows should be about as wide as they are deep. (If you plant two rows on each bed, it's best to work on one row at a time.) Cover the bottom of the furrow about 2 inches deep with a mixture of half compost and half well-rotted barnyard fertilizer, along with about 1 teaspoon of phosphate fertilizer for each foot of row. If you do not have access to barnyard fertilizer, use a complete fertilizer, such as 10-20-10, at the same rate as the phosphate. Next, apply about an inch of good soil to the bottom of the furrow so that the crowns won't be in direct contact with the banded fertilizer. Immediately before setting the crowns, form the bottom of the planting furrow into a slightly ridged mound.

Place the crowns 15 to 18 inches apart in the furrow. Avoid the temptation to space the plants closer together because the result will be a large percentage of smaller spears. When positioning the crowns, make certain the roots spread in an outward direction over the ridged mound. Don't worry about whether the crowns are upside down or not—it doesn't make any difference. Cover the crowns with 2 inches of soil as soon as possible so they don't dry out.

If you plant two rows per bed as recommended, stagger the crowns so that they are not directly across from each other in the rows. If you do as suggested and work on one row at a time, simply mark the position of two of the crowns on the first row planted. Start placing the crowns in the second row midway between these markers and continue setting them at 15- to 18-inch intervals.

After covering the crowns, water well. Within a few weeks, the first young spears will emerge. As they grow, gradually fill in the furrow with soil until it is level with the garden surface, taking care not to cover the asparagus foliage. This process probably will take several months, but should be accomplished by early summer. Once the furrow is completely filled, mulch around the plants with 2 inches of organic matter to conserve moisture and keep out weeds. Any weeds that do grow up should be removed as soon as possible.

Crooked spears can be the result of insect or wind damage and can be prevented by controlling insects and planting a windbreak, if necessary.

Care And Cultivation

Starting at planting and continuing through the first year, asparagus must have adequate soil moisture and fertility to encourage vigorous foliage growth and development of a strong root system. For the first two years your asparagus bed will require the equivalent of an inch of water per week during the growing season, applied either by you or Mother Nature. During this same period of time and prior to the emergence of the spears, a nitrogen fertilizer such as ammonium sulfate (21-0-0) should be applied at the rate of about 1/4 pound per 100 square feet of bed. If barnyard fertilizer is available, it can be scattered over the bed surface at the rate of about 50 pounds per 100 square feet of bed.

The asparagus plants will grow vigorously during spring and summer months but their growth will slow as temperatures cool in the fall. To encourage the production of spears in the spring, the tops must be removed. In the northern parts of Texas, this operation should occur after the foliage is killed by the first hard freeze. In areas where the temperatures are not severe enough to kill the tops, they should be removed when they turn yellow, which usually is in late fall or early winter. Use a sharp knife to cut the plant stalk near or just below ground level. After removing the tops, use a shovel or hoe to mound the asparagus rows. This will provide protection from extreme cold in the northern parts of Texas and will insulate the crowns from the unfavorably warm temperatures in the south.

Be careful when harvesting asparagus not to damage the plant. Use a kitchen knife or special aspargus knife to cut the spears just below ground level. At the end of the growing season, cut the plants back to about ground level.

About the time you decide to cut back the asparagus tops at the end of the first growing season, you also should consider removing those plants that produce berries. Asparagus produces both male and female plants and the female produces small, red berries. The female plants generally are few in number, less vigorous and produce smaller and fewer spears. Also, these berries will drop to the ground, germinate and produce additional asparagus plants that will act like weeds and cause crowded conditions. To avoid these problems, simply dig up the crowns that produce female plants. Those spaces left vacant can be replanted the following spring. Within two years after planting, all your asparagus plants should be male and potentially highly productive.

During these first two years, care and maintenance of your asparagus bed is fairly routine—watering, fertilizing, weeding and removing the tops in the winter, but no harvesting! However, if your patience runs thin and is aggravated by an overwhelming desire for a taste of your own garden-grown asparagus, you can cheat just a little and harvest a *mess* for the dinner table during the second year. But refrain from harvesting more than two spears from each crown.

The First Harvest

The third year in the life of asparagus plants (two years after planting 1-year-old-crowns), you'll need to modify your cultural and harvesting practices. In early spring (or when appropriate), harvest all the spears when they are about 6 inches tall, regardless of their diameter. Use a sharp kitchen knife or special asparagus knife and cut diagonally through the spear just below ground level. This will prevent a clump of woody stumps from developing above ground. Be careful when harvesting to avoid damaging nearby developing and emerging spears.

Regardless of where you live in Texas, this first harvest season should last only about four weeks. This will allow the continued strengthening of the storage root system. In following years, except for you folks in South Texas, the harvest season can be lengthened to as long as eight weeks. However, remember the importance of foliage growth, and refrain from literally "harvesting your asparagus to death." A good rule of thumb is to stop harvesting when the spears are less than 3/8 inch in diameter.

You also should be aware that the spears will emerge in three or four flushes, probably with two-thirds of the production occurring during the first half of the harvest season. During this period, you probably will have to harvest daily. However, don't be too concerned if the spear production tapers off as the season progresses.

From the third year (first clean harvest season) on, rather than fertilize before the spears emerge, apply the fertilizer about two weeks before the end of harvest. Use the same type of fertilizer but increase the rate to ½ pound per 100 square feet of bed area. Also, to make certain yields remain high for the next year, be sure the plants get enough moisture after harvest and when the ferns are developing. Continuing to mulch around the plants will help maintain adequate soil moisture.

Insects Not A Major Problem

Asparagus is one of the few vegetables grown in Texas that is not continually the target of numerous insects and diseases. Cutworms can be a problem and will attack the emerging spears, just as they do other plants such as tomatoes and peppers. The use of an approved insecticide applied to the soil before the spears emerge will give satisfactory control. Occasionally, and especially during dry years, grasshoppers will feed on the ferns, but cause little actual damage. However, severe infestations should be controlled. Asparagus beetles are not common in Texas, but if they do become a problem, they're easily controlled with a general purpose insecticide such as Sevin.

Occasionally, asparagus is plagued by a foliage disease that results in spots or lesions forming on the leaves, stems and sometimes on the spears. Cercospora leaf spot and rust can be controlled by applications of a fungicide containing zineb or maneb, applied at seven- to 10-day intervals.

Weeds in your asparagus bed must be controlled because they compete with the asparagus plants for nutrients and moisture. Mulching and hand pulling weeds that come up probably is the best method of control. If you use a hoe, be sure to cultivate lightly to avoid damaging developing spears. Also, avoid the fairly common practice of using table salt for weed control, even though asparagus is fairly salt-tolerant and most weeds are not. The long-term effect of continued applications of salt will take its toll, causing poor yields and early death of the asparagus plants.

Even though asparagus is a perennial, it will not live productively forever. In the northern areas of Texas, you can expect your asparagus bed to produce quantities of spears for 12 to 15 years. In South Texas, however, eight to 10 years of harvest should be anticipated.

With good cultural care, you should harvest an average of eight to 12 spears from each crown annually. Again, higher yields will occur in the northern part of the state.

Quick Problem Solver: Asparagus

Problem	Causes	Solutions
Weak foliage growth.	Used old, weak crowns at planting.	Consider replanting. Apply fertilizer and under no circumstances harvest until third season.
	Acid soil.	Top dress with limestone, lightly incorporate and water. Have soil tested.
	Poorly drained soil.	Dig crowns in late winter, apply additional organic matter/sand to bed and replant. Consider using raised beds.
Woody, fibrous spears.	Low fertility.	Apply fertilizer two weeks before end of harvest to eliminate problem next season and maintain good soil mixture.
Crooked, misshapen spears.	Damage by insects, windblown sand or during harvest.	Control insects early in season. Consider planting a windbreak, especially if you garden in West Texas. Use care when harvesting to avoid damage to adjacent, developing spears.
Small, spindly spears.	Crowns too close together.	Remove extra crowns to obtain correct spacing. Too wide a spacing is better than crowded conditions.
	Low soil moisture previous year.	Maintain good soil moisture, especially for several months following harvest.
	Harvesting too long.	Immediately stop harvesting.
Spots on stems, leaves.	Cercospora leaf spot or other fungal disease.	Apply a fungicide, such as maneb or zineb.
Seedling asparagus plants in bed.	Female plants producing berries.	Remove crowns of female plants and replant.
Declining production.	Poor cultural care.	Fertilize, water and mulch.
	Harvesting too long.	Reduce length of harvest to allow for longer foliage growth. Curb appetite!
	Warm weather conditions.	Consider establishing new asparagus bed. Move North!

BEANS

Scientific Name:
  Green Beans: *Phaseolus vulgaris*
  Limas: *Phaseolus lunatus*
Family: *Leguminosae*
Annual
Warm Season
Varieties:
  Green Beans: Tendercrop, Topcrop, Greencrop, Blue Lake, Improved Horticultural; (pole) Kentucky Wonder, Dade; (wax) Gold Crop, Cherokee Wax
  Limas: Fordhook 242, Jackson Wonder; (nematode resistant) Nemagreen; (pole) King of the Garden
Expected Harvest: 3 to 5 pounds per 10 feet of row

BEANS

Beans are among the oldest and most important food crops in the world, both nutritionally and economically. Various types of beans were common foods in the Old World long before Christopher Columbus discovered America. And when he finally did find the New World, Columbus also found two new types of beans, green beans and lima beans, which were commonly cultivated by the natives. Both types probably originated in Guatemala and were spread northward through Mexico and the Southwest United States by migrating tribes of Indians.

The word *bean,* like the word vegetable, is indefinite and commonly used to describe the seed of many different plants. However, from this point on, bean will refer to green, shell and dry beans, a common but somewhat confusing classification based on use.

Green beans usually are called garden, snap, wax and string beans. All are grown for their immature pods. Shell beans are grown primarily for their immature and tender, but large, seed. Dry beans are allowed to fully ripen before they are harvested and can be dried and stored.

Even with this explanation, classifications are still indefinite because some kinds of beans can be used in one or more of these forms. For example, the pinto bean can be enjoyed green, shelled or dried. To add to the confusion, beans also are classified according to their growth habit, which is either bush or pole. And green, shelled and dry beans all come in both bush and pole varieties.

Regardless of how beans are classified, used or grown, their culture is basically the same—with a few exceptions. But it's these exceptions that can cause you problems!

Beans And Beneficial Bacteria

Before we deal with their culture, let's discuss a little bean taxonomy and botany. Beans, peas and a number of other crops are members of the legume family, which makes them rather unique in the

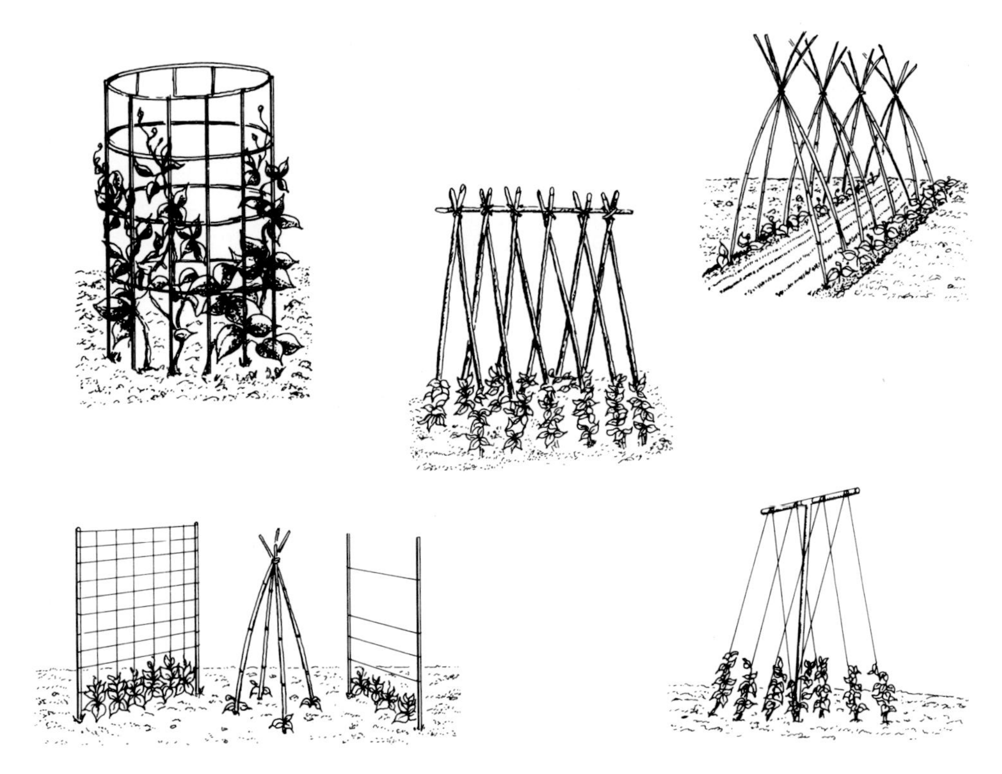

You can use many different structures to support pole beans, ranging from cages like those used around tomatoes to sticks tied together in the shape of teepees.

world of plants. Legumes have the remarkable ability to literally manufacture their own nitrogen. They do this by what is termed a symbiotic (mutually beneficial) relationship with a type of soilborne bacterium. The legumes' roots provide a satisfactory *home* for this bacterium. In return, the bacterium converts atmospheric nitrogen that is found in air spaces in the soil into usable nitrogen (food) for the plants. An indication that the nitrogen-manufacturing bacterium is present in a particular plant is the formation of lumps, or nodules, on the roots of legumes. This is actually the home of the bacteria. Generally, the roots with the most nodules produce the most nitrogen and, thus, the most vigorous plants.

The legumes are not the only plants to benefit from this unique relationship. When they have completed their life cycle, die, are turned under and start to decompose, legumes release nitrogen into the soil to be used by future crops.

This is a very simplified explanation of an extremely complicated process. The importance of this short lesson will become apparent later when we discuss fertility and planting.

Planting And Cultivation

Beans grow well in many soil types, but will do best when planted in light-textured soils. These soils warm up earlier in the spring and usually drain well. Beans planted in heavy type soils, which have a tendency to stay wet, may be late-maturing and low-yielding.

Regardless of your soil type, the addition of liberal amounts of organic matter, such as decomposed leaves, grass clippings, hay or any other suitable material, is desirable. Spread 2 to 3 inches of these materials over the area to be planted in beans and till.

Since legumes make their own nitrogen, beans normally do not require heavy fertilization. In fact, excessive fertilization may result in large, lush plants that have delayed maturity and low yields. Oftentimes, you do not need to fertilize at all before planting. However, if you have any doubts about whether your soil is fertile enough, it's best to work in about ½ to ¾ pound of a complete fertilizer, such as 10-20-10, per 100 square feet of area or for each 35 feet of row to be planted in beans. In addition, work about 50 pounds of well-decomposed barnyard manure, if it's available, into the same area.

Beans also do best in soils that have a pH between 6.0 and 7.5. If you live in East Texas and have had only fair results with beans, chances are you should lime your soil. (See page 394 for more information on adjusting your soil's pH level.) For you folks gardening in alkaline soils that have a pH above 7.5, adding a small amount of iron will prevent chlorosis, or yellowing, of the leaves and increase yields. Iron can be applied as copperous (iron sulfate) or, even better, as the sequesterene form usually available under the trade name of Geigy 138. It is formulated specially for high pH soils. Check the label for the correct amounts to apply.

When preparing your soil for planting, it's important to keep in mind that beans have a moderately deep-growing root system and under ideal conditions their roots will penetrate the soil to a depth of 3 to 4 feet. Of course, it's not necessary to till your soil to this depth, but it is a good idea to work your soil at least 8 to 10 inches deep. This will provide room for the development of a strong root system and will thoroughly incorporate the organic matter, fertilizer and other additives that you've applied to the soil.

As mentioned earlier, beans will do best in light-textured, well-drained soils that warm up early in the spring. For these very same reasons, it's good to plant beans on raised beds, especially if your soil is on the heavy side. By forming ridges and furrows, more surface area is exposed to the sun's rays, resulting in a warmer planting area. In addition,

Many Texans enjoy planting several types of beans in their gardens. Pinto beans (top left) and limas (bottom left) are quite popular, while yardlong beans (right) generally are grown as a novelty.

the raised beds will dry more quickly if, or when, heavy rains occur. Obviously, the warming effect is much more beneficial for an early spring planting than for a late summer or early fall planting. However, the benefit of improved drainage makes planting on raised beds a desirable practice throughout the year.

If your garden soil is a deep sand, planting on raised beds is not as important since poor drainage and slow warming of the soil are not problems. Yet, such soils often have a tendency to crust over following heavy rains, causing problems with soil aeration and resulting in poor plant growth. Crusting is not as severe on garden soils that have been ridged and furrowed, which makes it a beneficial practice on almost all Texas soils. Soils that crust over immediately after planting can cause real problems for lima and butter beans.

Your raised beds should be about 6 inches high and 30 to 36 inches apart, measured from the center of one bed to the center of an adjoining bed. The wider spacing is preferable. The planting area should be about 16 to 20 inches wide, with the remaining area serving as a water furrow. Use the flat side of a garden rake to form and smooth the surface of the bed in preparation for planting.

Don't Plant Early

Avoid the common mistake many gardeners make of planting beans, especially limas, too early in the spring! You derive absolutely no benefit from planting beans before the soil warms up enough to encourage germination, root development and plant growth. The result of planting too soon will not be an earlier harvest. Instead you'll end up making another trip to the garden center for more seed to plant.

Most bean seed planted in soils that have a temperature below 60 degrees at the planting depth will—at the very best—germinate and emerge very slowly. Limas prefer even warmer soils for germination and should not be planted until soil temperatures rise to 65 degrees. Bean plants subjected to unfavorably low temperatures during germination and seedling development often will appear stunted throughout their lives and usually will fail to produce well.

In addition to poor growth, cold soils at planting will cause the bean seeds and seedlings to be more susceptible to numerous soilborne fungus diseases whose symptoms are expressed by seed decay and seedling die-off, or damping- off, following emergence.

Once soil temperatures reach favorable levels for good germination, planting should begin. Additional plantings can be made at 10- to 14-day intervals to lengthen your harvest season. However, you should stop planting early enough so that the plants will not be blooming and maturing when average daytime temperatures are expected to exceed 70 to 75 degrees. Green beans often will produce pods at fairly high temperatures, but they will be small and of poor quality. Limas, though they do well at warmer temperatures than green beans, will drop their blooms when it's too hot, especially in combination with low humidity.

When planting beans for a fall crop, soil temperatures generally are not a problem because bean seeds germinate quite well at fairly high temperatures. Nevertheless, it's common to have difficulty in getting a stand of beans, especially limas, when soil temperatures exceed 90 to 95 degrees. Fall crops should be planted at a time to allow the pods to mature when daily temperatures average near 70 degrees. Additional plantings can be made up to 10 to 12 weeks prior to the first anticipated frost. How long it takes a crop to mature depends on the type of bean grown and how you plan to use it—green, shelled or dried.

Plant your beans in single rows on top of raised beds. Use the end of a hoe or stick to make a planting furrow in the center of the bed. The furrow should be about 1½ inches deep if your soil is sandy and loose and about 1 inch deep if your soil is heavy.

To ensure yourself a good stand, plant seed that has been treated with a fungicide to prevent seed and seedling diseases. Most seed that you purchase already has been treated, as evidenced by the pink or sometimes blue color of the seed. However, if you get untreated seed, you can treat it with an appropriate fungicide, following label directions. Simply put your seed in a paper bag along with the needed amount of fungicide, close and shake vigorously.

Inoculating Your Seed

In addition to treating your seed to prevent disease problems, you might consider inoculation, which is the process of applying nitrogen-fixing bacteria to the seed prior to planting instead of depending upon your garden soil as the inoculating source. If you've been successful for a number of years growing beans, peas or other legumes in your garden, or if native legumes grow abundantly in your area, inoculation may not be beneficial. However, it's so easy to do, it's probably worth the effort—just for insurance! Simply dampen (do not soak) the seeds, place them in a paper bag and apply the inoculating powder. If you choose to inoculate and treat your seed with a fungicide, both can be applied at the same time. However, you can treat the seed with a fungicide at any time, but inoculation must be done immediately before planting. If the damp, inoculated seeds are allowed to completely dry before planting, the nitrogen-fixing bacteria lose their effectiveness. Commercial inoculation powders are available from most garden centers and a number of mail-order firms.

Ideally, there should be sufficient moisture in the soil at planting time to result in germination and seedling emergence without your having to apply additional water. However, if your soil is on the dry side at planting time, simply apply water directly into the seed furrow. Apply enough water to saturate the soil beneath the seed furrow to a depth of 3 to 4 inches. You may have to water several times depending upon your soil type. After the water has soaked in, sow the seed at the rate of five to six seeds per foot of row and cover with dry soil. After covering the seeds, use the flat side of a hoe to firm the soil over the seed furrow. This practice will help conserve soil moisture and ensure good contact between the seed and the soil.

Pole beans should be planted in much the same manner as just described. However, because they produce large plants requiring support for their vining growth habit, they should be spaced farther apart. Pole beans commonly are planted in hills consisting of three to five seeds. The hills are spaced approximately 1½ to 2 feet apart down the row and the plants usually are trained to grow up canes, poles, teepees or a similar type of support structure. Pole beans also can be planted in rows and trellised on wires, nets, concrete reinforcing wire, chain link fences or almost anything your imagination can conjure up.

Most viable bean seed will emerge within seven to 10 days after planting. Avoid letting your soil crust during the time the seedlings begin to emerge, especially if you're growing limas. When beans emerge from the soil, the seedling stem emerges first and it literally pulls the primary leaves up through the ground. Limas have extra large primary leaves and if the soil is tight and crusted, damage to the seedling can occur. It's not uncommon for emerging limas to actually "pull their heads off" as they emerge from tight or crusted soils. To overcome the problem of crusted soils, sprinkle the bed with water when the emerging beans are first visible. Once a good stand is established, water thoroughly if the soil is on the dry side.

About a week after emergence, your stand of beans should be thinned to the proper in-row spacing. It's best to thin the rows two different times. This will provide a little insurance against any insects and diseases that might attack the seedlings. Thinning is best done by simply pulling up the unwanted seedlings. However, if thinning is delayed and the roots of the plants are intertwined, pinching or cutting off the plants at ground level is best.

Green beans should be thinned to a spacing of 3 or 4 inches between plants. Limas require a little more room and perform best at an in-row spacing of 4 to 6 inches. All types of pole beans grown in rows and trellised should be spaced at least 6 inches apart. When pole beans are planted in hills, spacing between plants is not critical due to the wide spacing between the hills. After thinning, it's a good idea to water thoroughly to settle any disturbed soil around the roots of the remaining plants.

Fertilize And Mulch

When the plants are 6 to 8 inches tall, stimulate their growth with a light application of nitrogen fertilizer. Use about 1 cup of fertilizer such as ammonium sulfate (21-0-0) or ⅔ cup of ammonium nitrate (33-0-0) for every 35 feet of row. Apply half the fertilizer to each side of the row about 6 inches from the plants, lightly work it into the soil and water. If your

Rust (left) and damping-off (right) are two common problems you may encounter when growing beans. Rust attacks mature plants and can be controlled with sulphur or Bravo. Damping-off attacks seedlings and can be prevented by planting treated seeds.

plants are healthy and growing vigorously, this *side-dressing* may not be necessary.

After side-dressing your beans, consider mulching around the base of the plants with 2 to 3 inches of hay, well-rotted grass clippings, compost or some other type of organic material. Mulching will conserve moisture, help control weeds, regulate the soil temperature and a dozen other things, all of which result in increased yields!

Contrary to popular belief, beans are fairly drought-tolerant and do not require a lot of moisture during their early growth. Even so, adequate moisture must be available to the plants while they're in bloom and as the pods begin to enlarge, or they will drop their blooms, and the pods that do set will be tough and stringy.

Common Insect And Disease Problems

Unfortunately, all beans are subject to problems caused by insects and diseases. The most common insect problems in Texas are aphids, stinkbugs and spider mites. Aphids often are a problem in late spring and fall. In addition to causing plant damage by sucking the plant's juices and stunting its growth, aphids transmit several diseases. Fortunately, aphids are controlled easily by early applications of malathion or diazinon.

Stinkbugs, whose feeding habits cause damage to the developing pods, can be controlled by applications of malathion, diazinon or Sevin. Be on the lookout for this pest when temperatures begin to warm in late spring and early summer.

Spider mites are probably the most destructive pest of beans in Texas. Although they prefer warm temperatures, spider mites can be a serious problem from early spring to late fall. The first symptom of a spider mite infestation is a slight yellowing and mottling of the lower leaves of the plants, which occurs because the mites suck juices from the plant tissue. Upon inspecting the surface of these leaves, very small, almost microscopic mites can be observed. As the population increases, a slight webbing occurs on the lower leaf surface. If the population of mites is allowed to develop to the webbing stage, they are very difficult to control. Satisfactory control can be achieved by early applications of the miticide Kelthane. Two to three applications at three-day intervals will be necessary to control both the feeding mites and those that hatch from eggs after the first application.

Numerous diseases pose problems to beans in Texas, but the most common are damping-off, rust, powdery mildew, bean mosaic virus and nematodes. As previously discussed, the symptoms of damping-off include seed decay and seedling death. It is caused by naturally occurring soilborne fungi, primarily *Pythium* and *Rhizoctonia spp.*, and is best prevented by planting treated seed. In addition, if damping-off has been a persistent problem in the past, you should apply a solution of an appropriate fungicide and water directly in the seed furrow immediately before planting. Chances of having problems with damping-off are increased by planting too early, deep planting, wet soils and incorporating non-decomposed, green plant material into the soil.

Rust is primarily a problem on mature plants and is characterized by reddish, dusty spots which occur mostly on the lower surface of the leaves, but also on the pods. The spores causing rust are spread by wind and gardening activities. Satisfactory control can be obtained by early detection and treatment with sulphur or the fungicide Bravo applied at seven- to 14-day intervals. Sulphur can cause severe injury to any cucurbit crops you may have in other parts of the garden, so be sure not to get it on those plants.

The first symptoms of powdery mildew are faint, discolored spots on the leaves which rapidly develop into a grayish, talcum-like powdery growth which will cover the entire plant. Yellowing of the foliage occurs, along with dwarfing of the plant and pods. Powdery mildew primarily occurs during warm, dry periods and usually attacks bean plants that are nearing maturity. Treating with a 95 percent wettable powder sulphur at the rate of 4 tablespoons per gallon of water will give good control if applications are begun early.

Bean mosaic virus is becoming more and more of a problem in Texas. Its symptoms include severe stunting of the plants, mottling, suckering and leaf die-back. Distortion and stunting of the pods are other symptoms. This disease can be seed-borne or spread from diseased plants to healthy plants by aphids and by people who handle healthy plants after working with infected ones. Control measures include planting healthy, disease-free seed (never save bean seed for planting), controlling insects and removing all bean plants exhibiting any of the above symptoms associated with bean mosaic virus.

Nematodes are a problem on beans just as they are on many other commonly grown vegetable crops. Symptoms of a nematode infestation on nearly all garden plants include slow growth, yellowing of the foliage and wilting. Upon examination, the roots of infected plants will exhibit elongated and round swellings (knots) on both the small and large roots. These knots are caused by the soilborne nematode entering through the root tissue, which causes a proliferation of cell development and swelling to occur. These knots make an accurate diagnosis of a nematode problem fairly easy—on most plants.

However, as discussed earlier, healthy bean roots also may have knots on the roots which are the home of the beneficial nitrogen-fixing bacteria. Luckily, it's simple to determine whether you have a nematode infestation or nitrogen-fixing bacteria. The nodules of the beneficial bacteria are loosely attached to the bean roots and can be removed easily. Nematode knots, however, are actually a swelling of the root tissue. If you determine your problem is nematodes, see page 408 for instructions on controlling nematodes in your garden.

When And How To Harvest

Harvesttime depends greatly on the type of bean grown and the season of the year. Most varieties of bush beans will be mature in about eight weeks, while the pole types will take 10 to 14 days longer.

Green beans should be harvested when the pods are young and tender, 3 to 4 inches long and the seeds within the pods are about one-third their full size. You should harvest every two to three days so the pods won't get overmature, which will decrease yields. Beans grown for shelling should be picked when the seeds are full-sized, the pods turn yellowish (or sometimes reddish depending upon variety) and when the seeds pop out easily if you press firmly on the pod seam with your thumb. Dry beans are left to fully mature on the plant before harvesting, which can be accomplished either by picking the individual pods or by pulling up the entire plant.

It's important to avoid harvesting your beans when the foliage is wet. In fact, any activity in the garden when the foliage is wet will spread various types of bean diseases from plant to plant.

Minor Bean Crops

Broadbeans—Commonly called fava beans or horse beans, this legume is not really a bean and is closely related to vetch. Broadbeans prefer cool weather and are best grown as a fall crop in Texas. They are cold-hardy and may overwinter during fairly mild winters in South Texas. Cutural requirements for broadbeans are similar to bush beans and the pods can be harvested as green, shell or dry beans.

Yardlong Beans—Also called asparagus beans by many Texans, this crop produces pods that may be 2 feet or more in length. It is actually a very vigorous, vining type of southern pea that must be trellised or supported in some manner. Yardlong beans are grown primarily as a novelty in Texas due to their low yields.

Mung Beans—Mung beans have the same basic requirements for growth as do southern peas—a loose, well-drained soil and warm temperatures. They do best in Texas when planted in late spring. The 2-foot-tall plants will produce to 2- to 3-inch-long pods about 90 to 100 days after seeding. The plants should be pulled and allowed to dry. The mature pods shatter easily and careful handling is necessary to prevent loss of the beans.

Edible Soybeans—Soybeans are a warm season crop and produce their pods on erect, bush-type plants. Their cultural requirements are similar to those of lima beans but they need a considerably longer period to mature, up to 120 days. They are sensitive to length of day with regard to flowering and fruit set, so time of planting and variety selection are very important. In general, seed soybeans about the same time you set out tomatoes and use only middle- or short-day-length varieties. Soybeans may be used as green pods, shelled or dried.

Quick Problem Solver: Beans

Problem	Causes	Solutions
Poor germination and emergence.	Old seed.	Replant with current season seed.
	Cold/wet soils.	Plant when soil temperature at seeding depth is 60 to 65 degrees.
	Soilborne diseases.	Use treated seed when planting and/or treat soil with an appropriate fungicide.
Damaged or missing seedling leaves.	Crusted soils.	Lightly sprinkle seed bed during emergence.
	Insect injury.	Treat plants with appropriate insecticide.
Slow seedling growth.	Cold/wet soils.	See above. Do not mulch until soil warms.
	Low fertility.	Side-dress with nitrogen fertilizer.
	Nematodes.	Examine root system for presence of "knots." (See appendix on nematode control.)
Seedlings die after emergence.	Damping-off (fungus).	Plant at appropriate time and use treated seed. Drench base of remaining plants with an appropriate fungicide, mixed as indicated on label.
	Cutworms, grubs.	Treat soil before planting with diazinon.
Necrotic areas on leaves/marginal burn.	Fertilizer burn.	Avoid excessive amounts of fertilizer and/or placing fertilizer too close to plants when side-dressing.
	High salts in soil.	Avoid overfertilizing and water deeply to leech soil salts downward.
	Root damage.	Avoid cultivating too close to plants.
	Sunburn.	Caused by intense sunlight following prolonged cloudy periods. No control; plants will recover.
Spots-lesions on leaves, stems and pods.	Fungal or bacterial diseases.	Treat with appropriate fungicides/bacteriacides. Limit garden activity until diseases are controlled, especially during wet periods.

Reddish spots on leaves, pods.	Rust.	Treat foliage with Bravo or maneb.
Talcum-like powder on plants.	Powdery mildew (fungus).	Treat with sulphur at 7 to 10 day intervals.
Bloom drop/failure to set pods.	High temperatures and/ or high humidity.	Plant at proper time and hope for cooler temperatures. Misting may help set pods.
	Insects feeding on blooms.	Examine blooms for presence of insects and treat with appropriate insecticides if necessary.
	Low soil moisture.	Maintain adequate soil moisture during bloom and pod formation.
Shriveled/small pods.	Low soil moisture.	Maintain adequate soil moisture during bloom and pod formation. Mulching will help conserve soil moisture.
Small holes in pods and seeds.	Insect damage.	Treat plants during pod formation with appropriate insecticide.
Yellowing of foliage, slow plant growth.	Low fertility.	Side-dress with nitrogen fertilizer.
	Wet soils.	Avoid overwatering, especially during early stages of plant growth.
	Spidermites.	Check underside of leaves for presence of mites. If necessary, treat with Kelthane as directed on label.
	Nematodes.	Check roots for presence of "knots." (See appendix on nematode control.)
Pods tough and stringy.	Low moisture during maturity.	Maintain adequate soil moisture during bloom and pod maturity.
	Overmature.	Harvest for green snap when pods are 3 to 4 inches long.

BEETS

Scientific Name: *Beta vulgaris*
Family: *Chenopodiaceae*
Biennial, grown as an annual
Cool Season
Varieties: Pacemaker II, Detroit Dark Red
Expected Harvest: 40 to 60 roots per 10 feet of row

BEETS

The beet, as we know it today, is a relatively new kid on the block in the historical world of vegetables. But it has ancestors that date back to prehistoric times. The original beet, which didn't have an enlarged and fleshy root, originated in the Mediterranean area. No one is sure when it first was utilized by man, but it was described in the writings of Aristotle and often mentioned by the Romans and Greeks, who called it *Beta.* At that time, its leaves were harvested from the wild and used as a potherb.

Beets with large, fleshy roots were unknown before the Christian era. It was the Romans in the second century who first began selecting beets with enlarged roots, reported they were edible and claimed they tasted better than cabbage. Despite this proclamation and the reputed authority of the mighty Romans, beets generated little interest. It wasn't until the 14th century that recipes calling for beet roots appeared in Europe. Even as late as the 1800s, only two types of beets were listed by English seedsmen and demand for the seed was almost non-existent. The first listing of beets in an American seed catalog occurred in 1806—a single variety uniquely named Red. It caused little interest and by the late 1800s only a few varieties of beets were available for planting.

Unfortunately, the beet still is considered a minor vegetable in the United States and is seldom included in Texas gardens. That's a shame because beets are easy to grow, highly nutritious and tasty.

That's right—tasty! Ironically, the reason why beets are not popular is because most folks don't like them—or at least *think* they don't. However, I suspect that most people who dislike beets simply haven't had them prepared right. Certainly, they haven't tried any right out of the garden. If you feel you might fit into this category, I suggest you check around for some good, old-fashioned recipes and pay close attention to the following guidelines on growing beets. I've got a feeling you'll change your mind about this delicious vegetable.

Before we deal with growing beets in Texas, an all-important principle regarding their successful culture needs to be explained. In reality, the beet's enlarged, fleshy root actually is an organ where excess carbohydrates manufactured by the plant's leaves are stored. These extra carbohydrates are made when factors affecting the plant's growth—such as light, water, fertility and temperature—are ideal and more plentiful than the plant needs to sustain normal growth. When these conditions occur, beet roots and tops develop rapidly and are tender and sweet. Conversely, if growing conditions are not conducive to rapid, luxurious growth, the leaves will be tough and bitter and the roots small and fibrous. Therefore, every effort should be made to encourage succulent growth of the beet plants if maximum yields and quality are expected.

Planting Time Is Important

To ensure the development of high-quality beet tops and roots, you must plant at the right time. You'll get the best quality roots and tops if the plants mature while daytime temperatures average between 60 and 65 degrees.

In the spring, planting can begin four to six weeks before the average last killing frost is expected in your area. Actually, beets are fairly cold-tolerant and planting could occur much earlier without hurting the young seedlings. However, planting too early should be avoided because other problems can occur, and usually do!

Beets are classified as biennials, which means they normally produce vegetative growth the first year, then flower and produce seed the second year. However, they can be tricked into crowding this two-year cycle into just a few months—if you plant too early!

If early planting is followed by moderate temperatures, the beet plants will grow rapidly. Then if cold weather sets in when the plants are 4 to 6 inches tall or larger, exposing them to temperatures of 45 degrees or below, they will cease growing and go dormant. If temperatures remain low for 10 days or longer, the plants will think they're in their second season when it turns warm again. Thus, they will act as if they have satisfied their biennial requirements. The flowering mechanism will be activated by the warm temperatures and longer days. Thus, bolting or seed stalk formation will occur. That's great if you're interested in raising beet seed or flowers for centerpieces, but not worth a flip if you're trying to raise beets to eat! The tops are bitter and the bulbs completely inedible.

Your initial planting can be followed by subsequent plantings at two- to three-week intervals to extend the harvest season. However, you

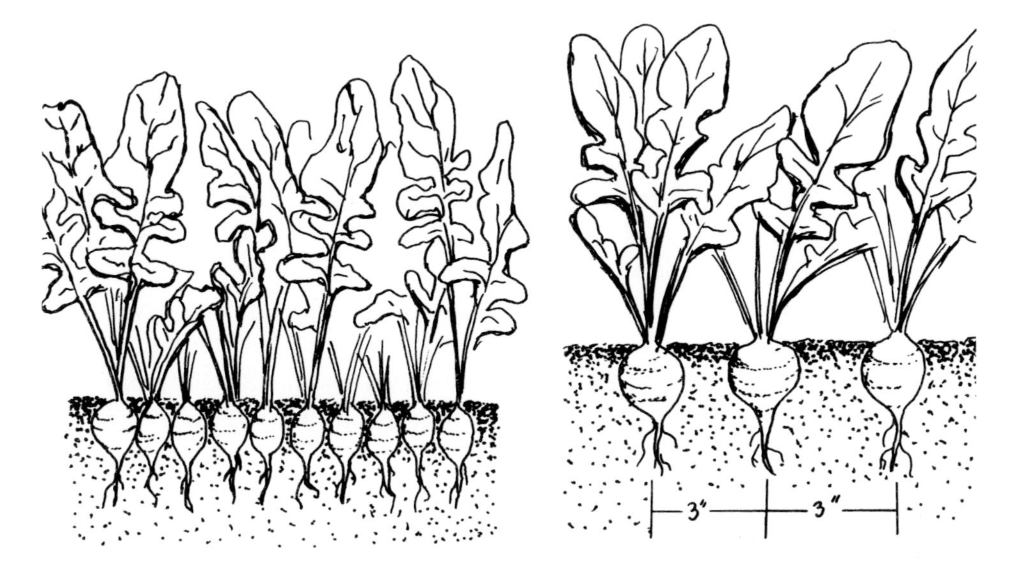

Once your stand of beets is established, you'll need to thin them to a spacing of 3 to 4 inches apart if you plan to eat the roots and to 2 inches apart if you only plan to eat the tops.

should stop planting 50 to 60 days before average daytime temperatures in your area are expected to exceed 80 degrees. High temperature conditions during maturity will result in the development of fibrous, poorly colored, low-quality roots and bitter, off-flavored leaves.

For a fall and winter crop, planting should begin when summer temperatures begin to moderate and again average near 80 degrees during the day. When your initial planting is made at this time, the beets should be maturing when average daytime temperatures are near 60 to 65 degrees or cooler. Again, successive plantings can be made, but should stop 70 to 80 days before temperatures are expected to reach the low 20s in your area. This means that in some areas of Texas such as the South Central, Gulf Coast and Rio Grande Valley regions, planting can occur right through winter. However, if you live in these warmer areas of our state, you must stop planting earlier in the spring and start planting later in the summer to be sure your beets mature when temperatures are cool.

It's also important to note that bolting, or flowering, as previously described, also can occur in beets planted in late fall or winter. Dormancy induced by cold temperatures below 45 degrees, followed by warm temperatures, may cause seedstem formation. This is a definite possibility if beets near maturity go dormant and are left to overwinter in the garden in anticipation of a late spring harvest. Under these conditions, the biennial requirements of the beet are fulfilled and flowering will occur.

Creating The Right Soil Conditions

Beets will grow on many soil types but, like all root crops, they will grow best in a deep, loose, fertile soil. Unfortunately, most Texans aren't lucky enough to have ideal soil and problems such as poor emergence, slow growth and rough, poor quality roots often occur. Most of these problems can be overcome by adding organic matter, fertilizing properly and, if necessary, correcting the pH of your soil.

Regardless of your soil type or where you garden in Texas, your efforts at growing great beets will be improved by adding liberal amounts of organic matter to the soil. If your soil is on the heavy side, organic matter will make it more friable and better suited for the development of beet roots. Organic matter also will help light, sandy soils to hold moisture and nutrients, thereby promoting the development of smooth, well-shaped beets.

When preparing your soil, spread 2 to 3 inches of organic matter, such as compost, grass clippings, leaves, hay or a similar material, over the surface of the area to be planted in beets. Till or spade it into the soil to a depth of 8 to 10 inches. As will all vegetables, beets will respond to the addition of barnyard manures. However, high levels of manure added just before planting may cause beets to develop rough, misshapen roots and should be avoided. Therefore, if you add manure to your soil, it should be done several months prior to planting. Work well-aged manure into the soil at the rate of about ½ pound per square foot, or 40 to 50 pounds per 35-foot row.

The primary benefit derived from the addition of barnyard manure is soil improvement although some nutrients, primarily nitrogen, are made available for plant growth. Usually, unless your soil already is fertile, beet yields and quality will be improved by the addition of commercial fertilizer.

Depending upon your soil's fertility level and type, use the equivalent of about 1 to 2 pounds of a complete fertilizer per 100 square feet or per 35 feet of row. Use the lower amount if your soil is fairly fertile or you garden in a sandy type soil. In East Texas and along the upper coast, fertilizers with a 1-2-2 ratio, such as 10-20-20, work well. In most other areas of our state, a fertilizer with a 1-2-1 ratio, like 10-20-10, is satisfactory. Scatter the fertilizer evenly over the area to be planted in beets and work it into the soil.

If you garden in East Texas and have had problems growing beets, your soil probably has too much acid and you should test its pH level. Beets will grow poorly in soils having a pH below 6.5. If low pH is the

Beets will be ready for harvesting about 55 to 80 days after planting.

problem, follow the quidelines for correcting acid soils given on page 394. Beets are a good test crop for acid soils and if you correct the pH problem, your efforts at growing all vegetables will be improved greatly.

Before you waste a lot of valuable time and effort, please note that organic matter, fertilizer and lime, if needed to correct your soil pH, all can be tilled or spaded into the soil at the same time. Some gardeners, however, prefer to till each time something is added to their soil to ensure proper mixing. What they're really doing is getting a little extra exercise. That's great, but unnecessary!

Forming Ridges And Furrows

After getting your soil in good shape, it's generally a good practice to form ridges and furrows, or raised beds, for planting, especially if your garden soil is on the heavy side. By planting your seed on top of the raised beds, problems with poor drainage and soil crusting will be lessened. Use a shovel or a tiller with a bedder to form the ridges and furrows. Ideally, the ridges should measure 30 to 36 inches apart from the top of one ridge to the top of an adjoining ridge. Next, use the flat side of a garden rake to flatten and smooth the ridge to form the planting bed. The top of the bed should be 16 to 20 inches across with the remaining area being the water furrow. After forming the beds, it's a good idea to use the flat side of your rake to tamp the bed top firm. This will help the planting beds hold moisture and ensure the lateral movement of water within them.

Beets can be planted in single rows, multiple rows or broadcast on top of the bed. Generally, it's preferable to plant in rows in the spring, because of the length of time it takes the beets to germinate and emerge. Weeds and grasses often will emerge before the beets and can be controlled more easily if your beets are planted in rows. Beets do extremely well when planted two rows per bed with the rows spaced 10 to 12 inches apart.

When it's time to plant your beets, there should be adequate moisture in the soil to encourage good germination. If your soil is dry, apply water several days before the anticipated planting date to provide the necessary moisture.

Use the end of your hoe, a stick or your hand to make the seeding furrow about 1 inch deep. Sow the seed along the bottom of the seed furrow using about eight to 10 seeds per foot. It's important to note at this time that the beet seed is really not a seed but a fruit containing several seeds. Therefore, it's not at all unusual to have several beet plants emerge where each seed was planted. Cover the seeds with soil, making certain they are planted no deeper than 1 inch in sandy soils and ½ inch in heavier soils. Use the flat end of your hoe to firm the soil over the seed to ensure good contact between the seed and the soil and to conserve the moisture in the soil.

Guaranteeing A Good Stand

Every experienced gardener knows one of the biggest problems in growing beets is getting a good stand. If you've planted at the right time and done a good job of getting your soil ready for planting, most of the concern about a poor stand has been eliminated. However, you can almost guarantee yourself a perfect stand of beets by soaking your seed in water at room temperature overnight, immediately prior to seeding, and by covering the seed at planting with compost or potting soil instead of garden soil. Soaking will initiate the germination process and covering the seed with compost or potting soil will provide it with optimum conditions during germination and emergence. In addition, crusting and packing of the soil, which pose very serious problems for seedling emergence, will no longer be problems.

At planting time, it's important to know that beet seeds germinate best when soil temperatures range between 45 and 85 degrees at the

For best results with your beet plants, soak the seeds in water overnight before planting. Then, sow the seeds about a half inch to an inch deep. When the seedlings are 2 inches tall, thin them as needed. When the plants are 6 inches tall, fertilize and mulch.

seeding depth, with faster germination and emergence occurring at the warmer temperatures. Emergence may take from as long as three weeks in the early spring to as short as five to seven days in the late summer.

After your stand of beets is established and growing, thinning will be necessary. It is best to thin when the plants have developed one or two true leaves and before they are more than 2 inches tall. If thinning is delayed, growth of the remaining plants may be affected. If you're growing the beets for both tops and roots, thin the seedlings to a spacing of 3 to 4 inches apart. If you're interested only in the tops for greens, leave the seedlings about 2 inches apart. Thinning is best done by gently pulling up the unwanted plants. If you are careful while thinning, the seedlings can be transplanted easily to other areas if needed.

Nematodes frequently attack beets and will cause them to be small and misshapen. A nematode infestation can be diagnosed by the appearance of small knots on the beet's feeder roots.

Fertilizer Requirements

As mentioned earlier, the secret to successfully growing beets is to maintain the growth of the plants at a rapid, luxurious rate. Therefore, it is critical that adequate fertility and moisture be available to the plants throughout their growth. To encourage growth, fertilize your beets when they are about 6 inches tall. Usually, about ½ cup of a nitrogen-containing fertilizer such as ammonium sulfate (21-0-0) or its equivalent for each 35 feet of row is sufficient. Apply half the fertilizer to each side of the row about 4 to 6 inches from the beets, lightly work it into the soil and water.

Mulch around your beets to conserve soil moisture and control weeds, especially if you live in the drier regions of Texas and garden on a sandy soil. After side-dressing and watering, apply 1 to 2 inches of organic material, such as hay, grass clippings or compost, around the base of the plants. In addition to conserving soil moisture and controlling weeds, mulching will tend to stabilize the soil temperature, which is highly desirable for the production of high-quality beet roots.

Regardless of how you water your beets, it's imperative that you never let the soil get too dry. It always should be in a moist condition. If the beets suffer from lack of soil moisture, the roots may become cracked and misshapen and the tops bitter and tough. Depending upon your soil type, where you live in Texas, the season of the year and rainfall, it may be necessary to water once or twice a week.

Insects And Diseases

As with any garden vegetable in Texas, insects and diseases probably will pose a serious threat to your crop of beets. Soilborne insects, such as wireworms and grubworms, that feed in the developing and mature roots literally can destroy a good crop of beets. And, worst of all, their damage often is not noticed until harvesttime. These pests must be prevented rather than controlled. When preparing the soil, if you see whitish grubs with dark heads and/or yellowish, slender, 1- to 1½-inch-long worms, resembling a jointed wire, apply diazinon to the soil as directed on the label. Diazinon also will help prevent cutworms, which can become a problem when they decide to help you thin your beets—usually much more than necessary!

The major foliage-feeding insect commonly a problem on beets in Texas is the flea beetle. These small, black, jumping beetles eat holes in the beet foliage and their damage is best described as a "shotgun hole effect." When the symptoms first appear, the application of Sevin, used as directed, will give effective control.

Cercospora leaf spot is the primary foliage disease that occurs on garden beets in Texas and is most common during cool, wet weather. It causes spots on the leaves that are brown to gray in color and have distinct reddish-purple borders. Early applications of a fungicide containing maneb generally will give good control.

Soilborne nematodes, which attack the roots of many plants can greatly affect the growth of beets and the quality of their roots, causing them to be small and misshapen. A nematode infestation can be diagnosed by the occurrence of small knots on the small feeder roots that arise from the fleshy, edible root. If you have nematodes, consult page 408 for a discussion on their control.

If corky, black areas occur within the roots of your beets, your garden soil is deficient in boron. This occurs primarily on alkaline soils and has been a problem in South Central and West Texas. If boron deficiency symptoms occur, treat your soil with 1/8 to 1/4 teaspoon of common borax mixed in 4 gallons of water. This is enough solution to treat 100 square feet of area or 35 feet of row. Use caution, because too much boron can cause toxicity to garden plants and is a good example of where the "cure" is worse than the problem.

Harvesting Your Beets

Depending on time of planting, season and their variety, beets will be ready to harvest about 55 to 80 days after planting. If you plant beets for the tops only, the leaves will be large enough to begin picking about five to six weeks after planting. The best quality beet roots will be those that are harvested before they are more than 2 inches in diameter. Beets should be pulled by hand and the tops twisted off rather than cut off. By twisting off the tops, they will bleed less and both the leaves and roots will be of higher quality.

Quick Problem Solver: Beets

Problem	Causes	Solutions
Poor stand.	Old seed.	Use only current season seed.
	Cold soils.	Plant when soil temperatures are above 45 degrees at the seed depth.
	Poor soil condition.	Smooth and firm seedbed. Add liberal amounts of organic matter to soil to improve soil aeration.
	Crusted soils.	Cover seed with compost, peat, etc., rather than soil.
	Planting too deep.	Plant seed ½ inch deep on heavy soils and 1 inch deep on loose, sandy soils. No deeper!
Plants die shortly after emerging.	Damping-off (fungus).	Use only treated seed when planting.
	Cutworms.	Treat around plants with appropriate insecticide.
Plants lack vigor, grow slowly.	Cold soils.	Avoid planting too early in the spring.
	Acid soils.	Add lime to raise soil pH.
	Nematodes.	Treat soil as discussed in appendix on nematodes.
	Low fertility.	Apply light application of nitrogen containing fertilizer to the side of the plants and water in.
Spot on leaves.	Cercospora leaf spot (fungus).	Treat foliage of plants with fungicide containing maneb.
Holes in leaves.	Flea beetles.	Treat foliage of plants with Sevin insecticide, following label directions.
Plants "bolt" or go to seed.	Dormancy induced during growth.	Avoid planting too early in the spring and allowing beets to "overwinter" in garden.
Roots are misshapen, cracked.	Low soil moisture.	Maintain soil in a moist condition during growth of plants.
Small, undersized roots.	Crowded growing conditions.	Thin plants to 3 to 4 inches apart for high quality roots.
Distinct "zones" or rings in interior of roots.	Overmature.	Harvest when roots are less than 2 inches in diameter.
	High temperatures during maturity.	Plant so beets will mature during cool temperatures.
Dark areas or spots in roots.	Boron deficiency.	Treat soil with borax, but avoid using too much.

BROCCOLI

Scientific Name: *Brassica oleracea (italica)*
Family: *Cruciferae*
Biennial, grown as an annual
Cool Season
Varieties: Green Comet, Emperor, Premium Crop
Expected Harvest: 15 to 20 pounds per 10 feet of row

BROCCOLI

Broccoli is a member of the *Cruciferae*, or cabbage, family and, like all its relatives, is a native of the Mediterranean area. In fact, a wild kale-like plant which geneticists believe is the original ancestor of the crucifer family still grows in that area. In 1860, plant breeders proved that different plants—resembling cauliflower, cabbage, kohlrabi and broccoli—could be developed from this wild kale.

Broccoli was a favorite of the Romans, who enjoyed it more than 2,000 years ago. However, it was just over 50 years ago that Americans began eating it. In the mid-1930s, Americans of Italian origin living near New York began growing broccoli in commercial quantities and shipping it across the United States. Today, broccoli is a very popular vegetable nationwide and its consumption increases each year.

The Perfect Garden Vegetable

Broccoli also is becoming more popular as a garden vegetable and is a favorite of Texans. And why not? It's productive, nutritious and tasty. Frankly, it just may be the perfect garden vegetable. After all, what other crop can you name that has the following characteristics?

- Once the main crop is harvested, it continues to produce large quantities of nutritious food for your dinner table.
- Not only is the head edible, but so are the stems and leaves.
- It can be grown in partial shade.
- It is tolerant of cold weather.
- It's as tasty after blanching and freezing as it is fresh from the garden.
- It's high in vitamin A.
- With a little effort, it's easy to grow!

It's true, broccoli is easy to grow. But only if you pay close attention to timing and to providing the necessary ingredients to promote rapid growth.

Timing is critical! Broccoli is classified as a cool-season vegetable, which simply means it will grow and produce best during cool weather. The highest quality broccoli is produced when temperatures range between 45 and 70 degrees. Therefore, to allow your spring crop of broccoli to mature under the best conditions possible, you should plant about two weeks before the last killing frost is expected in your area. If you plant earlier, the plants can be damaged, especially if temperatures drop toward the middle 20s. Also, problems can occur if temperatures remain 40 degrees or below for more than two weeks when the plants are 4 to 6 inches tall. Such temperatures will cause the plants to go dormant. Then when temperatures warm and growth resumes, the plants often will produce small heads and flower prematurely.

By the same token, if you plant too late in the spring and the broccoli is forced to mature when temperatures average above 75 degrees, the heads usually will be small and flower almost immediately.

For a fall crop of broccoli, planting should occur in the late summer or early fall, depending on where you live in Texas. Generally, your first planting should occur 10 to 12 weeks before the first hard killing frost is expected in your area. This should allow the broccoli to mature during ideal conditions. Additional plantings can be made, but should cease in time for the broccoli to mature before temperatures are expected to drop to the mid-20s. Obviously, if you garden in an area with mild winters, broccoli often can be harvested throughout the winter.

Getting Off To A Good Start

If you plant broccoli at the right time, you're on the way to growing a bumper crop. The next step is to make certain that the plants grow luxuriously and rapidly. If there is a secret to success with broccoli, it's to grow a large, vigorous plant before the head ever starts to form. The ingredients needed to encourage the development of such a plant are a well-prepared soil, adequate fertility and sufficient moisture.

Broccoli will do well in a variety of soil types but will do best in slightly heavy soils that have good drainage and a pH of between 6.0 and 7.5. If your soil pH is below 6.0, lime should be added to bring it up to the acceptable range. (See page 394 for details on adjusting the pH of soils.)

Regardless of your soil type, the addition of liberal amounts of organic matter is highly desirable. This is especially true if you garden in a light, sandy soil. The organic matter will enable such soils to hold fertility and moisture that is critical for success in growing broccoli. Spread 2 to 3 inches of organic matter, such as compost, grass clippings or leaves, over

In the spring, it's best to transplant broccoli, but in the fall you can plant from seeds with good success. Sow eight to 10 seeds per foot of row and cover lightly. Once the seedlings emerge and are 2 to 3 inches tall, thin them to about 6 inches apart.

the area to be planted in broccoli and till or spade it in to a depth of 8 to 10 inches. Also, if it's available, work aged barnyard manure into the soil at the rate of 1 pound per square foot or approximately 100 pounds per 35 feet of row. Since broccoli has a relatively shallow root system, with most of its feeder roots found in the top 12 inches of soil, it will respond quite well to the organic matter and barnyard fertilizer.

Success with broccoli is highly dependent upon fertility. Relatively high levels of fertilizer will encourage the development of vegetative growth, which is good when growing broccoli. Therefore, unless your soil is highly fertile, a commercial fertilizer should be added to your planting area, in addition to the barnyard manure.

Choosing A Fertilizer

The type of fertilizer to use depends upon where you garden in Texas and your soil type. In much of East Texas and along the upper coastal areas, fertilizers with a ratio of 1-2-2 work well. In most other areas, a fertilizer with a ratio of 1-2-1 is satisfactory. Scatter 2 to 3 pounds of the fertilizer over each 100-square-foot area or 35 feet of row to be planted in broccoli and work it into the soil. Use the lower rate if you have used barnyard fertilizer or if your garden soil is sandy. In the fall, you probably should consider using a fertilizer that contains only nitrogen, especially if you fertilized heavily with a complete mixture in the spring. One pound of ammonium sulfate (21-0-0) or ⅔ pound of ammonium nitrate (33-0-0) per 100-square-foot area or for each 35 feet of broccoli row should be sufficient. Ideally, the incorporation of the organic matter, fertilizer and lime (if needed) should occur several weeks prior to planting.

Preparing Your Broccoli Beds

Broccoli, due to its shallow root system and its preference for a well-drained soil, does best when planted on raised beds. Use a shovel, hoe or a tiller with a bedder to form ridges and furrows. The ridges should measure at least 36 inches apart from the top of one ridge to the top of an adjoining ridge. Use the back side of a garden rake to flatten and smooth the ridge to form the planting bed.

The bed should be 16 to 20 inches across and 6 to 8 inches high. The remaining area between the beds will be a furrow to facilitate watering and to provide drainage. This is especially valuable in the late summer and early fall when tropical storms or occasional hurricanes blow in from the gulf and cause drenching rains over much of South, Central and East Texas. If you garden on sandy soil, raised beds aren't as important since drainage usually isn't a problem. However, raised beds still may prove desirable because the soil doesn't crust as severely as it does with flat planting.

Broccoli can be planted in single or double rows per bed, but yields will be higher if you use the double-row system. The two rows should be 12 inches apart, and if you plant on raised beds, each row should be about 3 to 4 inches from the edge of the bed.

Spring broccoli does best in Texas when it's transplanted, not seeded, because broccoli seed is slow to germinate when soil temperatures are below 50 degrees, taking two weeks or longer to emerge. If you wait until the soil warms up to the optimum germination temperature of 75 to 80 degrees to sow seed, your broccoli probably will mature when temperatures are higher than optimum. Transplants often will mature as much as three weeks earlier than seeded broccoli. And, as mentioned earlier, it is imperative that your broccoli mature during cool weather if you expect high yields and good quality!

In the fall, broccoli can be seeded or transplanted with about equal success, since broccoli seed will germinate at soil temperatures near 100 degrees. If you decide to seed fall broccoli, begin about 10 to 14 days before time to set out transplants. At planting time, your soil should be fairly

Harvesting at the right time is important if you want to enjoy your crop of broccoli. It should be picked when fully mature as in the photo at top. If you wait too long to harvest, it will flower and will no longer be edible.

moist at the seeding depth, with good subsurface moisture. If you anticipate dry conditions at planting, you should pre-irrigate several days in advance to supply the desirable soil moisture. Immediately before planting, use the flat side of your rake to tamp and firm the planting bed. Sow the seed in planting furrows at the rate of eight to 10 seeds per foot of row and cover them 1/4 to 1/2 inch deep using the greater depth on lighter soils. Ideally, you should not have to water until after the seeds germinate and emerge, but this may not be possible. If you need to water, do so with repeated, light applications to prevent the surface of the soil from crusting and hindering emergence of the seedlings. Once the plants are 2 to 3 inches tall, thin them to the same spacing as indicated below for transplants.

Transplanting Is Your Best Bet

Spring or fall, transplanting broccoli is your best bet, simply because it's easier, there's less worry about getting a stand (and keeping it), and it will mature earlier. The key to success in transplanting is to begin with the right plant. The ideal broccoli transplant is 4 to 5 weeks old, has five to six true leaves, is medium-green in color, and free of insect and disease damage. Hopefully, the plant has never suffered from water stress and/or low fertility, either of which can cause it to remain stunted and perform poorly. Also, avoid transplants that appear to have a woody stem. They probably are old for their size and will never yield properly.

When it's time to set out your broccoli transplants, your soil should be moist, not too wet or too dry. Use a trowel or your hand to make the holes for transplanting. Broccoli plants should be spaced about 6 inches apart in the row, even if you use the double-row system just described. This in-row spacing is considerably closer than most recommendations you'll find in other garden publications, but is based on the latest research findings and is intended to maximize yields. In fact, there is considerable indication that broccoli will perform exceptionally well when spaced as close as 4 inches apart in the row—something that you might try just for fun. The obvious disadvantage is that you either have to grow or buy more broccoli transplants—but what's a few cents for additional seed or transplants compared to the reward come harvesttime?

After you've dug the transplant holes, pour 1 cup of starter solution in each hole and allow it to soak. Starter solutions are simply water-soluble fertilizers that supply transplants with needed nutrients as soon as you set them out and while they are developing a root system. There are many excellent starter solutions on the market. Follow the individual label directions when mixing.

The best time to set out transplants is on cloudy days and/or late in the afternoon—especially during late summer and early fall. Broccoli transplants should be set deeply, just below the first leaves. Place the transplants in the holes and then backfill with soil. Firm the plants in, leaving a slight dish-shaped depression around each one to hold water. Water thoroughly after setting out the plants.

It's vitally important for broccoli plants not to suffer any kind of stress during the first few days after transplanting. You may need to water daily. Also, protect the plants from excessive temperature extremes, drying winds and direct sun by placing boards, shingles, milk cartons or shade cloths over them. Broccoli plants that suffer stress when very young often will remain stunted and produce poorly.

Be Sure To Provide Enough Water

Adequate soil moisture is critical to broccoli, not just after transplanting, but throughout the growing season. Broccoli has a high moisture requirement but a limited and rather shallow root system, compared to crops such as tomatoes and squash. Therefore, to compensate for its limited ability to absorb subsoil moisture, the area around your plants should always be kept fairly moist. Water when the soil first begins to dry and mulch with 2 to 3 inches of organic matter to help maintain moisture. Mulching is not as critical in the spring when soils are cool and we usually get enough rainfall. However, with the hot and dry conditions

Broccoli will be ready to harvest about 60 to 80 days after transplanting. Use a sharp knife to cut through the stem about 6 to 8 inches below the top of the head. Following the first harvest, numerous sideshoots will be produced and can be harvested.

of late summer and early fall, mulching may mean the difference between success and failure.

Broccoli responds well to light applications of fertilizer during the growing season. Generally, it's a good idea to apply a side-dressing two weeks after transplanting or six weeks after seeding. Then, fertilize again just before the heads start to form. Use 1 cup of ammonium sulfate (21-0-0) or ⅔ cup ammonium nitrate (33-0-0) for each 35 feet of row, applying half the fertilizer to each side of the row. Work it into the soil lightly and water. Use the same rate and procedure for both single- and double-row plantings. After the first harvest, fertilize again to stimulate the production of large side-shoots or secondary heads.

Growing broccoli in Texas is not a problem-free endeavor. Various types of insects and diseases enjoy broccoli just about as much as you do. It often seems that these pests come with transplants or in the seed packets! However, most problems can be avoided or controlled if you take measures early.

Common Broccoli Pests

Several types of worms are the most common broccoli pests. Cabbage loopers, imported cabbage worms and several others feed on the foliage and heads, causing considerable damage if left uncontrolled. However, the biological insecticide *Bacillus thuringiensis*, sold under various trade names, such as Dipel, Thuricide and Biological Worm Killer, provide effective control.

Aphids, or plant lice as they're called by many gardeners, often are a problem on broccoli. These small, sucking insects come in several colors but usually are green. They can be winged or wingless and generally feed on the underside of the leaves. They reproduce so rapidly that they can multiply from just a few to thousands almost overnight. Therefore, at the first sign of aphids, apply diazinon or malathion, according to the manufacturer's directions.

Harlequin bugs are pretty critters that can cause lots of problems in a hurry if not controlled. These bright-colored, shield-shaped insects are related closely to stinkbugs and often attack broccoli. Begin control measures with malathion, according to manufacturer's directions, before their numbers get out of control.

Generally, diseases are not a major problem with broccoli in Texas. However, several different fungi and bacteria can cause damage, especially if prolonged wet periods occur when the plants are near maturity. Downy mildew, which causes small yellow spots on the leaves and heads that later

Worms (top left), cutworms (top right) and harlequin bugs (bottom) are major pests of broccoli but can be controlled if identified early and proper control measures are taken.

turn brown, can reduce yields greatly. Apply a fungicide containing maneb at the first sign of the disease. Black rot, which is a devastating bacterial disease, can be seed-borne but usually is caused by the bacteria overwintering in your soil on residue from previous plantings of members of the cabbage family. Symptoms of black rot are V-shaped yellow lesions on the margins of the older leaves and a black discoloration of the veins within affected areas. Broccoli heads will be dwarfed and the lower leaves often will fall off. Chemical controls are ineffective, but long-term crop rotations are beneficial. Therefore, to prevent the occurrence of black rot, you should never plant broccoli or any member of the crucifer family in the same spot in your garden more than once every three to four years.

Harvest In 60 To 80 Days

Depending on the variety and season, broccoli should be ready for the dinner table about 60 to 80 days after transplanting. Don't be greedy and try to see how big the heads will get. Most of the better hybrid varieties on the market will produce heads that are 6 to 8 inches in diameter when mature. If you delay harvesting until the small flower buds that make up the broccoli head begin to bloom and turn yellow, you've waited too long. To enjoy broccoli at its edible best, it must be harvested when the heads are tight and compact and the flower buds are immature.

Use a sharp knife to cut through the stem about 6 to 8 inches below the top of the head. Use caution when harvesting to avoid damaging the small, secondary heads that will form below the main head. As mentioned earlier, a light application of fertilizer after the first harvest will stimulate production. Be sure to water after fertilizing. This also will increase the size of secondary heads, which are smaller but just as tasty as the main crop. Usually, the yield of secondary heads is limited in the spring by the onset of warm temperatures. However, a fall crop of broccoli often will continue to produce tasty, nutritious, secondary heads for weeks or even months, depending upon the severity of winter.

Quick Problem Solver: Broccoli

Problem	Causes	Solutions
Seeds fail to germinate.	Cold soils.	Plant when soil temperatures are above 50 degrees.
	Planted too deep.	Plant ¼ to ½ inch deep.
	Old seed.	Use current season seed.
Plants die soon after emerging or transplanting.	Damping-off (fungus).	Always use treated seed, avoid keeping soil too wet, and plant at the right time.
	Cutworms.	Treat around base of plants with diazinon or Sevin.
Stunted, slow-growing plants.	Low fertility.	Apply light application of nitrogen fertilizer along side of plants and water.
	Soil too acid.	Adjust soil pH.
Holes in leaves.	Loopers.	Use the biological product, *Bacillus thuringiensis*, for excellent control.
	Flea beetles.	Apply malathion or diazinon for control.
Older, lower leaves infested with stinkbug like insects.	Harlequin bugs.	Use Sevin spray or dust for control. Do not let abandoned broccoli plants remain in garden.
Yellow, V-shaped lesions present on leaf margins.	Black rot (bacteria).	Remove severely infected plants and do not plant broccoli or other crucifers in area for at least three years.
Premature flowering.	High temperatures.	Time planting so that maturity will occur during cool temperatures.
	Plant stress—low moisture and fertility or temperature extremes.	Maintain adequate levels of moisture and fertility for plants to encourage rapid growth. Protect young plants from either high or low temperatures.
Hollow stems.	Excessive soil fertility.	Too much nitrogen available for plants. Reduce rate of application.
	Boron deficiency.	Use borax at the rate of ⅛ to ¼ teaspoon mixed in 4 gallons of water and apply to each 100 square feet of area before planting. Use caution as too much can be toxic.
Heads fail to make.	Wrong variety.	Use new hybrid varieties adapted to Texas conditions.
	Unsuitable climatic conditions.	Plant at right time of year.

BRUSSELS SPROUTS

Scientific Name: *Brassica oleracea (gemmifera)*
Family: *Cruciferae*
Biennial, grown as an annual
Cool Season
Varieties: Prince Marvel, Jade Cross
Expected Harvest: 1 to 1½ pounds of sprouts per plant

BRUSSELS SPROUTS

The Brussels sprout, a member of the crucifer family, is simply nothing more than a crazy, mixed-up cabbage. You can see this yourself by cutting a cabbage head in half from the top down through its center. Inside you'll find a short stem to which the leaves that make up the cabbage head are attached. Now, compare this structure to that of the Brussels sprout plant. It's identical, except that the leaves of the Brussels sprout are attached to an elongated stem. The cabbage, as a result of its short stem, forms a single, compact head. The elongated stem of the Brussels sprout produces a much taller plant with open leaves.

Don't be concerned about the buds that develop in the axils of the Brussel sprout's leaves. Similar buds are found along the cabbage stem, but they don't develop and enlarge. However, as many gardeners know, if the stump containing a few leaves is left in the garden after the cabbage head is harvested, it often produces several small, Brussels sprout-like heads. The similarity of these cabbage sprouts to real Brussels sprouts in appearance and taste is remarkable. Often, only a true connoisseur of Brussels sprouts can tell the difference.

Like all the crucifers, scientists believe the Brussels sprout originated in the Mediterranean area from a wild kale-like plant. However, the Belgians dispute this theory and claim it as their own. Supposedly, the Brussels sprout has been grown *forever* near Brussels, Belgium—hence its name. Without a doubt, it first gained prominence near Brussels and the first written reference to it appeared in Belgium literature nearly 400 years ago. No earlier description of a "tall, single-stemmed plant bearing numerous, small and highly tasty *caboches* (a French term meaning head, from which the word cabbage was derived)" can be found.

Regardless of where the Brussels sprout originated, it grows extremely well in most areas of Europe and is also a very popular garden item in the northern part of the United States. However, utter frustration and disappointment often are expressed when Texans get around to discussing growing Brussels sprouts in their gardens. And the reason why is simple—the weather.

Long periods of cool weather while Brussels sprouts are growing and maturing is an absolute must for success. When temperatures are too high, especially while the plants are near maturity, low yields (if any) and poor quality sprouts will result.

Nevertheless, Brussels sprouts can be grown in Texas. They just won't produce as much or for as long as they would farther north. But, if you realize the important effects of temperature on the plant's growth and provide a little tender, loving care during the growing season, you can enjoy a successful harvest of high-quality Brussels sprouts. To take advantage of temperatures close to ideal, Brussels sprouts must be planted in late summer or early fall, depending on where you garden in Texas. Planting in the spring will accomplish only two things: valuable garden space will be wasted and you will experience grief and frustration.

Always Use Transplants

It's important to point out that any reference to planting Brussels sprouts in a Texas garden always means setting out transplants. Transplanting eliminates the many problems associated with seed germination, emergence and seedling growth during high temperatures. Transplanting also will help ensure that the sprouts will develop and mature during favorable climatic conditions.

Ideally, Brussels sprouts should mature when temperatures average between 55 to 65 degrees or cooler, but no hotter! In Texas, these temperatures occur for an extended period of time only in the fall. Such ideal conditions do occur in the spring, but don't last long. In addition, the spring temperatures are rising. If Brussels sprouts mature at higher than ideal temperatures, the sprouts will be small, soft and often simply fail to head.

Low temperatures, however, also can be a problem. Even though Brussels sprouts are extremely resistant to cold, young plants that are exposed to temperatures below 40 degrees for an extended time will be induced to flower when temperatures become warm and the days lengthen. Also, temperatures below freezing will slow plant growth, thereby inhibiting sprout formation and lowering yields. Temperatures below 20 degrees that persist for an extended period of time may damage or even kill the plants. Therefore, a late fall or winter planting for an early spring harvest is, at best, a gamble and should be avoided.

Set Brussels sprouts transplants fairly deep, leaving a slight depression around each one to hold moisture. After planting, protect new transplants from the hot sun by placing newspapers on frames over the plants.

Time of planting is extremely critical. Every effort should be made to plant during what I call the Brussels sprout's "time window." Transplants should be set out in your garden eight to 10 weeks before the first hard frost is expected to occur in your area of Texas. If you plant much earlier, sprout formation will be affected by temperatures that are too high. Plant too late, and cold weather (or hot weather in South Texas) may be a problem.

Like all members of the cabbage family, Brussels sprouts will grow relatively well in a wide variety of soils, but prefer those that are on the heavy side and well-drained. Ideally, your soil pH should be between 5.5 and 7.5. Brussels sprouts will grow slowly and appear stunted if grown in soils having a pH lower than 5.5. Therefore, if you garden in an acid soil, such as that found in many areas of East Texas, and you've had trouble growing Brussels sprouts in the past, chances are you should lime your soil according to the directions given on page 394.

Your garden soil should be prepared several weeks prior to the anticipated planting date. Regardless of your soil type, the addition of liberal amounts of organic matter is desirable. Organic matter will improve aeration and drainage of heavy soils and help sandy soils hold moisture and fertility. Spread 2 to 3 inches of organic matter, such as decomposed leaves, compost or grass clippings, over the area to be planted. In addition, and if available, use barnyard fertilizer at the rate of about ½ pound per square foot or 50 pounds per 35 feet of row.

Add Commercial Fertilizers

Unless your soil is relatively fertile from previous applications and soil-improving activities, the addition of commercial fertilizer will prove beneficial. The type and amount of fertilizer you should use depends upon where you live and your soil type. Fertilizers with a 1-2-2 ratio usually are satisfactory in most of East Texas and along the upper coastal areas. In most other areas of Texas, a 1-2-1 ratio is satisfactory. Scatter about 1½ to 2 pounds of the fertilizer over each 100 square feet or 35 feet of row to be planted in Brussels sprouts. Use the lower rate if you used barnyard fertilizer or if your garden soil is sandy.

If the area where you decide to grow your Brussels sprouts was heavily fertilized in the spring with a complete fertilizer, the application of a fertilizer containing only nitrogen may be all that's needed. About ⅔ pound of ammonium sulfate (21-0-0) or ½ pound of ammonium nitrate (33-0-0) per 100 square feet or for each 35 feet of row should be sufficient.

This amount of pre-plant fertilizer is slightly less than that recommended for other crucifers, such as cabbage, cauliflower and broccoli. Excessive amounts of fertilizer applied prior to planting will produce a weak, spindly plant, which is highly undesirable for Brussels sprouts since their natural tendency is to grow fairly tall. Additional fertilizer will be applied as the plants grow.

Brussels sprouts are categorized as having a relatively shallow root system that rarely extends deeper than 18 to 24 inches, with most of the feeder roots found in the top 10 to 12 inches of soil. Therefore, after you've applied the organic matter, barnyard fertilizer, commercial fertilizer and lime (if needed) to the soil surface, till or spade them in to a depth of 8 to 10 inches. This will allow for the development of a strong root system and result in a well-prepared soil, adequately supplied with the necessary ingredients required to produce a bumper crop of sprouts.

Brussels sprouts, due to their relatively shallow root systems and preference for a slightly heavy but well-drained soil, will do best when planted in raised beds. Form ridges and furrows that are at least 36 inches apart when measured from the top of one ridge to the top of an adjoining ridge. Use the back side of a garden rake to flatten and smooth the ridge into a planting bed that is about 16 to 20 inches wide and 6 inches high. The remaining area will be a furrow to facilitate watering and provide drainage. After forming the bed, again use your rake to tamp the top of the bed until it's firm. Brussels sprouts, due to their limited root system but rather tall growth habit, need a firm footing or you will have problems maintaining the plants in an upright position.

The Ideal Transplant

As with any crop that's transplanted, success depends greatly on the quality of the plant. The ideal Brussels sprout transplant should be older and larger than those often described in other gardening publications because a more mature plant can better withstand the adverse weather conditions common in Texas during late summer and early fall. Plants capable of surviving our usual hot and dry weather conditions should be about 6 weeks old, have six to eight true leaves, dark-green in color and free of insect and disease damage.

Since the Brussels sprout is not a commonly grown garden vegetable in Texas, rarely do you find quality plants of the right varieties at the proper planting time at local outlets. Consequently, you may be forced to grow your own transplants. See page 396 for details on how to do so.

When it's time to set out transplants, your soil should be slightly moist near the surface and have good subsoil moisture. Since the time to plant Brussels sprouts in Texas usually coincides with dry weather conditions, you may need to pre-irrigate several days prior to planting to supply the necessary soil moisture.

Brussels sprouts should be planted in a single row in the center of a raised bed with an in-row spacing of 18 inches between plants. Use a trowel, hoe or your hand to dig holes for the transplants 3 to 4 inches deep and about as wide. Pour about a cup of starter solution in each hole and allow it to soak. Starter solutions are water-soluble fertilizers that usually are high in phosphorous, encouraging root development and providing transplants with a little kick immediately after planting. As indicated earlier, excess fertility should be avoided in the early growth stages so the plants won't become weak and spindly. Therefore, it's a good idea to use the starter solution at half strength, thereby benefitting from a slightly smaller kick but preventing spindly growth of the transplant.

During hot weather, the best time to set out transplants is on a cloudy day or late in the afternoon. Brussels sprout transplants should be planted deeply so that their first leaves are at ground level. Firm the soil around the plants, leaving a slight dish-shaped depression around each one to help hold water. After transplanting, water thoroughly.

It's important to protect your plants from high temperatures and drying conditions for about 10 days after planting or until they are solidly established. You may need to water daily and possibly provide the plants with shade and shelter from the Texas sun and drying winds.

Keep the soil around your Brussels sprout plants fairly moist

Harvest Brussels sprouts when they are 1 to 2 inches in diameter by pulling downward with a twisting motion. To encourage the remaining sprouts to mature at one time, you can top the plant when the first sprouts begin to size.

throughout their growth. As mentioned earlier, Brussels sprouts have a fairly shallow root system and, consequently, are unable to absorb deep, subsoil moisture. To compensate for their lack of a well-developed root system, water when the soil first begins to dry and mulch around the plants with organic matter immediately after planting.

When the plants are about 12 inches tall, apply a light application of fertilizer to stimulate growth and encourage high yields. Use 1 cup of ammonium sulfate (21-0-0) or ⅔ cup of ammonium nitrate (33-0-0) for each 35 feet of row, applying half the fertilizer to each side of the row. Lightly work the fertilizer into the soil and water thoroughly. If you're gardening on a light, sandy soil you should "hill-up" your plants at about this time. Hilling-up simply means to pull some soil toward the plants to provide stronger support for them as they grow.

Susceptibility To Insects And Diseases

As with all crops grown in Texas, Brussels sprouts often are subject to problems related to insects and diseases. The most common insect pests you will encounter are cabbage loopers, imported cabbage worms and aphids. Downy mildew and black rot are the most likely diseases.

Although an entomologist might tell you there are distinct differences between the habits and damage caused by loopers and cabbage worms, they are similar in one important area: their control is the same. At first sign of any type of worms on your Brussels sprouts, you should treat with the biological insecticide, *Bacillus thuringiensis*, which is sold under various trade names. Loopers or cabbage worms, left uncontrolled, will feed on leaves, stems and the developing sprouts, destroying any hopes for a good yield.

Aphids can become a serious problem, especially if they penetrate and feed inside the developing sprouts. When this occurs, the sprouts will fail to form properly and will become what is termed in the commercial trade as "blown." This is simply a description of an open, loose sprout. Applications of malathion or diazinon applied at the first sign of aphids will give adequate control.

Downy mildew is a foliage disease that can attack Brussels sprouts at any stage, from seedlings to mature plants. Downy mildew is most prevalent in cool, moist weather, which means it most likely will be a problem when your plants are nearing maturity. First symptoms include small, yellow spots that enlarge, turn brownish and may cause severe foliage damage and low yields. Treating your plants with Bravo or a fungicide containing maneb at the first sign of mildew will give satisfactory control. Repeated applications may be necessary, especially if cool, wet weather conditions continue.

Black rot, which can pose serious problems for Brussels sprouts and all other members of the cabbage family, is a bacterial disease. The absence of a good rotation program is its primary cause. Symptoms of black rot include V-shaped, yellow lesions on the leaf margins that enlarge and turn brown. In addition, the veins of the leaves and stems in the infected areas become discolored. To avoid this serious disease, you should not plant Brussels sprouts, or any member of the cabbage family, in the same area in your garden for at least three years. If symptoms occur, pull the infected plants up and throw them in your trash pile, not your compost pile! Composting infected plants will not kill the bacteria, but will serve as a source of infection when the compost is added back to your soil.

When To Harvest

Depending upon weather conditions and variety, your Brussels sprouts should begin producing 90 to 100 days after transplanting. And, depending on the weather, you should enjoy a good harvest for about one to two months. The sprouts will begin forming near ground level and progress up the stalk. If you plant a little early or summer-like temperatures persist longer than expected, blown sprouts may initially occur. As the weather moderates, high-quality sprouts will be produced.

Considerable controversy exists as to whether the lower leaves should be removed to encourage the development of large, firm sprouts. Clearly the answer is no. The leaves, as long as they are functioning by manufacturing food for plant and sprout growth, should be left on the plant. If an occasional leaf becomes yellow and sickly, or hampers harvesting, it can and should be removed.

If you want to have a lot of sprouts ready at one time for processing, you can top the plants, which is the removal of the plant's terminal growing point. Doing this will encourage the simultaneous development of a majority of the sprouts along the stem. Generally, you should not top your plants until several of the lower sprouts are ½ to ¾ inches in diameter. Waiting until some of the lower sprouts have size will help ensure that a majority of the still undeveloped sprouts will mature.

Topping also is an excellent way to make sure the sprouts develop during fairly optimum conditions. If, for example, you've enjoyed a good harvest but realize that unsatisfactory temperatures (high or low) are likely to occur before most of the remaining sprouts mature, the plants can be topped to encourage them to develop during more favorable conditions.

Brussels sprouts are mature and ready for your dinner table when they are 1 to 2 inches in diameter. Harvest by gently pulling downward with a twisting motion. If you live in an area with mild winters, make a light application of fertilizer after your first harvest to promote future development. In the northern areas, however, fertilizing late in the season may promote succulent growth and cold damage may occur.

When your Brussels sprouts have quit producing, remove them from your garden to prevent them from harboring unwanted insects and diseases.

Quick Problem Solver: Brussels Sprouts

Problem	Causes	Solutions
Plants die after transplanting.	Damping-off (fungus).	Drench soil around plants with an appropriate fungicide solution.
	Excessive heat.	Use larger plants and water frequently, lightly.
	Cutworms.	Treat soil with appropriate insecticide.
Plants spindly, weak.	Excess fertility.	Avoid heavy fertilization at planting.
Plants stunted, grow slowly.	Low fertility.	Apply light application of fertilizer and water.
	Acid soils.	Apply lime to soil.
	Dry soils.	Water and maintain soils in fairly moist condition.
Holes in leaves.	Cabbage loopers. Imported cabbage worms.	Treat plants with *Bacillus thuringiensis* for control of "worms."
Yellow or brownish spots/lesions on leaves.	Downy mildew (fungus).	Treat foliage with Bravo or maneb as directed.
V-shaped lesions on margins of leaves/veins discolored.	Black rot (bacteria).	Remove affected plants and discard. Do not plant cabbage family members in same area for three years.
Sprouts fail to develop.	Aphids.	Check for presence on or in sprouts. Treat with malathion or diazinon.
	High temperature.	Plant at proper time of year. Occurrence of cooler temperatures will cause sprouts to develop.
	Wrong variety.	Use recommended hybrid varieties.

CABBAGE

Scientific Name: *Brassica oleracea (capitata)*
Family: *Cruciferae*
Biennial, grown as an annual
Cool Season
Varieties: Early Jersey Wakefield, Sanibel, Gourmet; (red) Ruby Ball; (savoy) Savoy King
Expected Harvest: 10 to 20 heads per 10 feet of row

CABBAGE

Cabbage is by far the most important member of the crucifer family and just may be the original grandpappy of them all. Most scientists believe all the other crucifers, including broccoli, cauliflower, Brussels sprout, turnip, mustard, rutabaga, Chinese cabbage, collard, kale and several others, developed from a cabbage-like plant which still grows wild in the Mediterranean area.

Regardless of which came first, one thing is quite obvious: cabbage has been around in one form or fashion for a long, long time, perhaps for more than 4,000 years. The ancient Egyptians literally worshipped a type of non-heading cabbage, which later was described in detail in the writings of Theophrastus around 350 B.C. The types of cabbage we know today apparently were unknown until the time of Charlemagne and it wasn't until 700 years later that heading varieties were described clearly in European literature.

Cabbage first was planted on the North American continent in Canada by the explorer, Cartier, around 1541, but no records can be found to indicate that it was cultivated anywhere in the United States before 1669. By the mid-1700s, however, it was grown widely by the colonists and American Indians. In the early 1800s, several varieties of cabbage were described in seed catalogs and its cultivation quickly spread across the United States.

Cabbage rapidly is becoming a popular home garden crop in Texas. And why not? It's a nutritious vegetable that grows extremely well on a wide variety of soil types and under various climatic conditions. In addition, cabbage is one of the most diverse vegetables around, ranging in color from green to purple; in leaf character from smooth to savoy (crinkled); in head shape from flat to pointed. And if grown properly, cabbage can be one of the most economical and productive crops in your garden.

A Cool Season Vegetable

The crucifers are categorized as cool-season vegetables and cabbage is certainly no exception. Highest yields and quality will occur when cabbage matures during temperatures averaging between 60 and 65 degrees. Cabbage is one of the most cold tolerant crucifers and, if properly conditioned, often can survive temperatures in the low 20s. However, if the plants are not first hardened by cool temperatures, they can be damaged by a sudden light freeze. A more serious problem in Texas occurs when temperatures average above 75 degrees when the plants are nearing maturity, causing many of the heads not to form and those that do to be loose and puffy.

Cabbage can be grown in spring and fall in most of Texas and in the winter along the coastal areas and South Texas. Of course, if you're going to be successful in growing cabbage, you need to plant at a time that will allow it to mature under favorable temperatures.

In the spring in Texas, temperatures often go from cool—or even cold—to downright hot in a short time. Therefore, it's best to transplant rather than sow seeds. By transplanting, the cabbage will mature earlier. Generally, the ideal time to set out transplants in the spring is two to three weeks before the last anticipated frost.

In the fall, you can seed or transplant with about equal success, but transplanting still offers the advantage of an earlier harvest and you don't have to worry about getting, and keeping, a stand during hot and dry conditions. Begin seeding, transplanting, or both if you're interested in extending your harvest, about 12 weeks before the first hard frost is expected. Additional plantings can be made to extend your harvest into the winter, keeping in mind that extreme cold or warm temperatures may cause problems.

Another temperature-related problem exists when growing cabbage, one that commonly occurs in the spring all over Texas. Cabbages are biennials, which simply means they normally will flower and produce seed during their second year of growth. Even so, if cabbage plants are exposed to extended periods of temperatures below 40 degrees, dormancy will be induced. When temperatures moderate and the plants begin growing again, they think their biennial requirement has been met and often will bolt or go to seed.

This is especially true for those plants with stem sizes larger than a pencil. Therefore, seeding or transplanting should not occur too late in the fall or too early in the spring, unless you're interested in yellow flowers for your dinner table instead of slaw or sauerkraut. Large plants that overwinter almost always will bolt.

As mentioned earlier, cabbage will do well on a wide variety of soil types, but prefers fertile soils that are a little on the heavy side because they hold moisture better. Cabbage grown on such soils generally will produce larger, higher-quality heads than those grown on lighter soils. However, those soils that have poor internal drainage and tend to stay wet for prolonged periods cause slow growth and poor yields.

Preparing The Soil For Planting

In preparing your soil for planting, the first thing to check is the pH, or level of acidity. Cabbage will grow best on soils having a pH between 6.0 and 7.5. In soils with a pH below 6.0, cabbage will grow slowly and perform poorly. Such soils are common in East Texas and if you suspect your soil is too acid, apply lime as directed on page 394.

Most garden soils in Texas, especially light or sandy soils and those that tend to be droughty, can be improved by the addition of liberal amounts of organic matter, such as leaves, grass clippings, hay or compost. Spread 2 to 3 inches of organic matter and, if available, barnyard manure at the rate of 1 pound per square foot over the area to be planted. Then spade or till it in to a depth of 8 to 10 inches.

Fertilizer, especially nitrogen, promotes vegetative growth, which is exactly what you want when growing cabbage. After all, when you're growing a head of cabbage what you're really producing is a compact mass of leaves attached to a short stem or core. Relatively high levels of fertilizer, therefore, will encourage the formation of large, firm, well-shaped cabbage heads. However, be aware that over-fertilizing can cause excess growth, resulting in heads that often split open when mature.

Unless your soil is already highly fertile, cabbage will respond to the application of a commercial fertilizer in addition to barnyard manure. The type and amount you should use will depend upon your climate, your soil type and your soil's fertility. In much of East Texas and along the upper coastal areas, fertilizers with a 1-2-2 ratio work well. In most other areas, fertilizers with a 1-2-1 ratio are satisfactory.

Cabbage will respond to high fertility. It requires about the same preplant fertility as broccoli. Scatter 2 to 3 pounds of the fertilizer over each 100 square feet or 35 feet of row and work it into the soil. Use the lower rate if you garden on a sandy soil or if you have used barnyard fertilizer. In the fall, use only nitrogen fertilizer, especially if you fertilized your garden heavily in the spring with a complete fertilizer. One pound of ammonium sulfate (21-0-0) or ⅔ pound of ammonium nitrate (33-0-0) per

Two excellent types of cabbage for Texas gardens are the Ruby Ball (top) and New Jersey Wakefield (bottom) varieties.

100 square feet or for each 35 feet of row should be sufficient.

Spading or tilling in organic matter, barnyard manure, fertilizer and lime, if needed, all can be done in one operation. Ideally, the process of getting your soil prepared should occur several weeks prior to planting.

Raised Beds Are Best

Cabbage is relatively shallow rooted, with most of its feeder roots found in the top 12 inches of soil, so it will do best when planted on raised beds. Raised beds provide good drainage, a particular advantage when growing cabbage, since it grows during periods when heavy rains are common. If you garden on a loose, well-drained soil, planting on raised beds loses some of its importance unless your soil has a tendency to crust over following rains. Crusting is not as severe on raised beds as on flat beds.

Use a shovel, hoe or tiller with a bedder to form ridges and furrows that measure at least 36 inches from the top of one ridge to the top of an adjoining ridge. Next, use the flat side of a garden rake to flatten and smooth the ridges into planting beds. After forming the bed, tamp the bed top firm. This firming operation will provide good contact between the soil particles, ensuring good lateral movement of soil moisture and a better environment for seed germination and/or early root growth by the transplants. The bed should be about 16 to 20 inches across and 6 to 8 inches high. The remaining lower area between the beds will be a furrow to facilitate watering and to provide good drainage for rainfall.

Cabbage can be planted in single or double rows per bed. Total yields generally will be higher from the double-row system, but the individual heads will be somewhat smaller. If you're growing cabbage for processing and using one of the larger-headed varieties, your best bet is the single-row system. If you're primarily interested in cabbage for fresh use, the double-row system is preferable. The two rows should be spaced 12 inches apart, and if you plant on raised beds, the rows should be 3 to 4 inches from the edges of the bed.

When transplanting, it's important to get quality plants. In spring, the ideal cabbage transplant should be about 4 to 5 weeks old, have five to six true leaves and a stem diameter of less than pencil size. (Remember the concern about plant size, low temperatures and bolting.) In late summer and early fall, the plants should be older and larger to withstand the high temperatures common in most areas of Texas at transplanting time. For late fall and winter transplanting in the milder areas of Texas, the smaller, younger plants are desirable. Again, you should be concerned with the possibility of bolting if larger plants are exposed to prolonged temperatures below 40 degrees.

Finding good cabbage transplants of the right varieties and at the right time for planting often is a major problem in many areas of Texas, especially in late summer and fall. If this is a problem, consider growing your own transplants as described on page 396.

At the time of transplanting, your soil should be slightly moist and have good subsoil moisture. If your soil is dry, pre-irrigate several days prior to planting to provide the necessary soil moisture. Cabbage plants should be spaced 8 to 14 inches apart in the row regardless of whether you use the single- or double-row system. If you're growing the larger headed varieties, use the wider spacing. Dig the transplant holes about as deep as they are wide, pour in a cup of starter solution and allow it to soak in thoroughly. Apply a starter solution to provide the transplants with immediate fertility until they establish a root system. Starter solutions are nothing more than water-soluble fertilizers, and a number of excellent products are on the market. Be sure to follow the label directions when mixing.

The ideal time to set out transplants, especially during late summer and early fall, is on a cloudy day or late in the afternoon and when the wind isn't blowing. Cabbage transplants should be set rather deeply, just below the first leaves. Place the transplants in the holes and backfill with soil. Firm them in, leaving a slight dish-shaped depression around each one to hold water. Water immediately after transplanting.

Protection From The Elements

For the first week or so after transplanting, be prepared to provide the plants with protection from unfavorable conditions—excessive temperatures, wind and dry soils. Young cabbage plants that suffer from the elements often never fully recover, remain stunted and fail to head.

If you plan on seeding cabbage directly in your garden, pay close attention to the soil temperature at the time of planting, especially in the early spring. Cabbage seed will germinate within a wide range of temperatures, but will perform poorly if the soil temperature at the planting depth is below 50 degrees. At that temperature, it would take two or more weeks for plants to come up, if they come up at all. As soil temperatures increase, the time required for the seeds to germinate and emerge decreases. The optimum temperature for germination is 85 degrees and the maximum it can be is 100. High soil temperatures at planting time can be overcome somewhat by frequent, light applications of water that provide a cooling effect on the soil.

Use a hoe handle or another tool to make seeding furrows about ½ inch deep. Either make one row down the center of the bed, or one on each side if you opt to use the double-row system. If the soil is relatively dry at the seeding depth, apply water directly in the seed furrow and allow it to soak in thoroughly. Sow the cabbage seed at the rate of about eight to 10 seeds per foot to ensure a good stand. Cover with soil, making certain the seeds are about 1/4 to 1/2 inch deep. The greater depth is satisfactory for lighter soils. After covering, use the flat side of a hoe to firm the soil over the planting furrow. This will result in good contact between the soil and seed, thereby providing moisture for germination. Firming the soil also will help conserve soil moisture that otherwise might be lost by evaporation.

There should be enough moisture in the soil at planting time so that you don't have to water until after the cabbage seeds germinate and the plants emerge. This may not prove feasible, though, when planting during dry conditions of late summer or early fall. If necessary, use a sprinkler to apply light applications of water until emergence occurs.

About three weeks after seeding, the plants will need to be thinned, which should be done when the soil is slightly moist. To allow for the possibility of some loss due to cutworms, a neighborhood dog or damping-off, thin your plants two times, leaving them twice as thick as recommended the first time. About seven to 10 days later, thin the remaining cabbage plants to their final in-row spacing of 8 to 14 inches apart. If you're careful when removing the plants, they can be transplanted easily to vacant spots in your cabbage patch or to another part of your garden. After thinning, water to settle any disturbed soil around the remaining plants.

About two to three weeks after thinning or transplanting, apply a light application of fertilizer to promote vigorous and rapid vegetative growth, which is essential when growing cabbage. Use 1 cup of ammonium sulfate (21-0-0) or 2/3 cup of ammonium nitrate (33-0-0) for each 35 feet of row. Apply half the fertilizer to each side of the row about 6 inches from the plants, lightly work it into the soil and water. Repeat this sidedress application of fertilizer again when the plants first start to cup their leaves and form heads. This second side-dressing can be omitted if your plants are growing rapidly and appear healthy and vigorous. Excess fertility at this time may cause the heads to split as they near maturity.

As most vegetables, cabbage will respond very positively to mulching. Just after you make your first sidedress application of fertilizer in the spring is a good time to mulch around the plants with 2 to 3 inches of organic matter. This will give the soil a chance to warm up slightly before the mulch is applied. In the late summer and fall, mulch immediately after transplanting or after the plants emerge to help cool the soil and conserve moisture. When you side-dress mulched plants, simply pull back the material and apply the fertilizer.

Cabbage plants should never suffer from low soil moisture. As

Common problems you may encounter when growing cabbage are black rot (left) and the cabbage looper (right).

previously mentioned, maintaining your plants in a vigorous, rapid state of growth is highly desirable and this can be accomplished only with adequate soil moisture. Cabbage has a relatively shallow root system and, consequently, lacks the ability to absorb deep, subsoil moisture. Therefore, you frequently should check your garden soil about 1 to 2 inches beneath the surface to determine its moisture content. If it's relatively dry, water thoroughly, wetting the soil to a depth of at least 6 inches. Do not wait for the plants to wilt! Depending upon Mother Nature and your soil, it may be necessary to water once or twice a week. Mulching as just described will conserve soil moisture and is almost a necessity on sandy type soils, especially when you're trying to get your plants started during hot, dry conditions.

The Insect Attack

Sometime during the growing season, you can bet your cabbage crop will come under attack by insects, particularly the *cabbage looper.* Cabbage loopers got their name for two reasons: they love to feed on cabbage foliage and they don't have legs along their middle, which causes them to move in a looping or inchworm-like manner. Loopers can be a serious problem in Texas throughout the year, but are most common during late spring and early fall. Actually, loopers will do little significant damage to your cabbage until the plants begin to head. At that time, they must be controlled. Luckily, agricultural scientists have given us an organic product that provides excellent control. *Bacillus thuringiensis,* which is sold under various trade names, including Biotrol, Thuricide, Biological Worm Killer and numerous others, is available at most retail gardening outlets across the state. It's important to note that *Bacillus thuringiensis* controls only worms and not other types of insect pests. In addition, it usually takes about three days before the worms die, although they quit feeding almost immediately after ingesting foliage treated with this biological insecticide.

Aphids and harlequin bugs can become a problem at times and both must be controlled if you expect high yields of good quality cabbage. Early applications of diazinon or malathion initiated at the first sign of either pest normally gives good control.

Cabbage frequently is troubled by various types of fungal diseases that cause spotting of the foliage and, if left uncontrolled, can result in low yields and poor quality. Downy mildew and alternaria leaf spot are by far the most common foliage diseases and usually occur as the cabbage nears maturity—during cool, damp weather. The fungicide Bravo, or one containing maneb, applied at seven to 10 day intervals will give good control.

Another serious problem which literally can wreck your cabbage crop is black rot, a devastating disease caused primarily by soilborne bacteria. Black rot is most common on heavy soils that have poor drainage and have been planted frequently in cabbage or any of its crucifer relatives. It is characterized by the appearance of yellow, V-shaped lesions on the leaf margins, which eventually enlarge and may cause the lower leaves to fall off. Infected leaves and stems also exhibit discolored vascular tissue, which is the result of bacterial plugging. If plants become infected during their early stages of development, normal heading will not occur and plant death is common.

Unfortunately, there is no chemical control for black rot. The best cure is prevention, which can be achieved best by following sound horticultural practices, such as planting on raised beds to encourage improved soil drainage; removing nonproductive plants and plants that show early signs of possible infection from your garden and most importantly, rotating your crops.

Cabbage is ready for harvesting when the heads are firm and feel solid. Size is not a good indicator due to the great differences that exist between varieties. Depending upon variety and season of the year, cabbage will be ready anywhere from 65 to 120 days from transplanting. Cabbage will mature more quickly in the spring than in the fall and it's not at all unusual for a variety that takes 75 days to mature in the spring to require 100 or more days when planted in the fall. This difference is caused by the warming temperatures and increasing daylight hours that occur in the spring. And, as you might expect, larger heads from the same variety are common in the fall due to the cabbage's preference for maturing during cool conditions.

Splitting of the heads is fairly common, especially in early-maturing varieties or if you get a little behind on harvesting! This problem can be lessened if you avoid overwatering and fertilizing as maturity approaches. Also, you can utilize the old practice of root pruning to slow down the growth of the plants. Simply loosen the plants from your garden soil with a gentle tug, but do not pull the plant completely out of the ground. This action will break some of the feeder roots, effectively reducing the plant's rate of growth and splitting of the heads.

Harvesting is simple. Remove the head by cutting through the stem with a sharp knife just above the lower leaves. Leave a few of the coarse, wrapper leaves on the head as protection until it is ready for use. Provided the weather is suitable, and if it's fertilized and watered, the cabbage stumps may produce sprouts, which also can be enjoyed at your dinner table. And what more can you ask for—two crops for the price of one!

Quick Problem Solver: Cabbage

Problem	Causes	Solutions
Seeds fail to germinate and emerge.	Old seed.	Always purchase seed packaged for current year.
	Cold soils.	Seed when soil temperatures are 50 degrees or higher.
	Planted too deep.	Plant seed ¼ to ½ inch deep and no deeper.
	Low moisture.	Plant when soil moisture is sufficient to result in germination. Apply additional water if necessary.
Seedlings die/fall over.	Damping-off (fungus).	Always use treated seed and plant when temperatures are favorable for germination.
	Cutworms.	Check for presence of worms in soil at base of plant. If found, treat with soil insecticide.

Transplants die soon after setting out.	Stress.	Protect from winds, high or low temperatures and low soil moisture.
	Damping-off.	Drench around plants with a fungicide, according to label directions.
Plants grow slowly, lack good color.	Wet soils/poor drainage.	Plant on raised beds/add organic matter to improve soil drainage.
	Acid soils.	Correct soil pH according to directions on page 394.
	Cold soils.	Plant/transplant at right time of year.
	Low fertility.	Apply light application of nitrogen containing fertilizer.
Holes in leaves.	Loopers.	Treat with *Bacillus thuringiensis*.
	Flea beetles.	Control with applications of malathion.
Leaves cupped, wrinkled.	Aphids.	Treat with diazinon or malathion.
V-shaped lesions on leaf margins/vascular tissue discolored.	Black rot.	Plant on raised beds, remove infected plants, follow good rotation program.
Lesions/sunken areas on leaves, head.	Leaf spots (fungus).	Control with applications of a fungicide containing maneb.
Heads fail to form.	High temperatures.	Seed/transplant at right time of year.
	Stress.	Avoid any type of stress such as low soil moisture, low fertility, etc., when plants are young.
Heads split/crack open near maturity.	Rapid growth.	Avoid excess fertility late in season.
	Excess moisture.	Avoid overwatering as plants near maturity.
Plants bolt/flower prematurely.	Exposure to cold.	Avoid planting too early or late causing the plants to be exposed to temperatures below 40 degrees.
	Large transplants.	Use only transplants with a stem diameter less than pencil size.

CANTALOUPE

Scientific Name: *Cucumis melo*
Family: *Cucurbitaceae*
Annual
Warm Season
Varieties: Magnum 45, Perlita, TAM Uvalde, Dixie Jumbo
Expected Harvest: 3 to 5 fruits per hill

CANTALOUPE

Cantaloupe is cantaloupe, right? Not when it's grown in Texas! What we Texans know and enjoy as cantaloupes are not really cantaloupes at all; they're muskmelons.

The melons (excluding watermelons) are categorized into seven distinct types, three of which are quite popular throughout the world. Real cantaloupes have rough, warty exteriors that are not netted, are usually oblong in shape and are seldom grown in Texas. Muskmelons, which include *our* cantaloupes and Persian melons, have netted surfaces, distinct musky odors and flesh colors ranging from green to salmon-orange. The third category of popular melons usually have light-colored skins, which can be smooth or rough, but not netted, and lack distinctive, musky odors. Included in this group are honeydews, casabas and crenshaws.

The muskmelon probably originated in Persia (Iran), although there also is considerable evidence indicating it might have come from Africa. Egyptian drawings of what is supposed to be a muskmelon date back to around 2400 B.C. The first definite description of the muskmelon is attributed to the Roman philosopher, Pliney, in the first century A.D. Directions for its culture and use appeared in Roman literature in the third century. Culture of the muskmelon spread westward and was common in Spain by the 15th century. Columbus had muskmelon seed planted on Isabella Island in 1494 and is responsible for its introduction to North America. Its popularity spread rapidly and, by 1683, muskmelons had been introduced by the Spaniards into the area that is now California.

Enough said about muskmelons! Right or wrong, muskmelons are cantaloupes in Texas and this book is written for Texans about gardening in Texas. From this point on, our muskmelons will be referred to as cantaloupes, no matter what the rest of the world thinks.

Before we outline their culture, it's important to know that cantaloupes are members of the cucurbit family, which also includes watermelon, cucumber, squash, pumpkin, gourd and several other melons. And like all the cucurbits, or vine crops, success depends on the presence of bees for pollination. Most of the commonly grown cucurbits are monoecious, which simply means they have separate male and female flowers on the same plant. Bees transfer the pollen from the male to the female flowers (pollination) so that fruit set (fertilization) will occur. Cantaloupes are a little different in that they are andromonoecious, having male, female and "perfect" flowers on the same plant. Occasionally, a cantaloupe fruit will set without bees doing the pollinating, but not often.

Telling The Girls From The Boys

How do you tell the difference between a male, female or perfect cantaloupe flower? The female and perfect flowers are those that have the small, immature fruit located directly behind the flower petals and usually are borne singularly. Male flowers do not have the immature fruit behind the petals, are borne in clusters of three to five, and usually are the first to bloom.

The purpose of this brief discussion on plant morphology is to point out that if you've had trouble in the past getting cantaloupes to set a good crop of fruit, chances are it's because you didn't have enough bee activity. And not only must the bees be active, they must be active at the right time. Female cantaloupe flowers are only open and receptive to pollination for one day. If for any reason bees are not present the day the flower is open, it will not set fruit.

This may seem to be just a minor problem. After all, cantaloupe plants produce lots of blooms, right? True, but you still have a major problem. Unfortunately, most of the blooms are male, with the ratio of male to female blooms being as high as 20-to-1. So for high yields, you cannot afford to have many female blooms fail to set.

Another common problem with home-grown cantaloupe is that the fruit doesn't develop a flavor. Many folks believe poor flavor is caused by cantaloupes crossing with cucumbers or some other member of the cucurbit family but this simply cannot and does not occur. Under no circumstances will pollen from squash, cucumbers, watermelons or any other vine crop pollinate and cause cantaloupe fruit to set—let alone develop poor flavor. Poorly flavored fruit can be the result of selecting the wrong variety and can be solved by planting varieties recommended for Texas.

More than likely, though, poor flavor is related to excess soil

The female flowers on cantaloupes are the ones that have the small, immature fruit behind the bloom.

moisture, caused either by too much rainfall or your watering practices during the time the fruit is nearing maturity. The possibility of poor-flavored fruit can be lessened somewhat by good soil preparation, planting on raised beds and proper watering practices.

Cantaloupes will grow well on many garden soils, but perform best on loose, silty or sandy loam soils. These soils warm up early in the spring, drain well and, most importantly, encourage development and growth of the cantaloupe root system. It's important to note that the roots of the cantaloupe plant, if given the opportunity, will extend out as far as its vines and will penetrate the soil to a depth of 4 feet, with most of its feeder roots in the top 18 to 24 inches. To have high yields, these characteristics should be remembered when preparing your soil, fertilizing and watering.

Cantaloupes Need Room To Grow

Before planting, you must determine how much garden space you want to allot to cantaloupes. For best results, cantaloupe rows should be spaced at least 6 feet apart with 18 inches between hills. If your garden is small and you're contemplating planting just a hill or two of cantaloupes, leave at least 6 feet of space in all directions from the hill to allow space for growth.

After you've determined the size of your cantaloupe patch, till or spade the area as deeply as possible, especially on heavier type soils. Generally, working your soil 10 to 12 inches deep is sufficient to allow for good root development, but deeper tilling or spading would prove beneficial.

Like most vegetables, cantaloupes will respond to applications of organic matter worked into the soil prior to planting. The organic matter will help light, droughty soils hold moisture and nutrients and will help loosen up heavy, tight soils. Scatter 2 to 3 inches of organic matter, such as leaves, hay, decomposed grass clippings or compost, over the planting area. Also, if it's available, apply about ½ pound of barnyard fertilizer per square foot over the area.

In addition to the organic matter and barnyard fertilizer, cantaloupes usually will respond to the application of commercial fertilizer. Scatter 1 to 2 pounds of a complete fertilizer over each 100 square feet to be planted or for each 15 feet of cantaloupe row. Use a fertilizer, such as 10-20-20, if you garden in East Texas or along the upper coast and 10-20-10 in most other areas of Texas. A soil test is your best method of accurately determining your soil's fertility requirements.

If you live in East Texas, you need to be concerned with the pH of your garden soil. Cantaloupes will do poorly and appear stunted when grown on acid soils having a pH of below 6.0. If your soil is too acidic, you'll need to add lime to correct the problem. (See page 394 for directions on adjusting your soil pH.)

After you've applied the organic matter, barnyard fertilizer, commercial fertilizer and lime, if needed, spade or till them into the soil to a depth of 8 to 10 inches. The process of getting your soil ready should occur several weeks prior to the anticipated planting date.

At this time, it's necessary to point out that some garden publications recommend a simplified method of preparing the soil which consists of working up and fertilizing a 2- to 4-square-foot area and planting the cantaloupes in its center. Unless you have an ideal, highly fertile soil, this practice is not recommended. Cantaloupes have an extensive, spreading root system and their feeder roots will grow so rapidly that they will extend well beyond the small prepared area soon after planting.

Next, you'll need to make an important decision—whether or not to plant your cantaloupes on raised beds. If you garden on a soil that is

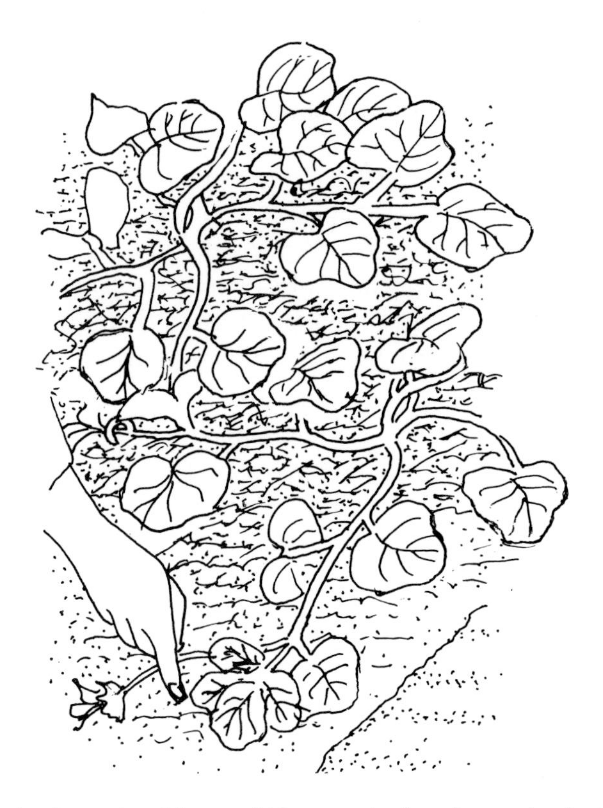

Once your plants begin to vine, it's a good idea to train them by gently placing the runners where you want them to be.

well-drained and warms up quickly in the spring, planting on raised beds may not prove worthwhile. If, however, your soil is on the heavy side, tends to stay wet and you garden in an area of Texas that normally experiences heavy rains, planting on raised beds will prove highly beneficial.

Raised beds can be formed in two ways. If you're planning a large planting of cantaloupes, you can make several ridges and furrows with your shovel or a tiller equipped with a bedder. The ridges should be about 36 inches apart, measured from the top of one ridge to the top of an adjoining ridge. Next, use the back of your garden rake to flatten and shape every other ridge into a planting bed that measures 20 to 24 inches across and plant only in these beds. About the time the plants start to vine, you will again use your shovel or tiller to bust up the unplanted beds, throwing the soil from them toward the planted beds. Use your rake to smooth, shape and tamp the tops of the beds firm. The new beds should now measure 40 to 48 inches across, with the remaining area serving as furrows to facilitate drainage or watering.

If you only have a small garden and want to grow only a few cantaloupe plants, you can use your shovel and rake to form a cantaloupe bed. As just described, the bed top should measure 3½ to 4 feet across.

Plant When The Soil Is Warm

Don't seed or set out transplants until soil temperatures are a minimum of 60 degrees at the planting depth. Planting when the soil is too cold will result in poor seed germination. Also, it will cause cantaloupe tranplants to grow slowly and to remain stunted throughout their existence. In addition, planting should take place when there is sufficient moisture in the soil to result in germination and emergence of the seed. If soil moisture is inadequate, you should consider pre-irrigating several days before the anticipated planting date.

Early soil warming can be hastened by covering the bed or planting area with black plastic and seeding or transplanting through it. The black plastic will warm the soil, resulting in better conditions for seed germination and/or transplant growth. It also will conserve soil moisture and help control weeds. If you're interested in using black plastic as a mulch, see page 397 for directions.

For a fall crop of cantaloupes, seeding and transplanting should occur about four months before the first anticipated killing frost. Remember, cooling temperatures and the decreasing day lengths of fall will cause most vegetables to take longer to mature than when planted in the spring. High soil temperatures, common during mid to late summer in Texas, generally are not a serious problem as optimum soil temperatures for cantaloupe seed germination range from 75 to 90 degrees. Planting through black plastic in late summer may result in excessively high temperatures and should be avoided.

Garden cantaloupes should be planted in hills, which are not raised areas but rather a horticultural term used to describe the technique of planting several seeds in one spot. Hill plant four to five seeds every 18 inches down the row. If you plant on raised beds, spread the seed down the center of the beds. If you're seeding through black plastic, use a bulb planter, sharp knife or razor blade to cut holes in the plastic at the desired spacing. Cover the seed from ½ to 1½ inches deep, using the greater depth on lighter soils. With ideal soil temperatures and sufficient moisture, the seeds should germinate and emerge from the soil within five to seven days.

Within two weeks after emergence, thin each hill to two of the

Cantaloupe can be raised on trellises and supported in some manner, such as with an old pair of panty hose. Shown here is the Israeli variety which is quite tasty, but is susceptible to diseases.

stronger, more vigorous plants. If you have too many plants, you also will have too much foliage, which makes it difficult for bees to carry out pollination. The obvious result is poor fruit set. Pinch the unwanted plants off near ground level, rather than pull them up, to avoid disturbing the roots of the remaining plants.

You can hasten the maturity of your cantaloupes by about two weeks if you set out transplants rather than seed. Oftentimes, though, healthy transplants of the right varieties are impossible to purchase, especially at the right time for setting out. If you're interested in growing your own transplants, see page 396.

The ideal cantaloupe transplant for setting out in your garden is about 3 to 4 weeks old and should be growing in some type of plantable container, such as a peat pot or pellet. Dig a hole 2 to 3 inches wide and just deep enough so that the peat pot or pellet will be just below the soil surface. Apply a cup of starter solution, mixed according to label directions, into the hole and allow it to soak. Place one or two plants in the center of the hole and backfill with garden soil. Firm the soil around the plants, leaving a slight dish-shaped depression to hold water. Water immediately after setting out the transplants.

If you're transplanting through black plastic, use exactly the same procedure as just described. However, make absolutely certain that the transplant stems are not in contact with the plastic sheeting, which can damage or actually cut through the tender stems when the wind blows.

Young cantaloupe plants grow best when nighttime temperatures remain above 55 degrees. These conditions can be almost assured by covering the transplants or the seeded area with hotcaps or some form of covering to provide warmer temperatures. Seed or transplant after danger of frost and utilize the coverings to provide additional warmth.

There's always the temptation to plant or transplant early and use the coverings to provide protection from frosty weather. However, research has shown that little if any benefit is derived from planting early, unless black plastic is used to warm the soil. Hotcaps, in combination with black plastic mulch, will result in environmental conditions which are conducive to early seeding or transplanting.

How To Plant Early

If you're interested in planting early, apply the black plastic three to four weeks prior to the frost-free date for your area of Texas. Wait seven to 10 days, depending upon the weather, before planting to give the black plastic time to warm the soil. Immediately after planting, place hotcaps over the transplants or the seeded area and hold them in place with soil. The response to the warm soil and air temperatures provided by the black plastic mulch and the hotcaps will be rapid germination and healthy, vigorous plant growth. You should remove the hotcaps when nighttime temperatures average about 60 degrees or, if necessary, when the plants need additional room for growth.

When the cantaloupe plants start to vine, or run, is a good time to apply a sidedress application of nitrogen fertilizer. Use 1 ⅓ tablespoons of ammonium nitrate (33-0-0) or 2 tablespoons of ammonium sulfate (21-0-0) per hill, applied in a circle around the plants about 8 inches from the plants. If you band the fertilizer to the side of the plants, use about ½ to ⅔ cup of fertilizer per 15 feet of row. Work the fertilizer very lightly into the soil and water. After side-dressing, apply an organic mulch around the plants to conserve moisture and help control weeds.

If you opt to grow your cantaloupes on black plastic, you have two choices regarding side-dressing. The band of fertilizer can be put down before planting and covering the bed with plastic, or you can roll back the plastic, apply the band of sidedress fertilizer and then put it back in place. Either system works well, but banding the fertilizer prior to planting and applying the black plastic obviously is preferable if you have a large planting.

A second side-dressing of nitrogen fertilizer at the same rate as just described should be applied when the plants first begin to set fruit, which generally is when the vines, or runners, are about 2 feet long. Again, apply the fertilizer in a band on either side of the plants approximately where the vines end, lightly work it into the soil and water. If you planted on black plastic, apply the fertilizer just outside the edge of the plastic.

It's important that cantaloupe plants have adequate moisture during early growth. Depending upon where you garden in Texas, your soil type and Mother Nature, it may be necessary to thoroughly water once a week to a depth of at least 6 inches. During this time, you are interested in developing a strong root system and vigorous foliage. However, once the fruits start to "net," if watering is necessary, make only light and frequent applications. Excessive soil moisture as the fruits near maturity will result in a poor flavor. If possible, avoid wetting the plants when watering because this may lead to the development of foliage diseases.

Now, here's a little more cantaloupe morphology, which can add fun and interest to growing this unique vegetable. The flowers that set fruit (perfect and pistillate) are borne on secondary or fruiting branches that normally develop when the primary branches are about 18 to 24 inches long. These fruiting branches can be encouraged to develop early by simply pinching out, or pruning, the growing tip of the primary branches at about the time the plant starts to vine. The result will be a concentrated set of cantaloupes that will be ready for harvesting at the same time, rather than over a long period of time. The practice of tip pruning cantaloupes is not only interesting, but practical, especially in the fall. Tip pruning can result in an increased number of melons maturing before freezing weather occurs, which will put an abrupt end to your cantaloupe harvest.

Train your plants as they grow and enlarge by encouraging the vines to remain on the bed tops or in the space provided for their growth. As the vines spread, gently move them around and direct their growth so that they will remain confined (as much as possible) to the desired area.

Common Diseases And Insects

Generally, diseases are a major problem when growing cantaloupes in Texas, as their foliage is subject to infection by a number of different plant pathogens. These foliage diseases must be controlled because it's the leaves that manufacture the carbohydrates, or sugars, that result in sweet, flavorful fruit. Without healthy, productive foliage, you cannot expect good quality, tasty cantaloupes—let alone high yields!

The most common foliage diseases that occur in Texas include downy mildew, powdery mildew and several other leaf spots. Generally, measures taken to control downy and powdery mildew also will control most of the other diseases that might attack cantaloupe foliage. Also, as a means of preventing foliage disease, every effort should be made to avoid wetting the plants when watering.

Downy mildew causes irregularly shaped, yellowish to brown spots to appear on the upper sides of the leaves, which oftentimes is followed by a moldy growth on the lower leaf surfaces. Infection nearly always begins at the crown or center of the plant on the older leaves and spreads outward. It is most common during humid conditions, such as in the early spring or in the late fall. Downy mildew can be controlled by applications of the fungicide Bravo, or one containing maneb, begun at the first sign of the disease.

Powdery mildew is favored by dry, hot weather. The primary symptoms include the occurrence of a white, powdery growth on the surface of the leaves which causes them to wither and die. Left uncontrolled, powdery mildew can eliminate any hope of a bountiful harvest in just a matter of days. At the first sign of the white, powdery fungus, apply Benlate or Bravo and repeat at seven to 10 day intervals.

Cantaloupes, like all cucurbits, are subject to infection by soilborne nematodes which enter the plant roots and prevent their normal growth and function. Symptoms include slow, stunted growth, knotted and swollen roots and, eventually, death of the plants. If your garden soil is infested with nematodes, see page 408 for information on their control.

Aphids, cucumber beetles and squash bugs are the insects that you can count on being a problem when raising cantaloupes in Texas. Aphids, or plant lice, usually feed on the stems and lower leaf surfaces, causing the leaves to curl and become distorted. Effective control results from early applications of malathion or diazinon.

Cucumber beetles and squash bugs basically do the same type of damage. They suck juices from the plants, causing them to wilt and sometimes die. Cucumber beetles are small, elongated, usually yellowish in color and can be either spotted or striped. Squash bugs usually are brownish, flat-backed bugs that can be ½ inch or more in length. They increase rapidly in numbers and can become a serious problem if not controlled. A sure sign of a serious squash bug problem is the presence of shiny, brick-red egg clusters on the leaf surfaces. Both cucumber beetles

Most cantaloupes are ready for harvest about 75 to 90 days after seeding. When the cantaloupe is mature it will slip from the vine.

and squash bugs can be controlled effectively by applying thiodan or Sevin at the first sign of their presence.

How To Harvest Cantaloupe

Most cantaloupe varieties produce mature fruit about 75 to 90 days after seeding. And the nice thing about cantaloupes is you don't have to count days or guess when they're ready. When a cantaloupe fruit is mature, it will slip from the vine. An abscission layer develops where the stem is attached to the fruit that easily separates, or slips, when the fruit is mature. Cantaloupe fruits should not be harvested until cracks are evident in the area where the stem is attached to the fruit, indicating the abscission layer is forming. At this time, they are fully mature or, "full slip," and can be removed easily from the vine with only slight pressure.

Contrary to popular belief, a cantaloupe fruit harvested before it is fully mature will not increase in sugar content. Its texture will improve as it softens, but not its flavor.

Quick Problem Solver: Cantaloupe

Problem	Causes	Solutions
Poor seed germination and emergence.	Old seed.	Use only current season seed.
	Cold soils.	Seed only after soil temperature is 60 degrees or above.
	Planted too deep.	Plant no deeper than ½ inch on heavier soils.
Seedlings/transplants die shortly after emergence or setting out.	Damping-off (fungus).	Use only treated seed and treat soil with a fungicide when planting and around transplants. Do not plant when soils are cold.
	Cutworms.	Treat with appropriate soil insecticide.
Plants grow slowly, appear stunted, foliage yellowish.	Cold soils.	Seed or set out plants only when soil temperature is 60 degrees or above.
	Acid soils.	If soil pH is below 6.0, add lime.
	Nematodes.	Check roots for presence of swollen area/knots. See appendix for control information.
	Low fertility.	Apply sidedress application of nitrogen fertilizer.
	Heavy soils/ poor drainage.	Add organic matter to loosen soils. Plant on raised beds.
Plants bloom but fail to set fruit.	Female blooms absent.	Male blooms always appear first. Be patient.
	Lack of pollinating insects—bees.	Never apply chemicals for insect and disease control during morning.
		Upset your neighbors—get a hive of bees!
	Excess foliage.	Next time, thin according to recommendations.
Seedlings/plants wither, "bugs" present.	Cucumber beetles/ Squash bugs.	If present, treat foliage with thiodan, according to label directions.
Leaves curled, distorted.	Aphids.	Check for presence on underside of leaves. Treat with diazinon or malathion as directed on label.

Yellowish spots on older leaves.	Downy mildew (fungus).	Treat foliage with fungicide containing Bravo or maneb.
Talcum-like powder evident on leaves which turn brown and wither.	Powdery mildew (fungus).	Treat foliage with the fungicides Bravo or Benlate.
Fruits small/poor quality.	Acid soils.	Treat soil with lime.
	Low fertility.	Side-dress with nitrogen fertilizer.
	Low moisture.	Maintain good soil moisture during early growth of plants.
Fruits rot on bottom side.	Soil fungi.	Mulch around plants to help keep fruit from contact with soil.
	Excess moisture.	Avoid overwatering near maturity. Plant on raised beds to help avoid problems caused by rainfall.
Fruits crack/split when mature.	Excess fertility.	Avoid over-fertilizing.
	Excess moisture.	Water lightly as fruits near maturity.
Fruits lack good "cantaloupe" flavor.	Fruit immature.	Harvest fruit at full slip stage of maturity.
	Excess moisture.	Avoid heavy applications of water as melons mature. Plant on raised beds if soils are poorly drained or you garden in East Texas (high rainfall areas).

CARROT

Scientific Name: *Daucus carota*
Family: *Umbelliferae*
Biennial, grown as an annual
Cool Season
Varieties: Imperator 58, Spartan Winner, Danvers 126
Expected Harvest: 70 to 80 roots per 10 feet of row

CARROTS

Carrots are among our most nutritious vegetables. Since the early 1900s, due primarily to the efforts of doctors and nutrition experts, carrots have been recognized as excellent sources of vitamin A. Before then, however, the carrot was a humble, obscure, but rather, tasty root. Occasionally, they were consumed by humans, but primarily were considered a delicacy for horses.

The carrot, in various colors and forms, has been around since ancient times and originated in Afghanistan. The first recorded use of carrots was by Greek physicians in the first century who prescribed them for various ailments of the stomach. Apparently, during the second and third centuries they were grown widely for medicinal purposes by the Greeks and Romans. Just how carrots went from being a medicinal tonic to an acceptable food source is not known, but during the 13th century they were grown in the gardens of France and Germany. In the early 1500s, European botanists and garden writers described in detail the occurrence and culture of red, yellow, white and even purple carrots. In the 17th century, plant breeders in the Netherlands, working with the red and yellow types, developed the orange-colored carrots which are grown today.

Carrots were brought to the United States by the very first colonists who settled in Jamestown, Virginia, in 1609. From that time on, they apparently were grown in every other settlement. The American Indians took a real liking to carrots and stories of skirmishes between tribes over the colorful, sweet roots are common. Due to their popularity among both the settlers and the Indians, carrots soon were found growing all across America.

The Modern-Day Carrot

Today, carrots are a Texas favorite and certainly rank as one of our most popular garden-grown vegetables. However, the Pilgrims and early

Indians might have a hard time recognizing our modern-day carrots. Plant breeders have done an excellent job of improving their shape, sugar content and deep color. Carotene, a pigment which our bodies convert into vitamin A, gives carrots their orange color. For those of you interested in a little garden nostalgia, white and yellow varieties similar to those grown hundreds of years ago are still offered in some mail-order seed catalogs.

To grow carrots successfully, you must meet two major requirements. First, carrots need virtually ideal growing conditions. The "root" we eat actually is a storage organ that will develop its desired characteristics only when the plant is grown under precise cultural and environmental conditions. Any negative conditions—low fertility, insufficient light, limited moisture, crowded spacing, improper soil and air temperatures or competition from weeds and grasses—will cause carrot roots to be misshapen, tough and poorly flavored.

The second growing requirement is properly prepared soil. Since the carrot's edible portion is produced below ground, shallow, tight, rocky or improperly prepared soils will not be conducive to the production of smooth, high-quality carrots.

Obviously, special attention must be given to planting time if your carrots are to grow and develop during ideal environmental conditions. Carrots produce best when temperatures during their growth range from a low of 40 degrees to a high of 85 degrees. For a spring crop, planting should terminate about 90 days before temperatures are expected to exceed 85 degrees. In the fall, planting should cease about 90 days before temperatures are expected to drop near 20 degrees. Obviously, if you live in an area of Texas that normally doesn't experience severe winters, planting can occur from late summer through early spring.

However, overwintering your carrots can cause problems, even in South Texas. The carrot is a biennial, which means it normally grows vegetatively during its first year, then flowers and produces seed the second year. If carrots grow for a period of time and then are exposed to temperatures of 45 degrees or below for several weeks, they will go dormant and become vernalized, or be induced to flower. When temperatures rise and the carrots resume growth, they will bolt or flower. Bolting is most likely to occur if dormancy is induced when the carrots' roots are more than 1/4 inch in diameter.

Carrot seedlings are fairly cold hardy and are not subject to vernalization if their roots are no larger than the 1/4 inch diameter. Therefore, planting can occur in either late winter or early spring,

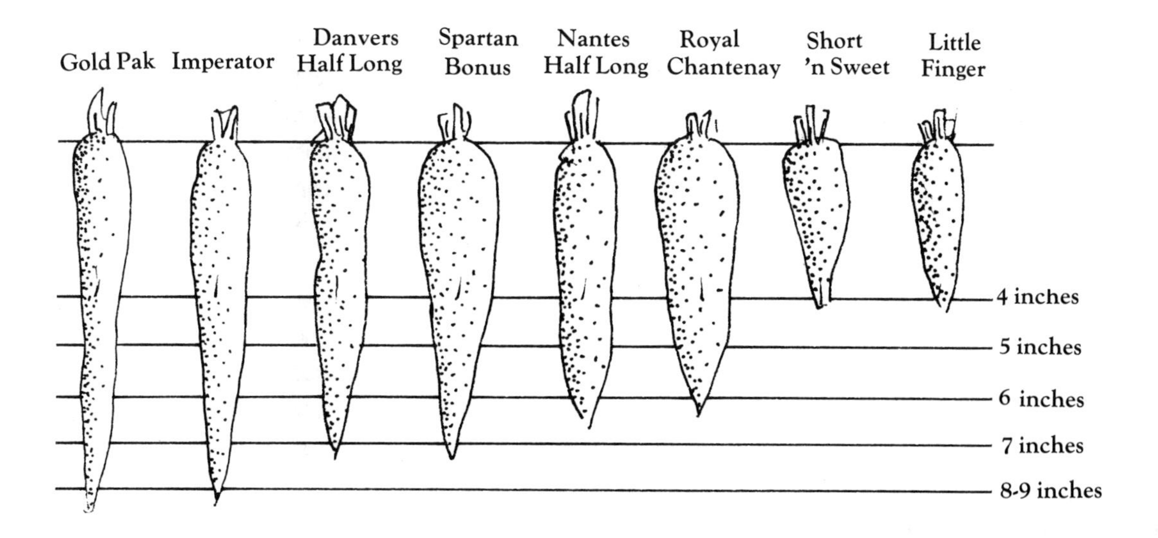

Carrots are available in many different varieties. Some produce carrots that are long and thin, while others are shorter and fatter. Select a variety that is best suited to your soil and growing conditions.

exposing the small plants to dormancy-inducing temperatures without fear of vernalization. However, temperatures near the low 20s can severely damage or kill the plants.

The Perfect Soil For Carrots

The ideal soil for growing carrots is a deep, well-drained, sandy loam. However, you can grow a successful crop of carrots in almost any soil—if it's properly prepared. Like most vegetables, carrots respond to the addition of organic matter to the soil. Spread 2 to 3 inches of leaves, grass clippings or compost over the area to be planted. The organic matter will loosen up heavy soils and help sandy soils hold moisture and nutrients. (Note: If you plan to use barnyard manure to improve your soil, it should be incorporated several months prior to planting or else the carrot roots may be rough and forked.)

When preparing your soil for planting, you should also consider its pH level. Carrots prefer a soil with a pH between 6.5 and 7.5. If you garden in East Texas and have had difficulty growing carrots (or other crops) in the past, your soil may be too acidic. Chances are lime should be added, according to the directions given on page 394.

Carrots normally do not require heavy fertilization prior to planting. In fact, if they follow a crop which was fertilized heavily, you may not need a preplant application of fertilizer. Excess fertility can cause your carrots to exhibit the "all top and little bottom" effect.

In most cases, however, a light application of preplant fertilizer usually is beneficial. Scatter about 1 pound of a complete fertilizer over each 100 square feet or 35 feet of row to be planted in carrots. A fertilizer such as 10-20-20 usually is satisfactory if you live in East Texas or along the coast, while 10-20-10 is adequate for most other areas of Texas.

After adding all the necessary ingredients and tilling them into the soil to a depth of 8 to 10 inches, consider planting your carrots on raised beds. By forming ridges and furrows measuring 30 to 36 inches apart and then shaping them into raised beds that are about 16 to 20 inches wide and 6 inches high, you will provide your carrots with better drainage and a deeper soil in which to grow. If your soil is loose and well-drained, planting on raised beds loses some of its significance. However, raised beds will warm up earlier in the spring because more surface area is exposed to the warming rays of the sun. This is of special value in the spring, as the warmer soil temperatures will result in quicker germination, emergence and, of course, an earlier harvest.

After getting your soil ready to grow carrots, you may feel it's not just right—perhaps still a little heavy or not quite deep enough. If so, you need to plant only those varieties with short or medium length roots and not the long-rooted types. Long-rooted varieties grown on shallow soils will be misshapen and often forked, whereas short-rooted types, grown on these same soils, will produce a good crop of quality carrots. If your soil is ideal, don't worry about root length.

At planting time, it's important to have adequate soil moisture and a fine, well-prepared seedbed to encourage good germination and emergence. If your soil is on the dry side, water several days prior to the anticipated planting date to ensure good soil moisture. Just prior to planting, use a rake to smooth, level and firm the planting area. At the same time, remove any trash, large clods and rocks.

Planting Methods

Carrots can be planted in a single row, multiple rows or broadcast. Raised beds are excellent for multiple row planting or broadcasting. If you plant in rows, use a stick, your hand or the edge of a hoe to make two seeding furrows about ½ inch deep—12 to 14 inches apart—on the top of the raised bed. If your soil still seems a little dry, apply water directly in the seed furrows and allow it to soak in before seeding. Sow the seeds at the rate of about three to four per inch and cover with ¼ to ½ inch of soil.

When broadcasting, scatter seeds evenly over the bed and lightly rake the surface to cover them. Always rake down the row, and not across the row, or all the emerging seedlings will be on the edge of the bed! If a number of seeds are visible after raking, use additional soil from outside the bed to adequately cover them.

After covering the seeds, whether you plant in rows or broadcast, use the flat side of your hoe to firm the soil over them. This will encourage moisture transfer from the soil to the seed and help conserve valuable soil moisture in the seeding zone. Every effort should be made after seeding to prevent the soil from crusting, which would hinder the emergence of the relatively weak carrot seedlings. If your soil tends to crust, consider covering the seed with compost or peat instead of soil. This will prevent crusting, maintain good soil moisture, provide the seed with a better germination medium and lessen the possibility of planting too deep. Applying frequent, light applications of water with a sprinkler also will help keep the soil surface moist and prevent crusting.

Carrot seed will germinate when soil temperatures range between 40 and 95 degrees at the seeding depth, with 80 degrees being optimum. As soil temperatures decrease, the time needed for germination and emergence will increase. Consequently, emergence of the carrot seedlings may take up to 21 days in the early spring when soils are cold, while taking a week or less in late summer or early fall.

Chances are that when your stand of carrots is established you'll have more plants than needed. Thinning will be necessary for carrots to develop to their full size and quality. When carrots are about 2 to 3 inches tall, thin them to about 1 inch apart by gently pulling up the unwanted plants. Later, when the plants are about 6 inches tall, thin again to a final stand of about 2 inches between plants. When you thin, the soil should be slightly moist so the carrots can be pulled from the ground easily. Water lightly after each thinning operation to settle any disturbed soil around the remaining plants.

A Side-dressing Of Fertilizer

Following the final thinning operation or when the plants are 6 inches tall, apply a sidedress application of nitrogen fertilizer. Use 1 cup of ammonium sulfate (21-0-0) or ⅔ cup of ammonium nitrate (33-0-0) per 35 feet of row. Apply half the fertilizer to each side of the bed (or row) in a band about 4 inches from the carrots. If you use the two-row planting system, band a third of the fertilizer between the rows. Lightly work the fertilizer into the soil and then water. To side-dress broadcast-planted carrots, evenly scatter the fertilizer over the bed (and around the carrots) and immediately water thoroughly to avoid the possibility of fertilizer burn.

Leaf blight (top) and nematodes often attack carrots and can destroy your crop if control measures are not taken.

After the final thinning and application the sidedress fertilizer, mulch around the carrots with a 2-inch layer of organic matter, such as leaves, hay or grass clippings. If soil temperatures are high when you plant, apply about 1 inch of organic mulch shortly after the seedlings emerge. This will provide better conditions for seedling growth and development. Mulching will help control weeds, warm (or cool) the soil and help conserve soil moisture, which is of great importance as the carrots mature.

How many times have you heard the saying: "If you dry your carrots down when they're about ready, they'll really get long by stretching and looking for moisture." Unfortunately, this is in error. If anything, just the opposite is true! Research has shown that carrot roots develop their length during the four- to six-week period following emergence—not as they near maturity! Ideally, the soil should be maintained in a slightly dry condition early in the growth of the carrots when excess soil moisture will cause the roots to lack good length. If you "dry your carrots down" as they mature, they most likely will be tough and have numerous feeder roots branching from the main root.

How often you need to water your carrot crop will depend upon your garden's soil type, where you live in Texas and Mother Nature. During dry periods and as the carrots near maturity, you may need to water weekly, especially if you have a sandy type soil. Regardless of the method you use to water, the soil should be kept in a fairly moist condition —not too wet or too dry. Allowing the soil to fluctuate from too dry to too wet will cause the carrots to split and to be of poor quality. Determine when to water by checking the soil. If it's fairly dry an inch or two beneath the surface, apply enough water to wet the soil at least 6 inches deep.

Soilborne Insects And Diseases

Carrots are a crop that, as you might suspect, are troubled most by soilborne insect and disease problems. The most common soil insect problems, such as wireworms, grubworms and cutworms, must be prevented or controlled before planting. Wireworms are well named in that they resemble a yellowish, jointed wire about 1 inch long and have a dark head. They do their damage by puncturing and tunneling into the carrot roots. Grubworms are usually yellowish-white with a fleshy, thick, legless body about ½ inch long. They feed on the developing roots and can do considerable damage in a short period of time. If you observe either of these worms when you're preparing the soil, you should apply diazinon before planting. Diazinon also will control cutworms, which do their damage at night by cutting off the carrot plants near ground level. They usually move down the row and often can be found just beneath the soil surface—near their next victim.

Root-knot nematodes are a common occurrence in many gardens and are by far the most serious problem encountered when growing carrots in Texas. Nematodes cause swellings, or galls, on the carrot roots, inhibiting them from carrying out their normal functions of absorbing water and nutrients. As a result, the roots often are forked, have a rough appearance and the plants are usually yellow and stunted. If you've been troubled in the past with slow-growing, stunted, poor- performing carrots (or other vegetables) that exhibit knotty roots, see page 408 for directions on nematode control.

Occasionally, various leaf-spotting fungal or bacterial diseases will attack the older foliage of carrots, especially during humid and/or wet conditions. Applications of the fungicide Bravo or one containing maneb at the first sign of yellow or brown spots on the foliage generally will give good control.

The really great thing about carrots is that they can be harvested at any time as long as they are of a usable size. And there's nothing quite like a young, sweet, tender carrot fresh from the garden. However, depending upon variety and season of the year, your carrots should be full size about 70 to 100 days after planting. Carrots will take longer to mature when planted in late summer or early fall. Cooling temperatures and decreasing day lengths slow their growth.

Since carrots usually are pulled from the ground, harvesting will be much easier if the soil is slightly moist. If the tops have a tendency to break off during harvest, use a garden fork to loosen the soil next to the carrots. In the milder winter areas of Texas or up until the soil is expected to freeze in your area, carrots can be left in the garden and harvested as needed. Carrots left in cool soils often will develop additional sweetness due to the conversion of starch to sugar that occurs in the roots. However, if prolonged wet periods are expected you should harvest your crop, as carrots probably will rot if left in the ground. Carrots placed in plastic bags and stored in your refrigerator will keep for an extended period of time.

Quick Problem Solver: Carrots

Problem	Causes	Solutions
Seedlings fail to emerge.	Old seed.	Use only current season seed.
	Planted too deep.	Plant ¼ inch deep on heavy soils; ½ inch deep on sandy, light soils.
	Cold soils.	Plant after soils warm above 45 degrees.
	Low moisture.	Maintain soils at fairly moist level to ensure moisture for germination.
	Crusted soils.	Sprinkle lightly to prevent crusting. Cover seed with compost, peat, etc. rather than soil.
Seedlings die after emergence.	Damping-off (fungus).	Use treated seed; plant when soils are above 45 degrees.
	Cutworms.	When preparing soil, treat with diazinon at recommended rates.

Seedlings grow slowly, lack vigor, color.	Wet soils.	Avoid overwatering; plant on raised beds.
	Cold soils.	Plant when soil temperatures are above 45 degrees; plant on raised beds for earlier warming.
	Acid soils.	Adjust soil pH.
	Low fertility.	Apply light application of nitrogen fertilizer and water lightly.
Plants all top, no bottom.	Excess fertility.	Avoid overfertilizing when preparing soil and side-dressing.
Carrots bent, forked, twisted.	Crowded growing conditions.	Thin carrots to 1 to 1½ inches apart.
	Soil poorly prepared.	Work soil to depth of 8 to 10 inches, add organic matter, remove all trash, rocks, etc.
	Fresh manure.	If manure is used, it should be worked into the soil several months before planting.
	Wrong variety.	If soil is shallow, use only short rooted varieties.
	Nematodes.	Control nematodes as indicated in appendix.
Carrots cracked, split.	Fluctuations in soil moisture.	Maintain soil moisture at a fairly constant level. Mulch to help conserve moisture.
Carrots "knotty," rough.	Nematodes.	Control nematodes as directed in appendix.
Plants flower or go to seed.	Improper time of planting.	Plant so as carrots with ¼ inch diameter roots will not be subject to prolonged temperatures below 45 degrees.
Carrots tough, lack flavor.	Low soil moisture.	Maintain soil at fairly moist level as carrots near maturity.
	Low fertility.	Side-dress when plants are about 6 inches tall.
	High temperatures.	Sugar in roots will not develop during high temperatures. Plant so as to encourage maturity during cool temperatures.
Carrots exhibit holes, tunnels.	Wireworms, grubworms.	Treat soil before planting with diazinon, as directed on label.
Spots on leaves, yellowish color.	Leaf spot (fungus or bacteria).	Treat foliage with appropriate fungicide, as directed on label.

CAULIFLOWER

Scientific Name: *Brassica oleracea (botrytis)*
Family: *Cruciferae*
Biennial, grown as an annual
Cool Season
Varieties: Snow Crown, Snow King
Expected Harvest: 5 to 7 heads per 10 feet of row

CAULIFLOWER

If you were to poll Texas gardeners on what family of vegetables they think is the most important—nutritionally and economically—few would name the cabbages. However, the cabbage family, which includes all the different types of cabbages, broccoli, cauliflower, collards, kohlrabi, turnips, mustard, kale, rutabaga and radishes, is highly nutritious. These cole crops, as they're commonly called, are all members of the crucifer family.

Now, if you were to ask gardeners what is the most difficult crucifer to grow, most would say cauliflower. This beautiful, tasty and nutritious vegetable causes frustration each and every gardening season for Texans.

Indeed, cauliflower is one of the most difficult of all vegetables to grow successfully, and it's almost impossible to produce a large, high quality head by accident. However, if you pay close attention to the following guidelines, you can grace your dinner table with some of the best cauliflower you've ever eaten—right from your own garden. Before I detail the fine art of growing cauliflower in Texas, let's examine its origin and history. That should tell you something about the cauliflower's cultural requirements. And, I sincerely believe the more you appreciate and understand a vegetable, the more likely you'll be able to grow it successfully.

Cauliflower, like the other members of the crucifer family, originated in the Mediterranean area, with the oldest record of its use as a food dating back to the sixth century B.C. It was grown for more than 2,000 years in Syria and Turkey, but was unknown in Europe until after the Dark Ages. In England, during the late 1500s, cauliflower was known as *Cyprus Colewarts,* suggesting that it might have been introduced into the British Isles from Cyprus. Commonly grown in most of Europe by the early 1600s, cauliflower migrated to the New World with the Pilgrims. Its culture and popularity spread rapidly, and as many as 12 varieties of cauliflower were listed in American seed catalogs more than 150 years ago.

Temperature Requirements

Having originated in areas of the world with a cool climate, the cauliflower still needs relatively cool temperatures for optimum growth. All the crucifers prefer cool weather, but cauliflower is by far the most demanding. Many gardeners appreciate its climatic sensitivity (and high price in the supermarket) and consider it the aristocrat of all the crucifers. Mark Twain, who must have been a pretty good gardener, knew of its demanding requirements and called cauliflower "the cabbage with a college education."

To successfully grow cauliflower, you must realize that it cannot withstand temperature extremes, either hot or cold. In the spring, you must plant early enough to allow the cauliflower time to mature before the average daytime temperature exceeds 75 degrees. If cauliflower matures when it's warmer, the heads will be either loose and poorly developed or not developed at all. In the fall, just the opposite is the case. Cauliflower can withstand freezing temperatures, but is the least cold hardy of all the crucifers. If it freezes when the plants are near maturity or before the plants have been preconditioned by several milder cold spells, they will be injured or killed.

You should make every effort to ensure that your cauliflower matures before the weather becomes too cold or too hot, if you expect to produce high-quality heads. This goal can be achieved if you use early-maturing varieties, prepare the soil properly, set out transplants at the right time and provide some tender, loving care as the plants grow.

Plant breeders have done an excellent job in recent years of developing high-yielding, fast-maturing hybrid varieties of cauliflower that are ideal for Texas. In the spring, these superstars will produce a 6- to 8-inch diameter head in about 60 days from transplanting. They require about two weeks longer to mature in the fall. Selecting one of these new hybrids will satisfy the requirement for an early-maturing variety and will go a long way toward ensuring a bountiful harvest of high-quality cauliflower.

When growing cauliflower, you must concentrate on producing the plant first and then the head. You simply cannot produce a large, high-quality head without first producing a large, vigorous plant. And this requires a well-prepared soil.

Cultural Requirements

Cauliflower, like most crucifers, will do well on a wide variety of soil types, but prefers one that is a little on the heavy side, well-drained and has a pH between 6.0 and 7.5. If you garden in an area where acid soils are common, such as in East Texas, and suspect your pH is below 6.0, see page 394 for information on adding lime to bring the pH of your soil up to an acceptable level.

Regardless of your soil type, the addition of liberal amounts of organic matter is highly desirable, especially if you garden in a light, sandy soil. Organic matter will help sandy soils hold fertility and moisture, which are critical to success in growing cauliflower. Spread 2 to 3 inches of organic matter, such as compost, grass clippings or leaves, over the area to be planted and till or spade it in to a depth of 8 to 10 inches. In addition, cauliflower will respond to the application of well-aged barnyard manure, which should be worked into the soil at the rate of 1 pound per square foot or approximately 100 pounds per 35-foot row.

Success with cauliflower depends greatly on fertility. Relatively high levels of fertilizer will encourage the development of desirable vegetative growth. Therefore, unless your soil is very fertile, commercial fertilizer, in addition to the barnyard manure, should be added when preparing your soil for planting.

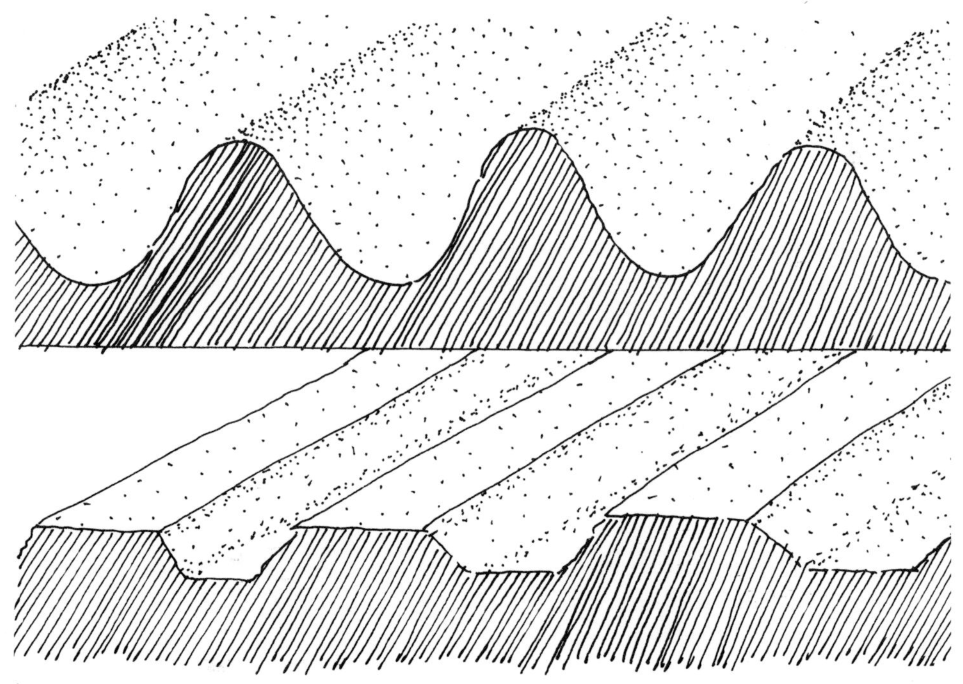

Cauliflower has a relatively shallow root system so forming ridges and furrows and shaping them into raised beds is a good idea.

The type and amount of fertilizer you should use depends upon where you garden in Texas, your soil type and its level of fertility. In much of East Texas and along the coastal areas, fertilizers with a ratio of 1-2-2, such as 10-20-20, work well. In most other areas, a fertilizer with a ratio of 1-2-1, such as 10-20-10 or 12-24-12, is satisfactory. Scatter 2 to 3 pounds of the fertilizer over each 100 square feet or 35 feet of row to be planted in cauliflower and work it into the soil. Use the lower rate if you have applied barnyard fertilizer or if your garden soil is sandy. In the fall, you probably should use a fertilizer that contains only nitrogen, especially if you fertilized heavily in the spring with a complete fertilizer. One pound of ammonium sulfate (21-0-0) or ⅔ pound of ammonium nitrate (33-0-0) per 100 square feet or for each 35 feet of cauliflower row should be adequate. Ideally, the incorporation of the organic matter, fertilizer and lime (if needed) should occur several weeks prior to planting.

Cauliflower, due to its relatively shallow root system and its preference for a well-drained soil, does best when planted on raised beds. Use a shovel, hoe or tiller with a bedder to form ridges and furrows. The ridges should measure at least 36 inches apart from the top of one ridge to the top of an adjoining ridge. Use the back side of a garden rake to flatten and smooth the ridge to form the planting bed. The bed should be 16 to 20 inches across and 6 to 8 inches high. The remaining area between the beds will be a furrow to facilitate watering and to provide drainage.

If you garden on a sandy soil, raised beds lose some of their benefit since drainage is not a common problem. However, they still may prove desirable. Raised beds don't tend to crust as severely as flat beds and they warm up more quickly in the spring, due to the increased amount of surface area that is exposed to the warming rays of the sun. Early warming will result in vigorous plant growth.

Start With Transplants

Transplanting in both the spring and fall is a requirement if you expect to successfully grow cauliflower in Texas. Hopefully, good, healthy transplants of the new hybrid varieties will be available from your local nurseries and garden centers at the right time for planting. If not, you should order seed and grow your own transplants as outlined on page 396.

In the spring, transplanting should occur about two weeks before the last anticipated killing frost. If you set the plants out earlier, damage can occur, especially if temperatures drop toward the middle 20s. Problems also can occur if temperatures remain 40 degrees or below for more than two weeks when the plants have a stem diameter greater than the size of a

As with all vegetables, it's important to plant cauliflower at the right time. If you plant too late in the spring, for example, cauliflower will "button," and form small plants with "ricey" heads. On the other hand, if you plant your cauliflower early enough in the fall and it's conditioned by several cold spells before it freezes, it can withstand freezing temperatures.

pencil. Such temperatures will cause the plants to go dormant. Oftentimes, when temperatures warm and growth resumes, they will produce small heads and may flower prematurely.

By the same token, if you transplant too late in the spring and your cauliflower is forced to mature when temperatures average above 75 degrees, the plants will be small and produce undersized, "ricey" heads of extremely poor quality.

For a fall crop of cauliflower, transplanting should occur in the late summer or early fall, depending again upon where you garden. Generally, transplanting should occur about 10 weeks before the first hard freezing weather is expected in your area of Texas. This should allow your cauliflower time to mature during ideal conditions. If you garden in an area with mild winters, you can make additional plantings and harvest cauliflower right through the winter. However, fairly large plants that overwinter are subject to dormancy and may flower when temperatures warm in the spring.

As mentioned earlier, transplanting is the rule when growing cauliflower in Texas and it's important to begin with quality plants. For early spring planting, the ideal transplant should be about 4 to 5 weeks old, have about six true leaves, and be healthy and vigorous. Avoid those plants that appear old for their size and have a stem diameter greater than pencil size. For late summer and early fall planting, the ideal plant should be somewhat older and larger to better withstand the hot weather prevalent in most of Texas during fall planting time. In South Texas and along the coastal regions, where late fall and winter plantings are common, use the younger, smaller plants to avoid premature flowering.

When it's time to set out transplants, spring or fall, your soil should be slightly moist and have good subsoil moisture. If your soil is on the dry side, water several days before you plan to plant.

Due to the size of the plants, cauliflower should be planted single row with the plants spaced about 15 to 18 inches apart. Dig the transplant holes about as deep as they are wide, pour in a cup of starter solution and allow it to soak. Using a starter solution will encourage vigorous and rapid early growth. Be sure to follow the label directions when mixing.

The best time to set out cauliflower transplants, especially when it's hot, is on a cloudy day or late in the afternoon and when the wind isn't blowing. Set the transplants deeply, just below the first leaves. Backfill with garden soil and firm the plants in, leaving a slight, dish-shaped depression around each one to help hold water. Water immediately after transplanting.

After transplanting, chances are your cauliflower plants may need protection from temperature extremes and dry conditions. You may need to water frequently and provide the plants with some form of shelter or shade from unfavorably cold or hot temperatures, drying winds and the Texas sun.

Tender, loving care, as I mentioned before, is very important to your transplants. Make every effort to be certain the transplants do not experience any checks in their growth. Any condition that causes them to quit growing, such as soils that get too dry or stay wet, low fertility, or excessive temperatures (high or low), can play havoc with your expected harvest. The cauliflower plants often will "button," which accurately describes the results, a small plant with a correspondingly small head.

Maintain the soil in a relatively moist condition—not too wet or too dry. As the plants grow larger, it may be necessary during dry spells to water once or twice a week. Shortly after transplanting and while the soil is moist, mulch around the plants with an organic material such as straw, hay or compost. Ideally, a light-colored mulch should be used when it's hot to reflect some of the heat and help cool the soil.

Approximately four to six weeks after transplanting, side-dress your cauliflower plants with 1 cup of ammonium sulfate (21-0-0) or ⅔ cup of ammonium nitrate (33-0-0) for each 35 feet of row of cauliflower. Apply half the fertilizer to each side of the row, lightly work it into the soil and water thoroughly.

Insects And Disease

As you might suspect, some insects enjoy garden-grown cauliflower almost as much as you do. Without doubt, the number one pest of cauliflower in Texas is the cabbage looper and its closely related "wormy" friends. These worms, with seemingly insatiable appetites, feed on both the foliage and the heads, causing considerable damage if left uncontrolled. You can control most worms that attack your cauliflower by using the biological insecticide *Bacillus thuringiensis.* It is sold under various trade names such as Dipel, Thuricide, Biological Worm Killer and several others.

Aphids, or plant lice as they're called by many gardeners, are often a problem on cauliflower. These small, sucking insects can be winged or wingless and generally feed on the underside of the leaves. Aphids reproduce very rapidly; and this means you should begin control measures when they are first observed, hopefully, when they are few in number. Diazinon or malathion, applied according to the manufacturer's directions, will give good control.

Soilborne insects, such as cutworms and grubworms, in addition to the brightly-colored harlequin bugs, may pose a threat to your cauliflower. Preplant applications of diazinon will control most soilborne insects and malathion usually will give good control of harlequin bugs.

Diseases of cauliflower usually are not a problem in Texas. However, several different fungi and bacteria can result in damage, especially if prolonged wet periods occur. Downy mildew, which first causes small yellow spots on the leaves that later turn brown, can reduce yields greatly. The mildew also can attack the developing heads, causing discoloration and decay. Applications of the fungicide Bravo or one containing maneb at first sign of the disease generally will give good control.

Purple cauliflower (top) is not nearly as common as the white-headed varieties, but is quite tasty. Most cauliflower is ready for harvest when the head is 6 to 8 inches in diameter and fully mature (bottom photo).

Blanching cauliflower will protect the head from the sun, enhancing its appearance. Blanching can be accomplished by pulling the leaves up to cover the head and either tying them or securing them with a clothespin.

Black rot, which is a devastating bacterial disease, can be seed-borne but usually is caused by a bacterium overwintering in the soil on residue from previously-grown crucifers. Symptoms of black rot are V-shaped yellow lesions on the margins of the older leaves and a black discoloration of the veins within affected areas. The plants often will be stunted, fail to head and may die. Chemical control is ineffective, but long-term rotations are beneficial. Therefore, to prevent the occurrence of black rot, you should never plant cauliflower, or any member of the crucifer family, in the same spot in your garden more than once every three to four years.

If you give your plants tender, loving care and adequate protection from insects and diseases, you'll soon notice the small, inner leaves of your cauliflower plants begin to cup or fold over. This is an indication that harvesttime is just around the corner. By gently separating these inner leaves you'll be able to see the small, immature head of cauliflower in its initial stages of development. At this time, you should gather up the larger, outside leaves over the head and tie them together with string or plastic tape. This blanching operation will keep light from reaching the heads, allowing them to remain white and tender. Depending upon the weather, the heads should be of suitable size for harvesting in about 10 days. If you're curious, take an occasional peek at the developing heads by carefully pulling apart the wrapper leaves. It's important to remember, however, that only a few minutes of exposure of the head to intense sunlight can cause discoloration. The discoloration, though, only detracts from the head's appearance and does not affect its taste.

Most of the better cauliflower varieties on the market will produce heads that measure 6 to 8 inches in diameter when fully mature. However, growing conditions often will affect size and the head can be smaller or much larger when mature.

If the head begins to become loose, pick it immediately, regardless of its size. If harvest is delayed, the head will not become larger, only looser and, consequently, of poorer quality. Use a sharp knife to cut through the stalk immediately beneath the head, leaving some of the wrapper leaves attached to provide protection until it's ready to be eaten.

Now you're ready to enjoy the flavor and quality of the "aristocrat of the cabbages." You'll soon understand why George Bernard Shaw in wrote in *The Apple Cart*: "What wise man, if you force him to choose between doing without roses and doing without cabbages, would not secure the cabbages?" There'll be no doubt in your mind that Shaw was referring to cauliflower—and truer words were never spoken.

Quick Problem Solver: Cauliflower

Problem	Causes	Solutions
Transplants die after setting out.	Damping-off (fungus).	Drench base of plants with a fungicide solution, according to label directions. Avoid excessive soil moisture.
	Wet/dry soils.	Avoid excessively wet soils. Plant on raised beds. In hot, dry conditions, it may be necessary to water frequently.
	Temperature extremes.	Plant at right time of year. Protect plants, if necessary, from cold, heat, winds, drying conditions.
	Cutworms.	Treat soil with diazinon as directed on label.
Slow plant growth, yellowish colored foliage.	Poor drainage.	Plant on raised beds and avoid overwatering.
	Low fertility.	Side-dress with nitrogen fertilizer.
	Acid soils.	Adjust pH of soil.
	Cold soils.	Plant at right time of year.
Holes in leaves.	Cabbage loopers and other "worms."	Treat foliage with *Bacillus thuringiensis*.
Leaves cupped, distorted.	Aphids.	Treat foliage with malathion at first sign of aphids.
V-shaped lesions on leaf margins.	Black rot (bacteria).	Remove infected plants. Do not plant cauliflower where other crucifers have been grown for at least three years.
Small plants form heads prematurely.	Cold temperatures.	Do not expose plants with stems larger than pencil size to prolonged temperatures 45 degrees or below.
	Large transplants.	Use small transplants in the spring (less than pencil size in diameter).
	Low fertility, dry or wet soils.	Avoid any condition that causes stress on the plants, resulting in checks in their growth.
Heads "ricey," rough or fail to form.	High temperatures.	Plant so cauliflower will mature before daytime temperatures average above 75 degrees.
	Excess nitrogen.	Avoid overfertilizing at planting and when side-dressing.
Heads discolored, yellowish brown.	Exposure to light.	Tie "wrapper" leaves above head to exclude sunlight.
Heads loose, rough.	Overmature.	Harvest when heads are tight, usually about 6 to 8 inches in diameter.

CELERY

Scientific Name: *Apium graveolens*
Family: *Umbelleferae*
Biennial, grown as an annual
Cool Season
Varieties: Utah 5270, Florida 683
Expected Harvest: 30 to 40 stalks per 10 feet of row

CELERY

Can you imagine celery wine? How about celery gum, a celery soft drink or even a crown made of celery for winners of athletic events? Well, it's true! These items and more were at one time or another made from celery.

Celery has had a long and distinguished, if not peculiar, history. In Homer's *Odyssey* of about 850 B.C., celery is believed to be the plant called *selinon*, which the ancient Greeks used to make a wine called *selinites*. Reportedly, it was used for medicinal purposes only. Celery's use as a food was first recorded in France in the early 17th century. Its popularity grew quickly and by 1806 at least four varieties were listed in American seed catalogs.

In the early 1900s, celery could best be described as a fad food. Sears, Roebuck & Co. offered a celery brew which they claimed was a great "nerve builder." Celery soft drinks were popular, as were celery-scented soaps and celery gum. In addition, nutritionists boosted celery's popularity by saying it was good for you. Some even claimed the more celery you ate, the thinner you got. Unfortunately, that's not true, but celery is a good food for dieters since each piece, or rib, contains only about 7 calories.

Today, celery is still extremely popular in the United States, ranking only behind lettuce and tomatoes as a salad vegetable. However, its popularity cannot be attributed to being easy to grow. Celery is, without a doubt, one of the most demanding of all vegetables. It requires particular climatic conditions and a great deal of one thing many gardeners lack—patience.

Commercial celery production is confined to relatively few areas in the United States, primarily California, Florida, the Michigan-Ohio area, New York and a small acreage in the Lower Rio Grande Valley. The reason it's grown in so few places is simple: celery requires up to five or six months of temperatures averaging between 50 and 70 degrees to produce high-quality stalks. And even in the great state of Texas, you'll have to look far and wide to find a place such as that!

Transplants And Patience

Celery can be grown successfully in Texas, but you must have patience and pay close attention to time of planting. You should always set out transplants, because then you won't need the full five or six months of 50- to 70-degree weather that you would need to grow celery from seed. However, even transplants require about 110 days to mature. Unfortunately, transplants are impossible to purchase in Texas, except in a few areas around San Antonio and in the Valley. Therefore, the persistent gardener must grow his own transplants, which is no simple matter. Celery plants take 12 to 16 weeks to reach transplanting size and also require precise conditions for seed germination and seedling growth, which I'll discuss shortly.

If you're still set on growing your own celery and are willing to accept the challenge, you must first determine exactly when transplanting should occur by studying the average weather patterns for your area. Determine what the temperature norms are for your area and base your planting dates on that information.

Celery must be considered a cool-season crop. It is cold hardy, but can be damaged by excessive or prolonged cold. Therefore, it needs to mature before temperatures drop much below 28 degrees. By the same token, celery that matures when temperatures average above 75 degrees usually will be tough and bitter.

In general, if you live in an area south of Austin, along the coastal regions, or in most of East Texas, you should transplant during mid- to late summer. For you folks in deep South Texas, the transplanting period can be somewhat later due to your mild winters. If you garden in Far West Texas, the Hill Country, North or North Central Texas, celery generally grows best as an early summer transplanted crop. Remember, celery requires cool temperatures for optimum growth and development, but should be set out early enough to mature before temperatures in the mid-20s are expected.

Another factor affecting when to transplant is that celery is a biennial, which means it normally produces vegetative growth the first year and flowers or produces seed during its second year. However, celery will be induced to flower prematurely if the plants are exposed to temperatures of 45 degrees or below for even a short period of time.

To grow your own celery transplants, seed in flats or peat pots 12 to 16 weeks before the anticipated transplanting date. When the seedlings are about 6 weeks old, transplant them into a small pot or flat. A cold frame is an ideal place to grow celery plants and to harden them off before setting outdoors.

Therefore, if you plant too early in the spring and the plants are exposed to cold temperatures, they will flower almost immediately when temperatures warm. The same thing may happen to you folks who garden in the milder areas of Texas and overwinter your celery.

As I mentioned earlier, it will be almost impossible to purchase celery transplants so you'll have to grow your own. About 12 to 16 weeks before you plan to set the transplants out in your garden, thickly sow celery seeds about a sixteenth of an inch deep into a seed flat containing a good potting soil. It's vital that the seeds be kept moist and at a temperature between 60 and 70 degrees until the seedlings emerge, which may take three to four weeks. Soaking the seeds overnight before planting will help improve germination. Cover the seedflat with wet burlap or place it in a plastic bag to help maintain adequate moisture.

Once the seedlings emerge, the flat should be placed in sunlight, hopefully at a slightly cooler temperature. About four weeks later, the seedlings should be transplanted into peat pots or pellets, then placed outside in the full sun to harden. Protect the plants from temperatures near the troublesome 45-degree mark. (Remember cold temperatures and their effect on flowering.) The ideal situation would be to place your plants in a cold frame where near optimum temperature and sunlight can be provided. If you're interested in learning how to build and operate a cold frame, see page 402.

After the initial transplanting and when the plants become established, water occasionally with a water-soluble fertilizer like Peters 20-20-20, mixed half-strength, according to the label directions. Also, it's important for celery plants not to suffer from low moisture at any time during their growth or they may remain stunted and perform poorly.

High temperatures during germination and seedling development will be a major problem if you set out transplants in late summer or early fall. Maintaining adequate moisture, misting occasionally and shading the seedlings from the hot Texas sun will provide some relief.

Fertility Requirements

For best production, celery requires a soil with a pH between 6.0 and 7.0 that is rich, moist, well-drained and deeply prepared. If your soil is too acid, its pH should be adjusted upward, according to the directions given on page 394. If you garden in alkaline soils, which are common in many areas of Texas, the addition of liberal amounts of organic matter will help bring your soil pH down to an acceptable level.

Next, scatter 2 to 3 inches of organic matter, such as compost or

You should mulch your celery transplants immediately after setting them out and watering. Mulching will help conserve moisture and control weeds.

peat, over the area. Also, apply well-aged barnyard manure at the rate of 1 pound per square foot. The organic matter will help loose, sandy soils hold moisture as well as fertility, and will improve drainage in heavier soils. The barnyard manure will provide the richness needed to grow good celery.

In addition, unless your soil is highly fertile, a commercial fertilizer should be added to your soil. The kind of fertilizer to use depends upon where you garden in Texas, your soil type and its level of fertility. In much of East Texas and along the coastal areas, fertilizers with a ratio of 1-2-2, such as 10-20-20, work well. In most other areas, a fertilizer with a ratio of 1-2-1, such as 10-20-10 or 12-24-12, is satisfactory. Scatter 2 to 3 pounds of the fertilizer over each 100 square feet or 35 feet of row to be planted and work it into the soil. Use the lower rate if your garden soil is sandy. Till all the added ingredients into the soil 8 to 10 inches deep. Ideally, your soil should be prepared four to six weeks prior to planting.

Due to its fibrous, shallow root system and its preference for a well-drained soil, celery does best when planted on raised beds. Use a shovel, hoe or a tiller with a bedder to form ridges and furrows. The ridges should measure at least 36 inches apart from the top of one ridge to the top of an adjoining ridge. Use the back side of a garden rake to flatten and smooth the ridge to form the planting bed. The bed should be 16 to 20 inches across and 6 to 8 inches high. The remaining areas between the beds will be furrows for watering and drainage.

Here is another system which works well, especially on light, sandy soils that drain well. First, apply the commercial fertilizer and lime, if needed, and work it into the soil. Then, dig a trench 8 inches deep, 20 inches wide and as long as needed. Backfill the trench about half full with

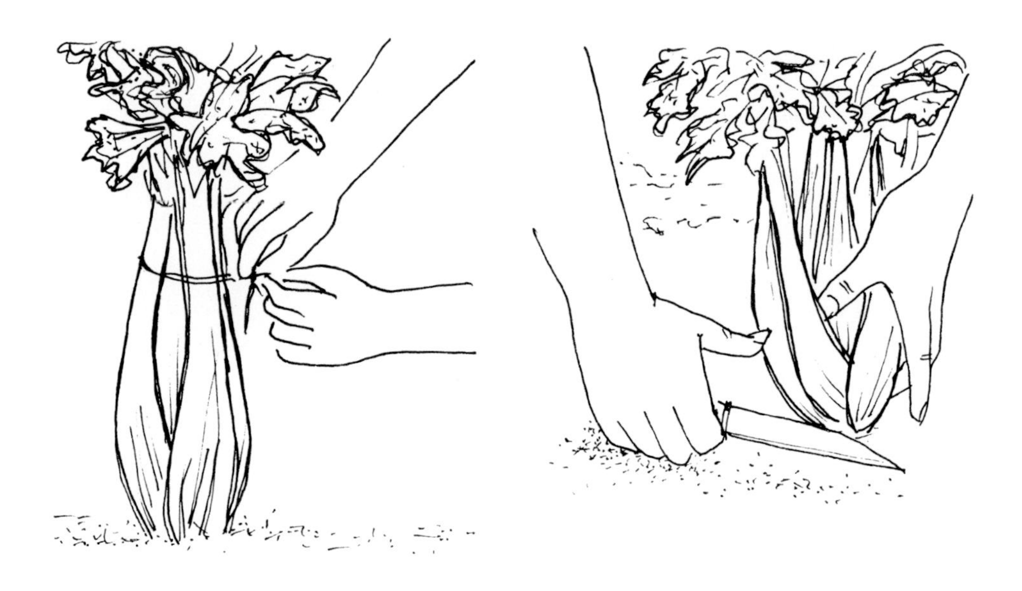

To encourage celery to form stalks, tie the stems together loosely. When harvesting, use a sharp knife to cut through the stalks near ground level.

a mixture consisting of equal parts of compost and barnyard manure. This mixture will help the loose, sandy type soils hold fertility and maintain good moisture in the immediate area around the celery roots. Finish filling the trench with garden soil for the transplants.

When you're ready to set out the transplants, the soil should be slightly moist near the surface and have good subsoil moisture. If you feel your soil is a little on the dry side, water several days prior to the anticipated planting date.

It's best to plant celery in a double row, with the rows spaced 10 to 14 inches apart and an in-row spacing of 6 to 8 inches between plants. Use a trowel or your hand to dig the holes about as deep as they are wide. Set the plants in the center of the holes, backfill with garden soil and water thoroughly. Avoid getting the crown of the plants below ground level or the plants probably will die. If possible, try to set your plants out on a cloudy day or late in the afternoon to reduce unnecessary stress and strain on you and the transplants! Mulching around your celery plants also is a good practice. Immediately after setting out the plants and watering thoroughly, apply about 2 inches of organic mulch, such as hay, grass clippings or compost, around the base of the plants. A light-colored mulch will reflect the sun's rays and result in somewhat cooler growing conditions.

More than likely, it will be necessary to provide the celery plants with protection from unfavorable conditions, especially when transplanting during high temperatures. Temperatures above 90 degrees may induce the celery plants to go dormant.

Under these conditions, it may be necessary to shade the plants for several weeks after transplanting, or until temperatures moderate. Special shading cloths, available at most garden centers, or common muslin work well. (Additional information on protecting plants from unfavorable weather is found on 407.) Tenderness and succulence, important characteristics of celery, are dependent upon adequate moisture during the growth of the plants. Therefore, depending upon soil type and Mother Nature, it may be necessary to water weekly during the early growth and development of the plants and perhaps twice a week as the plants mature. Regardless of how often you water, it is absolutely imperative that you maintain the soil in a fairly moist condition. This is especially important in warm weather and during the last six weeks before harvest, when celery grows rapidly and its demand for water is high.

You also should fertilize your celery lightly at three- to four-week intervals. Use ⅔ cup of ammonium sulfate (21-0-0) or ½ cup of ammonium nitrate (33-0-0) per 35 feet of row. Apply half the fertilizer to each side of the celery row in a band about 4 inches from the plants. If you use the two-row planting system, apply a third of the fertilizer between the rows when side-dressing the first time. And after each side-dressing, lightly work the fertilizer into the soil and water.

The close in-row spacing of 6 to 8 inches will help force the plants to grow upright and assume the normal appearance of a stalk of celery. Help the plants along by loosely tying the stems or ribs together just below the leaves. If you're interested in blanching your celery, place soil or newspaper up against the plants to exclude the light. This will cause the stems to be whitish rather than green. If you blanch with soil, avoid getting any soil between the stems, which may cause the plants to rot. Blanching is not practiced often today because unblanched, green celery is higher in vitamin A and more nutritious.

When your celery is large enough, tie the tops together to blanch the stalks.

Pests And Disease

During its growth, celery often is subject to various insect problems. Aphids and leaf miners are perhaps the most common insects posing a threat to your celery. Aphids suck juices from the plants and appear in large numbers on the foliage and on the inside surface of the stems. Leaf miners attack the foliage, forming tunnels, or mines, throughout the leaves and can cause defoliation. Both of these insects can be controlled by early applications of either malathion or diazinon. Occasionally, foliage-feeding worms can cause problems, but they can be controlled by applying the biological insecticide, *Bacillus thuringiensis.*

Various foliage blight or leaf-spotting diseases sometimes will attack celery during cool and wet weather. Generally, these diseases cause yellowish spots on the leaves, which soon darken and cause the infected tissue to die. Spraying the foliage at seven- to 10-day intervals with the fungicide Bravo or one containing maneb usually will result in good control. Soilborne nematodes will cause plants to be stunted, have poor color and wilt if they're subjected to only slight moisture stress. Nematodes, however, can be controlled by following the directions given on page 408.

Celery also is subject to nutritional deficiences. A deficiency of boron in the soil will cause the celery stems to crack and/or exhibit darkened areas on their inner surface. Soils with a high pH are most likely to have a boron deficiency. If your garden soil is alkaline and your celery exhibits the above symptoms and you've also noticed your broccoli has hollow stems, chances are your soil is deficient in boron. Before planting your next crop of celery, mix 1/8 to 1/4 teaspoon of borax in 4 gallons of water and apply the solution over each 100 square feet or 35 feet of row. Use caution because too much boron can be toxic to the plants.

Blackheart is a nutritional problem caused by a calcium deficiency. It occurs in the young heart leaves of the plant, causing them to appear water-soaked and darkened. Blackheart of celery is similar in nature to tip burn of cabbage and blossom-end rot of tomatoes. Blackheart can be controlled effectively by applications of calcium chloride applied to the foliage at the rate of 1 tablespoon per gallon of water.

Like many vegetables, celery can be harvested as soon as it reaches a usable size, but should be fully mature about 100 to 120 days after transplanting. If left growing in your garden too long, the celery will become pithy and lack good flavor. To harvest, simply cut through the root below where the stems are attached, lift the plant from the soil, and trim away excess roots, leaves and any undesired stems.

If you live in the milder winter areas of Texas and you're interested in growing celery seed, simply leave a few plants to overwinter in your garden. The following spring you'll have plenty of seed to use for flavoring your favorite recipes. The seed can be saved for planting, but this practice is not recommended since off-type plants often result.

Quick Problem Solver: Celery

Problem	Causes	Solutions
Transplants die after setting out.	Low soil moisture.	Maintain soil in moist condition, mulch around plants.
	High temperatures.	Shade plants from intense sunlight, mist occasionally.
	Cutworms.	Treat soil before planting with diazinon according to label directions. Check base of plants for worms.
	Damping-off.	Avoid overwatering.
Plants yellowish, appear stunted, grow slowly.	High temperatures.	Shade plants, maintain soil in moist condition.
	Acid soils.	Adjust pH.
	Low fertility.	Side-dress plants with nitrogen fertilizer.
	Wet soils/poor drainage.	Plant on raised beds, do not over water.
	Nematodes.	Check for "knots" on roots. If present, treat according to directions in appendix.
Plants fail to form upright "stalk."	In-row spacing too great.	Space plants 6 to 8 inches apart. Tie stems together with string, raffia, rubber bands.
Yellowish spots, lesions on foliage.	Blight/mildew (fungus).	Treat foliage with fungicide according to label directions.
Leaves discolored, poorly formed.	Calcium deficiency.	Treat foliage with calcium chloride.
Stems (ribs) cracked, discolored.	Boron deficiency.	Treat soil with borax before planting.

Bitter flavor.	High temperatures.	Celery should mature before temperatures exceed 75 degrees.
Stems pithy, tough.	Low soil moisture.	Maintain soil moist, especially during last 6 weeks before harvest.
	Low fertility.	Side-dress frequently with nitrogen fertilizer.
	Overmature.	Harvest while celery is still tender, succulent.
Trails in leaves.	Leaf miners.	Treat foliage at first sign of trails with malathion or diazinon.
Leaves cupped, distorted.	Aphids.	Treat foliage with malathion or diazinon.
Plants flower prematurely.	Exposure to cold temperatures.	Avoid exposing plants to temperatures 45 degrees or below —unless you're interested in producing seed.

COLLARDS/KALE

Scientific Name: *Brassica oleracea (acephala)*
Family: *Cruciferae*
Biennial, grown as an annual
Cool Season
Varieties: Blue Max, Champion; (kale) Blue Knight
Expected Harvest: 10 to 15 pounds per 10 feet of row

COLLARDS/KALE

Collards have one distinct advantage over most other vegetables; they actually taste better after a hard frost. And the same is true for kale, which is identical to collards except for the shape and form of its leaves. Both vegetables develop sugar in their leaves following frosty weather, which gives them a sweeter, milder flavor.

If you're a true connoisseur of greens, you'll probably disagree that collards and kale are just alike. Personally, I like collards better, but for all practical purposes they are identical. They have the same scientific name, require the same climatic conditions and culture, and are prepared in basically the same way. Thus, for simplification, let's assume they're synonymous. From this point on, we'll be talking collards, but all the information could just as easily apply to kale.

Collards are at least 2,000 years old and are thought to be the original non-heading, cabbage-like plant that gave rise to all the other members of the cabbage family of vegetables. The ancient Greeks and Romans grew several types of collards, including broad-leaved forms and those with curled leaves (probably the original kale). The first documented mention of collards in America was in about 1669, but due to their European popularity, it's believed they were introduced to the New World somewhat earlier. Collards gained wide popularity as a winter green and quickly became a favorite food of many Southern families. Being extremely high in vitamins and minerals, collards are credited for helping millions of Americans maintain acceptably nutritious diets during and after the Civil War and the Great Depression. Even today, the collard patch is commonplace across much of rural America and is gaining popularity in Texas.

Collards can be one of the easiest and most productive vegetables to grow—if you pay attention to planting dates, provide sufficient water and fertility, and protect the plants from occasional insect and disease problems.

Collards Do Best In Cool Weather

Collards require about the same growing conditions as cabbage, but are more hardy. They withstand both colder and warmer temperatures. They grow best between 40 and 75 degrees, but often can tolerate temperatures to near zero and as high as 100 degrees. Since collards are a member of the crucifer family, you'll get the highest quality greens when the edible leaves are harvested during cool temperatures. Therefore, collards usually are planted about six to eight weeks before the first anticipated frost in the fall, which allows for harvesting to occur during ideal conditions. In many areas of Texas, however, collards also can be planted four to six weeks before the last frost in the spring and can be harvested until the following spring, when they will flower, due to their biennial nature. Collards harvested during high temperatures have a strong flavor that is objectionable to some Texans, but enjoyed by many others.

Collards do well on a wide variety of soil types, even those that might be considered poor for most other vegetables. The *ideal* soil for collards, however, is a little on the heavy side, well-drained and with a pH between 5.5 and 7.0. If you garden in an area where acid soils are common, such as in East Texas, and suspect your pH is below 5.5, see page 394 for information on adding lime to bring the pH up to an acceptable level.

Regardless of your soil type, the addition of liberal amounts of organic matter is highly recommended. Organic matter will help light soils hold fertility and moisture, while improving drainage and aeration in heavy soils. Spread 2 to 3 inches of organic matter, such as compost, grass clippings or leaves, over the area to be planted and till or spade it in to a depth of 8 to 10 inches. In addition, collards will respond well to the application of barnyard fertilizer. If it's available, work well-aged manure into the soil at the rate of 1 pound per square foot or approximately 100 pounds per 35 feet of row.

Providing Adequate Fertility

A big harvest of tender, succulent leaves requires adequate fertility. Unless your soil is quite fertile, you should add a commercial fertilizer before planting. The type and amount of fertilizer to use depends upon where you garden in Texas, your soil type and its level of fertility. In much of East Texas and along the upper coastal areas, fertilizers with a ratio of 1-2-2, such as 10-20-20, work well. In most other areas, a fertilizer with a ratio of 1-2-1, such as 10-20-10 or 12-24-12, is satisfactory. Scatter 2 to 3 pounds of the fertilizer over each 100 square feet or 35 feet of row to be planted in collards and work it into the soil. Use the lower rate if you have applied barnyard fertilizer or if your garden soil is sandy. For a fall crop of collards, and especially if you fertilized your garden heavily in the spring with a complete fertilizer, you probably should use a fertilizer that contains only nitrogen. One pound of ammonium sulfate (21-0-0) or ⅔ pound of ammonium nitrate (33-0-0) per 100 square feet or for each 35 feet of row should be adequate. If possible, prepare your soil for planting several weeks ahead of time.

Collards, due to their relatively shallow root system and preference for well-drained soils, do best when planted on raised beds. Use a shovel, hoe or a tiller with a bedder to form ridges and furrows. The ridges should measure at least 36 inches apart from the top of one ridge to the top of an adjoining ridge. Use the back side of a garden rake to flatten and smooth the ridge to form planting beds. The beds should be 16 to 20 inches across and 6 to 8 inches high. The remaining area between the beds will be a furrow for watering and drainage when, or if, it rains. If you garden on a well-drained soil, preparing raised beds is not necessary since collards do well when planted "flat."

Regardless of whether you plant on raised beds or on flat ground, your soil should be fairly moist at the seeding depth and have good subsoil moisture at planting time. If you feel your soil is not moist enough, water several days before you expect to plant.

Collards can be transplanted, but generally do best when planted from seed because direct seeding will cause plants to develop a stronger, deeper-growing root system. If you decide to set out plants, collard transplants often are available at nursery or garden centers, or you can grow your own, as described on page 396.

Collards should be planted in single rows spaced at least 36 inches apart. Some publications suggest a much closer row spacing, but this practice should be avoided. Collards will yield better, be tastier and more nutritious when their leaves are exposed to as much sunlight as possible, which will not be the case under crowded conditions.

Use a stick, your hand or the edge of a hoe to make a seeding furrow about ½ inch deep. If your soil still seems a little dry, apply water directly in the seed furrow and allow it to soak in before seeding. Sow the seed at the rate of about six to eight seeds per inch and cover them ¼ to ½ inch deep. After covering the seed, use the flat side of your hoe to firm the soil over the seed. This encourages moisture transfer from the soil to the seed and helps conserve valuable soil moisture in the seeding zone.

Every effort should be made after seeding to prevent the soil from

Kale is identical to collards except for the shape and form of its leaves. Like collards, most people think kale tastes better after a freeze.

crusting over the seed. Crusted soil could hamper emergence of collard seedlings. If your soil has a past history of crusting, don't cover your seed with soil. Instead, cover them with compost or peat, which will prevent crusting, maintain good soil moisture, provide the seeds with a better germination medium and lessen the possibility of planting too deep. Frequent, light applications of water with a sprinkler also will help to keep the soil surface moist and prevent crusting.

Collard seeds will germinate when soil temperatures range between 40 and 90 degrees at the seeding depth, with 80 degrees being optimum. As soil temperatures decrease, the time needed for germination and emergence will increase. Consequently, emergence of the collard seedlings may take as long as two weeks or longer in early spring when soils are cold, and a week or less in late summer or early fall.

The Thinning Process

Once your stand of collards is established, you probably will need to thin them out, which should be done in two or three operations. The first thinning should occur when the seedlings are about 2 inches tall, leaving an in-row spacing of 4 to 6 inches between plants. If you're careful when pulling up these unwanted plants, they can be transplanted to other areas if needed. Then, when the leaves of the remaining plants become crowded, thin a second time to a spacing of 12 inches between plants. The plants you remove can be either transplanted or eaten. Whether or not you need to thin your collards a third time depends on how you plan to harvest them. If you intend to harvest the entire plant at one time, leave the plants spaced 12 inches apart. If, however, you plan on leaf harvesting your collards over an extended period of time, thin again when the plants begin to crowd each other, leaving a final spacing of 24 inches between plants. (Remember the discussion regarding spacing and adequate sunlight.) If you decide to use transplants, set them out at either the 12- or 24-inch spacing, again depending upon your harvesting method.

Shortly after the first thinning is a good time to begin side-dressing your collards with nitrogen fertilizer. Use ⅔ cup of ammonium sulfate (21-0-0) or ½ cup of ammonium nitrate (33-0-0) per 35 feet of row. Apply half the fertilizer to each side of the row in a band about 4 inches from the plants. After each side-dressing, lightly work the fertilizer into the soil and then water.

Fertilizing your collards every three or four weeks will encourage high yields of tender greens. *However*, if you garden in the colder areas of our state, do not fertilize within about three weeks of when temperatures are expected to drop toward the middle to lower 20s, or damage to the plants may occur.

Collards have a relatively shallow root system with most of their feeder roots found in the top 10 to 12 inches of soil. Therefore, it is important to maintain the soil in a fairly moist condition by watering every five to seven days, depending upon rainfall and soil type. However, it's also important to note that collards do not like wet feet and will turn yellowish and grow slowly (if at all) in overly wet soils. To help conserve soil moisture during hot, dry conditions, mulch around your collards with hay, straw, grass clippings or compost after watering in the first side-dressing of nitrogen fertilizer.

Insects And Diseases

Like all members of the crucifer family, collards are subject to problems related to insects and diseases, although not as much as their more popular relatives, broccoli, cauliflower and cabbage. Loopers are the most common foliage-feeding pests of collards, but can be controlled easily with applications of the biological insecticide *Bacillus thuringiensis*. Aphids also can be a problem, but early applications of malathion or diazinon usually result in effective control.

Downy mildew, a fungus disease, causes yellowish areas on the leaves that later become dark and necrotic. It is primarily a cool weather problem and can greatly reduce the quantity of edible greens. Applications of the fungicide Bravo, or one containing maneb, at the first sign of the disease and repeated at seven- to 10- day intervals will result in good control. Black rot, which is a devastating bacterial disease, can be seed-borne, but usually is caused by a bacterium which overwinters in the soil on residue from previously grown crucifers. Symptoms of black rot are V-shaped yellow lesions on the margins of the more mature leaves and a black discoloration of the veins within the infected areas. The plants often will be stunted, nonproductive and may die. Chemical control is ineffective, but long-term rotations are beneficial. Therefore, to prevent the occurrence of black rot, never plant collards or any other member of the crucifer family in the same spot in your garden more than once every three or four years.

Collards normally will be at a mature stage within about 90 days from seeding. However, as indicated earlier, you can begin enjoying collard greens at almost any stage. Harvesting usually is performed in one of two ways. Either the whole plant is harvested at a relatively young and tender stage, or the lower, more mature leaves are removed from the plant as they reach an edible stage. Most gardeners prefer the latter system since yields are greater and the harvest season is extended over a much longer period of time. If you practice this system, remove and discard any leaves that become discolored or appear over-mature. The final harvest will be a clump of succulent, tender leaves at the top of a bare stalk that is several feet tall.

Quick Problem Solver: Collards/Kale

Problem	Causes	Solutions
Seeds fail to germinate and emerge.	Old seed.	Always use current season seed.
	Cold soils.	Wait until soil temperature is above 40 degrees.
	Planted too deep.	Cover seed ¼ to ½ inch deep.
	Low moisture.	Seed when sufficient soil moisture is present at the seeding depth. Apply moisture if needed before planting.
	Crusted soils.	Cover seed with peat or compost rather than soil. Keep surface of soil moist.
Seedlings die/fall over.	Damping-off (fungus).	Use treated seed and plant when temperatures and soil moisture conditions are favorable.
	Cutworms.	Check base of surviving plants for cutworms. If present, treat with appropriate insecticide.
Plants grow slowly, lack color.	Wet soils/poor drainage.	Plant on raised beds rather than on flat ground. Add organic matter to improve soil drainage.
	Acid soils.	Adjust pH of soil.
	Low fertility.	Apply light application of nitrogen to side of plants and water.
	Cold soils.	Seed when soil temperatures are above 40 degrees.
Holes in leaves.	Loopers.	Check for presence of "inch worms." If found, treat with *Bacillus thuringiensis.*
Leaves cupped, wrinkled.	Aphids.	Treat with diazinon or malathion.
V-shaped lesions on leaf edges; vascular tissue discolored.	Black rot (bacteria).	Remove infected plants, follow 3 to 4 year rotation with all crucifers.
Yellowish spots on leaves which soon darken.	Downy mildew (fungus).	Begin applications of the fungicide Bravo or one containing maneb.
Leaves tough, bitter.	High temperatures.	Plant at right time of year to cause collards to mature during cool temperatures.
	Overmaturity.	Harvest leaves (plants) at a young, tender stage.
Plants "go to seed" or flower prematurely.	Exposure of plants to cold temperatures.	Plants exposed to prolonged temperatures below 45 degrees will often flower when temperatures warm.

CUCUMBER

Scientific Name: *Cucumis sativus*
Family: *Cucurbitaceae*
Annual
Warm Season
Varieties:
  Slicing: Dasher II, Slice Master, Sweet Slice, Sweet Success, Burpless
  Pickling: Liberty, Carolina
Expected Harvest: 8 to 12 fruit per plant

CUCUMBER

Cucumbers originated in India, somewhere between the Himalayan Mountains and the Bay of Bengal, long before the beginning of written history. Their culture and use is described in detail in ancient Greek, Roman and Chinese literature. Just how cucumbers spread across Asia and Europe is only speculation, but it is a well-known fact that Columbus introduced cucumbers to the New World when he planted them in Haiti in 1494. Their culture rapidly spread across the West Indies and then to America. An explorer, Fernando De Soto, reported cucumbers were cultivated widely in Florida in 1539. By the American Revolution, they were a common item in the gardens of American colonists.

Today, cucumbers are grown in nearly every home garden in Texas. One of the main reasons for their popularity is that they're easy to grow. Almost anyone can plant a packet of seed and, within a relatively short time, harvest a few cucumbers for the dinner table.

The key word in the above statement is "few." If you're an avid gardener, words such as few, fair, average and poor are totally unacceptable when it comes to describing yields from any garden vegetable. And there's absolutely no reason why such words should ever be used to describe your results in growing cucumbers.

Before we get into the "hows and whys" of growing cucumbers, it's important for you to determine how you want to use your crop. Are you going to enjoy your cucumbers fresh for your salad, pickled for your pantry, or perhaps both? You need to make this decision before you ever plant a seed in your garden. Why? Because all pickles are cucumbers, but not all cucumbers are pickles. There are cucumbers for pickling and there are cucumbers for slicing.

When mature, most slicing cucumbers are dark green, 8 to 10 inches or longer in length and usually about 1½ inches in diameter. Slicers have been developed for fresh use and are not intended to withstand a brining or pickling process. Pickling cucumbers generally are lighter green in color and considerably shorter in length. Most important, they have been developed with certain characteristics which allow them to go through the pickling process and still maintain a desirable internal structure. This is of special importance if you put up whole pickles, but of little value if you're making bread-and-butter pickles or a relish.

True, you can pickle a slicing cucumber—just like you can fry a hen! It can be done, and is done all the time, but if you're really interested in quality and you intend to put up pickles, grow pickling cucumber varieties. Likewise, if you want fresh cucumbers for garden salads, plant slicing cucumber varieties. However, I'll be realistic and offer a compromise. If you have limited garden space and want cucumbers both for salads and pickling, plant pickling varieties, which can be used for both purposes. If you have room, though, plant a few rows or hills of each type.

Getting The Soil Ready

Getting your garden soil right for growing cucumbers is the next important step. It's important to remember that cucumbers and other cucurbits have extensive root systems that may grow 2 to 3 inches each day, extend out as far as the vines grow and can reach a depth of 2 to 3 feet beneath the soil surface. Obviously a tight, compacted, poorly prepared garden soil will restrict root growth and development. The results will be expressed above ground as poor plant growth, delayed maturity, increased susceptibility to foliage diseases and, without a doubt, low yields of quality fruit.

Get your garden soil ready by working it as deeply as possible, at least 8 to 10 inches—the deeper, the better. Generally, cucumbers will do best on light, loamy soils, but they will do well on most any Texas soil that is loose, friable and, most important, well-drained. For best results, the pH of your soil should be between 6.0 and 7.0. If you garden in an area where acid soils are common, see page 394 for information on adjusting your soil's pH.

Regardless of your garden soil type, 3 to 4 inches of organic matter, such as well-rotted leaves, grass clippings or compost, spread over the area to be planted and then tilled or spaded in works wonders. The organic matter will help sandy-type soils hold moisture and nutrients. More importantly, if your soil is on the heavy side, the organic matter will loosen it up and provide better drainage and aeration, thereby encouraging the development of a strong and extensive root system.

All pickles are cucumbers but all cucumbers aren't pickles. Pickling cucumbers are smaller and have a different texture than the larger varieties used for slicing.

At the same time you're working in the organic matter, you probably should add some fertilizer. Cucumbers are relatively heavy feeders and the addition of nutrients in the form of commercial fertilizer and/or barnyard fertilizer generally is beneficial.

Ideally, both types of fertilizer should be used. An adequate amount is about ½ to ¾ pounds of well-rotted barnyard fertilizer, along with 1 to 1½ teaspoons of a complete fertilizer, distributed evenly over each square foot of area to be occupied by the cucumbers and their roots. For you folks with larger plantings, this figures out to be about 50 to 75 pounds of barnyard fertilizer and 1 to 1½ pounds of commercial fertilizer per 100 square feet of area. If your soil is sandy or is already fertile, use the lower rates.

If you're gardening in East Texas or along the upper coast, use a fertilizer with a 1-2-2 ratio, such as 10-20-20. In other areas of the state, a 1-2-1 ratio, such as 10-20-10, is satisfactory.

It seems appropriate at this time to point out that some garden publications recommend a simplified method of preparing the soil. This method consists of working up and fertilizing a 2- to 4-square-foot area and planting cucumbers in its center. Unless you have an ideal, highly fertile soil, this practice is not recommended. Because cucumbers have an extensive, spreading root system their feeder roots will grow so rapidly and vigorously that they will extend beyond the small prepared area within three to four weeks after planting. Therefore, it's far better to work up and fertilize the entire area the cucumber roots are expected to occupy—if you're striving for maximum yields.

After preparing your soil, it's generally a good idea to prepare raised beds for planting, especially if your garden soil is a little tight and on the heavy side. Not only will raised planting areas provide better drainage, but they also will warm up earlier in the spring since more surface area is exposed to the sun's warming rays.

Use your shovel, hoe or tiller with a bedder to form ridges and furrows that measure at least 36 inches from the top of one ridge to the top of an adjoining ridge. Next, use the back side of your garden rake to shape and smooth the beds into planting areas. The beds should be 6 to 8 inches tall and 16 to 20 inches wide across their tops, with the remaining area being a furrow for watering or drainage. After forming the beds, again use the flat side of your garden rake or something similar to tamp the beds firm. Firming will consolidate the soil particles and help ensure the lateral movement of water within the beds. After working up your soil and preparing the area, you're ready to plant.

When planting during summer or fall, soil temperatures are of little concern, as cucumber seed will germinate well at temperatures in excess of 100 degrees. Therefore, your only concern with regard to time of fall planting is that it should occur early enough to allow the plants to produce a good harvest before the first killing frost.

When it comes to spring planting, though, don't get over-anxious and plant too early. Cucumber seeds planted before the soil temperature is above 60 degrees may either rot in the ground or emerge as weak plants that are subject to attack by various soilborne fungi. Plants that do survive cold soils and poor growing conditions during their early development will never grow vigorously or produce anything close to a bumper crop of cucumbers.

Early soil warming can be hastened by covering the bed or planting area with black plastic and planting through it. Not only will the black plastic help the soil warm up earlier, but it also will conserve soil moisture and help control weeds. If you're interested in using black plastic as a mulch, see page 397 for directions.

Homegrown cucumbers usually are planted in hills rather than in rows, which are common in most commercial fields. Hilling does not refer to planting on mounds, as you might suspect, but rather to planting four

Cucumbers can be planted early in the spring if you protect them from the elements.

to six seeds, or plants, in clumps. Cucumber hills should be spaced 2 to 3 feet apart, either on top of raised beds or on flat ground.

Cucumber seed should be planted at a depth of 1 to 1½ inches, with the greater depth used on lighter soils. Enough moisture should be available at the planting depth to initiate germination. If the soil is dry at planting time, you should water several days in advance. Planting in dry soils, followed by watering, often results in the occurrence of soilborne seedling diseases and should be avoided if possible.

If adequate soil moisture is available and soil temperatures are satisfactory, the cucumber seedlings should emerge within five to 14 days, with the longer time required when soil temperatures are cooler.

About a week after emergence, each hill should be thinned to two plants. Remove the weakest looking plants and leave the larger, more vigorous ones. When thinning, it's better to cut or pinch off the unwanted plants near ground level. If you pull them from the soil, you could damage the roots of the remaining plants.

Although cucumbers usually are seeded in the garden, you can hasten your first harvest by about seven to 10 days if you set out transplants rather than direct seed. Oftentimes, good healthy transplants of the right varieties are impossible to purchase, especially at the right time for planting. If you're interested in growing your own transplants, see page 396.

The Ideal Transplant

The ideal cucumber transplant for setting out in your garden is about 3 weeks old and should be grown in a plantable container, such as a peat pot or pellet. Using the proper spacing, dig holes wide enough to hold the plants and just deep enough so that the peat pots or pellets will be just below the soil surface after planting. Apply a cup of starter solution, mixed according to label directions, into each hole and allow it to soak. If you're planting hills, place two plants growing in plantable containers in each hole and backfill with garden soil. Firm the soil around the plants, leaving a slight dish-shaped depression to hold water. Then water immediately.

If you're transplanting through black plastic, use exactly the same procedure as just described. However, make absolutely certain that the transplant stems are not in contact with the plastic sheeting. The plastic can damage or actually cut through the tender stems when the wind blows the plants back and forth.

Young cucumber plants grow best when nighttime temperatures remain above 55 degrees. These conditions can almost be assured by planting after all danger of frosty weather has passed and by covering the transplants or the seeded area with hotcaps or some form of covering to provide warmer temperatures.

If you're a typical Texas gardener and want to produce the first spring cucumbers on the block, you'll probably be tempted to seed or transplant early and use the coverings to provide protection from cold weather. However, unless you also use black plastic to warm the soil, research has shown that little, if any, benefit is derived from planting cucurbits early. Protective covers, in combination with black plastic mulch, though, will result in environmental conditions both above and below ground which are conducive to early germination or good transplant growth.

If you want to have the first cucumbers in your area, put the black plastic down three to four weeks prior to the frost-free date. Wait seven to 10 days, depending upon the weather, before planting to allow the black plastic time to warm the soil. Immediately after planting, place the protective covers or hotcaps over the transplants, or the seeded area, and hold them in place with soil. These measures should result in rapid germination and healthy, vigorous plant growth. You should remove the hotcaps or protective coverings when nighttime temperatures average above 60 degrees or, if necessary, when the plants need additional room for growth.

When your cucumber plants begin to vine, or run, you should consider side-dressing them with additional fertilizer to stimulate growth. Scatter about 2 tablespoons of ammonium sulfate (21-0-0) or 1⅓ tablespoons of ammonium nitrate (33-0-0) in a circle around each hill about 12 to 15 inches from the plants. Make sure you do not get the fertilizer on or too close to the plants, because it can damage or kill them. After applying the fertilizer, lightly work it into the soil, avoiding damage to the roots, and then water.

If you opt to grow your cucumbers on black plastic, you have two choices regarding side-dressing. You can put the fertilizer down before you cover the bed with plastic, or you can roll back the plastic, apply the side-dressing in a band beside the plants and then put the black plastic back in place. Either system works well, but applying the fertilizer before putting down the black plastic is best if you have a large planting.

If you don't use the black plastic as a mulch, apply an organic mulch around the plants after side-dressing. Well-decomposed hay, leaves, grass clippings or compost, applied about 2 inches thick, will stabilize the soil temperature, conserve moisture and help control weeds. Organic mulching materials also will help maintain the soil around the plants in a loose, friable condition and, when turned under, will improve the condition of your soil.

You must decide whether to allow your cucumber plants to grow over the surface of the garden or to train them to climb on a trellis. To me, the choice is obvious. Take advantage of the cucumber plant's ability to climb. Cucumber plants have grasping tendrils which develop in the leaf axils. Once the tendrils are about a third grown, they become very sensitive to contact and will wrap around almost anything they touch. This grasping and clinging characteristic gives the cucumber plant the ability to climb.

There are several advantages to growing cucumbers vertically. Your yields of cucumbers will be increased because of improved air movement around the leaves, keeping them drier and less susceptible to foliage diseases. And, if insects and diseases do occur, they're easier to see and control. In addition, upright plants are less susceptible to damage from heavy rains or hail—common problems in Texas. Another advantage of great importance to you folks with small gardens is that the plants take up far less space growing vertically than they do sprawled across the surface of your garden.

Many different structures can be used to support the upright growth of cucumbers, including trellises, pole teepees, fences and cages. I

Cucumbers have both male and female blooms and pollination must occur in order for fruit to set. As soon as your plants start to vine, you must decide whether to let them grow on the ground or provide them with some type of support. Cages, like those used for tomatoes, are excellent choices.

prefer to use cages and suggest you plant a hill or two of cucumbers, spaced about 3 feet apart, to allow room for cages made of concrete reinforcing wire or some similar material. Cucumber cages are identical to those used to provide support for tomato plants. Directions for making cages are given on page 398. Place a cage over each hill of cucumber plants after side-dressing and mulching. The plants will grow up the inside of the cage, although you may have to initially make sure the vigorously growing plants remain confined within the wire cylinder.

Cucumbers are extremely sensitive to moisture stress, especially during the early stages of growth and during fruiting. Insufficient moisture during these periods will result in stunted plants with poorly developed root systems and gourdy, misshapen fruit.

Mulching will help conserve soil moisture, but additional water usually must be applied. The best way to water your cucumber plants is either by furrow irrigation or by using a soaker hose or drip system. Make every effort to avoid wetting the foliage when watering because this will encourage the development of diseases. Depending upon Mother Nature, your soil type and the plant's stage of growth, you may need to water several times a week. When you do water, apply enough water to wet the soil to a depth of 6 to 8 inches.

Ensuring Adequate Pollination

Regardless of how well you grow your cucumber plants, your yield will be low without adequate pollination. Pollination is defined as "the transfer of pollen from the anther, or male part of a flower, to the stigma, or female part of a flower." In cucumbers, the male and female parts are found in separate flowers and, to add to the problem, not all cucumber varieties have both male and female flowers. In case you're wondering, the female blooms are those with the small, immature cucumber located directly behind the flower petals. The male blooms don't have the immature cucumber.

Varieties such as Poinsett, Liberty and National Pickling are monoecious, which means they have both male and female flowers on the same plants. Some of the newer varieties, such as Slice Master and Dasher II, produce only female blooms, meaning they're gynoecious. If you plant a gynoecious variety, a few seed of a monoecious variety are included in the seed packet to provide pollen producers. There are also parthenocarpic varieties, such as Sweet Success, which will set fruit without pollination. As a result, the fruit are seedless. Parthenocarpic varieties originally were developed for greenhouse culture, where honeybees are not welcome. If, however, you grow these varieties in your garden and pollination occurs, the fruit will contain seed.

As I've already indicated, the transfer of pollen from the male to the female flower (pollination) usually is accomplished by honeybees. And, the most common reason for poor fruit set in cucumbers is a bee shortage. Unfortunately, the parthenocarpic varieties, which don't need pollination, are not really heavy yielders. However, such varieties are a good choice for you folks living in urban areas where honeybees might not be abundant enough to carry out their important task.

Any condition or activity which limits honeybee activity in your garden almost certainly will result in low yields. Lots of blooms, but poor fruit set probably is due to one of the following reasons: prolonged cloudy, wet weather that greatly restricts honeybee activity; lack of naturally occurring honeybees for pollination; or misuse of pesticides.

There's not a lot you can do about cloudy, wet weather or the lack of honeybees in your neighborhood, other than hope for good weather and bring in a bee hive or two, which might not make your city neighbors too happy. However, you can play the part of the honeybee and do the pollinating yourself as detailed on page 399. You also can limit bee kill and encourage their activity by using pesticides only when absolutely necessary. If you must use pesticides, spray or dust only during late afternoon when honeybee activity is minimal.

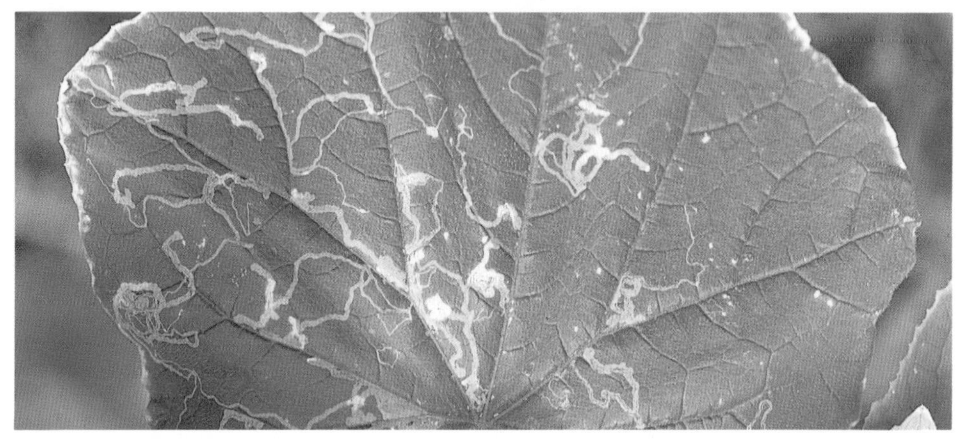

Cucumbers that suffer from moisture stress and low levels of fertility will be small and misshapen (top). Leaf miners also will do serious damage to your plants if not controlled. These small insects will tunnel between the upper and lower leaf surfaces and eventually cause the plant to defoliate. Leaf miners can be controlled with diazinon.

Insects And Disease

Without a doubt, insects and diseases will pose a serious obstacle to producing a bumper crop of tasty cucumbers. As a result, treating with the appropriate insecticides and fungicides probably will be necessary.

The most common insect pests of cucumbers are aphids, cucumber beetles, squash bugs, leaf miners and, on occasion, pickle worms. Aphids, or plant lice, usually feed on the stems and lower leaf surfaces, causing the leaves to curl and become distorted. Effective control can be achieved by early applications of malathion or diazinon.

Cucumber beetles and squash bugs basically do the same type of damage—they suck juices from the plants, causing them to wilt and sometimes die. Cucumber beetles are small, elongated, usually yellowish in color, and can be either spotted or striped. Squash bugs usually are brownish, flat-backed bugs that can be a half inch or more in length. If left uncontrolled, they can increase rapidly in number and will become a serious problem. A sure sign of a serious squash bug problem is the presence of shiny, brick-red egg clusters on the leaf surfaces. Both cucumber beetles and squash bugs can be controlled effectively by applying thiodan or Sevin at the first sign of their presence.

Leaf miners are aptly named because they do their damage by mining or tunneling between the upper and lower surfaces of the cucumber leaves. If left uncontrolled, these small larvae will completely defoliate your cucumber plants. Applications of diazinon begun at first sign of damage usually will result in good control.

If you've ever experienced the "thrill" of finding unwanted critters inside your home-processed dills or sweets, chances are they were pickle worms. However, don't let the name fool you—they enjoy cucumbers in any form and will feed on flowers, buds, vines and the fruit. Pickle worms generally will not be a problem on your early crop of cucumbers, but can be a serious threat to late spring plantings and those made during early summer and fall. Control measures must begin before the worms enter the fruit. Inspect flowers and buds for the presence of yellowish-white worms, ½ to ¾ inch long with a dark head. If found, immediately begin applications of malathion, diazinon or thiodan.

Diseases are a problem when growing cucumbers in Texas because their foliage is subject to infection by a number of different plant pathogens. Foliage diseases of cucumbers that commonly occur in Texas include downy mildew, powdery mildew and several other leaf spot diseases. In most cases, measures taken to control downy and powdery mildew also will control most of the other diseases that commonly attack the foliage of your cucumbers.

Downy mildew causes irregularly shaped yellowish or brown spots to appear on the upper surface of the leaves, often followed by a moldy growth on the lower leaf surface. Infection nearly always begins on the older leaves and is most common during humid conditions, such as in the early spring or in the late fall. Downy mildew can be controlled by applications of the fungicide Bravo, or one containing maneb, begun at the first sign of the disease.

Powdery mildew is encouraged by dry, hot weather and is almost always a problem when growing cucumbers in Texas. The primary symptoms include the occurrence of a white, powdery growth on the surface of the leaves, which causes them to wither and die. Left uncontrolled, powdery mildew can eliminate any hope of a bountiful harvest in just a matter of days. At the first sign of the white, powdery fungus, apply Benlate or Bravo and repeat at seven- to 10-day intervals.

Cucumbers, like all cucurbits, are subject to infection by soilborne nematodes that enter the plant's roots and prevent their normal growth and function. Symptoms include slow, stunted growth, knotted and swollen roots, and, eventually, plant death. If your garden soil is infested with nematodes, see page 408 for information on their control.

Harvesttime will be about 55 to 60 days after planting. Always pick the fruits as they reach a usable size. If you leave even one fruit on the vine too long, the plant will stop growing and producing. Once you begin harvesting, don't forget the fertilizer and water. Shortly after your first trip to the kitchen with a load of cucumbers is a good time to side-dress your plants again with nitrogen fertilizer. Also, during this critical period, make absolutely certain that adequate soil moisture is available to the plants. If you're forgetful or negligent, misshapen, gourdy and bitter fruit will be your reward.

Quick Problem Solver: Cucumbers

Problem	Causes	Solutions
Seeds fail to germinate, plants to emerge.	Old seed.	Always use current season seed.
	Cold soils.	Plant when soil temperatures at seeding depth is above 60 degrees.
	Planted too deeply.	Avoid planting deeper than 1 to 1½ inches.
	Insufficient soil moisture.	Soil should be moist enough at planting time to ensure germination and emergence.
Plants lack vigor, grow slowly.	Cold soils.	As above.
	Low pH.	Soil pH should be above 6.0 to ensure good plant growth. See page 394 for information on adjusting the soil pH.
	Low fertility.	Side-dress lightly with nitrogen fertilizer.

Plants die shortly after emergence.	Damping-off (fungus).	Use treated seed. Avoid cold, wet soils during time of planting.
	Cutworms.	Check soil at base of healthy plants for presence of cutworms. If found, use appropriate insecticide.
Plants bloom, but set few fruit.	Poor pollination.	Usually due to lack of honeybees. Avoid spraying garden in morning hours. Use parthenocarpic varieties (seedless) which do not require pollination.
Fruits gourdy, misshapen.	Low soil moisture.	Adequate soil moisture must be present during blooming and fruiting.
	Stress.	Any condition such as above, low fertility, high temperatures, foliage diseases will cause fruit to be of poor quality.
Yellowish spots on older leaves.	Downy mildew (fungus).	Treat foliage with Bravo or fungicide containing maneb.
Talcum-like fungus on leaves which turn brown, wither and die.	Powdery mildew (fungus).	Treat foliage with Bravo or Benlate.
"Worms" found inside fruit.	Pickle worms.	Inspect flowers for presence of small yellowish-white worms. If detected, treat with malathion or thiodan.
Tunnels or mines occur on leaves.	Leaf miner.	Treat foliage with diazinon.
Flat-backed bugs on foliage, fruit.	Squash bugs.	Treat foliage with Sevin or thiodan.
Knots on roots, plants stunted, grow slowly.	Nematodes.	See page 408 for information on nematode control.
Fruits "bitter."	Stress.	Plant at right time of year and maintain adequate soil moisture and fertility. Control foliage diseases.
Pickles soft, of general poor quality.	Improper variety.	If putting up pickles, use pickling varieties!

EGGPLANT
Scientific Name: Solanum melongena
Family: Solanaceae
Perennial, grown as an annual
Warm Season
Varieties: Florida Market, Midnight; (small fruited) Ichiban, Imperial
Expected Harvest: 7 to 20 fruit per plant

EGGPLANT

Was it a "fruit of love" or an "apple for the fool?" For a long time nothing was certain about the eggplant, except that it was thought of as a strange plant with mysterious powers. During the 16th century, the Spaniards cherished eggplants for their alleged strong romantic effects. In Northern Europe during this same period of time, eggplants were called *Mala insana*, or mad apple, and were thought to cause incurable insanity. We don't know how these completely unfounded beliefs came about, just as we also don't know why Americans thought eggplant was extremely poisonous and grew it only as an ornamental until about 75 years ago. It's hard to believe that such an attractive and tasty vegetable could have such a strange and unique history.

The eggplant belongs to the *Solanaceae* family of plants that also includes the tomato, pepper and potato. The large-fruited types originated in India while the smaller-fruited forms came from China. Although cultivated in these areas as a food for literally thousands of years, the first written accounts of the eggplant being consumed in the Western World are from Arabia and date back to the ninth century. The Moors carried the eggplant to Spain in the early 12th century and by the 1600s, round, oblong, pear-shaped and long-fruited types in many colors were common in Germany. The Spaniards introduced the eggplant into the Americas and by 1806, purple and white varieties were offered in seed catalogs for ornamental use only.

Just when we Americans first accepted the eggplant as being edible is not known and even today we don't eat much of it. However, while the eggplant is considered a minor crop in the United States, in the Orient it is more popular than either the tomato or potato. Most likely, eggplants have never become popular in the United States for two reasons: first, they're more difficult to grow than most vegetables; and second, most people aren't familiar with the many tasty ways they can be prepared. I'll have to leave the recipes to someone else, but as for the successful culture of eggplant, it's really not all that difficult if you'llpay close attention to its climatic needs.

The eggplant, having originated in tropical areas of the world, thrives in warm but not hot weather. It is extremely sensitive to frost or even mention of the word "cold." In the spring, planting should never occur until after the average daily temperature exceeds 65 degrees. If you plant before weather conditions are favorable, and the young plants are subjected to cool temperatures, they usually will remain small and nonproductive. Additional plantings can be made later in the year, but keep in mind that although the plant can thrive at high temperatures, any fruits that mature when average daily temperatures exceed 85 degrees often develop a bitter flavor, especially if the plants also are suffering from water stress.

Planting For A Fall Harvest

Oftentimes, spring-planted eggplants will survive the heat of our Texas summers and continue producing up until the first killing frost of winter. If, however, you plan on making a new planting for fall harvest, you should do so at least 120 to 140 days before the first freezing weather is expected. This will be early enough to allow the plants time to bloom and set fruit during favorable conditions and then produce a good crop before frosty weather. You must also realize that as the days get shorter and temperatures drop, it will take longer for the fruits to mature.

The eggplant will grow on a wide variety of soils, but prefers those that have a pH between 5.5 and 7.0, are high in fertility and well-drained. If you garden in an area of Texas where acid soils are common, such as in the eastern parts of the state, you should have your soil tested to determine if its pH is below 5.5. If so, lime should be added when preparing your soil to bring its pH up to an acceptable level. For information on adjusting the pH of your garden soil, see page 394.

The level of fertility in your garden soil should be high enough to ensure rapid, uninterrupted growth of the plants. Unless your soil is unusually fertile, chances are eggplants will respond to heavy applications of both barnyard manure and commercial fertilizer. Scatter about 1 pound of well-aged barnyard manure and 2 teaspoons of a commercial fertilizer over each square foot of area to be planted in eggplants. For you folks with larger plantings, this is the equivalent of 100 pounds of barnyard manure and 2 pounds of commercial fertilizer per 100 square feet or 35 feet of row. If you garden in East Texas or along the coastal regions, use a fertilizer with

It is important to till your soil before planting eggplant, working in organic matter and forming ridges and furrows.

a 1-2-2 ratio, such as 10-20-20. In the other areas of the state, a fertilizer with a 1-2-1 ratio is satisfactory.

In addition, and especially if your soil is on the heavy side and has a tendency to drain poorly, scatter 2 to 3 inches of well-rotted organic matter, such as grass clippings, hay, leaves or compost, over the area. These materials will improve aeration and drainage of heavy soils and help loose, sandy soils hold moisture and fertility.

After you've added all the necessary ingredients, till or spade the area 8 to 10 inches deep, thoroughly incorporating them. Soil preparation activities should take place several weeks prior to the anticipated planting date.

Small fruited varieties such as Ichiban and Imperial are well suited to Texas conditions.

Plant On Raised Beds

Eggplants usually do best when planted on raised beds. These beds will improve soil drainage and will warm up more quickly in the spring. If your soil is loose and well-drained, planting on raised beds loses some of its importance, although the plants still will benefit by the earlier warming of the soil.

If you decide to plant on raised beds, use your shovel or a tiller with a bedder to form ridges and furrows that measure at least 36 inches from the top of one ridge to the top of an adjoining ridge. Next, use the flat side of your garden rake to smooth and shape the ridges into beds for planting. The beds should be 6 to 8 inches high and 16 to 20 inches wide. Use the remaining areas as furrows to facilitate watering and drainage. After forming the beds, use the flat side of your garden rake to tamp the beds firm to facilitate the lateral movement of water within the beds.

You should seriously consider using black plastic sheeting as a mulch. This is a highly recommended practice in the spring, as the eggplants will respond to the warmer soils provided by the black plastic. In addition, regardless of what season it is, the black plastic will help conserve soil moisture, prevent compaction and control troublesome weeds. Directions for applying the plastic are given on page 397.

Planting eggplants in Texas always should refer to transplanting, although they can be directly seeded in your garden with some degree of success. Transplanting, though, usually results in an earlier harvest and allows fruits to develop and mature before temperatures become too hot or too cold.

Eggplant transplants usually are available at most nurseries and garden centers in Texas. If, however, you're interested in growing your own transplants, details are given on page 396. When purchasing eggplant transplants, select those that are 6 to 8 inches tall, have a vigorous appearance and a good green color. Avoid those plants with stems that appear hard and woody. Chances are they have suffered stress from low moisture and/or fertility during their growth and will perform poorly when set out in your garden.

Warm temperatures are critical to success with eggplants. Therefore, even though you're sure that the last of the cold weather is over, and in spite of the fact that all your gardening friends already have their eggplants in the ground, wait at least another 10 to 14 days before setting out your plants. Come harvesttime, you'll be glad you did.

When at last it's time to plant, your soil should be moist—not too wet or too dry. If it's on the dry side, water several days in advance of the anticipated planting date. Also, if possible, set out the transplants on a cloudy, windless day to avoid undue stress on the plants. This is of special importance when transplanting during hot, dry conditions.

Use a trowel or something similar to dig transplant holes that are about as deep as they are wide. For maximum production, eggplants should have an in-row spacing of 2½ feet between plants with the rows spaced no closer than 3 feet apart. Pour 1 cup of a starter solution in each hole and let it soak. Starter solutions are nothing more than water-soluble fertilizers that will supply the transplants with needed fertility until they develop a larger root system. Place a transplant in the center of each hole and backfill with soil. Unlike the tomato, eggplants do not have the ability to form roots along their stems, and so deep planting should be avoided. Firm in the plants leaving a dish-shaped depression around each one to hold water. Water immediately after transplanting.

If you use black plastic sheeting as a mulch, simply cut holes in the sheeting at the proper spacing and follow the planting procedure outlined above. However, make certain that the holes are large enough so that the stems of the plants do not come in contact with the plastic sheeting. The plastic sheeting actually can cut through the tender stems as the plants are blown back and forth by the wind.

Protecting Your Plants

Chances are your plants will need protection from the elements for a while after planting. Use newspaper, milk cartons, plastic sheeting, shingles or whatever is available to shelter the plants from high winds, intense sunlight, and either high or low temperature extremes. In the spring, even though you have no doubt been ridiculed by your gardening friends for setting your plants out late, it's a good idea to cover them with hotcaps or something similar for a week or two to provide even warmer growing conditions.

About three weeks after transplanting, begin side-dressing your plants with nitrogen fertilizer. Use 2 tablespoons of ammonium sulfate (21-0-0) or 1½ tablespoons of ammonium nitrate (33-0-0) for each plant. If you only have a couple of plants, apply the fertilizer in a circle about 12 inches from the plants. If you have a considerable planting, you can apply the fertilizer in a band on both sides of the row at about the same distance from the plants. Lightly work the fertilizer into the soil, avoiding damage to the roots, and then water. Repeat this procedure every three weeks during the season to maintain the plants in a vigorous state of growth. As the plants (and root systems) enlarge, apply each side-dressing of fertilizer at a slightly greater distance from the plants—but never at a distance greater than about 18 inches.

When side-dressing eggplants grown on black plastic, roll back the sheeting and apply the first application of fertilizer in a band as just discussed. Subsequent side-dressings can be made at the outer edge of the plastic mulch.

If you don't use the black plastic sheeting, mulch around the plants with organic matter after you apply the first side-dressing of fertilizer. Do not apply an organic mulch too early in the spring, though, or its insulating effect will delay warming of the soil. Apply 2 to 3 inches of well-decomposed hay, grass clippings, leaves or compost around the base of the plants.

The eggplant is a vegetable that needs a generous supply of soil moisture at all times. Depending upon soil type, the season, plant size and, most importantly, Mother Nature, it may be necessary to water as frequently as twice a week. Check your garden soil when deciding when to water. If it's relatively dry an inch or so beneath the surface, it's time to water. Apply enough water each time to wet the soil to a depth of 6 to 8 inches.

Depending upon variety and the season, your eggplants will be ready for harvesting about 70 to 90 days after transplanting. The fruits can be consumed at any usable size, but should be harvested before they become tough and the seeds begin to harden. The highest quality eggplant for your dinner table is about two-thirds its full size and its surface has enough elasticity that when gently pressed with your thumb, it springs back, leaving only a slight impression. Since the stems are woody and tough, harvesting is best accomplished with the aid of a sharp knife or pruning shears. As the season progresses and the plants become heavily loaded with fruit, you may need to support them with cages or stakes.

Controlling Insects And Diseases

Your expected bountiful harvest may become only a gathering of a few misshapen, poor quality fruit if insects and diseases are not controlled. The most common insect pests attacking eggplants in Texas are leaf miners, potato bugs, flea beetles and spider mites. The predominant diseases are nematodes, anthracnose, fruit rots and yellows.

Leaf miners are minute larvae that actually feed off the plant by tunneling between the upper and lower surfaces of the leaves. If left uncontrolled, they can severely reduce the leaves' photosynthetic ability and greatly reduce yields. Control can be achieved by the early

Kurame (top) and casper varieties of eggplant are highly productive.

Black Beauty is one of the most common eggplants and is used in many different recipes.

applications of malathion or thiodan, begun at the first sign of mines or tunnels.

Potato bugs and flea beetles feed on the foliage of eggplants and can cause considerable damage. It's the larvae of the well-known potato bug that does most of the damage by feeding primarily on the leaf margins. Flea beetles are aptly named because they bite small holes in the leaf surface, causing a "shothole" effect. Potato bugs can be removed by hand and destroyed but you'll seldom see the small flea beetles, though you will see their damage. Adequate control of both of these pests can be achieved by using Sevin, malathion or thiodan.

Spider mites can be a serious problem of eggplants, primarily during hot, dry conditions. These small plant "chiggers" do their damage by sucking the plant's juices, causing a yellow mottling of the leaves and a slight webbing on the leaves' lower surfaces. None of the miticides currently available are cleared for use on eggplants, but early applications of sulphur dust usually will give good control. Be careful using the sulphur dust; it can cause considerable damage to other vegetables growing in your garden, especially members of the cucurbit family.

Soilborne nematodes can put an end to your dreams of a bountiful harvest quickly and effectively. Nematodes enter the feeder roots and cause knots, or galls, to form, decreasing the roots' ability to absorb moisture and nutrients. The plants simply quit growing, flowering and yielding fruit. If the infestation is severe enough, the plants eventually will die. Control measures should begin with a long-term rotation program that includes not planting eggplant or any of its relatives—tomato, potato or pepper—in the same area of your garden for at least two or three years. Additional information on controlling nematodes in your garden is found on page 408.

Anthracnose is a fungal disease that causes small, sunken spots to appear on the surface of the fruits. If severe enough, and left uncontrolled, it will cause the fruits to drop to the ground. Anthracnose is caused by the fungus overwintering in the soil on residue from diseased plants. Several other fungal diseases also attack eggplants' foliage or fruit. A good rotation program as just described and applications of a fungicide containing maneb begun when the fruits start to form will result in satisfactory control of most diseases.

Yellows is a viral disease spread by feeding insects that results in the yellowing of individual leaves, a portion of the plant or the whole plant. It seldom kills the plants, but yields are reduced drastically. There is no satisfactory chemical control. If you have a large planting, those plants exhibiting the virus symptoms should be removed and destroyed. If you have only a few plants, a little tender, loving care in the form of extra fertilizer and water may mask the effects of the virus infection and result in a fair harvest.

As mentioned earlier, depending upon the care provided the plants and the severity of summertime temperatures, spring-planted eggplants often will survive the heat of our Texas summers and continue producing until the first killing frost of winter. However, if you garden in the hotter, drier areas of Texas—generally south of Austin—you should consider judiciously pruning back the plants and applying a small amount of fertilizer. This will stimulate new growth and flowering. Avoid over-pruning as the intense heat and bright sunlight can cause damage and prevent rejuvenation of the plants.

Flea beetles frequently attack eggplants and will bite many small holes in the leaves. They can be controlled with an appropriate insecticide. Another serious problem with eggplants is the threat of a disease call "yellows," which as its name indicates, turns the foliage yellow.

Quick Problem Solver: Eggplant

Problem	Causes	Solutions
Transplants fall over/cut off.	Damping-off (fungus).	Plant when soil is warm and avoid overwatering. Drench base of plants with a fungicide solution.
	Cutworms.	Check base of healthy plants for presence of worms. If found, treat with cutworm bait or approved insecticide.
Plants grow slowly, have poor color.	Cold weather/soils.	Do not set out plants until average daily temperatures are 65 degrees. Mulch with black plastic to warm soils.
	Low fertility.	Side-dress plants with nitrogen fertilizer.
	Acid soils.	Adjust pH of soils.
	Planted too deep.	Avoid setting plants too deeply.
	Poor drainage.	Plant on raised beds.
Blooms fail to set fruit.	Cool, cloudy weather.	Hope for better growing conditions.
	Temperature extremes.	Set out transplants at right time so blooming will occur before excessively high or low temperatures occur.
	Insects.	Check inside blooms for presence of small, active insects (thrips). If present, treat with malathion or thiodan.
	Low soil moisture.	Maintain adequate soil moisture, especially during flowering and fruit set.
Plants remain small, stunted.	Transplanting too early.	Wait 10 to 14 days after setting out tomatoes to set out eggplants.
	Woody, hard transplants.	Use healthy, vigorous plants.
Fruits small, misshapen.	Low fertility.	Side-dress frequently during growth and development of plants and fruits.
	Low soil moisture.	Maintain soil in fairly moist condition.

Fruits lack bright color, often brownish.	Overmature.	Harvest when fruits are ⅔ full size and bright in color.
	High temperatures.	Average daytime temperatures exceeding 85 degrees will often cause poor colored fruits at maturity.
Fruits off-flavored, bitter.	High temperatures.	Fruits that mature during high temperature conditions in combination with low soil moisture will often be bitter.
	Overmature.	Harvest fruits when ⅔ full size and of good color.
Individual leaves, plants yellow.	Yellows (virus).	Remove infected plants. If desired, fertilize and water to encourage fruit production—pray!
Holes in margins of leaves, reddish larva present.	Potato bugs.	Remove pests by hand or treat plants with malathion or thiodan.
"Birdshot" holes in leaves.	Flea beetles.	Treat foliage with Sevin, malathion or thiodan.
Trails, tunnels in leaves.	Leaf miners.	Treat foliage with malathion or thiodan.
Leaves mottled, webbing on lower surface.	Spider mites.	Wash off with strong stream of water/sulphur dust will help control. Do not get sulphur on other crops, especially cucurbits.

KOHLRABI

Scientific Name: *Brassica oleracea (gongylodes)*
Family: *Cruciferae*
Biennial, grown as an annual
Cool Season
Varieties: Grand Duke, White Vienna, Purple Danube
Expected Harvest: 20 to 40 bulbs per 10 feet of row

KOHLRABI

Kohlrabi is considered to be a relatively odd vegetable. A turnip-like "bulb" that sits squat on the ground with a few stemmy, spindly leaves protruding from its sides and top, it certainly is rather strange and different. Perhaps its unique appearance is the reason why kohlrabi has never been too popular, but it is tasty, remarkably productive and relatively easy to grow. It certainly deserves more attention from Texas gardeners.

Kohlrabi has been used as a human food source for less than 500 years, which makes it one of our newer vegetables. When translated literally from German, kohlrabi means "cabbage turnips." Apparently, it first was cultured as an edible crop in Northern Europe during the 15th century. However, like all members of the *Cruciferae* or cabbage family of plants, kohlrabi is thought to have its original roots in the Mediterranean area as an offspring, or mutant, of a wild form of cabbage. It was grown commercially for the first time in Ireland in 1734 and then in England in 1837. Just when kohlrabi first came to the New World is uncertain, but records indicate it was cultured here in the early 1800s.

A bumper crop of tender, tasty kohlrabi is easy to grow—if the plants are provided with conditions conducive to rapid, unchecked and succulent growth. These requirements are easy to appreciate if you know about the morphology, or structure, of the kohlrabi plant. What we call the bulb actually isn't a bulb at all. It's the enlarged, bulbous stem of the plant. In the plant world, one of the primary purposes of a stem is to support the aboveground portion of the plant. Thus, the stem often becomes fibrous and woody so it will be strong enough to provide this support. This is especially true when the plant ages or is subjected to stress. This also applies to the kohlrabi stem. If environmental conditions, soil moisture or fertility are inadequate, and therefore not conducive to growth and development, the edible stem will become tough and inedible. It also will be inedible if the stem is allowed to overmature.

You can either drill- or clump-plant kohlrabi. Either way, you'll need to thin the seedlings when they are about 1 to 2 inches tall by gently pulling them up from the ground.

Preparing The Soil

Obviously your garden soil and how it's prepared and fertilized will have a great influence on your success in growing kohlrabi. Although it will grow on a wide variety of soils, kohlrabi will do best on medium-textured, well-drained soils with a pH between 6.0 and 7.0. If you garden in areas of Texas known to have acid soils with a pH below 6.0 and have had trouble in the past growing kohlrabi (or other crops), you might need to raise the pH of your soil by adding agricultural lime. Consult page 394 for information on adjusting the pH of your soil.

Regardless of your soil type or where you garden in Texas, kohlrabi will do best if you add liberal amounts of organic matter to your garden area. If your soil is on the heavy side, the organic matter will make it more friable and enhance drainage, which will encourage vigorous plant growth. Adding organic matter also will improve the ability of light, sandy-type soils to hold moisture and nutrients.

When preparing your soil for planting, spread 2 to 3 inches of well-decomposed grass clippings, leaves, hay or other forms of organic matter over the surface of the area to be planted and work it into the soil. Like all other vegetables, kohlrabi responds well to the addition of barnyard manure. However, when growing kohlrabi the manure should be added to

Kohlrabi plants will produce large leaves but the bulb is only about the size of a tennis ball when mature.

the soil several months prior to planting. If it's added just before planting, it may cause kohlrabi to be rough and misshapen. Work the well-aged manure into the soil at the rate of about ½ pound per square foot or 50 pounds per 110 square feet of area to be planted.

The primary purpose of using barnyard manure is to improve your soil but it also contains nitrogen, which stimulates plant growth. Unless your soil is unusually fertile, you also should add a commercial fertilizer to ensure high yields and good quality.

Depending upon your soil type and its fertility level, use the equivalent of about 1½ to 2 pounds of a complete fertilizer per 100 square feet or per 35 feet of row. Use the lower rate if your soil is fairly fertile or sandy. In East Texas and along the coastal areas, fertilizers with a 1-2-2 ratio, such as 10-20-20, work well. In most other areas of our state, a fertilizer with a 1-2-1 ratio, like 10-20-10, is satisfactory. Scatter the fertilizer evenly over the planting area and work it into the soil 8 to 10 inches deep.

Before you waste a lot of valuable time and effort, please note that the organic matter, fertilizer and lime to correct your soil pH all can be tilled or spaded into the soil at the same time. Remember, barnyard manure should be added several months prior to planting.

If your soil is a little on the heavy side, it's generally a good practice to plant in raised beds formed by ridges and furrows. Plant on top of the raised beds to lessen problems with poor drainage and soil crusting. Use a shovel or a tiller with a bedder to form the ridges and furrows, making the ridges 30 to 36 inches apart. Next, use the flat side of your garden rake to flatten and smooth the ridges into the raised planting beds. Also use your rake to tamp the beds firm. Firming will consolidate the soil particles, which will help the beds hold soil moisture and aid the lateral movement of water within the beds. When completed, the top of each bed should be 16 to 20 inches wide and the remaining area will be the furrow for watering and to provide drainage.

Kohlrabi is classified as a cool-season vegetable, but is more tolerant of both low and high temperatures than its close relative, the turnip. Highest quality will result if your kohlrabi matures when daily temperatures average below 70 degrees. The plants can be stunted or killed, though, if temperatures drop into the low 20s (or sometimes higher), depending upon the duration of the cold spell. Thus, you need to time your planting so that the kohlrabi will be maturing when temperatures are favorable.

In the spring, your first planting should occur when nighttime temperatures average above 40 degrees. Kohlrabi can withstand much colder temperatures, but is a biennial and exposure to prolonged temperatures below 40 may induce dormancy. When temperatures moderate and the plants resume growth, they may bolt or flower prematurely. For that reason, earlier plantings should be avoided.

Since kohlrabi can be damaged by cold, fall plantings should not be made later than 50 days before temperatures are expected to drop toward the mid-20s. If you live in an area of Texas where milder winters occur, plantings can be made throughout fall and winter. Just keep in mind that low temperatures can cause bolting or flowering.

Plant Kohlrabi From Seed

Planting kohlrabi always should refer to *seeding* directly in your garden. Kohlrabi is transplanted easily, but the process usually causes a check in growth that often hurts its development, so seeding is preferred. If for some reason you do want to put out transplants, it's best to use very young plants.

Kohlrabi can be planted in a single row or two rows per bed. Broadcast planting should not be practiced because it can create crowded conditions that result in excess shading and competition for water and

Harvest your kohlrabi "bulbs" when they are about 2 inches or slightly larger in size.

nutrients from adjacent plants. This situation will cause your kohlrabi to be stunted and produce low yields.

The raised beds previously discussed are excellent for two-row plantings. Use a stick, your hand or the edge of a hoe to make two seeding furrows about ½ inch deep, 10 to 14 inches apart, on the top of the 16- to 20-inch-wide bed. At planting time, your soil should be moist enough at the seeding depth to initiate germination and emergence. If your soil seems a little dry, apply water directly in the seed furrow and allow it to soak in before seeding. Sow the seed at the rate of five to six per foot of row, or clump plant three to four seeds every 6 inches. Cover the seeds about ½ inch deep. After covering the seeds, use the flat side of your hoe to firm the soil over them. This will encourage moisture transfer from the soil to the seed and help conserve valuable soil moisture.

Every effort should be made after seeding to prevent the soil covering the seed from crusting, which will hamper seedling emergence. If your soil has a tendency to crust, consider covering your seed with compost or peat instead of soil. This will prevent crusting, maintain good soil moisture, provide a better germination medium and lessen the possibility of planting too deep. Frequent and light applications of water with a sprinkler also will help keep the soil surface moist and prevent crusting.

Kohlrabi seed will germinate when soil temperatures range from about 45 to more than 100 degrees at the seeding depth. About 75 degrees is optimum. Kohlrabi seedlings often will emerge from the soil in three to four days when soil temperatures are between 60 and 85 degrees.

You probably will need to thin the plants and the best time to do it is when the seedlings are 1 to 1½ inches tall. Gently pull up the unwanted plants, leaving an in-row spacing of about 6 inches between the remaining seedlings. When thinning, the soil should be slightly moist so that the seedlings to be removed can be pulled easily from the ground without disturbing the adjacent plants. This is especially true if you planted in clumps. Water lightly after thinning to settleany disturbed soil around the remaining plants.

The kohlrabi, like the turnip, is more drought tolerant than the other members of the *Cruciferae* family because it has a deeper penetrating and more extensive root system. However, during the first two or three weeks following emergence and while the root system is developing, the soil should be kept fairly moist. Once the plants are established, how often you need to water depends on soil type, climate and Mother Nature. Water when the soil is relatively dry about 1 inch beneath the surface and apply enough water to wet the soil to a depth of at least 6 inches.

When the soil is moist and you have completed the thinning process, mulch around the plants with a 1- to 2-inch layer of organic matter. Mulching will help conserve moisture, control weeds and stabilize the soil temperature. If you plant kohlrabi when soil temperatures are high, apply a thin layer of organic mulch shortly after the seedlings emerge to provide better conditions for their growth and development.

Apply A Fertilizer Side-dressing

A sidedress application of fertilizer is not always necessary since kohlrabi matures rapidly and has an efficient root system. Sometimes, though, a side-dressing is needed, especially if you receive a lot of rainfall, have sandy soil, or if the plants seem sluggish. Under these conditions, apply 1 cup of ammonium sulfate (21-0-0) or ⅔ cup of ammonium nitrate (33-0-0) for each 35-foot row of kohlrabi. Apply half the fertilizer to each side of the bed (or row) in a band about 4 inches from the plants. If you use the two-row-per-bed planting system, apply a third of the fertilizer between the rows. Lightly work the fertilizer into the soil and water.

Kohlrabi is subject to many insect and disease problems. Aphids and cabbage loopers are the worst insects you'll have to contend with and downy mildew is the most common disease of kohlrabi.

Aphids, or what many Texans call plant lice, will feed on kohlrabi during any stage of the plant's growth and in any season of the year. Aphids do their damage by sucking the plant's juices, thereby stunting its growth. If allowed to develop, feed and reproduce in large numbers (which they can do in an unbelievably short time), aphids can reduce your chances of a good harvest significantly. Malathion applied at the first sign of an aphid population usually provides good control.

Ragged holes in the foliage, along with the presence of greenish inchworms, can mean only one thing when growing kohlrabi—cabbage loopers. These ravenous feeders always seem to be a problem in Texas when growing any member of the cabbage family. If uncontrolled, loopers can put a quick end to any thought of garden-fresh kohlrabi. Fortunately, science has developed a safe and sure control for this seemingly ever-present pest, *Bacillus thuringiensis.* This biological insecticide is available at most garden centers and nurseries under various trade names, such as Dipel, Thuricide, Biological Worm Killer and several others.

Downy mildew is, by far, the most common disease affecting kohlrabi. This fungal disease, which is a problem primarily during wet weather, first occurs as small yellow spots on the upper surfaces of the leaves. These spots soon darken, causing a "downy" growth on the leaves' lower surfaces. If weather conditions favorable for its continued growth and development persist, downy mildew can seriously damage or kill the plants. Applications of Dithane begun at the first sign of the disease and repeated at seven- to 10- day intervals will result in satisfactory control.

If provided with adequate cultural care and protection from pests, your kohlrabi will be ready for the dinner table about 50 to 60 days after seeding. Highest quality will occur when the "bulbs" are about 2 to 2½ inches in diameter or about the size of a tennis ball. If you have kohlrabi that matures during high temperatures, you can overcome the effects of the adverse environmental conditions by picking the fruit when it's smaller without great loss in flavor and quality.

Quick Problem Solver: Kohlrabi

Problem	Causes	Solutions
Seed fails to germinate and emerge.	Old seed.	Use only current season seed.
	Planted too deep.	Never plant deeper than ½ inch.
	Low soil moisture.	Soil should be moist at time of planting.
	Cold soils.	Never plant seed until soil temperature exceeds 45 degrees at seeding depth.
	Crusted soils.	Cover seed with organic matter and/or sprinkle lightly to prevent crusting.
Seedlings grow slowly, lack good color.	Cold/wet soils.	Do not plant too early/plant on raised beds to improve soil drainage.
	Low fertility.	Apply light application of nitrogen fertilizer.
	Acid soils.	Lime should be added to raise pH of soil.
Seedlings die soon after emergence.	Damping-off (fungus).	Avoid planting too early and wet soils. Use only treated seed when planting. Treat base of seedlings with an appropriate fungicide.
	Cutworms.	Check for presence at base of healthy plant, just beneath soil surface. Treat with appropriate insecticide.
Plants stunted, fail to "bulb."	Transplanting.	Seed kohlrabi rather than transplant. If transplanting, always use small plants.
	Cold/wet soils.	Avoid temptation to plant early. Use raised beds to improve soil drainage.
	Low soil moisture.	Maintain adequate soil moisture during early stage of plant growth. Use a mulch to conserve moisture.
	Crowded conditions.	Thin seedlings early to a in-row spacing of 6 inches.
	Low fertility.	Apply a light application of nitrogen fertilizer to sides of plants, lightly work into the soil and water.

"Bulbs" tough, woody.	Stress.	Avoid unfavorable growing conditions; low soil moisture, high temperatures, low fertility, competition from other plants, etc.
	Overmature.	Harvest when "bulbs" are about 2 inches in diameter.
Plants flower or bolt prematurely.	Exposure to cold.	Avoid planting at a time which will expose the plants to prolonged periods of 40 degrees or below.
Holes in leaves, worms present.	Loopers.	Treat foliage with *Bacillus thuringiensis.*
Plants stunted, covered with numerous small insects.	Aphids.	Treat foliage with malathion as directed.
Yellow spots on foliage, later darkens.	Downy mildew (fungus).	Treat foliage with Dithane fungicide.
Bulbs rough, misshapen.	Fresh barnyard manure.	Do not add barnyard manure except several months before planting kohlrabi.

LETTUCE

Scientific Name: *Lactuca sativa*
Family: *Compositae*
Annual
Cool Season
Varieties:
- Crisp Head (Iceburg): Vanguard, Mission, Great Lakes types
- Romaine: Paris Island Cos, Romaine, Valmaine
- Butterhead: Bibb, Big Boston, Butterhead
- Leaf: Salad Bowl, Prize Head; (red) Ruby, Red Sails

Expected Harvest: 20 to 40 heads per 10 feet of row

LETTUCE

Due to the increasingly popular idea that "thin is beautiful," salads have experienced a meteoric rise in popularity in recent years. And, if there's one word that's synonymous with "salad" the world over, it's lettuce. No other item can come close to it as the main ingredient in our salads.

This leafy vegetable not only adds color and texture to salads, it's also tasty, rather nutritious and very low in those dreaded calories. A pound of lettuce contains only about 56 calories, but is in the same category as artichoke, asparagus, celery and cauliflower in nutrient value. Since it's attractive, tasty, nutritious, low calorie and relatively easy to grow, is there any wonder why you rarely see a home garden in Texas without a row or two of lettuce?

Lettuce began its ascent to stardom and "the top of the heap" (or salad bowl) in either Egypt or Iran at least 4,500 years ago, as evidenced by paintings on the walls of ancient Egyptian tombs. At that time, though, it was grown only as an oil seed crop. We don't know when lettuce first was cultivated as a food source, but we do know it was served at the tables of Persian kings in the sixth century B.C. Its popularity continued with the Greeks and Romans, who advanced its level of culture, use and, most importantly, acceptance. As a result, the consumption of various forms of lettuce was common in Europe by the early 1600s. Columbus introduced lettuce to the New World in 1494 when he planted it in the Bahamas. Also, the early colonists brought their own seed with them from England and, without doubt, lettuce was one of the first vegetables grown in what must have been considered their "survival" gardens.

To the uninformed, lettuce is just lettuce, but it's actually a very versatile vegetable. There are a number of different and distinct types of lettuce, each with a texture and flavor all its own, enabling the true connoisseur to prepare many different salads just by using different types of lettuce.

The Four Faces Of Lettuce

Four types of lettuce—leaf, butterhead, romaine and iceburg—are grown in Texas gardens. Let's discuss them in order of how difficult they are to grow, beginning with the easiest.

Leaf lettuce, as the name indicates, doesn't form a head—it grows up and out. It is the type of lettuce most often recommended for garden production in Texas. Some of the best varieties are Salad Bowl, Prize Head, Black-Seeded Simpson, and the colorful Ruby and Red Sails. These varieties will mature about 50 days after seeding.

Butterhead lettuce is best described as a "loosehead" type with soft, pliable leaves that barely overlap to form a head. The plants exhibit an open growth habit and the leaves characteristically have a dark green color. The better varieties, such as Bibb, Big Boston and Buttercrunch, will mature about 65 days after seeding.

The *romaine*, or cos, type of lettuce, is recognized easily by its upright growth habit that produces elongated heads, which are often 10 inches or more in height. The leaves form a rather firm head and have a coarse, ribby appearance that seems to contradict their tender, sweet flavor. Paris Island Cos and Romaine are the better varieties and they will mature at about the same time as the butterhead types.

Referred to by most Texans as *iceburg* or head lettuce, the crisphead type most commonly is found in supermarkets and grocery stores across the state. Crisphead varieties have large, firm heads that may weigh as much as 2 pounds and be 6 to 10 inches in diameter. The leaves are firm, crisp and distinguished by prominent veins and midribs. Vanguard, Mission and the Great Lakes varieties will mature about 90 days after seeding.

Which type of lettuce should you grow in your garden? The choice is yours, for each can be grown successfully in Texas if you pay close attention to planting time and provide a little cultural care. However, I firmly believe the leaf types should be planted in the greatest quantity, followed by the butterheads, romaines and crisphead types. There are two basic reasons for this belief: first, the leaf types are just as tasty as the others; second, and most important, the leaf types are much easier to grow since they mature more quickly and have much less demanding climatic requirements.

Of course, many people prefer a crunchy lettuce for their salads and sandwiches and it's true that the leaf, butterhead and romaine lettuces lack this *crunchiness*—or is it really *toughness*? Over the years, most of us have been programmed to expect lettuce to have a crisp texture, an

There are four major types of lettuce that can be grown in Texas. Clockwise from top left they are leaf, butterhead, romaine and iceburg. Though iceburg lettuce is the type people are most familiar with, it is the least well-adapted to Texas' growing conditions. The leaf varieties grow best here.

expectancy brought about by our past dependency upon supermarkets to supply us with lettuce. And the reason crisphead varieties dominate our retail sales outlets is not because they taste better, but because they ship better. Their firm, tight heads and crisp (tough) leaves with large midribs are far less likely to show the stress and strain endured from harvest to market. And, there's a 95 percent chance that the head of lettuce you purchase at your local supermarket was grown in California and shipped to Texas by refrigerated truck.

California produces most of the head lettuce consumed in the United States for one reason—its climate is ideally suited for the growth of this type of lettuce. Lettuce, especially the heading types, grows best when the humidity is low, and temperatures are relatively cool and constant. Temperature extremes during the early growth of the plants or when they're near maturity will affect lettuce greatly. High temperatures will cause heading types of lettuce to develop puffy heads, and cause all other types of lettuce to have a bitter flavor and "bolt," or send up a seedstem. Low temperatures can damage or kill the plants, especially if the plants are in the seedling stage or near maturity.

Consequently, the problem with growing head lettuce in Texas should be obvious. Since it requires up to 90 days or more to mature, head lettuce—if planted in early spring—will be reaching maturity when it's hot in most of Texas. The result will be puffy, poor quality heads—if heads form at all. If you plant head lettuce in late summer, high temperatures followed by cloudy and rainy conditions at maturity, will result in less than desirable quality. Using transplants in the spring and fall will help, but the results still may be disappointing. My suggestion is to grow leaf, butterhead and romaine lettuce in your garden and let the local retailers and California supply the head lettuce. Once Texans become accustomed to these better and easier-to-grow lettuces, California will have to look elsewhere for a place to sell its product.

Make sure you only plant varieties of lettuce recommended for Texas. If you decide to grow your own transplants, you should start them three to four weeks before you plan to set them out in the garden. Information on growing your own transplants is found on page 396.

Timing is extremely critical in growing lettuce. In the spring, direct seeding or transplanting should occur about four to six weeks before the date of the last average killing frost in your area, but hopefully after the last extremely cold weather has occurred. Temperatures in the upper 20s often will kill young lettuce plants or, in some cases, promote the premature development of seedstem formation when temperatures warm. In the fall, planting should occur about eight to 10 weeks before the first freezing weather is expected. Additional plantings can be made in both the spring and fall, but remember the limitations regarding both high and low temperatures. Spring planting should cease in time so that your lettuce will not have to mature under temperatures averaging above 80 degrees. In the fall, make sure your lettuce has a chance to mature before temperatures drop much below the freezing point.

If its climatic requirements are met, lettuce can be grown successfully on almost any type soil, as long as it is well-drained, yet not droughty, and has a pH above 6.0. The addition of liberal amounts of organic matter, along with some agricultural lime if your soil is too acid, will help most Texas soils meet these requirements.

Add Organic Matter To Soil

Spread 2 to 3 inches of organic matter, such as well-decomposed leaves, hay, grass clippings or compost, over the area to be planted and till or spade it into the soil to a depth of 8 to 10 inches. These materials will loosen up tight, heavy soils, while helping light, sandy soils hold moisture and fertility. If you garden in areas of Texas where acid soils are common and you've had trouble growing lettuce (and other crops) in the past, turn to page 394 for information on adjusting the pH of your soil.

Being a leafy crop, lettuce responds to relatively high levels of fertility. When tilling or spading in the organic matter, also work in about 1 pound of well-rotted barnyard manure and 2 teaspoons of commercial fertilizer for each square foot of area to be planted in lettuce. For you folks with larger plantings, this is the equivalent of 100 pounds of barnyard manure and 2 pounds of commercial fertilizer per 100 square feet or per 35 feet of row. If you're gardening in East Texas or along the coastal areas, use a fertilizer with a 1-2-2 ratio, such as 10-20-20. For the other areas of the state, a fertilizer with a 1-2-1 ratio, such as 10-20-10 or 12-24-12, usually is

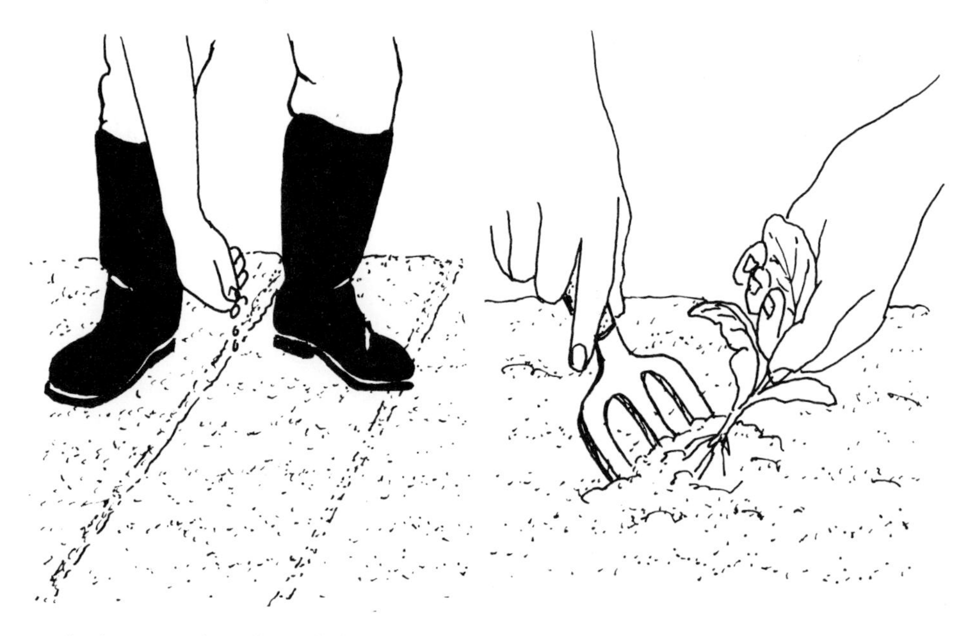

Usually, lettuce is directly seeded into the garden. To enhance germination, it's a good idea to cover the seeds with peat instead of soil. If you want to thin your stand and transplant some of the plants to other parts of your garden, carefully dig up the seedling and replant it immediately.

satisfactory. If you do not have access to barnyard manure, use the commercial fertilizer at the rate of 1 tablespoon per square foot or 3 pounds per 100 square feet.

Due to the lettuce plant's relatively shallow root system and its preference for damp but not wet "feet," planting on raised beds generally is a good idea. Use your shovel or a tiller with a bedder to form ridges and furrows that measure at least 36 inches from the top of one ridge to the top of an adjacent ridge. Next, use your garden rake to form and smooth the ridges into raised beds in preparation for planting. The beds should be 16 to 20 inches wide and about 6 inches high. The remaining lower areas will be furrows to facilitate watering and to provide good drainage.

Since lettuce seed is so small, a smooth, well-pulverized planting bed is highly desirable. Cloddy, rough soils may result in the seed being planted too deeply. Use your garden rake to smooth the planting area and remove any large clods, rocks or trash. Next, use the flat side of your rake to tamp the surface of the planting bed firm. This procedure will consolidate the soil particles, thereby helping to conserve soil moisture and aid the lateral movement of moisture within the planting bed.

Your garden soil should be moist enough at planting time to initiate germination and emergence of the lettuce seed. If your soil is on the dry side, water several days prior to the anticipated planting date. Ideally, you should not have to water again until after the lettuce seedlings have emerged from the soil.

Lettuce can be planted in single or double rows on top of the beds or the seed can be broadcast over the bed surface. Either system works well, but I prefer planting in rows, which makes it easier to remove weeds and grasses that may come up about the same time as your lettuce.

When planting rows, use the edge of your hoe, a stick or your hand to make the seed furrows. The 16- to 20-inch-wide beds easily will accommodate two rows of lettuce spaced about 10 to 12 inches apart. If you feel your soil is a little on the dry side, apply water directly in the seed furrow and allow it to soak in before seeding. The basic rule when planting lettuce is to use plenty of seed. Sow the seed at the rate of about 10 to 15 seeds per foot of row and cover them ¼ to ½ inch deep. Use the deeper planting depth only if you have a loose, light-textured soil or if hot, dry conditions exist, causing a moisture deficiency near the soil surface. This is what commercial vegetable farmers commonly refer to as "planting in moisture."

If you opt to broadcast plant, scatter the seed evenly over the bed and lightly rake the surface to help cover the seed. Always rake down the

Spacing of your lettuce plants is important to a good harvest. About one to two weeks after your seedlings emerge, they should be thinned to 2 to 3 inches apart. Two or three weeks later, thin them to 4 to 6 inches apart to ensure them with enough room to develop properly.

row and not across the row or all the seedlings that emerge will be on the edge of the bed. If a number of seeds are still visible after raking, use soil from outside the bed to lightly cover them. Tamp and firm the surface of the planting area, just as you would if planting in rows.

During the first few days following planting, every effort should be made to keep the soil covering the seed from crusting, which will hamper the emergence of the lettuce seedlings. If your soil has a tendency to crust, consider covering the seed with compost or peat rather than soil. Such a practice will help prevent crusting, provide the seed with better conditions for germination and lessen the possibility of planting too deep. Also, if necessary, light applications of water with a sprinkler will help keep the soil surface moist and prevent crusting.

Lettuce seed will germinate in soil temperatures ranging from freezing to over 85 degrees. The optimum temperature for germination, however, is about 75 degrees, at which emergence will occur in three to four days. However, if you wait until soil temperatures are optimal before planting in the spring, your lettuce probably will mature during adversely warm or even hot temperatures. Plant earlier, but not *too* early—unless you have the patience of Job. Lettuce seed will germinate at 32 degrees, but it may take as long as 50 days to do so!

Soil temperatures exceeding 78 degrees, which are common when seeding a late summer or fall crop in Texas, may stimulate the flowering mechanism of lettuce and result in premature seedstem formation. Therefore, if you do plant seed at that time, keep the soil moist and apply a light layer of organic mulch over the planting area to shade the soil from the intense Texas sun. Placing wet burlap or a similar material over the seed row and keeping it moist also is an effective cooling method. Remember to remove any covering as soon as the first seedlings emerge.

Extending Your Harvest

Lettuce is a crop that does extremely well when grown in protective enclosures and often will survive the winter in many areas of Texas with minimal care. If you're interested in extending your harvest and would consider building a cold frame or hotbed for extended production of lettuce, see page 402.

Within a few days your stand of lettuce will be established and you'll probably have more seedlings than needed. Thinning will be necessary and should be done in at least two operations, the first one occurring seven to 10 days after emergence. At that time, leave twice as many seedlings as you want. Thin the plants again in about two or three weeks. The final in-row spacing should be 4 to 6 inches apart for leaf lettuce, 8 inches apart for butterhead and romaine, and at least 10 inches apart for crisphead types. If you use the two rows per bed planting system, stagger the plants in adjacent rows to make maximum use of your garden space. This also provides the lettuce plants with optimum growing conditions. The thinned lettuce seedlings can be replanted to other areas in your garden or, since lettuce is edible at any stage, can be enjoyed at your dinner table.

As indicated previously, lettuce can be transplanted as well as seeded directly in your garden. When setting out transplants, try to do so on a cloudy, cool, windless day to avoid undue stress on the plants. Use a trowel, hoe or your hand to dig adequate-sized holes at the desired spacing for the transplants. Place a transplant in each hole, backfill with soil and firm the plants in, leaving a slight depression around each one to hold water. Due to the succulent nature of lettuce transplants, do not use a starter solution when transplanting. Water immediately after planting.

Approximately two weeks after transplanting or thinning to the final spacing, side-dress your lettuce with nitrogen fertilizer. A second side-dressing is advisable about three or four weeks later, especially if you're growing the romaine or crisphead types. Apply half the fertilizer to each side of the lettuce rows in a band about 4 inches from the plants. Use 1 cup of ammonium sulfate or 2/3 cup of ammonium nitrate per 35 feet of row. If you use the two-row-per-bed planting system, band one-third of the fertilizer between the rows of lettuce. Lightly work the fertilizer into the soil and then water.

If you planted your lettuce using the broadcast method, side-dressing is more difficult. Evenly scatter the fertilizer at the rates just described over the bed and around the plants, making an effort to avoid getting the fertilizer on the foliage. Water immediately, preferably by sprinkler, to wash any fertilizer off the foliage and to lessen the possibility of burn.

Maintaining Soil Moisture

Maintaining the soil in a moist condition is of paramount importance in growing lettuce successfully and as a result, rarely is it grown "dryland" in Texas. Supplemental water must be available when and if needed. Soil type, stage of growth of the plants, season of the year and Mother Nature will determine how often you'll need to water. Remember that lettuce has a shallow root system and is not capable of taking advantage of deep, subsoil moisture. Regardless of the watering method you use, apply water before the top inch of soil becomes dry. Do not allow the plants to severely wilt, as they may never fully recover.

Mulching around the lettuce plants is an excellent way to maintain soil moisture, especially during hot, dry periods. After thinning and side-dressing in the spring, apply 2 to 3 inches of organic matter, such as well-decomposed hay, straw, grass clippings or compost, around the plants. As mentioned earlier,when planting in late summer or fall, a light application of mulch over the newly planted seed row will help cool the soil and improve germination and emergence. Then, after thinning and fertilizing, more organic matter should be added. Not only will mulching conserve soil moisture, but it also will help control weeds, prevent soil compaction and erosion, and regulate the soil temperature.

Insects And Diseases

From planting to harvest, your lettuce will be subject to attack by various types of insects and diseases. The most common insects that feed on lettuce are cutworms, various types of caterpillars or "worms," and

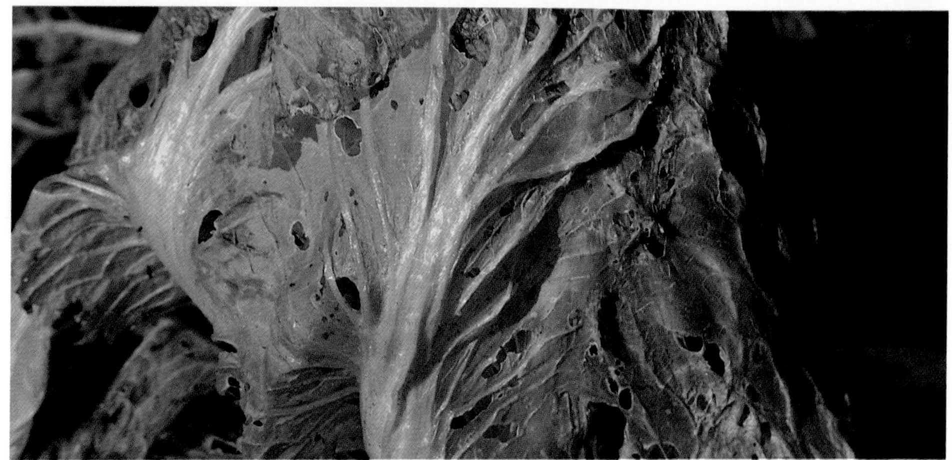

Temperatures have a great effect on lettuce plants. Cold temperatures, followed by warmer weather, can cause bolting (top photo). Extremely cold temperatures can cause freeze damage (bottom photo).

aphids. Although troubled by a large number of plant pathogens, the primary diseases you'll need to contend with in Texas are downy mildew and botrytis.

Cutworms seem to enjoy feeding on young, tender lettuce almost as much as we do. These nocturnal-feeding, darkish, inch-long worms attack newly emerged seedlings or transplants by cutting them off near ground level. Oftentimes, they can be found just beneath the soil surface near the base of a healthy lettuce plant, patiently waiting for nighttime so they can begin feeding. Control can be achieved by applying diazinon according to the label directions and, of course, by destroying any cutworms you might dig up.

Cabbage loopers, armyworms and numerous other worms can pose a quick and serious threat to your lettuce harvest if left uncontrolled.

Fortunately, control is relatively easy if you use *Bacillus thuringiensis*, which is sold under various trade names. When foliage treated with this biological insecticide is ingested by worms, their digestive system is paralyzed, causing death within two to three days. *Bacillus thuringiensis* is completely safe for your use and the lettuce can be eaten the same day it is treated.

Aphids, or plant lice, do their damage by sucking juices from the plants and, in some cases, by transmitting virus diseases. Applications of malathion or diazinon, applied at the first sign of a population build-up, will give satisfactory control. The key phrase in the above sentence is "at the first sign." Most types of aphids give birth to offspring who are already pregnant and capable of giving birth within just a few days. Obviously, early control is an absolute must!

Both of the most common lettuce diseases are primarily a problem during wet, humid weather conditions. Downy mildew first appears as yellowish or light green blotchy areas on the upper leaf surfaces, followed by a white, downy mold on the lower leaf surfaces. The spots eventually die, causing brown lesions on the leaves. If left uncontrolled and favorable climatic conditions exist, the fungus can kill the entire plant.

Botrytis can attack lettuce at any stage of maturity. This disease most often occurs when lettuce leaves are in contact with the soil, causing a slimy rot to spread upwards to the head or center of the plant. Botrytis is identified easily by the appearance of a dense, fuzzy, gray mold that occurs on the surfaces of affected areas. Since both downy mildew and botrytis can be soilborne, a good rotation program will aid in their control. In addition, applications of a fungicide containing zineb, begun at the first sign of a problem and repeated at seven- to 10-day intervals, usually will result in good control of both diseases.

Harvesting is a snap, because it can be done at anytime! All types of lettuce are edible the minute the plants emerge from the soil. However, the romaine and crisphead types usually are harvested by removing the entire plant after the heads form. The leaf and butterhead types can be harvested either by removing the entire plant or by using what's commonly called the "cut-and-come-again" technique, which is nothing more than removing the older, outer leaves as they mature. Regardless of how you harvest your lettuce crop, never make the mistake of waiting too long, especially as temperatures warm. Remember, lettuce is always best when harvested early, at its peak of edible quality.

Quick Problem Solver: Lettuce

Problem	Causes	Solutions
Seeds fail to germinate and emerge.	Old seed.	Always use current season seed.
	Cold soils.	Avoid planting too early. Seed approximately 3 to 4 weeks before frost-free date in the spring.
	High temperatures.	Seed may fail to germinate at soil temperatures above 90 degrees. Keep soil moist and apply light mulch over seed row to help cool soil.
	Planted too deep.	Lettuce seed should be planted ¼ to ½ inch deep and no deeper.
	Low soil moisture.	Maintain soil in moist condition during germination and emergence. Plant when soil is moist, firming soil over seed row.
Seedlings lack vigor, good color.	Cold soils.	Avoid temptation of planting too early.
	Low fertility.	Light application of nitrogen fertilizer, lightly work into the soil and then water.
	Acid soils.	Soil pH should be above 6.0.
Seedlings die shortly after emergence.	Damping-off (fungus).	Avoid planting too early. Plant on raised beds to improve drainage and warming of the soil. Always use treated seed. Spray base of plants with an appropriate fungicide.
	Cutworms.	Check for presence of worms beneath soil surface at base of healthy plants. Treat with appropriate insecticide.
Plants spindly, weak.	Crowded growing conditions.	Thin your stand to the recommended in-row spacing.
Plants fail to "head."	Variety.	Some lettuce varieties will not form heads.
	High temperatures.	High temperatures near maturity will cause lettuce to fail to head.
	Crowded growing conditions.	Provide plants adequate growing space to develop.

Plants bolt or flower prematurely.	Low temperatures.	Seedlings exposed to low temperatures will often be induced to flower early. Avoid planting too early in the spring.
	High temperatures.	High air temperatures and soil temperatures may stimulate lettuce to flower early. Avoid planting too late in spring and too early in summer and fall. Keep soil moist during high temperatures.
Heads "puffy."	High temperatures.	Plant so that lettuce will mature before daily temperatures average above 80 degrees.
Lettuce bitter, off-flavored.	Stress.	Low fertility, low soil moisture, high temperatures can cause bitter flavor. Usually related to low soil moisture and high temperatures.
Leaves ragged, torn, holes present.	Loopers.	Treat foliage with *Bacillus thuringiensis.*
Underside of foliage covered with "plant lice."	Aphids.	Treat foliage with malathion or diazinon according to label directions.
Yellowish spots on foliage, "downy" growth on undersurface.	Downy mildew (fungus).	Treat foliage with fungicide containing zineb. Follow good rotation program.
Fuzzy, gray mold on leaf surface, tissue decays.	Botrytis.	Treat foliage with fungicide containing zineb. Follow good rotation program.

MUSTARD GREENS

Scientific Name: *Brassica juncea*
Family: *Cruciferae*
Annual
Cool Season
Varieties: Tendergreen II, Florida Broad Leaf; (Curly) Southern Giant Curled, Green Wave
Expected Harvest: 5 to 7 pounds per 10 feet of row

MUSTARD GREENS

The term "greens" can refer to many different types of leafy vegetables. However, to most Texans and Southerners, it means mustard, turnip or collard greens, which when picked tender and fixed right, make for some mighty good eating.

Mustard greens are not a common item in most Texas gardens and the reasons for their lack of popularity aren't clear. Some have suggested that younger Texans simply don't know what mustard greens are or how to prepare them, while many older Texans enjoyed them all too often in the past and turned their gardening skills to growing other crops. In addition, some folks have an inherent dislike for all greens, primarily because they have been considered food for "poor folks." During hard times, such as during World War I and the Great Depression, many families in the South literally survived on a small patch of greens. Even today, it's not at all uncommon to see numerous plantings of mustard greens (and other greens) dotting the countryside as you travel across the South.

Mustard greens should be considered a first-class garden crop simply because they are tasty, highly nutritious, extremely productive, economical to produce and—best of all—easy to grow! Before dealing with their culture in Texas, it's interesting to note that mustard greens (leaf mustard) belong to the *Cruciferae* family of plants and, like all crucifers, is thought to have originated in the Mediterranean area. Mustard greens gained fame in India and the Orient, where many different and distinct forms developed, including white (*B. alba*) and black (*B. nigra*) mustard, which are grown for their seed to make the table mustard we put on hamburgers and hot dogs.

Minimal Soil Preparation

Greens, which is what we'll call mustard greens from this point on, are easy to grow and require almost no care from the time of seeding to harvest. In fact, most patches of greens are grown with little or no soil preparation, fertilization, irrigation or pest control. To maximize yields and quality of your greens, however, attention should be given to their cultural and environmental requirements.

Greens will grow well on almost any Texas soil but prefer sandy loams that have a pH between 5.5 and 7.0. If you live in an area where acid soils are common and your greens grow, but not like they should, your soil may be too acid. For information on adjusting your soil's pH, see page 394. If your soil is highly calcareous, add iron in the form of copperous or sequesterene, following the label directions, to improve foliage color and increase yields.

Like all vegetables, greens will respond to a well-prepared soil. Spread 2 to 3 inches of organic matter over the area to be planted. At the same time, apply about 100 pounds of barnyard manure per 100 square feet of area or per 35 feet of row to be planted. If your soil is fairly fertile already, you should not need to add any other fertilizer. However, if barnyard manure is unavailable, add 1 pound of ammonium sulfate (21-0-0) or ⅔ pound of ammonium nitrate (33-0-0) per 100 square feet or for each 35 feet of row. This is the equivalent of 1 teaspoon of ammonium sulfate or ⅔ teaspoon of ammonium nitrate for each square foot of area to be planted.

If you notice that your vegetables have good color, but seem to grow slowly and lack vigor even though your soil's pH is satisfactory, low soil phosphorous and/or potassium may be the problem. In that case, you should add a complete fertilizer to the soil, rather than just nitrogen, to ensure a healthy crop of greens. Use 2 pounds of a complete fertilizer, such as 10-10-10, per 100 square feet or for each 35 feet of row. If you only have a small planting, use 2 teaspoons per square foot of area to be planted. Till all the added ingredients into the soil to a depth of 8 to 10 inches.

Greens have an efficient, moderately deep-growing root system that may reach a depth of 3 to 4 feet. As a result, they will do well when planted either flat or on raised beds. If you choose to plant flat, simply use your garden rake to level and smooth the planting area. However, if your soil is on the heavy side, plant on raised beds to provide improved drainage. Form ridges and furrows that measure at least 30 inches from the top of one ridge to the top of an adjacent ridge. Next, use the flat side of your garden rake to form and shape the ridges into raised planting beds that are 4 to 6 inches tall and 16 to 20 inches wide. The remaining space will be the furrow to facilitate watering and aid in drainage. After forming the beds, tamp them firm to consolidate the soil particles. This will help

If you broadcast plant your mustard greens, scatter the seeds evenly over the surface of the soil. Then rake down the bed to cover the seeds.

conserve soil moisture and improve the ability of the water to move laterally within the beds.

Timing Is Important

Time of planting probably will influence your success with greens more than any other single factor. The highest quality greens will be those that mature during relatively cool temperatures. Your first planting should be made three to four weeks prior to the last killing frost in the spring. Additional plantings can follow, but should cease in time to allow the greens to mature before daytime temperatures average above 70 degrees. High temperatures in combination with increasing day length will cause greens to bolt or flower. And greens that are harvested just as they are about ready to bolt invariably will have a "hot," rather than a "piquant," flavor.

For fall and winter harvests, your first planting should occur six to eight weeks before the first anticipated killing frost. Additional plantings

Purple Osaka mustard is not only tasty but adds a touch of beauty to your garden area.

can be made and, of course, you don't have to worry about high temperatures, although low temperatures can cause problems. Greens are extremely cold hardy, but temperatures near 20 degrees can damage or kill the plants, depending upon duration of the cold and whether or not the plants were hardened previously by cold temperatures. However, with the possible exceptions of the far northern and western areas, greens can be grown and harvested throughout most winters across Texas.

Your garden soil should be moist enough at planting to initiate germination and emergence of the seedlings. If your soil is on the dry side, water several days prior to the anticipated planting date. Ideally, you should not have to apply water again until after the seedlings have emerged from the soil.

Greens can be planted in rows or the seed can be broadcast over the soil surface. Either system works well, but broadcast planting is ideally suited to greens. When using this system, scatter the seed as evenly as possible over the area to be planted. If you're a typical Texas gardener, you'll use too much seed. Therefore, plant only about two-thirds as much seed as you think you'll need. Chances are good you'll still have to do some thinning! Next, lightly rake the surface to cover the seed. Always rake down the row and not across the row or all the seedlings that emerge will be on the edge of the bed. If seeds are still visible after the raking, use soil from outside the bed to lightly cover them.

If you chose to plant in rows, use the edge of your hoe, a stick or your hand to make the seed furrows. The 16- to 20-inch wide beds previously discussed will easily accommodate two rows of greens spaced 12 inches apart. If you feel your soil is a little on the dry side, apply water directly in the seed furrows and allow it to soak in before planting. Sow the seed at the rate of about eight to 10 per foot of row and cover ¼ inch deep with soil.

Regardless of your planting system, after you cover the seeds, use the flat side of your hoe to firm the soil over them. This will encourage water transfer from the soil to the seed and help conserve valuable moisture in the seeding zone.

Unlike most vegetables, soil temperature at planting has little influence on seed germination of greens. Germination and emergence will occur in two to five days at soil temperatures ranging from 50 to 105 degrees, with the faster emergence occurring as soil temperatures warm. If you plant at the right time and the seedlings fail to emerge within one week, chances are you either planted too deeply or the seed was old. Replanting is advisable.

The disease white rust (top) and various foliage-feeding insects are common pests of mustard greens. Both can be controlled with an approved pesticide, used according to label directions at the first sign of problems.

Within 35 to 50 days after seeding, your greens will be ready for the dinner table.

Two to three weeks after they emerge, thin your greens to a spacing of 3 to 4 inches between plants. Greens are edible at any usable size and at this age they can help make a great salad, but lack the desired bulk and consistency for cooking. Remove the unwanted plants by gently pulling them from the soil. During thinning, the soil should be slightly moist to avoid disturbing the root systems of the remaining plants. Water lightly after thinning to settle any disturbed soil.

If you're growing greens in rows, mulching between the rows and to the side of the plants with organic matter will help conserve soil moisture and control weeds. Mulching between broadcast planted beds also is desirable, but is difficult due to the scattered and uneven distribution of the plants. However, the greens themselves actually will serve as a "living mulch" by shading the ground from the sun's rays. This will help prevent weed growth and conserve soil moisture by reducing evaporation.

Greens, due to their relatively efficient and deep-growing root system, can be grown successfully dryland (without supplemental water) in much of Texas. This is especially true for greens planted in early spring, late fall and during the winter. However, be prepared to water when the top 1 to 2 inches of soil is fairly dry, wetting the soil to a depth of at least 6 inches.

Within 35 to 50 days after seeding, your greens will be ready for the dinner table. You can harvest by removing the entire plant or by the cut-and-come-again technique of removing the older, outer leaves as they're needed. Either system works well, but I prefer harvesting the entire plant and utilizing the vacated space for another planting. Broadcast planting is best suited for whole plant harvesting and planting in rows is best for multiple harvesting.

If you use the cut-and-come-again harvesting technique, you should side-dress the plants with fertilizer soon after your first harvest. Use 1 cup of ammonium sulfate (21-0-0) or ⅔ cup of ammonium nitrate (33-0-0) for each 35 feet of row planted in greens. Apply the fertilizer in a band to the side of the beds or rows. If you planted two rows per bed and sufficient space exists between them, apply one-third of the fertilizer between the rows and the other two-thirds along the outer sides of the rows. After applying the fertilizer, lightly work it into the soil and then water.

Insect and Disease Problems

Besides being easy to grow, greens have few insect and disease problems. If some do occur, chances are they will be due to flea beetles, aphids or downy mildew.

Flea beetles are aptly named in that they are about the size of a flea and are highly proficient jumpers. Due to their mobility, flea beetles are seldom visible, but their damage certainly is apparent. They feed on the foliage, causing small holes over the leaf surfaces with a resulting "shotgun hole" effect. Aphids, or plant lice, occur primarily on the lower surfaces of the younger leaves and do their damage by sucking juices from the plants. Adequate control of both of these pests can be achieved by using Sevin or malathion at the first sign of their presence.

Downy mildew occurs during cool, moist weather and is first expressed as faint yellow spots that appear on the upper leaf surface. On the corresponding lower surface, a gray "downy" mold appears, causing the tissue to darken and die. If left uncontrolled and if favorable environmental conditions persist, your entire patch of greens quickly may become part of your garden's history. Being aware of the environmental conditions favorable for the development of this fungal disease and applying a fungicide containing maneb at seven- to 10-day intervals after symptoms appear usually will result in satisfactory control.

As indicated earlier, greens are edible at any usable size. The young, tender leaves are great for adding a little zest to your salads, while the more mature, outer leaves with a stronger flavor are best suited to cooking.

Quick Problem Solver: Mustard Greens

Problem	Causes	Solutions
Seeds fail to germinate and seedlings emerge.	Old seed.	Always plant current season seed.
	Planted too deep.	Never plant greens more than ¼ inch deep.
Seedlings grow slowly, lack good color.	Low fertility.	Apply light application of nitrogen fertilizer around plants, work into the soil and water.
	Low soil pH.	Adjust soil pH.
	Iron deficiency.	Add copperous or iron in sequesterene form to soil, according to label directions.
Plants spindly, stemmy.	Crowded growing conditions.	Greens should be thinned to 3 to 4 inches between plants.
Holes in leaves (shothole effect).	Flea beetles.	Treat foliage with Sevin or malathion.
Leaves ragged, worms present.	Cabbage loopers.	Treat foliage with *Bacillus thuringiensis.*
Yellow spots on leaves, moldy growth on lower leaf surface.	Downy mildew (fungus).	Treat foliage with fungicide containing maneb.
Plants bolt or flower.	High temperatures/ long days.	Plant at right time.
Leaves bitter, "hot."	High temperatures/ plants ready to bolt or flower.	Same as above. Greens should mature during cool temperatures.

OKRA

Scientific Name: *Hibiscus esculentus*
Family: *Malvaceae*
Annual
Warm Season
Varieties: Clemson Spineless, Emerald, Lee, Annie Okley
Expected Harvest: 20 to 30 pods per plant

OKRA

If there is a vegetable that's truly adapted to Texas and the South, it has to be okra. It's a good thing too, since we Southerners long have recognized okra as a true culinary delight. The same can't be said for many of our neighbors to the north. Those Yankees really don't know what they're missing by not occasionally sitting down at the dinner table to a serving of fried okra, gumbo or a dozen other tasty okra dishes.

A versatile plant, okra also is grown for a variety of different purposes in other parts of the world. In the Mediterranean area, its seed is used to produce an edible oil. In other areas, the seeds are roasted, ground and served as a substitute for coffee. In Turkey, the plant's tender shoots and leaves are eaten and also used in the preparation of an ointment to soothe and reduce inflammation. Edible, drinkable and medicinal—what more can you ask of any plant?

This truly remarkable vegetable originated in hot and arid Ethiopia, but little more is known about its early life. Historians, however, theorize that it was carried across the Red Sea into Arabia and then into Egypt by the Moslems during the seventh century. Its culture soon spread across North Africa, completely around the Mediterranean and, subsequently, to the rest of the temperate world. Okra first was introduced into this country by French colonists in Louisiana in the early 1700s. Thomas Jefferson indicated that okra was being grown in Virginia prior to 1781, and by the early 1800s, several different varieties were being grown in the United States.

Okra is adapted particularly well to Texas; nevertheless, patience is the key to its successful culture—especially when deciding what is the right time to plant.

Okra will produce a bumper crop only when planted and grown during warm environmental conditions. If planted too early in the spring and subjected to unfavorably cool weather, the plants will remain stunted and have low yields. If planted too late in the year, cool temperatures will reduce the amount of blooming and pod set. Therefore, you must attempt to provide your okra with satisfactory temperatures, both at planting and during the growth cycle.

Avoid the temptation of planting early. It's helpful to remember that okra is closely related to cotton and requires basically the same growing conditions. If you garden in a cotton-producing area of Texas, plant your okra when the farmers plant their cotton. If you garden in other areas, or just desire to be more precise, your first planting in the spring should not occur until the soil temperature at the seeding depth has warmed to at least 68 degrees and nighttime temperatures remain above 50 degrees for five consecutive days. If you show patience and follow these guidelines, your okra will emerge from the soil quickly, grow rapidly and produce heavily.

One planting in the spring generally is all that's needed since okra will continue to grow until the first killing frost of winter. Additional or later plantings can be made, but keep in mind the effect of cool temperatures on blooming and pod set. To ensure yourself a good harvest, the last planting of okra should be made about 90 days before daytime temperatures are expected to drop to and remain below 70 degrees.

Good Drainage Important

When grown under satisfactory environmental conditions, okra will produce a good crop on most Texas soils—if they are well-drained. Okra simply does not like wet feet and will perform poorly on soils that have a tendency to stay wet. By the same token, if grown on loose, sandy soils that are dry, okra may exhibit moisture stress during dry periods and will need to be watered.

If you garden in an area of Texas where acid soils are common, you may need to raise the pH of your soil by adding lime. Okra plants grown on acid soils having a pH below 6.0 will appear stunted and yield poorly. Those pods that are produced often will be puffy and misshapen. Additional information on adjusting the pH of your soil can be found on page 394.

Getting your soil prepared for planting is not as demanding for okra as for most other vegetables. Due to its extensive and deep-growing root system, okra is an efficient forager for nutrients and moisture. Consequently, it will do relatively well with minimal soil preparation. If your soil is already fairly fertile, all you may have to do is stick the seed in the ground. However, chances are your yields will be increased significantly if you add organic matter and fertilizer. Scatter 2 to 3 inches

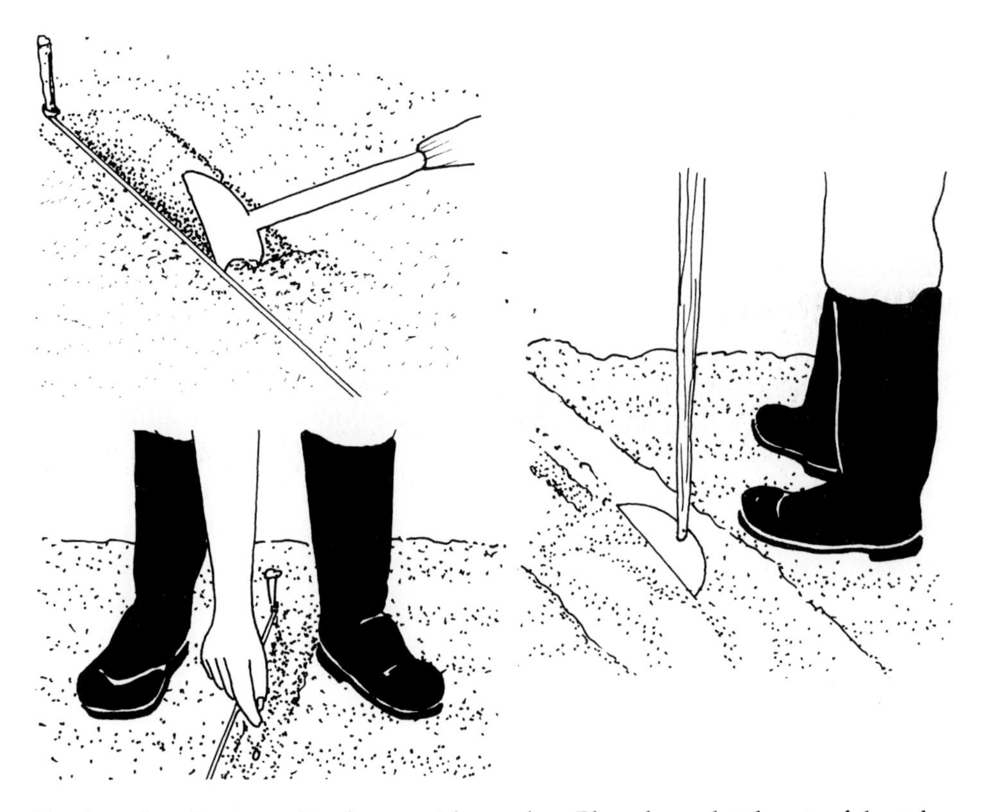

To plant okra, form a seeding furrow with your hoe. Plant the seed at the rate of about four or five per foot of row and cover them lightly. After planting, use the flat side of your hoe to firm the soil over the seeds.

of materials, such as hay, leaves, grass clippings or compost, over the area to be planted. If it's available, you also can apply barnyard manure at the rate of about ½ pound per square foot, which probably will provide all the preplant fertility that is needed. If barnyard manure is unavailable and/or your soil lacks good fertility, use a complete fertilizer, such as 10-10-10, at the rate of 1 pound per 100 square feet or for each 35 feet of row to be planted in okra. Till or spade all the added ingredients, including lime if it's needed, into the soil to a depth of 8 to 10 inches. This soil preparation should take place well ahead of planting time.

Next, you're ready to prepare the soil for planting. Regardless of whether you plant on flat ground or on raised beds, your rows of okra should be 3 to 4 feet apart, with the wider spacing being preferable. Okra is a sun-loving plant and even the dwarf or small plant types will produce relatively large plants. If grown under crowded conditions, the plants will compete with each other and your yields will suffer. In addition, if you plan to cut back the plants in late summer to rejuvenate their growth, the wider spacing will accommodate the bush-like plants that result. Perhaps most importantly, you'll greatly appreciate the wider row spacing come harvesttime.

Okra can be planted on flat ground or on raised beds. If you're fortunate enough to be gardening on a well-drained, loose-textured, ideal soil, all you need to do is use your garden rake to level and smooth the planting area. If, however, your soil is on the heavy side, you should plant in raised beds, which will improve drainage of tight, heavy soils and will warm up earlier in the spring due to the greater surface area exposed to the sun.

If you decide to plant on raised beds, use your shovel or a tiller with a bedder to form ridges and furrows that measure the desired 36 to 48 inches apart from the top of one ridge to the top of an adjoining ridge. Next, use the flat side of your garden rake to smooth and shape the ridges into planting beds. The beds should be 6 to 8 inches high and 20 to 24 inches wide with the remaining areas used as furrows to facilitate watering and drainage. After forming the beds, use the flat side of your garden rake to tamp them firm. This firming action will consolidate the soil particles and facilitate the lateral movement of water within the beds.

Always Plant Seed

Okra always should be directly seeded into the garden. It can be transplanted, but you will gain no real advantage from it. In fact, okra transplants grow slowly, if at all, for a considerable period of time after setting them out. As a result, directly seeded and transplanted okra often will produce mature pods at about the same time.

When temperatures are right for planting, your garden soil also should contain sufficient moisture to initiate germination of the seed and the resulting emergence of the young okra seedlings. If your soil seems dry, water several days in advance of the anticipated planting date.

Okra seed will germinate best when soil temperatures are between 75 and 90 degrees, and very poorly if temperatures are below 68 degrees. Provided with ideal temperatures and adequate soil moisture, emergence should occur within seven to 12 days. However, even under ideal conditions, germination is erratic, which causes uneven and sporadic emergence of the seedlings. It isn't unusual for the okra seedlings to emerge over a two-week period from the time the first seedlings appear. Soaking the seed in water at room temperature for 24 hours or for 1½ hours at 110 to 112 degrees prior to planting will improve germination and emergence.

When you're ready to plant, use the edge of your hoe, a stick or your hand to form seed furrows in the center of the raised beds or on the

You can expect to be harvesting okra soon after the first bloom appears. If you're tired of the plain old green okra, try growing one of the red varieties for a different look and taste.

flat ground. If the soil at the seeding depth still seems dry, apply water directly in the seed furrows and allow it to soak in before planting. Sow the seeds at the rate of four to five per foot of row. For you folks with larger gardens and a real hankering for fresh okra, this figures out to be about 1 ounce of seed for each 100 feet of row. After planting, cover the seed about ½ to ¾ inch deep.

Next, use the flat side of your hoe to firm the soil over the newly planted seed. This will help conserve valuable soil moisture and result in good soil-seed contact.

A short time after emergence, you will need to thin out the seedlings, preferably in two operations. When the seedlings are about 2 inches tall, thin your stand of okra to an in-row spacing of 6 to 9 inches apart. In a couple of weeks or when the plants are about 6 inches tall, thin again to a spacing of 12 to 18 inches apart. Use the wider spacing if you anticipate cutting the plants back later on to rejuvenate growth. Thinning is best accomplished by simply pulling up the unwanted plants. After each thinning, it's a good idea to water to settle any disturbed soil (and roots) around the remaining plants.

Shortly after the final thinning is an ideal time to side-dress your okra with a light application of nitrogen fertilizer. Use 1 cup of ammonium sulfate (21-0-0) or ⅔ cup of ammonium nitrate (33-0-0) for each 35 feet of row. Apply half the fertilizer to each side of the okra in a band about 6 inches from the base of the plants. Lightly work the fertilizer into the soil and then water. After the first harvest, side-dress again, but double the rate of fertilizer and band it about 12 to 15 inches from the plants. From this point on, chances are your okra will respond well to similar sidedress applications of nitrogen every three to four weeks. This is especially true if you're gardening on a light soil in a high rainfall area of our state, or if frequent irrigations are required during the growing season.

For spring-planted okra, mulch around the okra plants with 2 to 3 inches of well-decomposed organic matter after the first application of fertilizer. However, make absolutely certain you do not apply this mulch until the soil is warm. If it's applied to cold soils, it will act like a blanket and insulate the soil from the warming rays of the sun. As a result, the soil will warm slowly, which will have a negative effect on the growth of your okra. For later planted okra, the plants can be mulched soon after emergence.

Water Requirements

Due to its deep-growing and extensive root system, okra often can be grown successfully *dryland*—without supplemental water—in many areas of Texas. Watering if and when it's needed, though, will increase the possibility of a good harvest. Water when your soil is relatively dry 1 to 2 inches beneath the surface and apply enough water to wet the soil to a depth of at least 6 inches. As indicated earlier, okra dislikes "wet feet," so avoid overwatering or watering too frequently. Soils that are constantly wet will cause okra to perform poorly and often result in the complete deterioration of the root system.

Given just a little care and attention, you should make your first proud trip to the kitchen with garden-fresh okra about 70 days after planting. Okra pods should be harvested when they are 3 to 5 inches long, tender and easily snap from the plants. Generally, this stage of development occurs about four to six days after the flower blooms. Once your okra begins to produce, you should harvest at least every other day. If you allow pods to grow too big and remain on the plants, flowering and pod formation will cease.

Okra, even the so-called dwarf varieties, often will grow to a height of 8 to 10 feet or more when planted in the spring. This makes harvesting rather difficult, the plants become hard to manage and yields often decrease. These problems can be overcome by cutting back the plants to within about 24 inches of the ground during middle to late summer or at least about 90 days prior to the onset of cool temperatures. After cutting back the plants, side-dress the "stumps" with nitrogen fertilizer and water thoroughly. New growth will appear almost immediately and the resulting bush-like plants soon will be producing high yields of quality okra.

Toward middle or late summer, you can cut back okra plants to rejuvenate them and make harvesting easier. The resulting "bush-like" plant will continue to produce yields of quality okra.

Leafhoppers (top) and nematodes are common pests of okra.

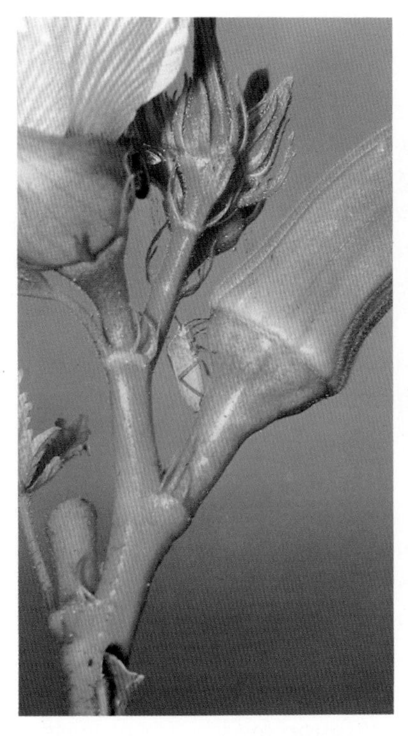

Stinkbugs feed on young, tender pods, which caused them to become crooked and poorly developed. Applications of Sevin usually provide good control.

Insects And Diseases

Fortunately, okra is not plagued by a vast array of insects and diseases. However, those that often do occur can literally destroy any hopes you might have for the proverbial bountiful harvest.

As mentioned earlier, okra is a close relative of cotton and therein lies the cause of a serious problem. If you live in a cotton-producing area of Texas and you've had okra that literally seemed to die overnight, the problem was cotton root rot. This disease is caused by a soilborne fungus for which there is simply no cure. Following a sound rotation program in your garden or planting your okra in a completely separate area may help. However, chances are if you've had this problem before, you'll have it again. It will be almost impossible for you to grow okra successfully in your garden and I would suggest that you devote the space and your time to growing other, more reliable vegetables.

Nematodes are the number one soilborne problem in Texas and okra is one of their favorite targets. Nematodes are microscopic eelworms that can be found to some degree in most Texas soils. They become a serious problem if their population increases so much that their feeding and reproduction habits interfere with the normal growth and function of the plant's root system. Nematodes enter the feeder roots of okra (and other vegetables), causing the formation of irregular swellings, or knots, which inhibit the plant's normal absorption of water and nutrients. When nematode-infested plants are pulled carefully from the soil, these knots can be found on the roots, giving them their name, root-knot nematodes. Symptoms of a nematode infestation are discoloration and yellowing of the foliage, abnormal wilting, slow growth, reduced yields and, oftentimes, death of the plants.

Control of nematodes can be achieved best by a combination of practices including a long-term rotation, summer fallowing and, if necessary, the use of chemicals. Detailed information on nematode control can be found on page 408.

Insects that occasionally trouble okra include stinkbugs, aphids and fire ants. Stinkbugs do their damage primarily by feeding on the young, tender pods, which causes them to be misshapen and poorly developed. Aphids, or plant lice, occur in large numbers and suck juices from the underside of the foliage and the tender stems. Fire ants, although they're not supposed to feed on plants, apparently have developed a taste for garden-grown okra. They oftentimes can be found feeding (or at least having a party) in large numbers inside the okra blooms and on the young pods. Needless to say, fire ants can make harvesting your okra an even more "stinging" experience than it is already. If these pests become a problem, applications of Sevin or malathion usually will give good control and help ensure a good harvest of quality okra.

Quick Problem Solver: Okra

Problem	Causes	Solutions
Seed fail to germinate/ plants do not emerge.	Old seed.	Only use current season seed or seed that has been properly stored (if you save seed from year to year).
	Planted too deep.	Plant okra seed ½ to ¾ inch deep.
	Lack of soil moisture.	Plant "in moisture" by watering several days prior to planting or by adding water directly to seed furrow at planting.
	Cold soils.	Never plant okra until the soil temperature is above 68 degrees.

Seedlings die shortly after emergence.	Damping-off (fungus).	Plant when soil temperatures are satisfactory. Use treated seed and avoid overwatering.
	Cutworms.	Check for presence of cutworms just below soil surface near healthy plants. If found, treat with appropriate insecticide/bait.
Plants grow slowly, lack good color.	Cold soils/growing conditions.	Okra will grow slowly if nighttime temperatures are 50 degrees or lower.
	Low fertility.	Side-dress with nitrogen fertilizer.
	Low soil pH.	Adjust pH of soil to above 6.0.
	Wet soils.	Avoid overwatering. Plant on raised beds for improved soil drainage.
Pods poorly shaped, puffy.	Low soil pH.	Adjust pH of soil to above 6.0.
Pods bent, twisted.	Insect stings on pods.	Treat foliage with Sevin or malathion to control insects.
Plants quit blooming, grow slowly.	Low fertility.	Side-dress with nitrogen fertilizer.
	Cool temperatures.	Hope for warmer weather. Remove plants and use space for fall/winter vegetables.
Plants lack good color, grow slowly, appear stunted.	Nematodes.	Check roots for galls or "knots." If present, before next crop treat soil for control of nematodes as outlined in appendix.
Plants literally die overnight, foliage remains on plant.	Cotton root rot (fungus).	No cure! Follow long-term rotation. Plant okra in another area and/or depend on friends and supermarkets to supply your okra needs.
Plants too tall, harvesting difficult.	Plant size.	Use dwarf varieties and/or cut back plants in mid- to late summer causing the development of a bush-like plant.

ONION

Scientific Name: *Allium cepa*
Family: *Amaryllidaceae*
Biennial, grown as an annual
Cool Season
Varieties:
- Bulb: Granno 502, Y1015 (SuperSweet), Granex; (red) Red Granex, Burgundy
- Green: Southport White, Beltsville Bunching, White Knight

Expected Harvest:
- Bulbs - 20 to 30 pounds per 10 feet of row
- Green - 3 to 5 pounds per 10 feet of row

ONIONS

Onions, and most of their smelly relatives like garlic and leeks, originated in Pakistan. They were an important food source and thirst-quencher in Egypt as long ago as 3200 B.C. A testimonial to the onion's value is found in the Bible, where it is referred to as an important part of the diet of the Israelites long before their exodus from Egypt. Onions were introduced into the West Indies by the Spaniards and their culture soon spread to all parts of the New World. Our first colonists in America grew lots of onions, which quickly became a favorite among the Indians. Today, the onion is by far our most important bulb crop as well as one of the world's most important vegetables. The United States leads the world in onion production, while Texas out-produces every other state. Indeed, Texas is known around the world for its production of large, high-quality, sweet onions.

But while our commercial onion growers are very successful, most home gardeners have difficulty growing a good crop. The reason for their failure usually can be attributed to one of two things. Either they planted the *wrong* variety and/or planted at the *wrong* time.

Let's talk about bulbing and the importance of using the right varieties. Onions bulb in response to the length of daylight hours and are categorized into three classes: short-day, intermediate-day and long-day types. Within each of these classes are numerous varieties. The short-day varieties require 10 to 11 hours of daylight to initiate bulbing; the intermediate varieties need 12 to 13 hours; and the long-day varieties need 14 to 16 hours. The importance of this classification becomes obvious when one realizes that in the southern regions of Texas, the longest day is less than 14 hours, which means the long-day varieties will never bulb, but make giant green onions instead. Even the intermediate-day varieties grown in this area usually produce relatively small bulbs, because only their minimal day length requirement is met. If grown in North Texas where the summer days are longer, however, long-day varieties will

Providing adequate space of onions to develop in is one of the most important factors in making good sized onions.

produce bulbs, but the intermediate-day varieties invariably produce larger ones. The short-day varieties, if planted at the right time, will make large bulbs wherever you garden in Texas. Obviously, then, you should plant short-day varieties. Another reason to plant short-day varieties is that they generally are not as pungent, or hot, as long-day types. The sweet onions Texas is famous for are all short-day varieties.

Most of the short-day varieties are simply called *Bermudas,* but you need to be more specific in choosing a variety. Use of the term Bermuda to describe an onion variety is analogous to someone asking you what kind of car you drive and you respond, "General Motors." The obvious next question would be: "What kind of General Motors car?" And you must decide what kind of Bermuda onion to grow-Grano 502, Granex or Y1015, the new Texas A&M release that is being promoted as Texas Super Sweet, are the best choices. Each of these varieties produces softball-size bulbs regardless of where you garden in Texas, if they're planted at the right time.

Planting At The Right Time

From this point on I'm going to assume you'll plant the right varieties in your garden and move onto another critical factor—timing. Remember, onions bulb in response to day length, not age or size of the plants. The importance of this fact should be quite obvious: if the onion plant is small when bulbing is initiated, the result will be a small bulb. Generally, if it's a larger plant, you'll get a larger bulb. The size of the onion is determined by its rings, which are the fleshy base of the plant's leaves. In general, the larger the plant, the more leaves you have and the larger the bulb. Bulb size also is determined by the thickness of the rings, which is influenced by fertility and moisture, which we'll discuss later.

How do you go about having the right size plant in your garden at the right time? The best way is to set out transplants that are pencil-size, or slightly smaller, about four to six weeks before the average frost-free date for your area. By doing this, the plants will be about optimum size at the same time the day length is sufficient to induce bulbing.

In the southern half of Texas, you can plant onion seed in the fall, and overwinter the plants to initiate bulbing in the spring. The best time for seeding varies, but should occur sometime between late September and mid-November. Your goal should be to have plants that are less than 1/4 inch in diameter when dormancy-inducing temperatures occur, but large enough not be be damaged by cold weather. Overwintering onions is not recommended in the colder regions of the state where cold weather can damage the plants.

Even in warmer parts of Texas, the advantage of seeding directly in your garden and overwintering the onion plants is questionable, for several reasons—the length of time they will occupy space in your garden; the possibility of cold injury during severe winters; and, most importantly, the distinct possibility that the plants may bolt or produce a seedstem.

Onions are biennials, which means they normally grow vegetatively for one season; then, following a cold-induced dormancy, flower and produce seed the second year. Dormancy will be induced though, if plants that are larger than 1/4 inch in diameter are exposed to prolonged temperatures below 45 degrees.When the temperatures rise and the plants resume growth, bolting or seedstem formation will occur. When bolting occurs, both bulb size and quality is reduced greatly. In addition, even short-term storage is almost impossible, due to the presence of the seedstem within the bulb.

Setting out transplants, though, is no guarantee against bolting or seedstem formation. First of all, nearly all the onion transplants available at garden centers and nurseries are produced in South Texas and may have been subjected to dormancy-inducing temperatures before you purchased them. You can lessen this possibility by only setting out transplants that are pencil-size or smaller. Onion plants smaller than the magical 1/4 inch diameter can go dormant, but will not be induced to bolt or go to seed. You also can grow your own plants in a protected area, such as a greenhouse or cold frame. Information on growing transplants and building a cold frame can be found on pages 396 and 402. Onion plants also can be induced to bolt after you set them out in your garden if they are exposed to extended periods with temperatures below 45 degrees, which is a good reason for not setting them out too early.

Sets, or small mature bulbs usually less than 1/2 inch in diameter, can be used to grow bulb onions, but this practice has not been successful in Texas. Most of the sets are northern-grown and usually are long-day varieties. In addition, they often have been stored at temperatures that will induce bolting from the time they were harvested until being shipped to market. If you decide to try your luck planting sets, use only those 1/2 inch or less in diameter (larger ones are almost sure to bolt) and plant them about the same time as you would transplants.

Care And Cultivation

Onions can be grown successfully on most Texas soils, if they're prepared properly. Soils that are heavy and tight, with poor internal drainage, or those that are droughty will not produce high yields of quality bulbs. To compensate for those problems, you should work 2 to 3 inches of well-decomposed organic matter into the soil.

Onions will not grow well in soils with a pH below 6.0 and if your soil has too low of a pH, lime should be added to bring it up to a satisfactory level. Information on testing and adjusting your soil pH can be found on page 394. Onions also will do better if you add barnyard manure to the soil. Apply the manure over the planting area at the rate of about 1/2 pound per square foot. Till or spade the necessary ingredients into the soil to a depth of 8 to 10 inches.

Planting onions on raised beds is a good practice, especially if your soil is a little on the heavy side. Raised beds will improve soil drainage and they will warm up more quickly in the spring because more surface area is exposed to the sun. Use a shovel or a tiller with a bedder to form ridges and furrows that measure at least 30 inches apart. Next, use the flat side of your garden rake to shape and form the ridges into raised beds about 6 inches tall and 16 to 20 inches wide.

Onions range from red to yellow and can be harvested "green" or when fully mature. Be sure to select transplants of suitable size.

A reference was made earlier to the fact that fertility and moisture influence the thickness of the "rings" and, consequently, the size of the bulb. With this in mind, you need to be aware of the fact that onions have a rather shallow and limited root system—nearly all the roots will be directly beneath the plant, and hopefully, eventually beneath the bulb. This characteristic is of major importance with regard to fertilizing as well as watering onions.

After forming the raised beds, evenly scatter about ½ pound of a complete fertilizer, such as 10-20-10, over each 50 square feet of bed surface. Thoroughly mix the fertilizer into the top 2 inches of the bed and then use your rake to reshape and smooth the beds. Tamp the beds firm to consolidate the soil particles which will help moisture move laterally within the beds. Prepare and fertilize the soil several weeks prior to planting.

Whether you're using seed, sets or transplants, the soil should be slightly moist at planting time. If it has been dry, water several days before planting. The 16- to 20-inch-wide beds easily will accommodate two rows of onions spaced 10 to 14 inches apart. When seeding, make the seed furrows about ½ inch deep. If your soil seems dry, apply water directly in the seed furrow and allow it to soak in before planting. Sow eight to 10 seeds per foot of row and cover them with soil. Firm the soil over the planted seed to ensure good soil/seed contact.

Onion seed will germinate at a wide range of soil temperatures and if those temperatures are between 50 and 85 degrees, the seedlings should emerge within seven to 14 days. As the plants grow, they should be thinned gradually to an in-row spacing of 3 to 4 inches. Use the larger thinnings as green onions. Be sure thinning is completed before the remaining plants give any indication of beginning to bulb.

When setting out transplants, use the same between-row spacing as for seed. Use a short stick, or dibble, to make holes 3 to 4 inches apart and about 1 inch deep to accommodate the transplants. Set the transplants in the holes, firm them in and water immediately to settle the soil around them. If you opt to use sets, plant them about 3 to 4 inches apart and about 1 inch deep using the same in-row spacing as with seed or transplants.

About three to four weeks after transplanting, emergence of the sets or after the first thinning, side-dress the plants with 1 cup of ammonium sulfate (21-0-0) or ⅔ cup of ammonium nitrate (33-0-0) per 35 feet of row. Apply the fertilizer in a band to each side of the bed, about 4 inches from the plants. If you planted two rows per bed, apply ⅓ of the fertilizer between the rows of onions. Work the fertilizer into the soil surface and water lightly.

Adequate Moisture Important

For maximum-size bulbs, your onion plants should be kept growing vigorously and steadily, without any setbacks. That means adequate soil moisture must be available to the plants. Keep the soil moist enough to encourage vigorous growth, especially after bulbing begins. Research has shown that the greatest water use by the onion occurs from bulb initiation until it begins to mature. If soil moisture is lacking during this period, bulb size will be reduced greatly. Therefore, depending upon soil type and Mother Nature, you may need to water at least once a week, applying enough water to wet the soil to a depth of at least 6 inches.

Mulching around the plants with 2 to 3 inches of organic matter will help conserve soil moisture and control weeds. A good time to mulch is shortly after the first sidedress application of fertilizer. For the second side-dressing, rake back the organic matter from the side of the plants, apply the fertilizer and re-apply the mulch. This should be done when the plants first start to bulb.

Once the plants begin to mature, which will be signaled by a slowdown in their growth and a softening of the neck just above the bulb, begin to let your soil dry. Excessive moisture during this time will inhibit proper curing of the bulbs and result in significant losses, due to decaying that takes place after harvest. When bulb onions are fully mature, their necks soften, causing their tops to fall over while the leaves are still green. At this stage, they should be pulled up and placed in a dry, protected area to cure for several days. After curing, clip off the roots and tops, leaving about 1 inch of the stem attached to the bulbs to prevent entry of decay-causing organisms.

Contrary to popular belief, it doesn't do any good to "walk the tops down," as practiced by some gardeners who believe that knocking the tops over will force the roots to nourish the bulbs rather than the foliage. In theory, this would cause the onions to mature more quickly and grow larger. However, it's the foliage, not the roots, that manufactures the plant's food, causing the bulb to size. Without the foliage, there's little need for the roots.

Insects And Diseases

You won't have to worry about harvesting, let alone about how large the bulbs will be, if you fail to control insects and diseases.

Thrips are the most damaging insects that attack onions in Texas.

Exposure to improper environmental conditions will cause onions to produce a seedstem and flower.

These minute insects have rasping mouthparts and their feeding results in whitish blotches on the leaves. Eventually, the tips of the leaves turn brown and die. If thrips are left uncontrolled and allowed to increase in number, yields will be reduced greatly. Applications of malathion or diazinon begun at the first sign of thrips will give good control.

Cutworms are often a problem when growing onions and do their damage by cutting the plants off near ground level. If you experience this problem, it's important to know that these pests are nocturnal and seldom are seen during the day—unless you dig around near the base of a healthy plant. Oftentimes, you'll find an inch-long dark worm just waiting for an evening meal. Diazinon applied to the soil before planting will give good control. If your plants are established and growing, you can use cutworm baits.

Purple blotch (left) and pink root (right) can damage you onion crop. Purple blotch causes lesions on leaves and pink root reduces root growth. Both conditions will reduce yields.

Several different types of foliage diseases also pose a threat to your crop of bulb onions. Downy mildew is a cool, wet-season disease that causes spots on the leaves that change from pale green to brown. As the disease develops, the older leaves fall over and become dry. Purple blotch, as the name indicates, causes large, purplish lesions on the leaves that have a "target spot" appearance. Often, this disease will reduce yields, but the worst damage occurs when the fungus enters the bulb through the neck, eventually causing a watery decay that usually becomes apparent after the onions are harvested and stored. Both downy mildew and purple blotch can be controlled by preventive applications of Bravo or a fungicide containing maneb. They should be applied at seven- to 10-day intervals during periods of wet, cool weather. Several different types of soilborne bulb rots can occur and are best controlled by planting on raised beds to improve soil drainage, providing adequate fertility to encourage vigorous plant growth and utilizing a long-term rotation program.

Quick Problem Solver: Onion

Problem	Causes	Solutions
Seed fail to germinate, seedlings emerge.	Old seed.	Onion seed lose viability quickly if not stored properly. Use current season seed.
	Planted too deep.	Plant seed ½ to ¾ inch deep using greater depth on loose soils.
	Cold soils.	Onion seed may fail to germinate if soil temperature below 50 degrees.
	Lack of soil moisture.	Soil should be moist at planting time.
	Crusted soils.	Onion seed are weak germinators. Prevent soil from crusting by sprinkling lightly as emergence time nears.
Seedlings weak, lack good color.	Cold soils.	Growth will be slow until soils warm.
	Wet soils.	Avoid excessive soil moisture. Plant on raised beds to provide better drainage.
	Acid soils.	Soil pH should be above 6.0.
	Low fertility.	Side-dress lightly with nitrogen fertilizer.
Seedlings die shortly after emergence.	Damping-off (fungus).	Avoid cold/wet soils and plant treated seed.
	Cutworms.	Check soil at base of healthy plants for dark worms. If found, treat with appropriate pesticide.
Plants sluggish, grow slowly.	Low fertility.	Side-dress with small amount of nitrogen fertilizer.
	Lack of soil moisture.	Water frequently to encourage vigorous growth. Mulch around plants to conserve soil moisture.
Plants fail to bulb, those that do are small, poor quality.	Wrong variety.	Plant only short day varieties. Intermediate day length varieties can be planted in North Texas.
	Planted at wrong time.	Pay close attention to time of planting/variety.
	Low soil moisture.	Once bulbing begins, maintain soil moist enough to encourage vigorous plant growth.

	Heavy and/or droughty soils.	Add liberal amounts of organic matter to soils to provide good conditions for plant growth and development.
	Planted "sets."	Sets are usually not the right varieties for Texas. Good way to grow green onions, however.
	Low fertility.	Side-dress frequently.
Plants bolt or send up a seedstem.	Plants overwintered.	Seeded or transplanted onions overwintered will usually bolt if exposed to extended cold.
	Purchased transplants already exposed to dormancy-inducing temperatures.	Grow your own transplants. Set out only those plants having a diameter of less than ¼ inch.
	Transplanted too early.	Transplants exposed to cold after setting out will often bolt. Avoid planting too early.
	Planted sets.	Use only sets less than ½ inch in diameter.
Tips of leaves brown, wither. Foliage spotty.	Thrips.	Control with malathion or diazinon.
Brownish spots on leaves, older leaves fall over.	Downy mildew (fungus).	Treat foliage with Bravo or a fungicide containing maneb.
Purplish lesions on leaves.	Purple blotch (fungus).	As above.
Bulbs rot in ground.	Soilborne fungi/ bacteria.	Plant on raised beds and follow good rotation program.
Tops fall over.	Normal sign of maturity.	Harvest bulbs and place in dry protected area to cure for several days.
Bulbs rot in storage.	Immature bulbs.	Harvest when mature as indicated by fall of tops.
	Fungi/bacteria.	Cure properly. Leave at least 1 inch of neck on bulb to prevent entry of decay-causing organisms.

PEAS

Scientific Name: *Pisum sativum*
Family: *Leguminosae*
Annual
Cool Season
Varieties:
English: Wando, Alaska, Progress No. 9
Edible Podded (snow): Dwarf Gray Sugar, Melting Sugar
Snap: Sugar Snap, Sugar Ann, Sugar Bon
Expected Harvest: ½ to 2 pounds of pods per plant

PEAS

Man has eaten and appreciated peas since before the beginning of recorded history. And the same is certainly true today, for there's nothing quite like fresh peas, picked at their very peak of quality and served soon after harvesting. Indeed, peas are best when prepared within hours, or even minutes, after being picked. To most folks, including yours truly, peas belong in the same unique category as tomatoes, sweet corn and green beans—their taste and flavor is simply superb when enjoyed fresh from the garden.

Unfortunately, however, this culinary delight doesn't belong on the Texas' "Top Ten" list of easy-to-grow vegetables. In fact, peas consistently are one of the most difficult crops to grow in Texas, but it can be done, if you'll pay close attention to their demanding environmental requirements.

Before we continue, it's important to note that the peas we'll be talking about in this chapter all have the scientific name *Pisum sativum.* These are the true peas and are only closely related to the very popular southern pea in that both are legumes. Southern peas, such as the blackeye, crowder and purple hull, actually are beans and are covered in their own chapter.

Peas are classified in at least three ways: seed type (smooth or wrinkled); growth habit (dwarf, semi-dwarf or vine); and how they are consumed, which is how they're most commonly identified by Texans. The garden, English or shelled pea is grown only for its seed. Snow or Chinese peas are harvested when the pods are full-size but before the seeds enlarge. The entire pod is eaten, hence their other name, edible-podded peas. The third and newest type is the snap pea. Both pods and seeds of snap peas can be enjoyed until the pods become tough and fibrous. At this stage of development, they're shelled and only the large, tender and very sweet peas are consumed.

The World's Oldest Vegetable

Considered to be the oldest cultivated vegetable in the world, peas have existed in one form or another since the Stone Age. Archaeologists working near the Burma-Thailand border found fossilized peas and carbon-dated them to 9750 B.C. The Chinese believe the pea first was determined as suitable for human consumption 5,000 years ago by Emperor Shen Nung, who also is credited with bringing rice and wheat into cultivation. Although widely cultivated in much of the world, peas generally were not grown in Europe until the Norman Conquest of England. In the Middle Ages, English botanists developed improved varieties and perfected their culture. At that time, peas usually were dried and kept for times of shortage, hardship and famine. Later, dried peas were an essential food for immigrants preparing to sail to the New World because they would keep indefinitely and required little storage space. Without a doubt, peas were one of the very first vegetables planted in the gardens of the English colonists.

Being strictly a cool-season vegetable, peas will do best in Texas when planted for late fall, winter and, if you garden in South Texas, early spring harvest. Ideally, planting should occur about eight to 10 weeks prior to the first expected freeze in your area of the state. The peas will not be damaged or killed by the cold, unless the temperature drops into the low to mid-20s. However, it's important for you to remember that even though the plants can withstand considerable cold, freezing temperatures during bloom will cause the flowers to abort. In the milder winter areas of our state, additional plantings can be made through the winter, until 10 weeks before daytime temperatures are expected to exceed 75 degrees.

Peas can be grown for late spring harvest but, at best, are a poor risk. Planting must occur at a time to ensure that the peas mature and develop a good crop before maximum daytime temperatures are expected to exceed 75 degrees. Consequently, planting should take place as soon as the soil can be worked in the late winter or early spring. And only fast-maturing varieties should be planted. Even the combination of using fast-maturing varieties and planting early, though, will not always ensure success. If the soil is too cold at time of planting the seed may not germinate. If you plant early and do get a stand, you still must be concerned about the effect of frosty weather during flowering.

Peas are as indifferent about the soil they grow in as they are particular about the weather. They will grow well on any soil as long as it does not stay wet and soggy for extended periods of time. Generally, peas grown on sand will produce earlier, while those grown on heavier soils usually produce higher yields.

Immediately after seeding, some type of support should be provided to meet the peas need to climb. Snow fence, chicken wire, picket fence and tomato cages work well.

A soil pH of between 6.5 and 7.5 is considered ideal, so if you garden in an area were acid soils are common, you may find it necessary to add lime to your soil. Additional information on adjusting the pH of your soil can be found on page 394.

Regardless of your garden's soil type, you should work in liberal amounts of well-decomposed leaves, grass clippings or compost. Spread 2 to 3 inches of such organic matter over the surface of the soil. At the same time, scatter a small amount of fertilizer evenly over the area to be planted —unless your soil already is adequately fertile. Peas, like all legumes, enjoy the rewards of a mutually beneficial relationship with a type of soilborne bacterium that causes small nodules to form on the legume roots and has the unique ability to fix nitrogen from the atmosphere. The nitrogen is utilized by both the bacteria and peas for their growth. As a result, peas normally need only a small amount of fertilizer to produce good yields.

Fertility Requirements

If your soil already is fertile due to previous applications of commercial fertilizer and/or barnyard manure, it may not be necessary to apply any preplant fertilizer. However, moderately increasing the amount of fertility usually will prove beneficial. Use about 1/4 pound of barnyard manure per square foot or 3/4 pound of a fertilizer low in nitrogen, such as 10-10-10, per 100 square feet or for each 35 feet of row to be planted in peas. Excessive fertility should be avoided; it will encourage foliage growth and delay flowering, neither of which is conducive to high yields!

For you folks gardening in alkaline soils with a pH above 7.5, the addition of a small amount of iron to your soil will prevent chlorosis, or yellowing, of the leaves, which can reduce yields. The iron can be applied as copperous (iron sulfate) or even better as the sequesterene form usually available under the trade name of Geigy 138, which is formulated specially for high pH soils. Check the label for the correct amount to apply. Till or spade all organic matter, fertilizer, barnyard manure, lime and iron into the soil to a depth of 8 to 10 inches, preferably doing so several weeks prior to planting.

Sugar snap peas are an excellent choice for any home garden.

Chicken wire provides excellent support for pea vines and makes harvesting easier.

As mentioned earlier, peas will do well on most soils as long as they are well-drained. If your soil is a little on the heavy side, you should consider planting on raised beds. If your garden soil is a deep sand, planting on raised beds may lose some of its importance since poor drainage usually is not a problem. However, such soils often have a tendency to crust over following heavy rains, causing problems with soil aeration and resulting in poor plant growth. Crusting is not as severe on raised beds.

To make raised beds, use your shovel or a tiller with a bedder to form ridges and furrows that are 30 to 48 inches apart measured from the top of one ridge to the center of an adjoining ridge. The between-ridge or final between-row spacing depends upon the characteristics of the particular pea variety you're planting. Generally, the distance between rows should equal the expected height of the peas. Use the flat side of your garden rake to flatten and smooth the ridges into raised beds. The bed top, or planting area, should be about 16 to 24 inches wide with the remaining area serving as a water furrow to facilitate drainage and watering.

At planting time, your soil should be moist enough to initiate germination and the subsequent emergence of the seedlings without applying additional water. If your soil is on the dry side, apply water several days prior to the anticipated planting date.

This seems an appropriate time to discuss an interesting fact about pea seeds, which are either smooth or wrinkled. Varieties which have wrinkled seed have a higher sugar content and thus, produce sweeter tasting peas. The smooth-seed varieties are more cold-hardy and if you garden in the colder winter areas of Texas, you should take advantage of this horticultural curiosity. Select varieties with wrinkled seed for early fall planting and smooth seeded varieties for those plantings that will mature when it's colder.

A Desire To Climb

Before actually planting, several important items need to be discussed. First, it's important that you realize all peas, including the dwarf, semi-dwarf and vining types, have an inherent desire to climb. They produce tendrils which actually are modified leaves that can grasp and hold. Therefore, you always should plan to support the plant growth of your peas in some way. Obviously, the taller the plant, the higher the support should be. Snow fencing, chicken wire, concrete reinforcing wire, trellises made by stringing wire between poles or almost anything your imagination can conjure up will work. In addition, the dwarf and semi-dwarf types should be planted two rows per bed so that the plants can intertwine and provide themselves with additional support.

Secondly, to ensure yourself a good stand, plant seeds that have been treated with a fungicide to prevent seedling diseases. Most seeds that you purchase already have been treated, as evidenced by the pink- or blue-colored fungicide on them. However, if your seeds are not treated, do so yourself, using an appropriate fungicide. Simply put your seeds in a paper bag along with the amount of fungicide recommended on the package's label, close and shake vigorously.

Thirdly, you also should consider inoculation, which is simply the process of applying the beneficial bacteria we discussed earlier to the pea seed prior to planting, rather than depending upon your garden soil as the inoculating source. If you've been successful for a number of years growing beans, peas or other legumes in your garden, or if native legumes grow abundantly in your area, inoculation may not be necessary. It's so easy to do, though, it's probably worth the effort just for insurance. Simply dampen (do not soak) the seed, place them in a paper bag and apply the inoculating powder. If you choose to inoculate and treat your seed with a fungicide, both can be done at the same time. However, you can treat the seed with a fungicide at any time, but inoculation must be done immediately prior to planting. If the damp, inoculated seeds are allowed to dry completely before planting, the nitrogen-fixing bacteria lose their effectiveness. Commercial inoculation powders are available from most garden centers and a number of mail-order firms.

Use your hoe, a stick or something similar to make seed furrows that are about 1 to 1½ inches deep. As mentioned earlier, the dwarf and semi-dwarf types should be planted double-row per bed with the rows spaced about 12 to 14 inches apart. The large vining types are planted single-row and should have a between-row spacing of at least 4 feet.

If your soil still seems dry after making furrows, simply apply water directly into them. Apply enough water to saturate the soil to a depth of 4 to 6 inches. You may have to apply the water at several different times, depending upon your soil type. After the water has soaked in, sow the seed at the rate of six to eight seeds per foot of row and cover them with dry soil. After covering the seed, firm the soil over the seed furrow. This practice will help conserve soil moisture and ensure good contact between the seed and the soil.

Most viable pea seed will emerge within about seven to 12 days after planting, depending primarily upon soil temperature. However, as indicated earlier, if the soil temperature is too cold (below 50 degrees) at the seeding depth, the seeds may either fail to germinate or take several weeks to emerge.

Immediately after planting is the best time to set up the support structures for your peas to climb on as they grow and develop. If you wait until the seedlings are up to do so, you risk damaging the plants or their root systems.

Once the seedlings begin to emerge, it's important to prevent your soil from crusting. When legumes emerge from the soil, the seedling stem emerges first and it literally pulls the primary or cotyledonary leaves up through the ground. It's not uncommon for pea seedlings to actually "pull their heads off" as they emerge from tight or crusted soils. To overcome the problem of crusted soils, sprinkle the bed with water when the emerging seedlings are first visible. Once a good stand is established, water thoroughly if the soil is dry.

Within a week after emergence, your stand of peas should be thinned to an in-row spacing of 2 to 3 inches apart for the dwarf and semi-dwarf types and about 5 inches apart for the vining types. Rather than

Powdery mildew (left) and insect damage (right) can destroy your pea crop. Control measures should be taken at the first sign of any disease symptoms or insect infestation.

thinning to the proper spacing the first time, it's best to do the thinning twice. This will provide a little insurance against any insects, diseases or birds that might attack some of the seedlings. Thinning is best done by simply pulling up the unwanted seedlings. However, if thinning is delayed and the roots of the plants are intertwined, pinch or cut off the plants near ground level. After thinning, water lightly to settle the soil around the remaining plants. Next, apply an organic mulch around the base of the pea plants. A 2- to 3-inch layer of well-decomposed leaves, grass clippings or compost will help stabilize the soil temperature, control weeds and conserve valuable soil moisture.

Within about 45 to 50 days after emergence, your pea plants will begin to bloom. From this point on, you should make every effort to be sure your plants have an adequate water supply. Insufficient soil moisture while peas are blooming will cause the plants to shed many of their blooms and to produce small, poor quality peas. Avoid moisture stress by watering your peas when the soil about 1 inch beneath the surface is relatively dry. Regardless of the watering method you use, apply enough water each time to wet the soil to a depth of 6 to 8 inches.

All your peas need from this point on is a little tender, loving care which, among other things, means controlling weeds, grasses, damaging insects and diseases. Mulching will help prevent many unwanted weeds and grasses but those that do come up should be removed by hand-pulling or lightly cultivating with your hoe. When cultivating, only scratch the surface of the soil to prevent damage to the plant roots.

Insect And Disease Problems

Fortunately, insects and diseases are not a major problem when growing peas in Texas. The only common insect pest is the aphid. Aphids appear in large numbers and cause great damage by feeding on the under surface of the plants' leaves. Occasionally, other foliage-feeding insects can be a problem but most of them, including aphids, can be controlled by applications of malathion or diazinon.

In recent years, plant breeders have done an excellent job of incorporating disease resistance into many of the newer pea varieties. However, you still can depend on the occurrence of powdery mildew, which if not controlled, literally can put you out of the pea business in a hurry. Powdery mildew is characterized by the formation of a white, talcum-like mold on the leaves, stems and pods. Humid, windy conditions encourage the development of the fungus and cause it to spread to other areas on the plants or to uninfected plants. The probability of your peas becoming infected with powdery mildew can be reduced greatly by providing adequate space for the growth of the plants, which encourages good air circulation. Also, control the problem by not handling the foliage when it is wet; and by avoiding overhead watering. If problems do occur, applications of sulphur begun at the first sign of the disease and applied according to label directions usually will provide good control.

Harvesting should occur when the appropriate stage of maturity is reached and, of course, this depends upon the type of pea you're growing. The first harvest of English or shelling peas usually will occur about 20 to 25 days after the first blooms set. The peas should be harvested when the pods appear plump and the peas within are full-size but still tender. The pods should be bright green and velvety to the touch. Edible-podded peas are picked when the pods are full-size, yet still tender, and the peas within the pods are about the size of BBs. If allowed to overmature, they can be shelled and eaten like English peas. The snap pea requires the least amount of timing, as they can be harvested and enjoyed at almost any stage of development. However, they develop their maximum sweet flavor if allowed to fully ripen on the vine.

To harvest, grasp the vine just below the pod and pull the pod off. By holding the vine secure, you avoid damaging the plant. It's best to harvest just before you plan to cook the peas, since their sugar is converted quickly to starch. If the peas are to be stored for a while, harvest in the early morning, place the peas in a moisture-proof bag or container and put them in the refrigerator. To maintain highest quality, English peas should not be shelled until just prior to their being prepared. If you produce a bountiful harvest, peas are easily canned or frozen for long-term storage. However, as good as home canned or frozen peas are, they won't compare with those prepared fresh from your garden.

Quick Problem Solver: Peas

Problem	Causes	Solutions
Seeds fail to germinate, seedlings emerge.	Old seed.	Always use current season seed.
	Planted too deep.	Peas should be seeded 1 to 1½ inches deep using the greater depth on sandier soils.
	Soil too cold.	Seed will fail to germinate or germinate very slowly if soil temperature is below 50 degrees.
	Lack of soil moisture.	At planting, soil should be moist enough to initiate germination.
Many seedlings emerge "headless."	Crusted soil.	Sprinkle soil lightly at first indication of seedling emergence to prevent soil from crusting.
Seedlings die soon after emergence.	Damping-off (fungus).	Use treated seed. Avoid overly wet soils. Plant at right time to encourage rapid germination and emergence of seedlings.
	Cutworms.	Check beneath soil near base of healthy plants. If worms found, treat with appropriate insecticide.
Plants sluggish, grow slowly, lack good color.	Soil pH too low.	Add lime to soil to raise pH above 6.5.
	Low fertility.	Add small amount of fertilizer to side of plants, lightly work into soil and water.
	Poor soil drainage.	Plant on raised beds and add organic matter to soil to improve drainage.

Foliage yellowish, leaf veins green.	Chlorosis.	Add small amount of iron to soil according to label directions.
Plants fail to "climb."	Low temperatures.	Tendrils will often fail to grasp and hold if temperatures are below 50 degrees.
Blooms fail to set, drop from plant.	Excess fertility.	Avoid over-fertilizing, especially prior to planting.
	Cold temperatures.	Frosty weather will cause blooms to fall from plant.
	High temperatures.	Hot, dry temperatures will cause peas to fail to set.
	Moisture stress.	Avoid low soil moisture during blooming.
White, talcum-like substance on leaves.	Powdery mildew (fungus).	Use resistant varieties; avoid crowded growing conditions, overhead watering; treat foliage with sulphur.
Foliage wrinkled, small insects present on undersurface of leaves.	Aphids.	Treat foliage with diazinon or malathion.
Foliage mottled, plants stunted.	Virus.	Discard affected plants.
Peas "starchy," lack sweet flavor.	High temperatures.	Peas should mature before daytime temperatures exceed 75 degrees.
	Overmature.	Harvest peas at peak of quality.
Pods tough, fibrous.	Overmature.	For edible podded varieties, harvest before peas begin to enlarge and while pods are tender.

PEPPERS

Scientific Name:
(mild) *Capsicum annuum*
(pungent) *Capsicum frutescens*
Family: *Solanaceae*
Perennial, grown as an annual
Warm Season
Varieties:
Mild: Bell Tower, Shamrock, Big Bertha, Valley Giant, Gypsy, Large Red Cherry, Sweet Banana
Pungent: Jalapeno, Serrano, Long Red Cayenne, Hungarian Wax
Expected Harvest: 1 to 3 pounds per plant

PEPPERS

Peppers are among our most versatile garden vegetables. Depending on the variety, peppers can produce fruit that ranges in size from barely bigger than a pea to larger than a softball. Flavors vary from firey hot to sweet; colors range from glossy greens to bright yellows to the reddest of reds. And, gardeners' opinions on growing peppers are as diverse as the vegetable itself. Some think peppers are the most satisfying and rewarding vegetables to grow; others find them to be the most frustrating. Those frustrations, however, can be eliminated by following a few simple techniques. Before examining those techniques, though, let's spend a little time on the pepper's interesting history.

The pepper belongs to the genus *Capsicum* and is in no way related to the true pepper, *Piper nigrum*, from which we make the common black pepper used for seasoning. Then why do they both have the same name? The reason can be traced back to Christopher Columbus, who on his first voyage was looking for a shorter route to the East Indies and their highly prized spices. When he found the natives of the West Indies growing and using the firey forms of *Capsicum*, he thought they were some types of peppers. Upon his return to Spain, his discovery of a new "pepper" caused great interest.

Subsequent explorers discovered numerous types of peppers throughout the New World, but most were found in Central and South America. Some peppers were described as large and sweet, while others were termed "edible only by fools with cast iron innards."

Today, there may be more varieties of peppers than ever before, but no matter what their sizes, shapes and colors are, all peppers are grown in basically the same way. Since the bell, or green, pepper is by far the most common type grown in Texas, we'll concentrate on it, but at the end of this chapter we'll briefly discuss some of the other types grown in Texas gardens.

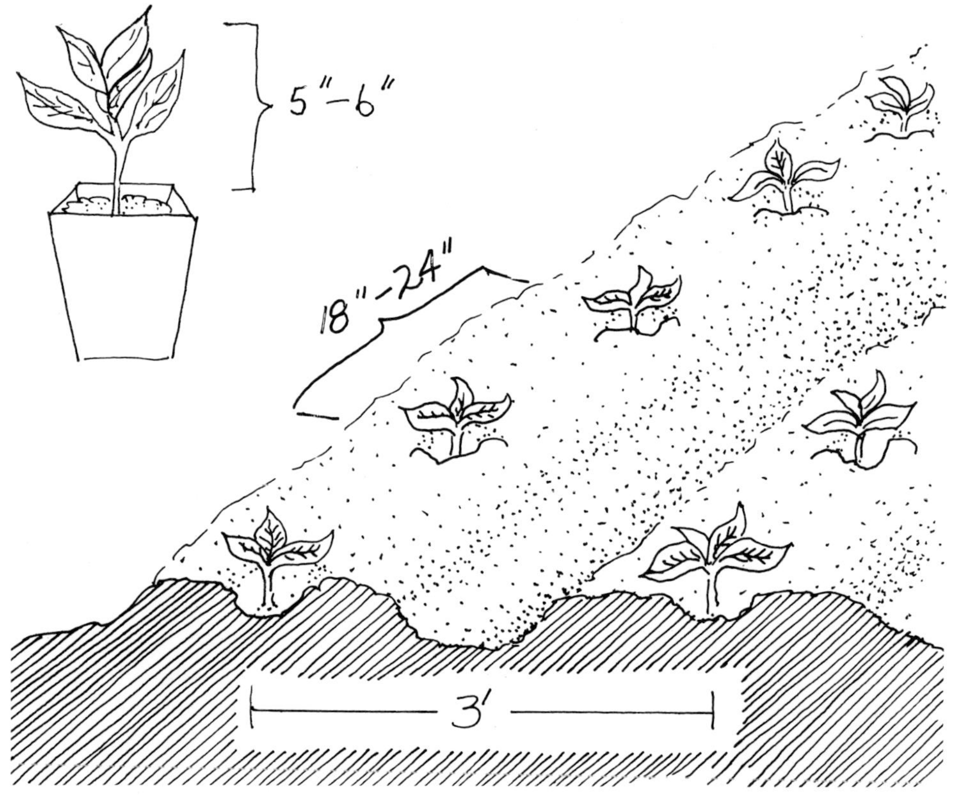

The ideal pepper transplant is 5 to 6 inches tall, dark green and free of insect and disease damage. Space the transplants 18 to 24 inches apart in the row on rows that are 36 inches apart.

The Basic Facts About Peppers

Let's look at some pepper basics. First of all, pepper plants must be grown in the full sun. High yields of quality fruit will not result if sufficient light is not available every possible minute. Secondly, the soil must be well-drained. Pepper plants will grow well in heavy soils, but they cannot stand "wet feet." Thirdly, and perhaps most important, the plants need lots of attention. Your shadow in the garden is an absolute must if a bountiful harvest of peppers is expected. If you can meet these prerequisites, you're ready to learn how to grow peppers—Texas style!

Peppers will grow in a wide variety of soils, but will do best in loamy types that have been enriched with liberal amounts of organic matter and have a pH between 5.5 and 7.5. If you garden in an area of Texas where acid soils are common, you should have your soil tested to determine if its pH is below 5.5. If so, add lime to raise its pH up to an acceptable level. Information on adjusting the pH of your soil can be found on page 394.

Get you soil ready to grow peppers by scattering about 2 inches of well-decomposed leaves, grass clippings, hay, compost or other organic matter over the planting area. At the same time, apply barnyard manure at the rate of about 50 pounds per 100 square feet. Unless your soil is already highly fertile, also add a complete commercial fertilizer at a rate of 2 to 2½ pounds per each 100 square feet. Use the lower rate if you also use barnyard manure. For you folks with only a few plants, this is the equivalent of ½ pound of barnyard manure and about 2 to 2½ teaspoons of fertilizer for each square foot of area.

If you live in East Texas or along the upper coastal regions, use a fertilizer with a 1-2-2 ratio, such as 10-20-20. Elsewhere in the state, use a fertilizer with a 1-2-1 ratio, such as 10-20-10. Till or spade the organic matter, barnyard manure, fertilizer and lime, if needed, into the soil at least 8 to 10 inches deep—the deeper, the better.

Unless your soil is near perfect, you should plant peppers on raised beds, which are made by forming ridges and furrows. Planting peppers on raised beds has several advantages. Peppers like to have warm feet (roots) and, as mentioned before, don't like wet feet. And with raised beds, the soil will drain better and warm up more quickly because more surface area is exposed to the sun. The obvious result of planting peppers on raised beds is drier, warmer feet, and peppers love it.

Use your shovel or a tiller with a bedder to form the ridges and furrows, making the ridges at least 36 inches apart. Use the flat side of your rake to shape and form the ridges into raised beds. The top of the beds should be 16 to 20 inches wide. The lower furrow area makes watering and drainage easier. In the spring, prepare the beds 10 to 14 days before your anticipated planting date to give the soil time to warm up a little.

You can help the soil warm up more quickly by covering the raised beds with black plastic sheeting. This also will help conserve moisture and control weeds. Simply lay the plastic sheeting over the planting area, making certain it's wide enough to extend over the edge of the bed so that soil can be used to hold it in place. Be sure your soil is relatively moist when you put down the plastic or you may have difficulty getting soil moisture to move laterally within the beds. Additional information on mulching with black plastic can be found on page 397.

The Importance Of Transplants

For maximum yields, peppers, like tomatoes, always should be transplanted rather than seeded directly in your garden so that the plants will have time to mature and produce before it gets too hot. Peppers will

For an earlier crop of peppers, you can put black plastic over your planting rows to help heat up the soil. Before setting transplants out, soak them in a bowl of water to make sure the peat pots or pellets they're growing in are wet.

set fruit best when the nighttime low is above 60 degrees and the daytime high is below 80, and such weather conditions don't last very long in most areas of Texas. When temperatures are outside this range, peppers usually begin to shed their blooms and any fruit that does set will be small, thin-walled and poorly shaped. The pungent types of peppers generally will set fruit at somewhat higher temperatures, but all varieties will quit setting if temperatures get much above 90 degrees. If you were to plant pepper seed, the plants would bloom during high temperatures and few, if any, fruit would set. By transplanting, and using early maturing varieties, you can be sure (as much as is possible in Texas) the peppers will bloom and set fruit during favorable weather conditions.

If you plant peppers for a fall harvest, you still need to be concerned about temperatures, both high and low. Transplants must be set out at a time to avoid the problems associated with high temperatures, but early enough for fruit set and maturity to occur before the first killing freeze. It takes about 45 to 60 days from the time a pepper flower is pollinated until the pepper fruit reaches its maximum, green, mature size.

The ideal pepper transplant should be about 7 to 8 weeks old, 5 to 6 inches tall and have dark green foliage that is free of any indication of insect damage or disease. Hopefully, such transplants of the right varieties will be available from nurseries at the right time. If not, you can always order seed from a reputable seed company and grow your own. Of course, you'll have to start the plants seven to eight weeks prior to the planting time. Information on raising your own transplants is found on page 396.

In the spring, most gardeners set out their pepper plants at the same time they set out tomato plants, which is a mistake. Tomatoes should be planted on or just prior to the date of the average last frost. They can stand considerable cold weather and still produce a good crop, but peppers can't. Exposure to temperatures in the low 40s for only a short time can stunt peppers, causing them to remain small and nonproductive. Therefore, resist the temptation to plant early. Wait until the weather warms a little, perhaps seven to 10 days after setting out your tomatoes, before planting peppers.

To be even more precise, check your soil temperature with a soil thermometer. Pepper roots will not grow and may be damaged if transplants are set out when the soil temperature is below 55 degrees. The plants may live and begin to grow when the soil warms up, but the damage already will have been done and the plants may never fully recover. Wait until the temperature about 2 inches beneath the surface is 55 degrees or higher for three consecutive days, then transplant.

In much of Texas, peppers set out in the spring will survive our summer weather and continue to produce up until the first killing frost of winter. However, in most of Central and all of South Texas, the heat can take its toll. The plants will live, but even after fertilizing and pruning them back to promote new growth, production will be minimal. If you live in these areas and want a fall crop of peppers, it's best to start anew by setting out transplants about 100 days before the first killing frost is expected.

At planting time, the soil should be slightly moist. If it's on the dry side, water several days before you set out the peppers. The ideal day to set out the plants would be cloudy and windless to avoid undue stress on the plants. If your transplants are growing in a plantable container, such as one composed of peat, it's a good idea to set them in a shallow pan of water for a few minutes before planting to make certain the peat is thoroughly wet. If the peat containers are dry when planted, they may remain dry, even after being watered thoroughly and early root growth and development will be restricted.

Pepper plants will grow best if spaced 18 to 24 inches apart in the row. If you use a black plastic mulch, use a bulb planter or a sharp knife to cut 2- to 3-inch diameter holes in the sheeting at the proper spacing. Use a trowel or your hand to dig holes for the transplants about 3 inches deep and about as wide.

Getting Off To A Good Start

To ensure vigorous early growth, pour about 1 cup of starter solution in each hole prior to planting. Starter solutions are available at most nurseries and garden centers and are simply water-soluble fertilizers that will supply the transplants with nutrients until they establish a larger root system.

After the starter solution soaks in, set the transplants in the center of the holes, backfill with soil and firm them in, leaving a slight depression around each one to hold water. Unlike tomatoes, peppers do not have the ability to initiate roots along their stems; therefore, deep planting should be avoided. If planted too deep, the plants may never grow vigorously, if they grow at all.

Water thoroughly after setting out your transplants. It's also a good idea to protect them from the weather for a few weeks, both in the spring and in the summer. Almost anything your imagination conjures up can be used to protect the plants from the intense sun, wind, and high or low temperatures.

About three weeks after planting, peppers should begin blooming, which is a critical time in the life of a pepper plant. If a pepper plant sets its first bloom and adequate soil fertility is not available to encourage vigorous growth, the plant usually will remain small and stunted. The plant is simply not large enough to produce more fruit and it will shed subsequent blooms. To avoid this possibility, apply a side-dressing of fertilizer when the plants first bloom. Use 1 cup of ammonium sulfate (21-0-0) or ⅔ cup of ammonium nitrate (33-0-0) for each 35-foot row. Band the fertilizer on both sides of the plants (down the row) about 12 to 14 inches from their bases. If you're only growing a few plants, apply 2 tablespoons of the ammonium sulfate or 1½ tablespoons of ammonium nitrate in a circle around each plant.

If you're using black plastic mulch, place the fertilizer at the edge of the sheeting. Don't worry about the fertilizer being too far from the plants —pepper roots often extend out 3 feet or more in all directions. Lightly work the fertilizer into the surface of the soil and then water. Additional side-dressings should be made at about three-week intervals.

If you don't use the black plastic as a mulch, place 2 to 3 inches of

Southern blight (top) and sunburn (bottom) are two common problems you're likely to encounter when growing peppers.

organic matter around the plants after side-dressing. Avoid applying these mulching materials too early in the spring, though, or they will act as an insulating blanket and the soil will remain cold. During hot, dry weather, mulch immediately after setting the plants out in your garden.

If you're really interested in growing a bumper crop, consider fertilizing your peppers using the "Texas Pot Method." This method uses containers placed between the plants as a means of side-dressing and works extremely well. (For more information on the Texas Pot Method, see tomato chapter.)

For maximum yields of large, thick-walled, high-quality peppers, adequate soil moisture is absolutely essential. When you water is far more important than how you apply the water. Avoid letting your garden soil get dry enough to cause the plants to wilt, especially during bloom and as the fruits mature. During these periods, you may have to water twice a week, depending upon your soil type and the generosity of Mother Nature. Check your soil to decide when to water. If it's fairly dry about 1 inch beneath the surface, it's time to water.

Insects And Diseases

Insects and disease problems are common, especially leaf miners, spider mites, leaf-spotting diseases and nematodes.

Leaf miners are aptly named because the mines, or trails, they create are the result of larvae of a small, fly-like insect that literally tunnels between the upper and lower surface of the leaves. If numerous enough and left uncontrolled, they can cause defoliation of your pepper plants. If just a few leaf miners are present, simply mashing the large end of the mine in the leaf will destroy the developing larvae. However, early applications of diazinon or Cygon will result in good control and will help prevent them from getting out of control.

Spider mites are usually a warm-weather problem and the first indication of their presence is yellowish areas on the older leaves. Close examination of the lower leaf surface will usually reveal small, almost microscopic spiders. These "plant chiggers" do their damage by sucking the plant juices. Three treatments with the miticide Kelthane, applied at three-day intervals, will result in good control, but only if the treatments are begun at first sign of the mites.

Peppers are subject to numerous different types of leaf-spotting diseases that cause brown or yellowish spots to form on the leaves. Applications of the fungicide Bravo or one containing maneb usually will provide good control. If left uncontrolled, though, these diseases eventually can defoliate and kill pepper plants.

By far the most serious problem you may have to contend with is pepper mosaic virus, which is actually a complex of several different viruses that is spread from one plant to another by foiliage-feeding insects. Symptoms include stunting of the plants, twisting and mottling of the leaves and just a few, small, misshapen fruit. There is no satisfactory control except to plant resistant varieties and researchers at Texas A&M University are close to releasing several high-yielding resistant varieties. The TAMU Mild Jalapeno is one of the first of the virus-resistant peppers. Until resistant varieties are available for all types of peppers, maintain your plants in a vigorous state of growth and provide adequate insect control. As hard as it is to do, pull up and discard in the trash any plants that exhibit virus symptoms.

Nematodes can be a serious problem but are not as common on peppers as they are on other garden vegetables, such as tomatoes, okra, beans and the vine crops. Symptoms include stunted, nonproductive plants and the development of the characteristic knots on the plant's root system. Information on the control of nematodes can be found on page 408.

Depending upon the type of pepper you're growing, season of the year and stage of maturity, you'll harvest about 65 to 80 days after transplanting. Bell or sweet peppers can be harvested at any usable size, but are best when they reach full maturity. The pungent types of peppers develop maximum flavor when they reach full size and normal mature color, which depends on the variety.

Pepper plants are relatively brittle and can be damaged easily during harvest, so it's a good idea to pick peppers late in the afternoon when the plants are less turgid. When harvesting, it's usually best to use a sharp knife or pruning shears to remove the fruit from the plants rather than to pull them off. Oftentimes, when you attempt to pull or snap the fruit from the plants, they will be accompanied by a considerable portion of the plant.

It's important to note that all types of peppers eventually turn red during their normal ripening process. Contrary to popular belief, pungency does not increase as the fruits ripen and turn from green to red.

Other Peppers

Ancho (Poblano)—Ancho is the most common dried pepper in Mexico and also is used to make the popular chiles rellenos. It does not grow exceptionally well in Texas, as it prefers cool, dry weather. Its flavor ranges from almost mild to hot. In the Poblano, or green, stage of development, it is skinned before using.

Peppers come in many shapes and sizes, including the Jumbo Serrano (top left), the mild jalapeno (top right), cayenne (bottom left) and the well-known green bell pepper (bottom right).

Other types of peppers include the Chili (left) and ornamental peppers.

Anaheim—A group of peppers having a wide variation in degree of pungency, the anaheims include the true chiles. They prefer warm, dry weather for best growth and primarily are used in preparation of chili powder and paprika. The anaheims grow best in far West Texas.

Cayenne—The cayenne pepper is the primary flavoring used in the preparation of many spicy Cajun dishes. It grows well in all areas of Texas, producing fruits from 4 to 12 inches in length. It's very pungent and is a good substitute for the Jalapeno and Serrano.

Cherry—The Cherry pepper gets its name from its similarity in shape and size to a cherry. When mature, colors range from a light orange to a deep red. The fruit can be hot or sweet, large or small. The Cherry pepper is a favorite for canning, but high moisture content makes it unsuitable for drying. Cherry peppers grow well all across the state and have ornamental value.

Chili Piquin—Often called birdseye pepper, the Chili Piquin is a South Texas favorite. It's extremely hot! The best way to describe this pepper is to say a little goes a long, long way. In South Texas, the Chili Piquin grows as a perennial in that it will freeze back in the winter, but resprout the following spring.

Habanero—This pepper looks like a rather plump Jalapeno, but is twice as pungent. When mature, the fruit are bright yellow-orange. One plant may be all that's required to supply your entire neighborhood with hot peppers. It will grow well in most areas of Texas and prefers warm, humid growing conditions.

Jalapeno—Easily the best-known and most widely grown hot pepper in Texas, the Jalapeno can be used fresh or pickled and adds zest to many Texas recipes. The new, highly productive TAMU Mild Jalapeno is half as hot as a regular Jalapeno and has good disease resistance, making it highly suitable for culture in Texas. The Jalapeno grows well in all areas of the state.

Serrano—This pepper looks similar to the Jalapeno, but is smaller and usually not as broad at the top. It's very pungent, the plants are quite large and it's well-adapted to all areas of our state.

Tabasco—Tabasco is not widely grown in Texas, but is well-adapted to culture across the state, especially East Texas. It's certainly one of the most pungent of all peppers, explosively hot! Tabasco requires more than 100 days from transplanting to mature red fruit. One plant will produce enough hot peppers to supply your family's needs for years, if not for life!

Quick Problem Solver: Peppers

Problem	Causes	Solutions
Transplants sluggish, lack vigor.	Cold soils.	Wait until soil is above 55 degrees to set out transplants. Use black plastic mulch.
	Wet soils.	Plant on raised beds, avoid excessive watering.
	Low fertility.	Use starter solution when setting out transplants.
	Acid soils.	Soil pH should be above 5.5 for peppers.
Plants spindly, weak.	Low sunlight.	Peppers must be planted in full sun for good growth.

Problem	Cause	Solution
Plants stunted, lack good growth.	Setting out too early.	Do not set out transplants early. Low temperatures will stunt plants. Soil temperature should be above 55 degrees.
	Dry plantable (peat) containers.	Soak roots/container before planting.
	Low fertility.	Side-dress plants with nitrogen fertilizer.
Plants bloom, but set few fruit.	Low fertility.	Side-dress with nitrogen fertilizer at first bloom.
	High temperatures.	Fruit set is best when temperatures are between 60 and 80 degrees. At above 90 degrees, bloom drop is common.
Fruits small, misshapen, thin walled.	High temperatures.	As above.
	Low fertility.	Side-dress with nitrogen fertilizer. Add additional preplant fertilizer next time.
Spring set-out plants fail to produce, but do well in the fall.	Set out too late.	High temperatures caused blossom drop, fruit set occurred with cooler conditions for fall.
Trails in leaves.	Leaf miners.	Control with malathion, diazinon or cygon.
Yellowish areas on lower leaves, minute spiders on lower surface of leaves.	Spider mites.	Control with repeated applications of Kelthane.
Brownish or yellowish spots on leaves.	Leaf-spotting diseases (fungi or bacteria).	At first sign of disease, treat foliage with maneb or Bravo.
Leaves twisted, mottled, plants stunted.	Pepper mosaic virus.	Destroy infected plants. Control insects and use resistant varieties.
Plants stunted, knots on root system.	Nematodes.	Treat soil with appropriate nematicide.
Water soaked areas on side of fruit.	Sunscald.	Caused by exposure to hot rays of sun. No control possible except to provide fruits protection.
Fruits develop chocolate color.	Normal ripening.	Pepper fruit change color as they ripen, eventually turning red.

POTATO

Scientific Name: *Solanum tuberosum*
Family: *Solanaceae*
Perennial, grown as an annual
Cool Season
Varieties:
Red: LaSoda, Pontiac
White: Kennebec
Russet: Norgold
Expected Harvest: 10 to 20 pounds per 10 feet of row

POTATOES

Potatoes are truly remarkable plants. They first were cultivated some 2,000 years ago, and since then we have striven to find ways of increasing their yields and improving their quality. The results have been absolutely fantastic. Today, the potato is the most important, most widely grown and most consumed vegetable in the world.

Potatoes originated in the higher elevations of Chile and first were grown as a food crop in Peru. Yields from those early crops were extremely low and the potatoes harvested were small, rough and yellow-fleshed. Eventually, the Incas, who depended upon potatoes, or *papas*, for their very existence, began the process of selecting and improving upon the original wild potato. They dried the potatoes, and ground them into a product called chuno which was used to make flour.

Following Pizarro's conquest of Peru, the potato was introduced into Europe in the late 1500s. It was grown as a novelty for more than a century, until the Irish recognized its value as a food crop. They improved upon its yield and quality and by 1693 it had become Ireland's most important food crop. Hence, it became known as the Irish potato. Irish immigrants who settled in Londonderry, New Hampshire, in 1719 are believed to have grown the first crop of potatoes in the United States.

Today, our potatoes have either red or white skin, white flesh, shallow eyes, and are large, smooth and of very high quality. Nationwide, commercial yields exceed 20,000 pounds per acre and the figure increases yearly. And, unlike the Incas, we prepare our potatoes in countless ways, including baked, fried, mashed and boiled. As hard as it is to believe, each and every Texan consumes more than 120 pounds of potatoes each year. And that, my gardening friends, is just a whole lot of "taters."

Nevertheless, potatoes are not widely grown in Texas gardens, primarily because the yields often are disappointing. However, if you pay close attention to variety selection, planting time and adequate cultural

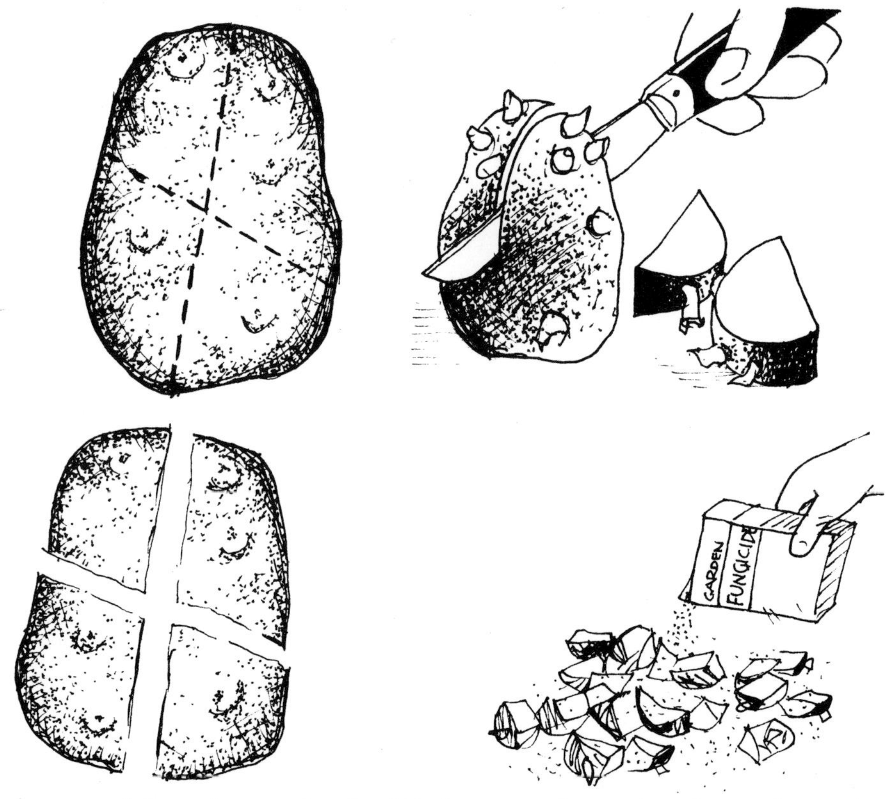

Purchase a good size seed potato that should be large enough to cut into three or four seed pieces. Each piece should have at least one eye or sprout. After cutting, treat the seed pieces with a fungicide and cure for several days before planting.

care, potatoes can be one of the most productive and rewarding vegetable crops in your garden.

Variety Selection Very Important

To grow a bumper crop of potatoes, it's imperative to plant the right varieties. The best ones for Texas are the red-skinned LaSoda and Pontiac, and the white-skinned Kennebec. If you garden in the Panhandle or in far West Texas, you can grow the high quality Norgold Russett successfully. Although all four of these varieties can be prepared in many ways, LaSoda and Pontiac generally are ideal for mashing or boiling, while Kennebec or Norgold Russett are best for baking or frying.

While discussing varieties, it's important to note that "seed" potatoes often are sold as Minnesota Blues or Nebraska Reds rather than by variety name. These names refer only to the state in which they were grown and the color designation indicates they are certified seed potatoes, which is certainly a desirable characteristic. You always should purchase certified seed potatoes because they will produce true to variety and are disease and insect-free. Given the choice, you should purchase seed potatoes bearing the blue certification, which means they are as clean and pure as possible.

Remember that seed potatoes are for planting only and should not be eaten because they may have been treated with chemicals while in storage. Likewise, table-stock potatoes are for eating only and not for planting. Such potatoes often are not the right varieties, can carry diseases or may have been treated to prevent sprouting.

Any discussion regarding planting potatoes is always lively, interesting and usually argumentative because there's considerable controversy about the right time for planting, especially in the spring. Some Texans plant potatoes by the dark of the moon, while others feel the only proper time to plant is on George Washington's Birthday. Fortunately, either time is just fine since the right time to plant in the spring is about four weeks prior to the last killing frost. And in a good portion of Texas, that date is close to both Washington's Birthday and the dark of the moon. However, if you garden in the northern areas of Texas you might plant a week or two later to be on the safe side. Even though newly emerged potato plants often can survive frosty weather, research and experience has shown that potato plants damaged by low temperatures often recover, but generally produce lower yields.

However, you also need to keep in mind that planting too late in the spring is just as bad as planting too early, especially if you garden in the southern areas of our state. Potato plants grow and produce best when temperatures range between 60 and 75 degrees during the day and between 45 and 55 degrees at night. In addition, for a good harvest, potatoes must set and size their crop before soil temperatures reach 85 degrees, the temperature at which potato initiation ceases. Obviously, if you wait too long to plant, causing the plants to grow and set potatoes during excessively warm temperatures, yields and quality will be disappointing.

The same temperature requirements also must be considered when growing a fall crop of potatoes. Planting should occur as late as possible to avoid high temperatures, but still early enough to allow time for the plants to produce potatoes before the first killing freeze. Unfortunately, in most areas of Texas we go from excessively high temperatures to below freezing conditions in a relatively short time, which reduces the time available for the potatoes to develop. Generally, the best time to plant a fall crop in most of Texas is about 90 days before the first expected freezing weather. Unless we have a late winter, a fall crop of potatoes usually will be less productive than a spring crop but just as tasty!

Cultural Requirements

Having discussed varieties and time of planting, let's talk about growing potatoes. Since we're growing potatoes for their edible tubers, which are produced underground, the soil is of utmost importance. Acid soils that are fertile, loose and well-drained are ideal for growing potatoes. If you garden where acid soils are common, it's best not to add lime to the area where you'll be growing potatoes, unless your soil's pH is below 4.8. If you add too much lime to acid soils or garden in alkaline soils, you may have trouble with potato scab, a very serious problem that we'll discuss later.

Heavy clays or soils with little water-holding ability should be avoided, unless they are enriched with liberal amounts of organic matter. If you don't have ideal soil, spread 3 to 4 inches of well-decomposed leaves, grass clippings, hay or compost over the area to be planted. Do not add barnyard manure to your soil—especially if your soil has a high pH. It is alkaline and, like lime, may cause potato scab.

Potatoes are heavy feeders and require high levels of fertility to produce good yields of quality tubers. And unlike most vegetables, all the fertilizer the potatoes will need should be worked into the soil prior to planting. Side-dressing with fertilizer after the plants are up and growing has little, if any, beneficial effect and can cause excessive foliage at the expense of the potatoes' sizes.

The amount and type of fertilizer you should use varies according to your soil type, level of fertility and where you garden in Texas. Generally, about 3 pounds of commercial fertilizer per 100 square feet or for each 35 feet of row is adequate. If you garden in East Texas or along the upper coast, use a fertilizer with a 1-2-2 ratio, such as 10-20-20. In the other areas of the state, a 1-2-1 ratio, such as 10-20-10 or 12-24-12, is satisfactory. Scatter the fertilizer evenly over the area to be planted in potatoes and till or spade it, along with the organic matter, into the soil to a depth of 8 to 10 inches. Your soil is now ready for planting. All you need now is the seed potatoes.

Selecting Seed Potatoes

When you go to a local nursery or garden center to purchase your seed potatoes, there's a good chance you'll have to make a choice between whole seed and pieces of seed. Always purchase whole seed potatoes. Unlike most garden vegetables, potatoes commonly are propagated or grown vegetatively from stem cuttings rather than from true seed and the potato you eat or the seed potato actually are swollen underground stems

Potatoes can be planted underground in rows or in a well-prepared mound of mulch and compost, allowing the tubers to form above ground as shown in photo at right.

or tubers. Like all stems, it has buds or *eyes*, and if you look closely you'll see that each eye has an eyebrow, which is a leaf scar where a leaf might be if this stem were above ground. Eventually, the aboveground portion of the potato plant develops from the eyes. If you plant a piece of this stem that does not contain at least one eye or bud, a potato plant will not develop. The problem with pre-cut seed pieces is that they are cut mechanically and may not have an eye. For this reason alone, it's a good idea to purchase whole seed potatoes. Also, research has shown that for maximum yields, each seed piece should weigh about 2 to 3 ounces and have two or three eyes. Obviously, by purchasing whole seed potatoes and cutting them into pieces yourself, you can make certain they meet the above criteria.

One thing you absolutely should avoid is purchasing or using potato eyes for planting. The potato sprout literally exists for a period of time on the portion of the tuber to which it's attached. The smaller the portion, such as a scooped-out eye, the less satisfied you're likely to be come harvesttime. Conversely, large seed pieces with many eyes may produce more potatoes, but not necessarily better potatoes. Each eye that sprouts produces foliage above ground and sets potatoes. The crowded conditions, however, cause competition for light, moisture and nutrients, which causes most of the potatoes to be small.

Purchase your seed potatoes about five to seven days before the anticipated planting date and immediately cut them into seed pieces. After cutting and before curing them, treat the pieces with sulphur to help prevent soil-related disease problems. A simple method for applying the sulphur is to place the seed pieces in a paper bag, add the appropriate amount of sulphur and shake vigorously.

Allow the cut seed pieces to cure until the day of planting, ideally at a temperature near 65 degrees and at a high humidity. Putting the seed pieces in a well-ventilated crate or box, placing them in a garage or a similar protected area and covering them with wet burlap works well. At planting time, a good seed piece should be slightly shriveled, have a well-healed cut surface and slightly enlarged eyes. If properly cured, the seed pieces can be kept safely for a reasonable period of time if weather conditions keep you from planting. If planting is delayed, however, be especially careful when handling the seed pieces to avoid damaging any sprouts that have elongated.

When it's time to plant, the soil should be moist but not too wet. If Mother Nature has been a little skimpy with rainfall and your soil is on the dry side, water thoroughly several days before planting to supply the desired soil moisture.

Planting Methods

Potatoes can be planted several ways—on raised beds, on the *flat* or, as we'll discuss shortly, on top of the ground. If your soil is heavy and poorly drained, it's generally best to make ridges and furrows and then shape them into raised beds about 4 to 6 inches high. However, if your soil is even anywhere close to average, planting on flat ground is satisfactory. Regardless of the method you use, the rows of potatoes should be no closer than 30 inches apart.

Use your garden rake to smooth and level the planting area. Mark off the rows with a hoe handle or, if you want to get fancy, with string and wooden stakes. Next, use your hoe to make planting furrows about 2½ to 3 inches deep. Firm the seed pieces into the bottom of the planting furrow, using an in-row spacing of 8 to 12 inches. Some folks like to place the seed pieces with the cut surface down and the eyes up, feeling root formation will be facilitated and the plants will emerge more quickly. However, the orientation of the seed piece makes little or no difference. After covering, firm the soil over the seed pieces to ensure good soil/seed piece contact and to conserve soil moisture.

Within three to four weeks, depending primarily upon soil temperature, the potato plants will emerge from the soil and begin growing rapidly. When they are about 5 to 6 inches tall, you must perform a very important task; the plants must be *dirted.* Use your hoe or shovel to throw about 3 to 4 inches of soil to the base of the plants. Your ultimate goal by dirting or hilling the plants is to end up with the seed piece being about 6 to 8 inches beneath the soil surface. In essence, you're building a raised bed in which the potatoes will develop.

Now seems an appropriate time to briefly discuss how the plant produces potatoes or tubers. When a potato eye sprouts, it produces a main stem, which grows upward, emerges from the soil and becomes the plant foliage. Along the underground portion of this main stem are initiated stolons, which are small, secondary, underground stems. These stolons grow laterally for short distances and then their ends begin to swell, eventually forming the tubers. It's very important for you to realize that all the tubers produced by the potato plant are initiated along the underground stem between the seed piece and the surface of the soil. Therefore, the deeper the seed piece is beneath the soil surface, the greater the opportunity for tuber initiation and development. However, please don't accept this statement literally and end up burying the seed pieces a foot or more beneath the soil surface. Maximum stolon initiation and tuber formation occurs when the final seed piece depth is 6 to 8 inches.

You might be wondering why you need to dirt the plants rather than just initially planting the seed pieces that deep. You can do that, and some years you'll be successful. However, if the soil stays cold and wet for an extended period of time, emergence will be slow, subjecting the plants to soilborne pathogens that can cause the seed pieces to rot in the ground. By planting fairly shallow and dirting the plants later, you can almost assure yourself of a good stand of strong, healthy plants.

For a fall crop, planting often occurs during high soil temperatures, so plant the seed pieces slightly deeper to take advantage of cooler soil temperatures at the greater depth. It's also advisable to apply a layer of organic mulch over the soil to provide additional protection from the summer heat. When dirting the plants, rake the mulch back, apply about 2 to 3 inches of soil and reapply the mulch.

The potato beetle will feed on the foliage of your potato plants and can be controlled with applications of an approved insecticide. Sometimes, your potatoes flower and even set fruit. Don't worry. This is a natural occurrence caused by cool weather.

If all this dirting sounds difficult and you've only got a small planting, you might consider growing your potatoes above ground. Follow the above guidelines up to the point of making the planting furrow. Instead of forming the furrow and covering the seed pieces with a couple of inches of soil, simply firm them into the soil and cover with about 6 inches of organic matter. After the plants have emerged, and the organic matter has settled, dirt them again with organic materials. The potatoes will develop in the organic matter and will be extremely easy to harvest. This system is well-adapted to the more humid areas of our state, but also will work well in the drier regions, if the mulch in which the potatoes are developing is not allowed to become too dry.

Adequate moisture is critical for the successful production of potatoes, whether you're growing them above ground or in the conventional manner. For maximum yields of smooth potatoes, it's imperative that adequate moisture be available from the time the tubers are initiated, which often begins about three weeks after the plants emerge, until they are fully mature. Never let the soil get excessively dry during this period. If the soil is allowed to fluctuate from being too dry to too wet—especially as the potatoes near maturity—regrowth will occur and cause them to become knobby and otherwise misshapen. Depending upon soil type and rainfall, you may need to water every five to seven days.

Regardless of whether you use furrow irrigation, an overhead sprinkler or a drip system, always apply enough water to wet the soil to a depth of at least 6 to 8 inches. If you grow your potatoes above ground, watering with a sprinkler is best because as the water filters down through the mulch and keeps it moist.

Any discussion of soil moisture and its importance in successfully growing potatoes is not complete without also stressing the value of mulching around the plants. Potatoes respond tremendously to the application of 2 to 3 inches of well-decomposed grass clippings, leaves, hay or other organic matter around the base of the plants. Not only will such a mulch conserve soil moisture, it also well help cool the soil—both of which are conducive to high yields. In the spring, apply the organic matter before the soil temperature exceeds 65 degrees. For a fall crop, as mentioned earlier, mulch immediately after planting.

Given just a little care and attention, your potato plants should grow vigorously and before long may produce flowers. Contrary to popular belief, there is no correlation between flowering and tuber initiation or development. Cool temperatures are conducive to both occurrences and during cooler periods, Texas-grown potato plants may flower profusely, but tubers will be formed regardless of whether or not flowering occurs. Occasionally, the flowers actually will set a small, green fruit. Rest assured that your potato plants are not beginning to produce tomatoes. Inside the fruit you often can find true potato seed, but don't waste your time and effort saving and then planting these seeds. If they do germinate, the results will be small, very weak plants that will only produce a few, small potatoes—if any at all.

Flowering, fruiting and setting seed, therefore, may seem of little importance to you, but they actually have great significance. Plant breeders utilize the potato's ability to flower and produce seed to make controlled genetic crosses between strains of potatoes. Plants from the resulting seed are grown in a greenhouse and the small potatoes produced are harvested. These potatoes are then field grown much like regular potatoes and evaluated for their potential as a new and improved variety.

Insect Troubles

Potatoes, like all vegetables, are subject to attack by insects. Pillbugs and grubworms apparently enjoy the environmental conditions created by organic mulches and moist soils that are conducive to tuber growth and development. Therefore, it's often a good idea to treat the soil with diazinon before planting and again just before dirting the plants. Wireworms, which are an inch long, yellow to orangish-colored and hard, do their damage by eating many small pits in the potatoes. Applications of diazinon before planting will give good control. Occasionally, aphids and potato bugs can become a problem but are easily controlled by treating the foliage with thiodan, malathion or Sevin.

Diseases generally are much more of a serious threat to potatoes grown in Texas than are insects. Early blight and late blight, the disease which caused Ireland's infamous potato famine during the mid-1800s, first are evidenced by spots on the leaves and stems which spread rapidly. If not controlled, the plants will die. The fungicide Bravo or one containing maneb, applied at the first sign of either of these diseases and continued at five- to seven-day intervals, usually will give good control. If you've had problems with either of these troublesome foliage diseases in the past, chances are you'll have them again. Therefore, begin preventive fungicide applications when the plants are 4 to 6 inches tall. By far, the most serious threat to your potatoes are the soilborne diseases, such as scab and various types of wilt. Nematodes also are a major concern. Potato scab, as mentioned earlier, is primarily a problem in areas of Texas having alkaline soils, but also can occur on acid soils where lime has been applied. It causes rough, corky, scab-like areas over the surface of the potatoes. The various types of wilt-causing diseases, such as fusarium wilt, bacterial wilt and southern blight, all cause basically the same symptoms—sudden death of the plants. Control all the soilborne diseases by a combination of practices: setting up a system of long term rotations; planting certified, disease-free seed potatoes; treating the seed pieces with sulphur before planting; and by not adding barnyard manure or other alkaline forming substances to the planting area.

Nematodes are a serious garden problem in Texas and can cause disappointment when it comes time to harvest your potatoes. These soilborne, microscopic worms enter the developing potatoes, causing a pimpling appearance over their surface. In addition, they also attack the root system, causing the roots to become swollen and knotty and, thereby, unable to absorb moisture and nutrients. The obvious result—low yields of poor quality potatoes. Control of nematodes is difficult but can be achieved by a combination of practices as outlined on page 408.

When To Harvest

Potatoes are one of the more exciting vegetables to harvest. You never know what's hiding beneath the soil. Also, there's concern as to whether they're really ready or not. Although potatoes can be consumed at any usable size, they're usually full-sized and mature about 90 to 120 days after planting—whether you planted by the moon or otherwise.

Spring-planted potatoes also indicate their maturity by the plants yellowing and starting to die. Your spring crop should be harvested as soon as they're mature, due to the possibility of warm temperatures and rainy weather which cause potatoes to rot in the ground. If you're growing a large patch of spring potatoes and are interested in storing a portion of your crop for later use, cut the plants off at ground level and leave the potatoes in the soil to cure for about three to five days. If the potatoes are mature, the skin will *set* and toughen, greatly increasing the likelihood of successful storage.

For your fall-planted potatoes, the first hard frost will kill back the plants without harming the potatoes. As long as they are mature, the soil doesn't freeze and it remains fairly dry, the potatoes can be left in the garden and harvested as needed. However, in most areas of Texas, garden curing in the fall is not practiced because the first hard frost often kills the plants before the potatoes are fully mature and wet conditions are common. If your area of the state experiences an early winter and the plants are killed by the cold, don't be upset—you're about to harvest and enjoy some of the best new potatoes you've ever eaten!

Harvesting is simple. Plunge a spading fork into the soil about 12 inches from the plant (or where the plant was if you cut them back), lift up and—at the same time—gently pull the plant from the ground. Remove any tubers that are adhering to the plant and then harvest those remaining in the soil. Dig around—there just may be some whoppers hidden down in the soil. Most of the tubers will be within about 10 to 12 inches of the main stem of the plant.

For you folks growing your potatoes above ground, harvesting is somewhat like hunting Easter eggs. Simply dig down into the organic matter with your hands and gently remove the potatoes. If desired, you can harvest only the larger potatoes and leave the smaller ones still attached to the growing plant so that they can continue to enlarge. Unfortunately, you will not be able to continue this selective harvesting forever, for either hot or cold temperatures will curtail sizing of the potatoes.

Certified seed potatoes are very difficult to find for fall planting. Therefore, it's advisable to save some of the smaller potatoes from your spring crop for fall planting. However, freshly harvested potatoes have a natural dormancy often lasting several months which prevents them from sprouting. A problem exists in that in many areas of Texas, the time to plant a fall crop is less than two months after the spring potato harvest. Fortunately, this dormancy can be broken by subjecting the fall seed potatoes to alternating temperatures. Put the small, unwashed potatoes in a well-ventilated box or crate and place them in a cool area such as your garage or, ideally, under your house. About 30 days prior to the anticipated fall planting date, place them in a refrigerator and leave them for about two weeks. At the end of this time, again place them in your garage until time to plant. The eyes should have begun to enlarge, indicating the dormancy has been broken. In the fall, it's best to plant the whole, small potatoes rather than cut them into pieces to avoid rot diseases associated with high soil temperatures.

Following harvest, potatoes can be stored for several months by putting them unwashed in a cool, humid place—ideally at a temperature as close to 40 degrees as possible.

Quick Problem Solver: Potatoes

Problem	Causes	Solutions
Seed potatoes fail to sprout.	Natural dormancy.	Subject seed potatoes saved from spring to alternating temperatures.
	Soil diseases.	Treat seed pieces prior to planting. Use certified seed.
	Cold, wet soils.	Avoid planting too deeply and use raised beds.
	No "eyes" (cut seed pieces only).	Make certain each piece has at least one eye before planting.
Plants spindly, lack good color.	Too crowded.	Plants should have an in-row spacing of 8 to 12 inches.
	Low fertility.	Soon after emergence, side-dress with fertilizer containing nitrogen.
	Cold wet soils.	Plant on raised beds, do not mulch until soil warms.
Plants large, excessively lush growth.	High temperatures.	Plants will grow best at temperatures between 45 and 75 degrees. Avoid planting too late in the spring.
	Excessive nitrogen.	Avoid overfertilizing at planting. Do not side-dress unless plants lack vigorous growth.

Plants flower, may set fruit.	Cool weather.	Natural occurrence during cool seasons. Plants are not producing tomatoes!
Striped bugs/holes in leaves.	Potato beetles.	Apply thiodan or malathion for control.
Foliage curled, yellowing. Small green insects on underside of leaves.	Aphids.	Control with applications of thiodan or malathion.
Brown/black spots on leaves, stems.	Blight (fungus).	Early applications at first sign of disease using Bravo or fungicide containing maneb will give control. Repeat at 5- to 7-day intervals.
Plants wilt, die suddenly.	Various soilborne fungi.	Rotation, certified seed and treating seed prior to planting will provide some protection.
Potatoes corky, rough.	Potato scab (fungus.)	Common on alkaline/over limed soils. Avoid use of barnyard manure.
Potatoes rough, "pimply," usually small.	Nematodes.	Before planting potatoes next year, consider treating soil with nematacide.
Potatoes rough, small pits over surface.	Wireworms.	Must be controlled by preplant applications of diazinon.
Potatoes knobby, misshapened.	Heavy soils.	Incorporate liberal amount of organic matter into soil. Plant your potatoes above ground (see text).
	Fluctuating soil moisture.	Maintain soil uniformly moist, never let it get too dry, especially near time of maturity.
Yields disappointing, potatoes small.	Wrong variety.	Red LaSoda and Pontiac are preferred red varieties. Kennebec is a good white potato.
	Late planting.	Plant early. Potatoes fail to set tubers at soil temperatures above 85 degrees.
	Improper planting depth.	Final seed piece depth should be 6 to 8 inches. All potatoes are formed from main stem above seed piece.
	Plants frosted after emergence in spring.	Avoid planting too early and risking late cold weather.
	Early first frost of winter.	Common occurrence—enjoy great "new potatoes!"

PUMPKIN

Scientific Name: *Cucurbita sp.*
Family: *Cucurbitaceae*
Annual
Warm Season
Varieties: Spirit, Big Max, Jackpot, Connecticut Field
Expected Harvest: 2 to 5 fruit per hill

PUMPKIN

Do you realize a pumpkin is actually a big, overgrown squash? Most gardeners know that pumpkin and squash are members of the cucurbit family of plants and, therefore, are closely related, but few realize the relationship is so close that most of the commercially canned pie "pumpkin" is really squash, as are many of the "pumpkins" available at local markets around Halloween and Thanksgiving.

However, don't feel deceived, for there are only a few minute differences between pumpkins and some of the larger fruited varieties of squash. And even those differences are not consistent. In fact, plant taxonomists literally have spent lifetimes trying to come up with a simple method of accurately determining whether a pumpkin is really a pumpkin or a squash. Generally, you can tell the difference when purchasing a pumpkin or when harvesting one from your garden, with a fair degree of accuracy. Most true pumpkins have angular, tough stems while squashes have round, rather tender stems. But, unless you're a stickler for the "real thing," it really doesn't make any difference because their appearance and taste are identical.

Whether they're pumpkins or squash, from this point on we'll be discussing pumpkins as you and I know them—those large, orange-colored fruit that make great pies and spooky Jack-o'-lanterns.

What we know as pumpkins originated in either Mexico or Peru some 5,000 to 7,000 years ago. Their culture was spread northward by migrating tribes of Indians and were first grown in what is now the United States about 1,000 years ago. The first explorers of the New World described vigorous plants that produced many large fruits growing both wild and under cultivation by the Indians. The early colonists found them an enjoyable food crop and, before long, pumpkins were widely cultivated in settlements all along the Eastern seaboard. Just how this large, colorful fruit obtained its name is unknown, but the word pumpkin is believed to stem from the French word *pepon*, which dates back to the 17th century.

Today there still is a lot of uncertainty regarding pumpkins (or squash). However, one thing that *is* absolutely certain about growing them in your garden—you've literally got to get into it in a big way. A single hill of pumpkins may extend out vines, or runners, 12 to 15 feet in all directions and require as much as 200 square feet of garden space. Obviously, pumpkins are strictly an item for larger gardens, unless of course you've got a kid or two who would get a thrill out of growing and picking their very own "Great Pumpkin." Then, any garden's just the right size!

Soil Requirements

Pumpkins, like all cucurbits, have extensive root systems. Consequently, they grow best on loose, coarse-textured soils that encourage the development of their strong root systems. Tight, compacted soils that have poor internal drainage will result in slow plant growth, increased susceptibility to foliage diseases and the production of small, misshapen, poor quality fruit. However, with adequate soil preparation, which should take place several weeks prior to planting, pumpkins can be grown successfully on most Texas soils.

The first item of concern should be your soil's pH, or level of acidity. Pumpkins will do very poorly on soils having a pH lower than 5.5. They *will* grow on highly acid soils, but don't expect much from them. Good yields of anything resembling quality pumpkins will be almost non-existent. Therefore, if you garden in an area of our state where soils having a pH below 5.5 are common, you may need to add lime to your soil. Information on adjusting the pH of your soil can be found on page 394.

Most Texas soils can be improved by working in liberal amounts of organic material, such as well-decomposed leaves, grass clippings, hay or compost. These materials will help loose, droughty soils hold moisture and nutrients, while loosening up tight, heavy soils.

Spread 2 to 3 inches of organic matter over the area to be planted in anticipation of incorporating it into the soil. At the same time, you should add some fertilizer. Pumpkins are relatively heavy feeders and usually benefit from the use of both commercial fertilizer and barnyard manure. Generally, an adequate amount is about 2 to 3 pounds of a complete fertilizer, such as 10-20-10, per 100 square feet. If you use barnyard manure, apply about ½ pound per square foot and use the lower rate of commercial fertilizer. Till or spade the fertilizer, along with any other ingredients, into the soil to a depth of 8 to 10 inches.

Some garden publications recommend preparing and fertilizing a

Pumpkins should be planted in hills, which simply means you place four to six seeds in the same spot. Cover the seeds lightly with soil. Shortly after the seedlings emerge, thin the hill to two plants by pinching off the unwanted seedlings.

2- to 4-square-foot area and planting pumpkins (and other cucurbits such as watermelons and cantaloupes) in its center. This may work in other states, but unless you have ideal soil conditions, this practice is not recommended for Texas. As previously pointed out, pumpkins have an extensive, spreading root system. Consequently, their feeder roots will grow so rapidly and vigorously that they will extend well beyond the small prepared area within a matter of just a few weeks after planting. Therefore, it's far better to work up and fertilize the entire area the plant's roots are expected to occupy.

After getting your soil prepared, you're ready to plant. Due to the extensive and rapidly growing root system of pumpkins, you don't need to plant on raised beds, unless your soil is extremely heavy and has drainage

Pumpkins planted in midsummer should be ready in time for Halloween Jack-O'-Lanterns and Thanksgiving pies.

problems. Therefore, when it's time to plant, all you need to do is rake the planting area to make it smooth and level.

Although pumpkins can be planted any time after the last killing spring frost, most folks want to time their planting for a fall harvest to enhance their enjoyment of Halloween or Thanksgiving. The variety you select to grow greatly determines the optimum planting time for a fall harvest. If you select a variety that requires 100 days to mature, determine the desired harvest date, or the date of the average first killing frost for your area of Texas, and count back 100 days. From this date, count back another 20 to 25 days to allow for the possibility of unfavorable weather conditions which might delay maturity and to ensure against the likelihood of an early frost. Planting can occur earlier and the pumpkins can be stored for later use, as we'll outline later. If you want to plant in the spring, wait until all danger of frost has passed and the soil temperature at the seeding depth is at least 70 degrees.

Pumpkins usually are planted in hills, which are not raised areas, but rather a horticultural term used to describe the technique of planting a number of seeds in one area or spot. Hill plant four to five seeds every 6 feet in rows that are at least 8 feet apart. If you're only going to grow a hill or two of pumpkins, plant about 3 feet from the edge of your garden. Avoid planting any vegetables within 6 feet of the hills. As the plants enlarge, you can train or direct the vines to grow away from your garden, which will save some valuable space. Depth of seeding should be 1 to 1½ inches, with the greater depth used on lighter-textured soils. Pumpkins can be transplanted if grown and set out in some type of plantable container, such as peat pots or pellets. However, transplanting results in little if any benefit and is not a recommended practice.

Germination And Emergence

The pumpkin seedlings should germinate and emerge within five to seven days—provided you haven't planted too deeply and soil temperatures range between 70 and 95 degrees at the seeding depth. Soil temperatures outside this range may result in poor germination, or no germination at all. To avoid this problem, plant when soil temperatures are above 70 degrees. Also, when planting during high temperature conditions, spread a thin layer of organic matter over the seeded area to help cool the soil.

Within seven to 10 days after emergence, thin each hill of pumpkins to two of the stronger, more vigorous seedlings. Thinning is best accomplished by pinching off the seedlings at ground level rather than pulling them from the soil. This is due to the rapid root development of the pumpkin seedlings, which often results in an intertwining of their roots. If the seedlings are pulled from the soil, damage to the roots of the remaining plants often will occur and should be avoided.

If you're planting during high soil temperatures and haven't already applied a layer of organic matter over the seeded area to help cool the soil, do so after thinning. If you're planting during early spring, this is the ideal time to mulch. The mulching material will stabilize the soil temperature, help prevent the appearance of unwanted weeds and grasses and conserve valuable soil moisture.

Although pumpkins are fairly drought-tolerant, overly dry soils should be avoided during the early growth of the seedlings and during bloom and fruit maturity. Obviously, dry soils during seedling growth are much more likely when planting occurs toward midsummer. During these times, weekly applications of water may be necessary. Overly dry soils during bloom often will cause the flowers to abort and, if dry conditions persist, those fruit that do set oftentimes will be misshapen and "gourdy." Again, weekly watering may be necessary. Regardless of the method used, apply enough water on each occasion to wet the soil to a depth of at least 6 inches.

About three weeks after thinning, side-dress the plants with a small amount of nitrogen fertilizer. Use 3 tablespoons of ammonium sulfate (21-0-0) or 2 tablespoons of ammonium nitrate (33-0-0) applied in a circle around each hill about 24 to 36 inches from the plants. Work the fertilizer into the top inch of soil and water lightly. If you mulched around the plants, simply pull the organic matter back, apply the fertilizer and work it into the soil, water lightly and then put the mulch back in place.

About 50 days after planting, depending upon the weather and variety you grow, your pumpkin plants should begin to flower, which should mean your first pumpkin pie or Jack-o'-lantern is on the way. Unfortunately, however, such is not always the case.

Pollination And The Bees

Pumpkins, like most other cucurbits, produce male and female blooms on the same plant. For those of you needing a little garden "sex education," the female blooms are those with the small, immature fruit located directly behind the flower petals. The male flowers are those without the immature fruit. For fruit set to occur, pollen must be transferred from the male to the female blooms. If pollination does not occur, the female bloom and immature fruit simply withers and dies.

The important job of transferring the pollen from the male to the female bloom generally is carried out by honeybees. Therefore, an adequate supply of honeybees is a must when growing any of the members of the cucurbit family. However, when growing pumpkins, a lack of honeybees during bloom spells doom to any hope of a bountiful harvest. This is simply due to the relatively small number of female blooms produced by pumpkins compared to most other cucurbits.

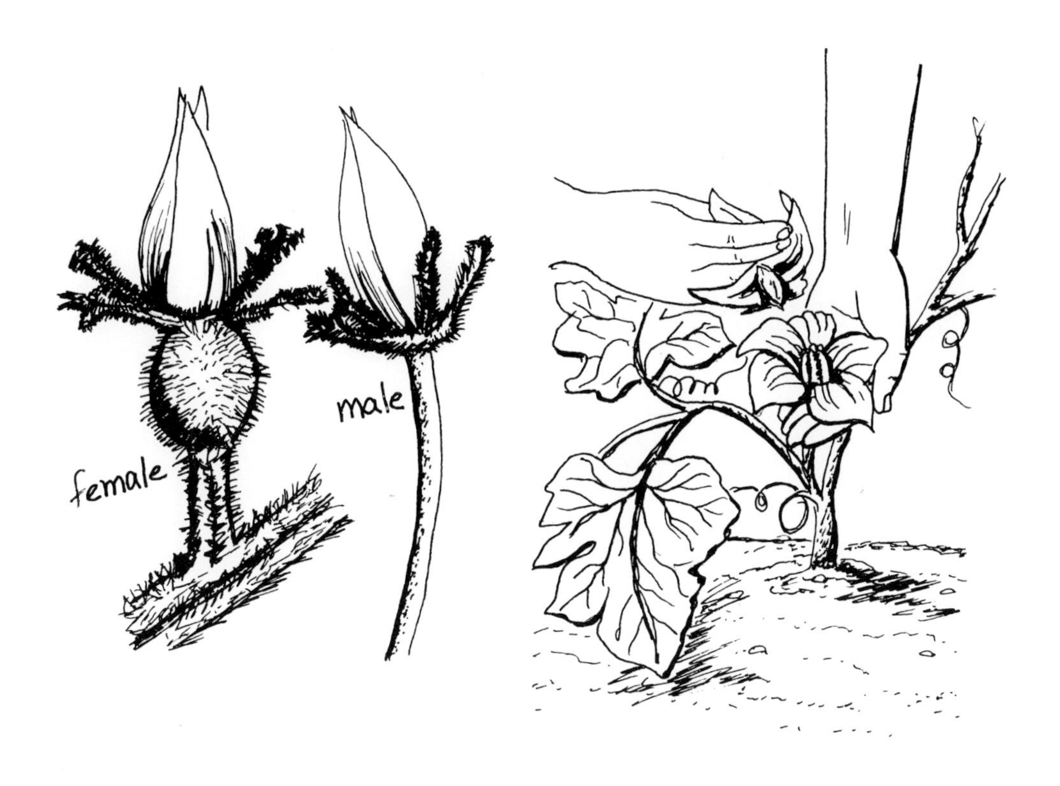

For fruit set to occur with pumpkins, pollen must be transferred from the male to the female blooms. You can play "honeybee" by transferring the pollen yourself.

There are several reasons for a lack of honeybee activity, including cloudy and wet weather; a natural absence; and misuse of chemicals. Not a lot can be done about the weather, except pray it gets better. However, if lack of naturally occurring honeybees is the problem, you might consider obtaining a beehive and placing it in the vicinity of your garden. If you garden in an urban area, though, your neighbors might object—unless they also happen to be gardeners! However, most pollination problems related to low honeybee activity can be avoided simply by applying pesticides only during the late afternoon when honeybee activity is at a minimum. Such a practice will avoid directly killing honeybees and help prevent honeybees contaminated with pesticides from returning home and causing great harm to their hives.

You can help ensure fruit set of your pumpkins by playing the role of a honeybee. Use a small brush or cotton swab to transfer the pollen

Powdery mildew (top) and downy mildew are fungal diseases that attack the plant's foliage and must be controlled with an appropriate fungicide.

Several types of viruses attack pumpkins and can destroy your harvest.

from the male to the female blooms, or simply remove a male bloom and dab it on the female bloom. One male bloom generally will provide enough pollen for eight to 10 female blooms. It's important to note that the female pumpkin blooms are only open and receptive to pollination for one day—the day they first open. Therefore, take a lesson from the honeybees. Do your pollinating during early morning when it's cool and when the blooms are fully open and most receptive to pollination.

Pumpkins Susceptible To Disease

From planting to harvest, pumpkins are susceptible to various problems related to insects and disease. However, unlike most garden vegetables grown in Texas, pumpkins are much more likely to be seriously troubled by diseases rather than insects.

By far the most common disease of pumpkins is powdery mildew. This foliage disease is most common during hot, dry weather and generally occurs about the time plants begin to set fruit. Powdery mildew is characterized by the appearance of a white, talcum-like fungus growth, which occurs on the upper surface of the leaves. If left uncontrolled, the fungus will spread rapidly and quickly put an end to your pumpkin patch.

Applications of a fungicide containing benomyl, begun at the first sign of the disease, usually will result in good control.

Downy mildew is a common foliage disease of pumpkins that occurs primarily during wet, humid weather. Symptoms of this disease are the development of yellowish areas on the upper leaf surface which are accompanied by a "downy," oftentimes purplish fungus growth on the corresponding lower leaf surfaces. The infected areas enlarge and darken, causing the infected leaves to wither and die. Downy mildew generally begins near the crown or older leaves of the pumpkin plant and spreads rapidly to the newer leaves. The fungicide Bravo, or one containing maneb, applied at the first sign of the disease usually will provide satisfactory control. If the plants have set a number of fruit and humid, wet weather occurs, applications of either of these fungicides is often a good preventive measure.

Another disease of pumpkins, which has become much more serious in recent years, is mosaic virus. Mosaic viruses, of which there are several types, primarily are spread by cucumber beetles feeding on the plant foliage. Infected plants usually are stunted and produce mottled, often distorted leaves. Fruit set is poor and the fruit that does reach maturity is often small and misshapen. Good insect control and the early removal of plants exhibiting symptoms of virus infection are the only means of prevention. There is no effective control once the plants are infected. Generally, if your pumpkin plants exhibit symptoms of virus infection during their early growth, pulling them up and devoting the garden space to some other crop is the best remedy.

Cucumber beetles, aphids, vine borers and the ever-present squash bugs are the insect pests most likely to attack your pumpkin plants. Cucumber beetles, which often are guilty of spreading viruses, do their damage by sucking juices from the pumpkin plants. Aphids, or plant lice, generally occur in large numbers on the undersides of the leaves. Both of these insects can be controlled adequately by early applications of malathion. Squash vine borers are the result of a colorful, wasp-like moth that lays her eggs on the vines, generally near the crown of the plant. The eggs hatch and the small larvae tunnel into the plant stems where they feed and enlarge. Severely infected plants wilt and eventually die. Early applications of the insecticide thiodan, applied when the adult moths and/or her eggs are first observed and hopefully before the larvae enter the stems, will result in effective control. Thiodan also will give good control of squash bugs—if applications are begun before their population gets out of control. If it does, two bricks may be your only effective means of control!

When harvesting pumpkins, leave several inches of stem attached to the fruit. If you don't, the area will be an inviting entrance for decay-causing organisms.

If provided a little "T.L.C.," which includes cultural care and protection from the disease and insect pests just described, your first pumpkin should be mature about 90 to 120 days after planting. Harvesting should occur when the fruit are vine ripe as indicated by a deep orange or orange-yellow color, a woody stem and a rind hard enough to resist scratching with your thumbnail. When harvesting your pumpkins, always cut the fruit from the vine, leaving a 3- to 4-inch-long portion of the stem attached to the fruit. If pumpkins are pulled from the vine, the stem often separates from the fruit leaving an inviting area for the entrance and development of decay-causing organisms.

Fall pumpkins can be left in the garden until after "the first frost," without damage to the fruits. However, harvest your pumpkins if temperatures below 30 degrees are predicted as injury to the fruit can result. Those fruit that are physically mature but lack good color will continue to develop color off the vine. If long-term storage is planned, first cure the pumpkins by setting them in the sun for seven to 10 days and then store them in a cool, dry area.

Quick Problem Solver: Pumpkins

Problem	Causes	Solutions
Seed fail to germinate.	Old seed.	Always use current season seed.
	Cold soils.	Wait until soil temperatures at seeding depth is above 70 degrees to plant.
	Planted too deep.	Seed should be planted 1 to 1½ inches deep. Use greater depth on loose, sandy soils.
	Lack of soil moisture.	Soil should be moist at planting.
Plants die after emergence.	Damping-off (fungus).	Always use treated seed. Avoid planting when soils are too cold.
	Cutworms.	Check base of healthy plants for dark worm just below surface. Treat with appropriate insecticide if found.
Plants stunted, lack vigor.	Low soil pH.	Pumpkins grow poorly if grown on acid soils. Add lime to raise pH above 5.5
	Low fertility.	Apply small amount of nitrogen fertilizer in circle around hill, lightly work into soil and water.
	Cold soils.	Pumpkins grow slowly until soils warm.
	Heavy, poorly drained soils.	Plant on raised beds. Add organic matter.
Leaves mottled, distorted.	Virus.	Remove and discard plants exhibiting symptoms of virus infection.
Flowers bloom, but fruits fail to set.	Lack of pollination.	Usually due to lack of honeybee activity. (See text.)
	Low soil moisture.	Maintain fairly moist soil during bloom.
Fruits small, misshapen.	Low soil moisture.	Maintain soil relatively moist as fruits mature.
	Virus infection.	Remove plants exhibiting symptoms of virus infection.
	Heavy, poorly drained soils.	Plant on raised beds and add liberal amounts of organic matter to the soil.

White talcum-like growth on leaves.	Powdery mildew (fungus).	Treat foliage with benomyl at first sign of the disease.
Older leaves exhibit yellow spots, wither and die.	Downy mildew (fungus).	Treat foliage with Bravo or a fungicide containing maneb.
Small "plant lice" on lower leaf surface.	Aphids.	Treat foliage with malathion.
Plants wilt suddenly, worms in stems.	Squash vine borer.	Apply thiodan when adult moths appear to lay eggs.
Numerous brown insects present.	Squash bugs.	Control with early applications of thiodan.
Spotted or striped beetles on foliage.	Cucumber beetles.	Malathion applied early will give good control.
Fruits rot quickly after harvesting.	Improper storage.	Cure in sun for several days and then store in cool, dry area.
	Pulled from plant.	Always harvest by cutting stem with sharp knife. Leave 3- to 4-inch-long stem attached to fruit.

RADISH

Scientific Name: *Raphanus sativus*
Family: *Cruciferae*
Annual or biennial, grown as an annual
Cool Season
Varieties: Red Prince, Champion; (white) Icicle, Diakon; (winter) Black Spanish, China Rose
Expected Harvest: 4 to 10 pounds per 10 feet of row

RADISHES

Radishes have the reputation of being the easiest of all vegetables to grow. There's even an old saying that "if you can't grow radishes, you can't be helped." And truer words were never spoken! In fact, the radish's genus name, *Raphanus,* is a Latinized form of an old Greek expression, *raphanos,* which freely translated means "easily reared."

Radishes have been grown since prehistoric times and originated in China, with a secondary center of origin in Middle Asia. Ancient Egyptian records indicate radishes were grown there even before the pyramids were built. Early Roman scholars described many different radishes including those that were mild, pungent, round, long, small and very large. Apparently, Europeans preferred the larger types, as indicated by the fact that a German botanist in 1544 reported radishes weighing 100 pounds. Columbus is believed to have introduced the radish into the New World during his first voyage since they were being grown in Mexico about 1500 and in Haiti by 1565. Radishes commonly were cultured in England during the late 1500s and were one of the most popular vegetables grown in the gardens of the early English colonists. Their popularity continues today: radishes are one of the most common vegetables grown in gardens across Texas and the rest of the United States.

Despite how easy it is to grow, the radish is a complicated and highly diverse vegetable. There are two basic types of radishes—the summer and the winter, each of which comes in various sizes, shapes, colors and "flavors."

The summer radishes are most commonly grown in Texas gardens. They generally mature in a relatively short period of time, some as quickly as three weeks after planting. Commonly eaten "in hand" and in salads, summer radishes usually have globular or cylindrical shaped roots with red, white, or red-and-white skin color. Winter radishes take longer to mature than the summer types. They also have various shaped roots which usually are either white, black or pink skinned. These radishes often have a somewhat pungent flavor and can be eaten fresh or used as an ingredient in various tasty recipes.

We'll begin our discussion by admitting that many gardeners often have trouble getting their radishes to grow and probably take exception to my earlier statement on how easy it is to grow them. Radishes can cause you much frustration—unless you know the simple keys to their successful culture. Two requirements must be met. First, the plants must be encouraged to grow rapidly and succulently. Second, sufficient space must be provided to accommodate the enlargement of the radish root. Keep these requirements in mind as we continue and you'll soon be able to grow radishes like never before.

Obviously, planting must occur at the right time to encourage the desired growth habit. Begin planting summer varieties as soon as soil temperatures are above 45 degrees in the spring. Additional plantings can be made up until 30 days before maximum daytime temperatures are expected to exceed 80 degrees. They shouldn't be planted any later because high temperatures during maturity often cause radishes to be pithy and develop a hot flavor. In addition, the summer type radishes are annuals and high temperatures, in combination with longer days, will cause them to bolt or flower. Late summer and fall plantings should begin

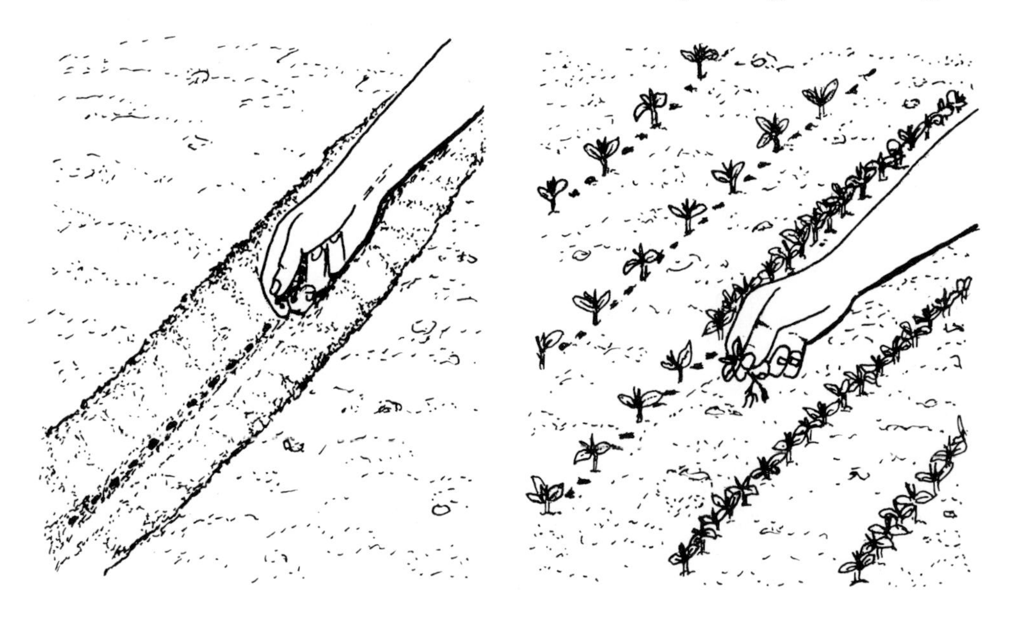

Sow your seed in furrows at the rate of three or four seeds per inch and cover them lightly with soil. About two or three days after emergence, thin you stand of seedlings to the appropriate in-row spacing.

when maximum daytime temperatures fall below 80 degrees and can continue until the nighttime temperatures drop to near 40 degrees. Radishes often can withstand considerable cold, but those that are developing when daily temperatures average below about 55 degrees will grow slowly and sometimes develop an off-flavor.

The winter type radishes can be planted in late winter or early spring. However, if you choose to plant during this time, be sure to use varieties adapted for late spring or summer harvest. As their name implies, winter type radishes prefer cold temperatures. Make your first fall planting about the same time as your first planting of summer type radishes. Additional plantings can be made until about 60 days before nighttime temperatures are expected to drop to near 20 degrees. Spring plantings should cease at least 60 days before maximum daytime temperatures are expected to exceed 80 degrees.

Obviously, in many areas of Texas radishes can be grown right through the winter without fear of cold damage, especially the winter types. However, you should be aware that winter type radishes are biennials, which means they normally take two years (one period of cold-induced dormancy) to go from "seed to seed." But if the plants are exposed to prolonged temperatures of 45 degrees or lower, dormancy will be induced. When temperatures warm and re-growth begins, they will bolt or flower. Premature flowering also is the reason why winter radishes often do poorly when planted in late winter or early spring. Low temperatures at planting and during seedling growth and development, followed by warm spring days, almost certainly will mean lots of flowers for your dinner table centerpiece—rather than radishes for your salads.

Preparing The Soil

Radishes will do well on a wide range of soil types, but grow best in a soil that is deep, loose and fertile. Unfortunately, many Texas soils fail to meet these requirements and must be improved. Ideally, you should get your soil ready for planting several weeks before the anticipated planting date.

Regardless of your soil type or where you garden in Texas, your efforts at growing radishes will be enhanced greatly by adding liberal amounts of organic matter to your garden soil. If your soil is on the heavy side, the organic matter will make it more friable and better suited for the development of smooth, well-developed radishes. Organic matter will improve sandy soils by increasing their ability to hold moisture and nutrients.

The edible portion of the radish does grow above ground.

When preparing your soil, spread 2 to 3 inches of organic matter, such as compost, grass clippings, leaves or hay, over the surface of the planting area. Till or spade it into the soil to a depth of 8 to 10 inches. Barnyard manure added to your garden soil will help radishes flourish. However, high levels of manure added to the soil just before planting may cause the radishes to be rough, cracked and misshapen. Therefore, it should be tilled or spaded into the soil several months prior to planting at the rate of ½ pound per square foot or 40 to 50 pounds per 35 feet of row.

Unless your soil is unusually fertile, radish yields and quality will be improved by the addition of a small amount of commercial fertilizer. Use about 1 to 1½ pounds of a complete fertilizer per 100 square feet or per 35 feet of row. Use the lower amount if you also used barnyard manure or if you garden in a sandy type soil. In East Texas and along the upper coastal areas, fertilizers with a 1-2-2 ratio, such as 10-20-20, work well. In

Spacing is extremely important when growing radishes. You must thin the seedlings soon after they come up, allowing enough space for the plants to "radish" properly.

most other areas of our state, a fertilizer with a 1-2-1 ratio, like 10-20-10, is satisfactory. Scatter the fertilizer evenly over the area to be planted and work it into the soil.

If you're growing the long-rooted or winter type radishes, the fertilizer can be worked into the soil along with the organic matter to a depth of 8 to 10 inches. However, when growing the small, fast-maturing, summer type radishes, the fertilizer should be worked into the soil after you till in the organic matter, and then only to a depth of 4 to 6 inches. Concentrating the fertilizer closer to the soil surface will compensate for the radishes' relatively inefficient and shallow-growing root systems.

In addition to adequately preparing and fertilizing your soil, you should be concerned about its pH. Radishes will do poorly when grown on soils having a pH of below 6.0. If you garden in an area of Texas where acid soils are common, you should have your soil pH tested. If it is too acid, the addition of lime will raise its pH and greatly improve your efforts at growing radishes (and other vegetables). Additional information on adjusting you soil's pH is found on page 394.

After getting your soil ready for planting, it's generally a good practice to form ridges and furrows to make raised planting beds, especially if the soil is on the heavy side. By planting on top of the raised beds, problems with poor drainage and soil crusting will be decreased. Also, more soil will be exposed to the sun and will warm up more quickly. This is of special value for your late winter or early spring plantings.

Use a shovel or tiller with a bedder to form the ridges and furrows. Ideally, the ridges should measure 30 to 36 inches apart from the top of one ridge to the top of an adjoining ridge. Next, use a garden rake to smooth, flatten and shape the ridges into raised planting beds. The top of the beds should be 16 to 20 inches across with the remaining lower areas between the beds serving as water furrows. After forming the beds, it's a good idea to use the flat side of your rake or something similar to tamp the bed tops firm. This will help the soil hold moisture and also ensure the lateral movement of water within the beds.

When it's time to plant, your soil should be moist enough to allow for germination and seedling emergence—without applying additional water. Planting "dry" and then watering can result in the development of various seedling diseases and should be avoided if at all possible. If your soil is dry, water thoroughly several days before planting.

Before planting, make sure the soil temperature is satisfactory. At the seeding depth, the temperature should be no lower than 45 degrees. If it is, it may take three to four weeks for the seedlings to emerge—if they emerge at all! At soil temperatures between 55 and 90 degrees, your radish seedlings should be up and growing in less than a week.

Planting Methods

Radishes can be planted either in rows or broadcast, but planting in rows is preferable for two reasons. First, the depth of seeding is more consistent, resulting in uniform seedling emergence; second, planting in rows makes the job of thinning easier. Thinning results in less competition between the plants for light, moisture and nutrients.

Raised beds are excellent for multiple-row planting. Make seeding furrows about ¾ inch deep. The 16- to 20-inch-wide bed easily will accommodate as many as four rows of radishes spaced about 4 inches apart. If you opt to plant two rows per bed, space the rows about 10 to 12 inches apart. Generally, the wider row spacing will result in somewhat larger radishes. If your soil still seems a little dry, apply water directly in

Radishes usually are a favorite crop of young gardeners because they're fast maturing and easy to care for.

the seed furrows and allow it to soak in before seeding. Sow the seeds at the rate of about three to four per inch and cover them with soil. Next, use the flat side of your hoe to firm the soil over the seeds. This will help conserve valuable soil moisture in the seeding zone and result in good soil/seed contact which encourages moisture transfer from soil to seed.

So far we've concentrated on timing, soil preparation, fertility and planting—items which will help ensure the rapid and succulent growth of the radish plants. Now we must emphasize how important it is to provide sufficient space for radishes to grow properly. Once the seedlings emerge from the soil, they must be thinned within two to three days. The reason for this is relatively simple, but understanding it requires a short lesson in botany. The radish *root* that we eat is not a root at all, but rather the hypocotyl of the radish plant. The hypocotyl is that part of the plant directly below the primary leaves but above the root which, in radishes, characteristically enlarges. Being a type of storage organ, it depends on adequate sunlight, fertility and moisture for development. Being above ground, though, the hypocotyl also is affected greatly by lack of adequate space for enlargement—especially during its early development. Since many varieties of radishes will mature within 20 to 30 days after planting, early thinning is an absolute must! If you wait two weeks or more after seedling emergence to provide adequate room for the radish "roots" to develop, you've waited too long. This also should help explain why some, but not all, of your plants develop properly. It's normally a variation in available space. Those that have adequate room "radish," while those that are too crowded don't.

When thinning, the expected size of the radish should determine the final in-row spacing. The smaller radishes should be thinned to at least 1½ to 2 inches apart. The larger types should be spaced 4 to 8 inches apart. Simply pinch off or pull up the unwanted plants. After thinning, water lightly to settle the soil around the roots of any plants you may have disturbed.

From this point on, all you need to do to ensure that your radishes develop properly is keep the soil relatively moist. Always water before the top inch of soil becomes dry. Mulching around the plants with a layer of organic matter will help conserve soil moisture and control weeds and grasses. Due to the rapid development of most types of radishes, side-dressing with fertilizer usually is not necessary. However, if the plants seem sluggish, apply a small amount of nitrogen fertilizer, such as ammonium sulfate (21-0-0) or ammonium nitrate (33-0-0), to the sides of the plants and water.

Insects And Diseases

Fortunately, radishes are bothered little by insects and diseases, but occasionally flea beetles and aphids will become problems. Flea beetles are small, black, jumping insects that eat holes in the leaves, causing a "shotgun hole" effect. Aphids generally are found on the underside of the leaves where they suck the juices from the plants. Both of these insects can be controlled easily by early applications of diazinon or malathion. The few diseases that sometimes attack radishes in Texas can be controlled best

If your children don't care for boiled eggs, try planting a crop of Easter Egg radishes, which come in many colors, for them to hunt on Easter.

through good cultural practices, such as garden sanitation and crop rotation.

The most common problems related to radishes at harvesttime are due to the fact that it's impossible to eat a 100-foot row of radishes in one day! Harvesting must occur early, at the peak of maturity, if you expect high quality and this is especially true of the summer type radishes. If left in your garden too long after they mature, radishes obviously will be pithy, poor flavored and often downright hot! To avoid having too many radishes all at once, make several small plantings a few weeks apart instead of one large, single planting. Then harvest your radishes as they mature.

The winter types often can be left in the garden and harvested as needed. If you garden in the colder winter areas of Texas, you should mulch around the plants with organic matter to provide protection from extremely low temperatures.

Quick Problem Solver: Radishes

Problem	Causes	Solutions
Seed fail to germinate.	Old seed.	Always use current-season seed.
	Cold soil.	Wait until soil temperature is above 45 degrees plant.
	Planted too deep.	Radish seed should be planted ½ to ¾ inch deep. Use greater depth on lighter soils.
Seedlings have poor color, lack vigor.	Acid soils.	Soil pH should be above 6.0. If soil is too acid, add lime to raise pH.
	Wet soils.	Plant on raised beds. Avoid overwatering.
Foliage has "shotgun hole" appearance.	Flea beetles.	Treat foliage with malathion or diazinon, according to label directions.
Small, greenish insects on underside of leaves.	Aphids.	Treat foliage with diazinon or malathion, according to label directions.
Radishes fail to "radish."	Crowded growing conditions.	Thin stand to correct in-row spacing within 2 to 3 days after emergence.
	Insufficient light, fertility, moisture.	As above.

Radishes "pithy," off-flavored.	High temperatures.	Radishes should mature before temperatures exceed 80 degrees during the day.
	Overmature.	Harvest radishes at peak of maturity.
	Low temperatures.	Temperatures should average above 50 degrees for highest quality.
Radishes cracked, misshapened.	Overmature.	Harvest at peak of quality.
	Barnyard manure.	Avoid using barnyard manure immediately before planting. Apply several months earlier.
Plants bolt or flower prematurely.	High temperatures, long days.	Plant at right time of year.
	Cold-induced dormancy.	Winter-type radishes should not be grown during prolonged periods below 45 degrees.
Radishes "hot."	Overmature.	Harvest on time!

SOUTHERN PEA

Scientific Name: *Vigna sinensis*
Family: *Leguminosae*
Annual
Warm Season
Varieties:
- Blackeye: California No. 5
- Purple Hull: Pink Eye Purple Hull, Purple Hull
- Cream: Cream 40, Zipper
- Crowder: Mississippi Silver, Calico, Colossus

Expected Harvest: 4 to 8 pounds per 10 feet of row

SOUTHERN PEAS

Southern peas, cow peas, field peas! Call them what you will; in Texas they all mean the same thing. And that's mighty good eating. Yet up north, there are a lot of folks who think that what we Texans commonly call southern peas are not fit for human consumption and only suitable for livestock feed. What a treat they're missing. It's hard to imagine life without some sliced, vine-ripe tomatoes, hot corn bread and a plate full of garden fresh blackeyed peas.

The southern pea originated in India long before recorded history. Its culture spread to Arabia and then down into Africa. It was brought from Africa to Jamaica in 1675 by slave traders who carried it as food for the slaves and as seedstock. Southern peas first were brought from the West Indies to Florida about 1700. George Washington is considered one of the first pea farmers in the United States since he planted 40 bushels of seed on his farm in Virginia in 1791.

Due to their wide adaptability to the warm growing conditions in the South, the popularity of the southern pea grew there by leaps and bounds. However, in the cooler regions of the north, they grew poorly and never caught on there. Today, southern peas are a tradition in the South and certainly are a favorite of most Texans.

Before we get into how to grow them in Texas, it's important to point out that there are several different types of southern peas, including blackeyes, purple hulls, creams and crowders. Peas are classified by their pod and seed characteristics. Southern peas also are characterized by their two basic plant types: bush and semi-vine. The culture, though, is basically the same for all types. Also, to most Texans, the word "pea" is synonymous with southern pea, so from this point on we'll simply refer to them as peas.

Minimal Soil Preparation

Peas will do well on most Texas soils. In fact, poor soils usually will produce a fairly good crop of peas. They'll do *best*, though, on loose, sandy type soils enriched with moderate amounts of organic matter. Spread about 1 to 2 inches of well-decomposed leaves, hay, grass clippings or other organic matter over your future pea patch and work it into the soil.

Though not particular about soil type, peas are sensitive to the pH level of the soil and will grow best if it's between 5.5 and 7.5. If you live in East Texas where acid soils are common and have had only fair results with peas, chances are you should add lime to your soil to raise its pH up to an acceptable level.

If your soil's pH is above 7.5, you should add sulphur to lower the pH and make iron in the soil more available to the plants. This helps prevent chlorosis or, yellowing, of the leaves, which is so common in alkaline soils. Additional information on adjusting your soil's pH can be found on page 394. Iron also can be applied as copperous (iron sulfate) or as the sequesterene form usually available under the trade name of Geigy 138, which has been formulated specially for alkaline soils. Check the label for the correct amounts to apply.

Moderate amounts of barnyard manure may provide all the nutrients your peas need. A common problem with peas is that they "go to vine" instead of producing pods, which is caused by too high a level of soil fertility. Excess fertility also can cause pod shattering and delayed maturity.

Peas are legumes, which means they have the unique ability to utilize atmospheric nitrogen from the air spaces in the soil for their growth and development. This process is carried out by bacteria in the small nodules found on the pea's root system. Therefore, if your soil is fairly fertile, you may not need to apply any preplant fertilizer. If you think some additional fertility is needed, though, apply 1/4 to 1/2 pound of barnyard manure per square foot of planting area. If barnyard manure is unavailable, use a commercial fertilizer, such as 10-20-10, at the rate of about 1/2 pound per 100 square feet or for each 35-foot row. Till the fertilizer, along with any other needed additives, into the soil to a depth of 8 to 10 inches.

Peas are susceptible to various types of soilborne fungi which cause damping-off of newly emerged seedlings. Problems with damping-off are recognized easily. Stem tissue at ground level becomes water-soaked and the plants just seem to fall over. These fungi are present in most of our soils, but become more of a problem for peas if the soil contains organic matter that is not yet decomposed. For this reason, you should prepare your soil at least three or four weeks before planting to allow the organic matter time to decompose.

Cream peas (top left), blackeyes (top right) and purple hulls are all popular varieties of southern peas.

With regard to time of planting, don't be in too big of a hurry in the spring. Pea seed germinates poorly if the soil is too cold and any seedlings that do emerge will not perform well. Wait until the soil temperature at the seeding depth is at least 65 degrees for three consecutive days before planting. Planting when it's too cold also will cause more problems with damping-off.

Peas are fairly tolerant of high temperatures and usually will grow well through midsummer. However, they probably will not develop pods when temperatures are extremely high and the days are long. Instead, they grow vegetatively and produce "running vines." These same plants, if allowed to continue to grow, often will bloom and set pods when the days become shorter and the temperatures lower.

Not all pea varieties react in this manner to high temperatures and long days, but many do. Consequently, you should make your first spring planting as soon as the soil is sufficiently warm (above 65 degrees) and all danger of frost has passed. Additional plantings can be made later, so long as the plants have time to set pods before the days become too long and hot. For a fall crop, plant about 90 to 100 days before the first killing freeze is expected.

As we noted before, peas do best on light-textured, sandy-type soils that warm up early and provide good drainage. Raised beds will provide the same advantages and should be used if you have heavy soil. Ridges and furrows, shaped into raised beds, allow more surface area to be exposed to the sun's rays, creating a warmer planting area. Raised beds also will dry more quickly when it rains. Even if you have well-drained, sandy soil, you probably should plant on raised beds, because such soils often crust over following rains, which causes poor aeration and hinders plant growth. Crusting is not as severe on raised beds.

The raised beds should be at least 4 to 6 inches high and 36 to 48 inches apart, measured from the center of one bed to the center of an adjoining one. The wider spacing is preferable for vining varieties. The bed top, or planting area, should be about 16 to 24 inches wide, with the remaining area serving as a water furrow.

Plant Treated Seed

Always plant seed that has been treated with a fungicide to help prevent seedling diseases. Most commercial seed has been treated, as will be evidenced by pink or blue powder on the seeds. If your seeds have not been treated, though, treat them with an approved fungicide, according to label directions. Simply put your seed and the fungicide in a paper bag, close and shake vigorously.

You also should consider inoculating your seed, which is the process of applying nitrogen-fixing bacteria to the seed instead of depending on your soil to do the job after planting. If you've been successful growing peas or other legumes in your garden, inoculation may not be beneficial. The process, though, is easy. Simply dampen (don't soak) the seed, place them in a paper bag and apply the inoculating powder. If you choose to both inoculate and treat your seed with a fungicide, both can be done at the same time. However, treating the seed with a fungicide can be done at any time, while inoculation must be done immediately before planting. If the damp, inoculated seed are allowed to dry completely before planting, the nitrogen-fixing bacteria will lose their effectiveness. Commercial inoculation powders are readily available.

Ideally, when it's time to plant, there should be enough soil moisture to result in germination and seedling emergence without watering until the seedlings appear. If your soil is on the dry side, water several days prior to planting.

Plant your peas in single rows on top of the raised beds. Make a planting furrow about 1½ inches deep if your soil is sandy and about 1 inch deep if it's heavy. If the soil still seems dry, apply water directly into the seed furrow immediately prior to planting. Apply enough water to saturate the soil to a depth of at least 6 inches. Depending on how fast your soil absorbs moisture, you may need to water several times to get the soil wet enough. Allow the water to soak in before planting.

The common practice of soaking the seed in water prior to planting to ensure germination is of little value with peas, especially in the spring. When planting a fall crop, however, conditions usually are drier and an overnight soaking is beneficial. If you opt to soak your seed, do so before treating or inoculating them.

Sow the seeds at the rate of four to five per foot of row and cover them with dry soil. Next, use the flat side of a hoe to firm the soil over the planted seeds. This practice will help conserve soil moisture and ensure good contact between the seed and the soil.

Within seven to 10 days your pea seedlings will emerge from the soil. When they are about 3 to 4 inches tall, thin them to an in-row spacing of 4 to 6 inches if they're bush types and about 8 inches if they're semi-vining. Rather than pull the unwanted seedlings from the ground, pinch them off to avoid damaging the roots of the remaining plants. It's usually a good idea to water lightly to settle any soil that might have been disturbed during the thinning operation.

Mulching is not as important for southern peas as with other crops because they prefer warm soils and have a deep-penetrating, extensive root system. However, mulching with a layer of organic matter will help control weeds and conserve soil moisture during dry periods. Apply the mulching materials in the spring when the soil is warm and fairly moist. In the fall, apply a layer of mulch soon after the seedlings emerge or after thinning.

Most of the commercially grown peas in Texas are grown dryland (without irrigation or supplemental water) and some years they produce quite well. It all depends upon Mother Nature. Peas prefer fairly dry soils during their growth cycle up to the time they begin to bloom. In fact, if the soil is too wet throughout the pea's life cycle, the plants may continue to grow vegetatively and not produce. On the other hand, if it's excessively dry when the plants are blooming, they will shed their flowers and yields will be reduced greatly. Keep the soil fairly moist while peas are blooming and you'll have a good harvest. During this period, water your peas when the soil becomes fairly dry about 1 inch beneath the surface. And, each time you water, wet the soil to a depth of at least 6 inches.

Harvesttime

Depending upon variety, season of the year and stage of maturity when harvested, your peas will be ready to eat about 70 to 90 days after planting. Peas can be harvested at three stages of maturity: green snap, green mature and dry. Peas for snapping should be harvested when the pods are about two-thirds full size and before the seeds begin to size. When peas reach the green, mature shelling stage, the pods will change to a light yellow, reddish-purple or silver color, depending upon variety. For dry peas, the pods are left to fully mature on the plants, then are shelled and stored for later use.

Obviously, when harvesting you'll find pods in several different stages of maturity, but hopefully not many that are fully mature—unless you're growing them for dry peas. For maximum yields, peas should be harvested either as green snap, green mature or both. If pods are left on the plants to mature, yields will decrease dramatically.

After harvesting your first mess of peas, lightly side-dress the plants with a nitrogen fertilizer. Use ⅔ cup of ammonium sulfate (21-0-0) or ½ cup of ammonium nitrate (33-0-0) for each 35-foot row. Put the fertilizer out along the drip line of the plants, work it into the very top of the soil and water lightly.

Look Out For Insects

To ensure yourself a bumper crop of garden-fresh peas, you'll need to be on the lookout for insects. Cutworms apparently love peas and often are looking for a meal when the young seedlings emerge. If you've had problems with cutworms in the past, the best thing to do is to avoid the problem by applying diazinon to the soil before planting.

Thrips often attack the young seedlings shortly after emergence, causing the leaves to become twisted, curled and otherwise misshaped. The developing plants look like they either have some type of virus disease or have been mistakenly treated with a weed killer. The plants usually recover, but yields will be reduced if these pests are not controlled. Begin treating the plants with malathion or diazinon at the first sign of a problem.

The cowpea curculio and the pea weevil both feed on the blooms or pods and lay eggs that eventually end up as larvae in the pea seed—

which is obviously highly undesirable. Fortunately, applications of Sevin during bloom usually control these pests.

Rust, fusarium wilt and various types of foliage-spotting diseases may pose a threat to your peas. Rust causes reddish spots on the foliage and can result in defoliation of the plants if uncontrolled. Sulphur dust or a fungicide containing maneb, applied at the first sign of the problem, usually will result in good control. Other leaf-spotting diseases may occur occasionally, but most can be controlled by maneb.

Fusarium wilt is a soilborne disease that causes the plants to suddenly wilt and die. Damage to the roots as a result of deep cultivation aggravates the problem and should be avoided. The only effective control is to plant resistant varieties and to practice a long-term rotation by not planting any peas or beans in the same area of your garden for at least three years.

Nematodes are a problem on peas, just as they are on many other commonly grown vegetable crops. Symptoms of a nematode infestation include slow, stunted growth, yellowing of the foliage and wilting. Infected

Chlorosis (top left), thrips (bottom left) and stinkbugs (right) are common pests of southern peas.

plants will exhibit elongated and round swellings, or knots, on both the small and large roots. These knots make an accurate diagnosis of a nematode problem fairly easy on most plants, but not on beans and peas.

Healthy peas also may exhibit knots on the roots which are the home of the beneficial nitrogen-fixing bacteria we discussed earlier. Luckily, it's simple to determine whether you have a nematode infestation or a good supply of nitrogen-fixing bacteria. The nodules formed by the beneficial bacteria are loosely attached to the pea roots and can be removed easily, whereas nematode knots are actually a swelling of the root tissue. If you determine your problem is nematodes, see page 408 for instructions on controlling them.

Quick Problem Solver: Southern Peas

Problem	Causes	Solutions
Poor germination and seedling emergence.	Old seed.	Pea seed lose viability quickly. Always use current-season seed or store in refrigerator.
	Cold soils.	Never plant if soil temperature is lower than 65 degrees.
	Planted too deep.	Plant pea seed 1 to 1½ inches deep, using greater depth on lighter textured soils.
	Crusted soils.	Avoid crusted soils by lightly watering with a sprinkler just as first seedlings begin to emerge.
Seedlings die shortly after emergence.	Damping-off (fungus).	Plant when soils are warm and avoid overwatering. Always use treated seed. Add organic matter to soil several weeks prior to planting—decomposing organic matter increases problems related to damping-off.
	Cutworms.	Check soil at base of plants for presence of dark "worms." If found, treat with appropriate insecticide.
Seedlings lack vigor, have poor color.	Cold soils.	Plant when soils are warm.
	Acid soils.	Soil pH should be above 5.5. Add lime to raise soil pH.
	Wet soils.	Plant on raised beds to improve soil drainage. Adding organic matter wil loosen heavy soils.

New leaves yellowish, veins green.	Chlorosis (lack of iron).	Add iron to soil as copperous or Geigy 138, following label directions. Lowering soil pH by adding sulphur will make naturally occurring iron in soil more available to plants.
Bottom leaves yellowish, plants lack vigor.	Low nitrogen.	Inoculate seed to encourage nitrogen "fixing" bacteria to develop. Side-dress with small amount of fertilizer containing nitrogen.
	Cold/wet soils.	Raised beds, liberal amounts of organic matter, avoiding overwatering and good weather will help.
Large vines but few blooms.	High temperatures/ long days.	Plant at right time to promote flowering and pod set.
	Excess soil moisture during early stages of growth.	Avoid overwatering. In high rainfall areas, avoid mulching too early in season.
	Excess fertility.	Avoid too much preplant fertilizer.
Plants drop their blooms, few pods.	Moisture stress.	Do not allow soil to get too dry when plants are blooming.
Seedlings twisted, leaves curled.	Thrips.	Control with malathion or diazinon.
Larvae in pods, seed.	Pea weevil or pea curculio.	Prevent by applications of Sevin during bloom.
Lower leaves discolored, slight webbing on lower surface.	Spider mites.	Control with Kelthane or sulphur.
Reddish spots on leaves.	Rust (fungus).	Control with sulphur or with a fungicide containing maneb.
Spots on leaves.	Fungus.	The fungicide maneb will control most leaf spotting fungi.
Plants wilt suddenly, die.	Fusarium wilt (fungus).	Resistant varieties and rotation are the only means of control.
Plants stunted, knots on roots.	Nematodes.	Use a nematicide for control prior to planting.
Plants quit producing.	Mature pods left on plants.	Harvest frequently, removing all usable pods.

SPINACH

Scientific Name: *Spinacia oleracea*
Family: *Chenopodiaceae*
Annual
Cool Season
Varieties: Melody, Hybrid 7, Iron Duke, Dixie Market, (spring) Bloomsdale Longstanding, America
Expected Harvest: 4 to 6 pounds per 10 feet of row

SPINACH

Would you believe the cartoon character, Popeye, and Texans have a lot in common? Well, it's true. They're famous for their association with spinach—Popeye for his love of it and Texans because the state produces so much of it. In fact, Texas produces most of the spinach consumed in the United States and almost half of the world's supply.

Crystal City, Texas, the "Spinach Capital of the World," is located about 100 miles southwest of San Antonio in Zavala County and the largest spinach canning plant in the United States is found there. Large commercial fields of spinach grown for canning and for fresh market distribution are scattered throughout the area. As you can imagine, the growing, processing and marketing of spinach is big business in and around this small South Texas community.

Just how Crystal City became the world's spinach capital is an interesting story, which actually began more than 2,000 years ago. Spinach originated in Iran where it was grown even before the birth of Christ. Its culture spread eastward to China and then into Europe during the 12th century. Just when spinach first was introduced into the New World is unknown, but it was commonly grown in the United States during the early 1800s.

By the late 1800s, spinach was well-known in Texas, and was grown primarily in very small acreages to be sold at local markets. It also was popular in home gardens. It grew extremely well and it wasn't long before our early vegetable farmers realized that spinach was ideally suited for commercial production in Texas. By the early 1900s, a relatively large amount of acreage devoted to spinach was located around the Austin area. In 1917, a small, 4-acre test plot was planted near Crystal City and it produced suprisingly high yields of good quality spinach. As a result, within just a few years, almost all the commercial production of spinach in Texas was centered in Zavala, Dimmit and Webb counties. The spinach grown in this area proved so superior that Crystal City soon became the center of most of the world's supply. It also became the home of spinach's most famous advocate, Popeye. A large statue of this spinach-eating cartoon hero stands prominently in Crystal City.

Even though history has shown that spinach is a natural for Texas gardens, its successful culture requires a reasonable amount of effort. Careful attention must be given to variety selection and time of planting. How you intend to use your spinach, for canning or fresh use, is an important factor in variety selection. Spinach comes in varieties that are flat- or smooth-leafed, semi-crinkled leafed (semi-savoy) or crinkled-leafed (savoy). Although these three types can be used interchangeably, the smooth-leaved types are best suited for canning and the savoy and semi-savoy types are best for fresh use.

Your choice of spinach varieties also should depend greatly upon time of planting. Spring crops of spinach are well-known for going to seed shortly after planting. This is due to the effect of temperature and day length on the developing plants. Warm temperatures and long days are conducive to bolting, or flowering, of spinach. When bolting occurs, the production of leaves ceases and an off-flavor, or bitterness, usually results.

Spinach is a cool-season crop and should be planted at a time to allow it to mature during cool or even cold conditions. However, in many areas of Texas, planting can and should occur not only in late summer and early fall but throughout the winter and even into early spring. For these late winter and early spring plantings, you must choose varieties that are resistant to bolting.

For fall planting, Melody, Iron Duke, Hybrid 7 and Dixie Market are excellent choices. For late winter and early spring plantings, use the bolt-resistant varieties, such as Bloomsdale Longstanding or America. All of these varieties are high yielding and, given good cultural care, will reward you with a bountiful harvest.

Soil Conditions And Preparation

Spinach will grow well on most Texas soils and there's nothing really unique about preparing your soil for planting, but there are two facts you do need to know. First, spinach is relatively shallow rooted, which will affect your fertilizing and watering practices. Second, spinach will not grow well on acid soils. Therefore, if you are gardening in an area of Texas where acid soils are common and you've had trouble in the past growing spinach (or beets), chances are your soil should be limed to raise its pH to near 6.5. Information on adjusting your soil's pH is found on page 394.

Regardless of your soil type, you should incorporate liberal

After planting, firm the soil over the seed furrow to ensure good contact between the soil and seeds. Later, about two weeks after thinning the seedlings, you should side-dress with a light application of nitrogen.

amounts of organic matter into it. Scatter 2 to 3 inches of decomposed grass clippings, hay or compost over the area to be planted in spinach. This organic matter will help loose, sandy soils hold moisture and nutrients, while loosening up tight, heavy soils. Like all vegetables, spinach will respond to the addition of barnyard manure, which should be applied at the rate of about ½ pound per square foot or 50 pounds per 35 feet of row. The manure will add nitrogen to the soil and serve as an additional source of organic matter.

Unless your soil is unusually fertile, your spinach will respond to the application of a small amount of commercial fertilizer. Evenly scatter about 1 pound of a complete fertilizer over each 100-square-foot area or for each 35-foot row. In East Texas and along upper the coastal areas, a fertilizer with a 1-2-2 ratio, such as 10-20-20, works well. In most other areas, a fertilizer with a 1-2-1 ratio, such as 10-20-10, is satisfactory.

If you've been using a complete fertilizer in your garden on a regular basis, you probably should use a fertilizer containing only nitrogen. About ½ pound of ammonium sulfate (21-0-0) or ⅓ pound of ammonium nitrate (33-0-0) per 100 square feet or for each 35 feet of row should be adequate. After adding all the necessary ingredients, including lime if it's needed, till or spade them into the soil to a depth of 8 to 10 inches. You should prepare your soil well in advance of the anticipated planting date.

Spinach is a popular garden crop, especially in Crystal City, Texas, where a statue of spinach's most famous fan, Popeye, stands.

It's a good idea to bed your soil prior to planting, especially if the soil is a little heavy and tends to stay wet for prolonged periods of time. Use your shovel or tiller with a bedder to form ridges and furrows that are about 36 inches apart from center to center. Use the flat side of a garden rake to smooth and shape the ridges into planting beds that measure about 16 to 20 inches across and 6 to 8 inches high. The remaining lower areas will be furrows to facilitate watering and provide drainage.

Now you're ready to plant, but as mentioned earlier, make absolutely certain the time is right. Spinach seed germinates very poorly in warm soils and may actually go dormant if temperatures exceed 77 degrees at the planting depth. To avoid a poor stand, make your first fall planting when soil temperatures are 75 degrees or below. Soil temperatures in this range will occur in most areas of Texas about eight to 10 weeks prior to the first anticipated fall frost. Additional plantings can be made until about six to eight weeks before temperatures are expected to drop to near 20 degrees, at which spinach is often damaged or even killed.

In the milder winter areas of Texas, planting can continue right through winter and into early spring. Keep in mind, however, the effect of high temperatures and long days on spinach. If your spinach is expected to mature during warm temperatures and long days, remember to use the bolt-resistant varieties, but even they will do poorly if planted too late. Therefore, you should stop planting about six weeks before daytime temperatures are expected to average above 75 degrees.

Plant Spinach From Seed

Spinach should always be directly seeded in your garden. Ideally, there should be sufficient moisture in your soil at planting time to result in germination and emergence of the seedlings without having to apply additional water. If your soil seems dry, water several days before planting. Applying water after planting, but before germination occurs, often causes seedling diseases and should be avoided if possible.

Gardeners often experience difficulty in obtaining a good stand of spinach, especially if they plant when soil temperatures are high. This problem can be overcome by placing the seed in a container filled with water and setting it in your refrigerator for 24 to 48 hours just prior to planting. The seed's absorption of the cold water will help initiate germination and avoid the possibility of seed dormancy being induced. The result will be improved germination and the rapid emergence of the spinach seedlings.

When planting, the seed can be scattered or broadcast over the top of the bed, or it can be planted in rows. Planting in rows usually is preferable, because weeds which might come up along with the spinach seedlings can be removed more easily. If your planting bed is about 20 inches wide, two, three or as many as four rows of spinach can be seeded across the top, leaving plenty of room for the plants to develop.

Use the edge of your hoe, a stick or your hand to make the seeding furrows. If the soil seems dry, apply water directly in the seed furrows and allow it to soak in before planting. Sow the seeds at the rate of about eight to 10 per foot of row and cover them about ½ inch deep. Next, use the flat side of your hoe to firm the soil over the newly planted seeds. Consolidating the soil particles will help conserve soil moisture and also result in good soil-seed contact, ensuring moisture transfer from the soil to the seed, which is necessary for germination.

Depending primarily upon soil temperature, the seedlings should be up in about seven to 10 days. About two weeks after emergence, thin the seedlings to a spacing of 4 to 6 inches apart. After removing the unwanted plants, water lightly to settle the soil around any plants that might have been disturbed during the thinning operation.

About two weeks after thinning, stimulate the growth of your spinach with a light application of nitrogen fertilizer. Use about ½ pound of ammonium sulfate or ⅓ pound of ammonium nitrate for each 35 feet of row. Band the fertilizer 4 to 6 inches to the side of the plants. If you use the multiple-row planting system and room permits, apply a portion of the fertilizer between the rows. If possible, lightly work the fertilizer into the soil and then water lightly.

As your crop of spinach grows, it's important that you maintain sufficient soil moisture to encourage good, vigorous growth of the plants. Remember that spinach has a rather shallow and limited root system, with most of the feeder roots in the top 8 to 10 inches of soil. You also should be aware of the fact that moisture stress during warm weather will encourage flowering or seedstalk formation. Therefore, regardless of the method used to apply the water, frequent applications may be desirable to maintain the soil in a slightly moist condition. Mulching around the plants with 2 to 3 inches of organic matter will help conserve soil moisture and control weeds.

Spinach is fairly cold-hardy and, when planted in late fall, often will overwinter in most areas of Texas. The possibility of this occurring will be greatly increased by applying a heavy layer of organic mulch around and over the plants prior to the onset of temperatures in the middle to lower 20s. When temperatures moderate, the layer of mulch can be pulled back and the spinach plants will resume their growth.

Insect And Disease Problems

Without a doubt, your spinach will serve as a delectable delight for numerous hungry insects and troublesome diseases. Aphids, or plant lice, are the number one insect problem but can be controlled easily if they're detected early. *Early* is the key word—one aphid today can become thousands next week. Malathion, applied when the aphids are first detected and still in small numbers, will give good control.

Various types of worms, including cabbage loopers, armyworms and a host of others, occasionally pose a threat to your crop of spinach. Fortunately, the biological insecticide *Bacillus thuringiensis* will give excellent control of these pests.

One of the most serious insect threats to your spinach does its damage beneath the soil surface. If while preparing the soil for planting, you unearth a number of hook-shaped, inch-long grubs with a dark posterior, you should treat the soil prior to planting with diazinon, according to the label directions. If present in large numbers and left

White rust (top) and bolting (bottom) are two problems to watch out for when growing spinach.

uncontrolled, these white grubs, or grubworms, can devastate your spinach planting overnight.

The most serious disease threats to your spinach are the foliage diseases, white rust and blue mold, along with the soilborne disease, fusarium wilt. White rust is identified easily by the formation of white, blister-like pustules which primarily occur on the lower leaf surface, along with development of a yellowish discoloration on the corresponding upper leaf surface. White rust is most commonly a problem during periods of cool, humid nights and mild days. Blue mold or downy mildew causes yellowish areas on the upper leaf surface, followed by the development of a grayish mold on the lower surface. Affected areas soon turn black and die. If left uncontrolled and if cool, moist weather conditions persist, your entire spinach crop will quickly become only a memory. Removal of infected leaves and early applications of a fungicide containing maneb, begun at first sign of disease symptoms, usually will result in good control of both white rust and blue mold.

Fusarium wilt is a soilborne fungus which can affect spinach at any stage of development and causes the plants to be stunted, turn yellow, wilt and often die. When the taproot of infected plants is cut diagonally with a sharp knife, the vascular system appears dark, due to the plugging action of the developing fungus. The only effective control of fusarium wilt is the use of a long-term rotation. Avoid planting spinach, beets or Swiss chard in the same area of your garden for at least three years.

Within approximately seven to 10 weeks after planting, depending upon variety and the weather, it's harvesttime. You'll note as temperatures cool, your spinach will take a little longer to fully mature and will grow more upright. Generally, spinach that matures when temperatures average between 50 and 60 degrees will be fuller-bodied and of higher quality.

Harvesting usually is done by either removing the older, outer leaves, often described as the cut-and-come-again method, or by pulling up the whole plant. A third method that works quite well is to harvest the foliage with a sharp knife, leaving the crown of the plant and roots in place so that a second crop can be produced by the same plant. A light application of fertilizer and water should follow this type of harvesting to encourage new leaf growth. This method is good for late summer and fall plantings, but should not be practiced for later plantings.

There you have it—a sure-fire way to grow spinach. With just a little cultural care, and within a short period of time, ole' "Popeye the Sailor Man" just might look right at home standing knee-deep in all your homegrown spinach.

Quick Problem Solver: Spinach

Problem	Causes	Solutions
Seed fail to germinate.	Soils too warm.	Do not plant spinach until soil temperature is 75 degrees or lower.
	Soils too cold.	Soil temperature should be about 45 degrees or germination will take 3 to 4 weeks and seed may rot in soil.
	Old seed.	Always use current season seed.
	Planted too deep.	Spinach seed should be planted about ½ inch deep, slightly deeper on sandy soils.
	Low soil moisture.	Soil should be moist enough at planting to ensure germination.

Seedlings die shortly after emergence.	Damping-off (fungus).	Always use treated seed. Plant when soil temperature is adequate and avoid excessively wet soils.
	Cutworms.	Check beneath soil near healthy plants. If worms found, treat with appropriate pesticide.
Plants grow slowly, lack good color.	Cold soils.	Plant at right time of year.
	Acid soils.	Add lime to raise pH of soil to above 6.5.
	Low fertility.	Side-dress plants with small amount of nitrogen fertilizer.
	Wet soils.	Plant on raised beds to improve soil drainage. Avoid overwatering.
Plants "stemmy," lack good body.	Too crowded.	Thin to 4 to 6 inches between plants to allow for full development of plants natural characteristics.
Leaves have off-flavor, bitter.	Plants about to bolt or flower.	Plant at right time of year.
Plants stunted, poorly developed leaves.	Aphids.	Treat foliage with malathion at first sign of small insects on underside of foliage.
Foliage develops white pustules on lower surface.	White rust (fungus).	At first sign of disease, treat foliage with fungicide containing maneb.
Grayish mold develops on underside of leaves, yellowish areas on upper leaf surface.	Blue mold (fungus).	Remove infected leaves and treat foliage with fungicide containing maneb.
Plants stunted, yellowish, often die.	Fusarium wilt (fungus).	Chemicals ineffective. Use long-term rotation—avoid planting beets, chard or spinach in same area for at least three years.
Holes in foliage, worms present.	Cabbage loopers.	Treat foliage with *Bacillus thuringiensis.*
Small holes in foliage, no worms present.	Flea beetles.	Treat foliage wih malathion.
Plants go to seed or flower prematurely.	High temperatures/ long days.	Plant at right time of year and use bolt-resistant varieties for planting in late winter, early spring.

SQUASH

Scientific Name: *Cucurbita sp.*
Family: *Cucurbitaceae*
Annual
Warm Season
Varieties:
- Summer Squash: (yellow) Dixie, Hyrific, Multipik; (green) Elite, Classic, Seneca Gourmet; (patty pan) Peter Pan, Green Tint
- Winter Squash: (acorn) Table King, Table Ace; (butternut) Waltham, Early Butternut

Expected Yield: Variable - 3 to 5 hills of any one variety per family of four should be sufficient

SQUASH

Squash is easy to grow, nutritious, low in calories and versatile. And what other vegetable can you grow in your garden that can be prepared and eaten in so many ways? Squash can be served raw in salads or with dips, fried, boiled, steamed, used in soups and casseroles, baked, or made into pies and breads. In addition, there are many varieties to choose from: yellow crookneck (and straightneck), zucchini, patty pan, cushaw, acorn, butternut, hubbard, spaghetti and turban, to name a few. Without a doubt, the squash is a real superstar of the vegetable world.

All the squashes are native to the Western Hemisphere and originated in the southwestern region of the United States (maybe even Texas) and Mexico. Archaeologists have discovered squash stems, fruit and seeds in ancient cliff dwellings dating as far back as 6000 B.C. They were very popular with the American Indians and the name *squash* is thought to have come from the Indian word *askutasquash*, which means "eaten raw or uncooked."

We don't know what the first squash was or what it looked like, but today there are so many different types and kinds that it's difficult just to categorize them. Most taxonomists put the squashes into three confusing and non-distinct species. For simplification, we'll classify squash into either summer or winter types, both of which can be grown either as bush or vining plants.

Summer squashes are eaten at an immature stage, when the seeds are not fully developed and the rind is still tender. The winter squashes are harvested and eaten when they are fully mature and their rind has hardened, making them suitable for storing. (Please note the winter types also can be grown in the spring and certainly are not cold-hardy, as their name seems to imply.)

Pollination Problems

The most common problem gardeners have with growing squash is a lack of pollen transfer. Without pollination, your squash plants can bloom profuse but never set any fruit.

All types and varieties of squash are monoecious, which means they all have separate male and female flowers on each plant. The female flower has a small, immature fruit directly behind the flower petals and the male flower does not. For fruit set to occur, pollen must be transferred from the male to the female flower. No pollen transfer means no squash for your dinner table.

Honeybees do an excellent job of pollinating, if there are enough of them and if no other factors interfere with their activity. Cloudy, wet weather or misuse of garden chemicals can keep the bees from doing their job. Sometimes, though, there simply aren't enough bees in the neighborhood, in which case you may consider bringing in a hive or two. But that may or may not make your neighbors happy, depending on whether or not they're gardeners. In any case, you can avoid killing or driving off the bees you do have. If you have to spray with pesticides, do so late in the afternoon when bee activity is at its lowest level.

As a last resort, you can solve your pollination problems by playing the role of the honeybee and doing the job yourself. Just how this is done is detailed on page 399. Before you play honeybee, however, make certain the problem of poor fruit set really is caused by lack of pollination. Check to see if some of the flowers are females. If all the flowers are male, which sometimes happens when the plants first begin to bloom, transferring the pollen is a waste of time and effort. Wait until the female flowers bloom; then, if fruit set fails to occur, it's time to hand pollinate. Female blooms are open and receptive to pollination for only one day, so you need to check your plants and pollinate them often.

Variety Selection

Several factors must be considered in deciding what kind of squash to plant, including how much space the plants require and how big your garden is. The bush-type squashes, such as the yellow straightneck, crookneck and zucchini, should be planted in rows at least 3 feet apart with an in-row spacing of 24 to 30 inches between plants. The vining types, such as acorn, butternut and hubbard, need much more space—an in-row spacing of 36 to 40 inches with the rows at least 6 to 8 feet apart. Give careful consideration to the amount of garden space needed to grow a particular type of squash, compared to its expected yields.

Squash does best on a loose, sandy-type soil, but can be grown successfully on almost any soil if it's well-drained and properly prepared. You should add a liberal amount of organic matter, which will help loose, droughty soils hold moisture and nutrients, while loosening up and

Depending on the type of soil you have, you can plant squash in raised beds or on flat ground. With either method, you need to be sure to measure between rows and provide adequate space for the plants to grow.

aerating heavy soils. Scatter 2 to 3 inches of well-decomposed leaves, grass clippings, hay or compost over the planting area. At the same time, add fertilizer to the soil. Squashes are heavy feeders and the addition of nutrients in the form of commercial fertilizer or barnyard fertilizer will boost the plants' productivity. Apply 50 to 75 pounds of barnyard fertilizer and 1 to 1½ pounds of commercial fertilizer per 100 square feet of area or for each 35-foot row. If you plant a vining type of squash that needs to be spaced further apart, use that same amount of fertilizer for each 15 feet of row. If your soil is sandy or already quite fertile, use the lower rates. If you're gardening in East Texas or along the upper coastal areas, use a fertilizer with a 1-2-2, ratio such as 10-20-20. In other areas, a 1-2-1 ratio, such as 10-20-10, is satisfactory. Prepare your soil several weeks in advance of planting.

Depending on what type of squash you plant, you may want to build raised beds. The vining squashes have a deep-growing, extensive and rapidly spreading root system and don't have to be planted in raised beds, unless your soil is heavy and poorly drained. The bush squashes have a moderately deep-growing, less massive, root system and it's wise to plant them on raised beds, especially if you have poor drainage.

To make raised beds, use your shovel or a tiller with a bedder to form ridges and furrows. The ridges should be at least 36 inches apart for bush types and 72 inches apart for the vining types, measured from the top of one ridge to the top of an adjacent one. Next, shape and smooth the ridges into beds measuring 16 to 20 inches wide and about 6 inches high. Next, tamp the beds firm. This will consolidate the soil particles, thereby ensuring good lateral movement of moisture within the beds. If you decide to plant flat, all you need to do is use your garden rake to smooth and level the planting area and remove any large clods, rocks or trash that might interfere with emergence of the seedlings.

Squash Sensitive To Weather

All the squashes are sensitive to low temperatures during all stages of growth and development. Do not plant in the spring until all danger of frost is past and the weather has started to warm. You will gain absolutely nothing by planting earlier; squash plants subjected to low temperatures may never recover and will remain stunted and nonproductive. Plant when the soil temperature is above 60 degrees and the daily maximum temperature is approaching 65. You can help the soil warm up more quickly and ensure vigorous early plant growth by using black plastic sheeting as a mulch. It will warm the soil, conserve moisture and help control weeds. Information on using black plastic as a mulch can be found on page 397.

For plantings later in the spring and summer, temperature is not a problem, since squash seeds germinate and the plants grow well when it's hot. However, if you're growing squash for a fall harvest, plant early enough for them to mature before it gets too cold. The onset of cool and cloudy weather will cause squash to grow slowly. Depending upon the type of squash you're growing, you may need to plant 120 to 140 days prior to the first killing frost.

At planting time, the soil should be moist enough to allow the seed to germinate and emerge without having to apply more water until after the seedlings appear. If your soil is dry, water several days in advance of planting. Also, if it's hot and dry at planting time, soak the seed in water before planting. This will decrease the time it takes for the seeds to sprout and emerge. Information on this procedure is given on page 403.

Garden squash usually is planted in hills, a horticultural term used to describe placing a number of seeds in one area or spot. Hill plant three or four seeds every 24 to 30 inches for the bush-type squashes and every 36 to 40 inches for the vining types. Depth of seeding should be 1½ to 2

There are many varieties of both summer and winter squashes. The summer types (top) include yellow squash, zucchini and patty pan. The winter types include hubbards, acorn and turbin.

inches, using the greater depth on lighter soils. If you use the black plastic as a mulch, simply cut a hole through the sheeting with a bulb planter or sharp knife and then plant.

If you're dryland gardening and soil moisture is short, which is common in midsummer in Texas, you may find it desirable to plant deeper so that the seeds are in moist soil—perhaps as deep as 2½ to 3 inches. If so, place the seeds fairly close together so that they can help each other push their way to the surface. If you garden in a heavy soil, after three or four days, scrape away some of the soil to allow for easier emergence. Make certain you do not injure the emerging seedlings while performing this task.

Depending upon soil temperature, your squash seedlings should be up within five to seven days. When the seedlings have two or three true leaves, thin each hill to one or two healthy, vigorous plants. Thin by pinching off the unwanted plants near ground level, rather than pulling them up, to avoid damaging the roots of the remaining plants.

After thinning your spring crop, mulch around the plants with 2 to 3 inches of organic matter (if you haven't used the black plastic). Avoid mulching too early or the soil will stay cool longer, causing the plants to grow slowly. When planting in middle to late summer for fall harvest, a thin layer of organic matter can be applied immediately after planting to help cool the soil and conserve moisture. As soon as the plants are up, additional mulch can be applied for increased insulation. Don't use black mulch for summer plantings because it will create conditions that are too hot for the squash to grow.

Squash can be grown by setting out transplants, rather than directly seeding in your garden, but its value is questionable. Setting out transplants in the spring hastens maturity by only three to five days. If you do use transplants, set them out at about the same time you normally plant seed. During high temperatures, transplanting offers little, if any, advantage because of the rapid germination, emergence and growth of the plants when they're direct seeded.

Depending upon what type of squash you're growing, the plants will begin to bloom about 35 to 60 days after planting. When the first blooms appear, side-dress them with nitrogen fertilizer. For the bush-types, apply the fertilizer about 14 to 18 inches from the plants or between rows. For the vining types, apply the fertilizer about 3 feet from the plants. If the vines have grown beyond this point, gently move them to apply the fertilizer.

For the bush types planted on rows 3 to 4 feet apart, use 1 cup of ammonium sulfate (21-0-0) or ⅔ cup of ammonium nitrate (33-0-0) for each 35-foot row, applying half the fertilizer to each side of the plants. If you're growing the vining types and your rows are 6 to 8 feet apart, apply this same amount of fertilizer for each 15-foot row. If you're only growing a few hills of squash, apply the fertilizer in a circle around the plants using 3 tablespoons of ammonium sulfate or 2 tablespoons of ammonium nitrate per hill. If you mulched with black plastic, apply the fertilizer at the edge of the sheeting for the bush types and at a 3-foot distance for the vining types. Lightly work the fertilizer into the surface of the soil and then water.

One tip that will help you when fertilizing and handling your squash vines is to train them during their early growth, which simply means moving and directing the vines to encourage them to remain in the space you have provided for them.

Unless Mother Nature is exceptionally generous, you'll need to water your squash plants during their growth and development. The best way to apply water is by furrow irrigation or by using a soaker hose or drip irrigation system. Every effort should be made to avoid wetting the foliage, which will encourage the development of foliage and fruit rot diseases. When watering, apply enough water on each occasion to wet the soil to a depth of at least 8 inches. Frequency of watering will depend on rainfall, soil type and size of the plants, but may be necessary as often as twice weekly during dry periods. Please note that it is normal for squash plants to wilt slightly on hot, dry days, but they should perk up by evening. If not, water thoroughly and look for insect or disease problems.

Harvesting Your Squash

The summer squashes should be harvested while their skin is tender and before the seeds become hard. Pick yellow straightneck or crookneck types when they're 4 to 6 inches long; scallop or patty pan when 2 to 4 inches in diameter; and the zucchini when 6 to 8 inches long. Squash will reach these sizes within only three to six days after the female bloom is pollinated. To keep the fruit from overmaturing on the plants, which greatly reduces yields, you should harvest every two or three days, especially during warm weather.

The winter squashes should not be harvested until the fruits are fully mature, which is when they are hard and their skin impervious to scratching with your thumbnail. Some of the winter squashes, such as the butternut and hubbard, will require four months from planting to maturity (60 to 80 days from bloom and pollination) with most of their fruit ready at the same time. If desirable, the mature fruit can be left in your garden after a frost has killed the plants to be harvested as needed. However, these squashes can be damaged by a hard freeze, so plan on gathering your crop if temperatures in the mid-20s are expected. Always harvest winter squashes with a sharp knife or clippers, leaving a short piece of stem attached to the fruit to help them keep longer.

For storing, brush the dirt off the fruit (do not wash) and place them single layer in a dry area where temperatures range between 50 and 65 degrees. Under these conditions, you'll be enjoying winter squash from your garden for four to six months.

Insects And Diseases

You won't have any squash to harvest, let alone store, if you fail to control the numerous different insects and diseases that are a common problem in Texas gardens.

Vine borers and squash bugs would be at the very top of every squash grower's "most unwanted list" of garden insects. If you've ever been proud of your squash plants one day, then they look a little wilted the next day and are dead the third day, you've experienced vine borers. The vine borer is the offspring of a colorful red-and-black, wasp-like moth that is attracted to the yellow squash flowers. The moth then lays her eggs on the leaves or stems of the plants. When they hatch, the small larvae bore into the stems of the plants, usually near ground level. As the larvae grow, their feeding literally destroys the tissue inside the stem and, of course, the plant dies. Once the larvae enter the stems, chemical control is ineffective. Slitting the stem with a sharp knife or razor and physically removing the borers is effective—if done soon enough and you don't have anything else to do! However, applications of Sevin or thiodan, if begun at first bloom, will provide effective control.

Squash bugs always seem to be a problem. These grayish, ½-inch-long, flat-backed bugs do their damage by sucking the plant juices from the leaves and stems. If uncontrolled, they will cause the plants to wilt and sometimes die. These pests are difficult to control, especially if fully mature adults occur in large numbers. However, if applications of thiodan are begun when the squash bugs are first detected, good control is possible. Destroying the clusters of bright red eggs that occur on the leaves also will help keep their population in check.

Several different diseases also can play havoc with your squash plants. Powdery mildew is a commonly occurring, warm-weather fungal disease that causes a white, talcum-like growth on the surface of the leaves. If uncontrolled, the fungus will spread quickly, causing the leaves to wither, turn brown and eventually die. Bravo, or a fungicide containing benomyl, applied at the first sign of white spots on the upper surface of the leaves, usually will result in good control.

Downy mildew is a cool weather problem that usually begins on the older leaves. Yellowish, irregularly shaped spots first appear on the upper leaf surfaces and often are accompanied by a purplish, downy growth on the corresponding lower surface. These spots can increase in size rapidly, causing the leaves and plants to die. The fungicide Bravo (chlorothalonil) applied early and continued at seven- to 10-day intervals as long as favorable conditions exist, will give satisfactory control.

Another common disease that attacks the immature squash fruit is choanephora fruit rot, which is favored by high moisture conditions. Symptoms of this fungal disease are shriveling and decay of the immature fruit, accompanied by the development of a bread mold-like, whiskery growth on the infected area. Control is best achieved by prevention: planting on raised beds to improve soil drainage; proper plant spacing to avoid crowded conditions; and good watering practices. Chemical control has not been proven to be effective.

Nematodes also are a serious threat to your squash, causing knots or swellings on the roots which inhibits their ability to take up water and nutrients. The plants then become stunted, yellowish and nonproductive. Information on the control of nematodes can be found on page 408.

How many times have you heard a gardener say: "I planted my squash and cucumbers too close together and they cross-pollinated causing my squash fruit to turn green?" Well, that just can't happen. Squash readily crosses with other squash, but will not cross-pollinate with cucumbers, cantaloupes or watermelons. What these gardeners have experienced is squash mosaic virus, a disease transmitted by insects. Squash mosaic virus causes yellow squash fruit to turn green or develop green spots over their surface, or it can cause green fruit to exhibit yellow coloration. In addition, virus-infected plants usually are stunted and often have mottled, distorted leaves. Chemical control is ineffective. Your best bet is to practice prevention by controlling insects and pulling up and discarding any plants exhibiting the above symptoms.

Powdery mildew (top left), mosaic virus (top right), vine borers (bottom left) and squash bugs (bottom right) are among the most destructive squash pests. All except mosaic virus can be controlled chemically. Your best bet to avoid the mosaic virus is to control insects, which carry it, and by pulling up any plants exhibiting symptoms.

Quick Problem Solver: Squash

Problem	Causes	Solutions
Seed fail to germinate, emerge.	Old seed.	Always use current-season seed and/or store seed in refrigerator.
	Cold soils.	Wait until soil temperature is at least 60 degrees before planting.
	Planted too deep.	Plant squash seed 1½ to 2 inches deep, using greater depth on loose, sandy soils.
	Low soil moisture.	Soil should be moist at seeding depth when planting. Water in advance of date of planting to supply soil moisture.
Seedlings lack vigor, grow slowly, lack good color.	Cold/wet soils.	Plant at right soil temperature (above) and use raised beds to improve soil drainage. Avoid overwatering.
	Low soil pH.	If pH of soil is below 5.5, lime should be added to soil to raise pH.
	Low fertility.	Side-dress plants with light application of nitrogen containing fertilizer.
	Low soil moisture.	If soil is dry, water thoroughly. Mulch around plants to conserve moisture.
Knots on roots, plants stunted.	Nematodes.	Control with appropriate nematicide.
Plants wilt slightly, recover in early morning.	Normal reaction to Texas heat.	
Plants wilt, fail to recover completely.	Low soil moisture.	Water thoroughly and use an organic mulch to conserve moisture.
	Nematodes.	Treat with nematicide.
	Vine borers.	White "grubs" in stems of plants near ground level. Control by using thiodan or Sevin, applied when plants first bloom.
	Squash bugs.	Flat-backed bugs in large numbers on plants. Control with thiodan as directed on label.

Plants bloom, fail to set fruit.	Male flowers only found on plants.	Normal occurrence when first flowers appear. Wait for occurrence of female flowers.
	Lack of pollination.	Pollinating honeybees not active for several reasons—cloudy, wet weather, misuse of pesticides, natural lack of honeybees. Play honeybee yourself—transfer pollen with swab or small brush.
Fruits shrivel, fail to enlarge.	Lack of pollination.	As above.
Fruits rot, "whiskers" develop on infected areas.	Fruit rot (fungus).	Chemical control is not effective. Plant on raised beds, avoid overcrowding and wetting foliage when watering.
Fruit multi-colored, leaves distorted, motled.	Squash mosiac (virus).	Control transmitting insects and remove plants showing typical symptoms to help prevent disease spread.
Talcum-like growth on leaves.	Powdery mildew (fungus).	Control with early treatment of chlorothalonil or benomyl.
Yellowish areas on older leaves, soon turn brown.	Downy mildew (fungus).	Control with applications of Bravo (chlorothalonil).
Fruits tough, seed hard.	Summer squash—overmature.	Harvest every 2 to 3 days to avoid fruits overmaturing on plants. Yields will be greatly decreased if fruits are left on plants to mature.
	Winter squash—normal.	Winter squash should not be harvested until skin hard and seed are mature.

SWEET CORN

Scientific Name: *Zea mays (saccharata)*
Family: *Gramineae*
Annual
Warm Season
Varieties: Sweet G90, Guardian, Florida Staysweet; (white) Silver Queen, Seneca Paleface
Expected Harvest: 1 to 2 ears per plant

SWEET CORN

There's no doubt that many Texans prefer field corn, or roasting ears, to sweet corn. It's also true that most of these good folks have never enjoyed fresh sweet corn picked at its peak of quality and cooked within hours, or even minutes, after being harvested.

Field corn cannot compare with high-quality, garden-fresh sweet corn. Yet, I'll certainly agree that low-quality sweet corn is objectionable, if not inedible. The herbalist, Gerard, in 1597 described corn as "of hard and evil digestion, a more convenient food for swine than man." If you didn't know better, you might suspect that he had just eaten some tasteless, chewy sweet corn like we all have eaten at some time. Of course, he was talking about the original, unimproved corn, or Indian maize, that Columbus found in the New World and took back to Spain. Various types of corn with sweet flavor originated in South America as a result of mutations from field corn thousands of years ago. Migrating tribes of Indians carried these sweet types northward, but they were not commonly grown or accepted, probably because of their relatively low yields and problems with storing. Sweet corn first gained prominence with the arrival of the white man in the New World and, according to most historians, Americans were first introduced to it in 1779 by Indians who lived along the Susquehanna River in Pennsylvania.

Today, even after tremendous advances and great improvements by plant breeders and horticulturists, Gerard still might have difficulty developing a taste for much of today's sweet corn, especially if he purchased it at a local grocery store. But, let's put the blame where the fault lies. The cause of poor flavor in most store-bought sweet corn is neither varietal, cultural nor, as some would have you believe, the result of the use of chemicals by farmers. Poor tasting sweet corn is due primarily to the corn's stage of maturity at harvest, the length of time it takes the ears to go from the field (or your garden) to your dinner table, and how they are handled in between.

Sweet corn is different from field corn because it has the ability to produce and retain sugar in its kernels. This ability is a genetic characteristic, as is sweet corn's tendency to send up suckers, or secondary shoots, from the base of the plant and to produce wrinkled seed when dried. However, another characteristic of sweet corn is that once it reaches its peak, it quickly begins to deteriorate, whether it is still on the plant, in transit or in storage.

Once an ear of sweet corn reaches its prime, especially during high temperatures, the sugar in the kernels is converted rapidly to starch. Studies have shown that significant losses in sugar content and, therefore, flavor can occur in just a matter of minutes, let alone the days or even weeks, it takes to get corn to market.

New, extra sweet varieties, modern post-harvest handling techniques and rapid transit systems have resulted in better quality sweet corn on the market today. Still, as every connoisseur of sweet corn will tell you, there's just no way that store-bought sweet corn can compare with garden-fresh sweet corn, enjoyed at its peak of quality and freshness.

Corn Deserves A Place In The Garden

Hopefully, you'll agree that you should try planting sweet corn, but you'll still need to learn how to grow it successfully. Gardeners in all areas of Texas experience considerable difficulty in producing high yields of good quality sweet corn. Comments like "little, undeveloped ears," "stunted, nonproductive stalks" and "all cob and no kernels" are commonly heard. But, you need not experience these or other disappointments—if you'll pay close attention to the following advice.

Sweet corn will grow best in a loamy type soil that has good drainage, but will do well in most Texas soils that have been well-prepared by adding organic matter and the proper amount of fertilizer. The soil pH should be between 6.0 and 7.0. If you garden in areas of East Texas where low pH soils are common, it may be necessary to raise your soil's pH by adding lime, as discussed on page 394.

Getting your garden soil ready for growing sweet corn is just as important, but not as demanding, as it is for most other vegetables. Sweet corn has a rather limited and shallow-growing root system and, as a result, deep tillage is not necessary but is desirable. Scatter 2 to 3 inches of well-decomposed organic matter, such as hay, leaves, grass clippings or compost, over the area designated for your corn patch, along with barnyard fertilizer at the rate of about ½ pound per square foot. Unless your soil is highly fertile, also scatter about 1 pound of a complete fertilizer

The best way to plant corn is in blocks, which will help ensure that adequate pollination will occur.

over each 100 square feet of area to be planted in corn. If you garden in East Texas or along the upper coastal areas, use a fertilizer with a ratio of 1-2-2, such as 10-20-20. For the rest of the state, a fertilizer with a 1-2-1 ratio, such as 10-20-10, generally is satisfactory. After applying the organic matter, barnyard manure, fertilizer and lime, if needed, spade or till the soil to a depth of 6 to 8 inches, thoroughly incorporating the added ingredients. For best results, prepare your soil several weeks before planting time.

Two Common Mistakes

Before we discuss planting, let's talk about a couple of mistakes commonly made by many gardeners: planting sweet corn in long rows and planting too early in the spring.

It's not uncommon to see one or two rows of sweet corn planted along the north side of a garden with the obvious intention of trying not to shade lower-growing vegetables. This is an excellent example of "doing good, but doing wrong." Planting tall crops on the north side of your garden will keep them from shading lower-growing crops, but if the corn is planted in a single row, pollination will be hindered, resulting in poorly filled ears.

Pollination occurs when pollen produced by the tassels (the male part of the plant) is transferred to the silks found protruding from the ends of the ears (the female part). In botanical terms, the silks are the styles of the female flowers, which are located on the cob. Each flower on the ear has its own silk. Therefore, for the ears to fill properly, a grain of pollen must land on each silk, germinate, grow down the silk and fertilize the ovary of the flower, which eventually becomes the kernel. Complete pollination and the resulting fertilization will result in well-filled ears. Since sweet corn is primarily wind-pollinated, the wind may blow the pollen away from the silks if you plant in just one or two long rows. Planting in blocks, though, will help ensure that sufficient pollen will be available from adjacent plants. This will help you avoid the problem of "all cob and no corn" come harvesttime.

The second common mistake made by Texas gardeners is planting too early in the spring. You should never plant sweet corn until the soil temperature at the seeding depth is above 50 degrees and all danger of frost has passed. If you use one of the new, extra sweet varieties, delay planting until the soil temperature is above 60 degrees. Cold soils delay germination and often cause the seed to rot, meaning you will have to re-plant. In addition, even if germination and emergence occurs, research has shown that planting in cold soils may not result in an earlier harvest, but can cause smaller, less productive plants, especially with the extra sweet varieties. A piece of excellent advice to follow when deciding when to plant corn comes from an old saying: "Plant your sweet corn when the leaves on oak leaves are as big as a mouse's ear."

To extend your harvest period, additional plantings can be made or make a single planting using varieties that mature at different times. Keep in mind that your sweet corn will mature more quickly at higher temperatures. The time between seeding and maturity of sweet corn may vary as much as two to three weeks, depending upon temperature. As a result, sweet corn planted several weeks apart may be ready for your dinner table at the same time. To avoid this possibility, make your subsequent plantings when the previously seeded plants are 10 to 12 inches tall, rather than by the calendar. However, be aware that your best quality sweet corn will result when you plant at a time which will allow maturity to occur when daytime temperatures average between 68 and 75 degrees.

For a fall crop of sweet corn, planting should occur early enough to allow for the corn to mature before freezing temperatures, usually about 80 to 90 days prior to the first anticipated killing frost. Regardless of when you plant, you should be aware that if daytime temperatures average much above 90 degrees during tasseling and silking, pollination may not occur due to pollen sterility caused by the heat.

When it's time to plant, the soil should be slightly moist to encourage good germination and emergence. If your soil is on the dry side, water several days in advance of the anticipated planting date.

Choosing A Planting Method

Several different types of planting systems commonly are used. Sweet corn can be planted on raised beds, on the "flat," or in furrows between slightly raised beds. The furrow system generally is preferable, as it provides the young seedlings with some protection from adverse weather and allows for ease in "dirting" the plants, which will be discussed shortly. Regardless of the system you use, your rows of sweet corn should be no closer than 30 inches apart.

Although sweet corn usually is directly seeded in the garden, it can be transplanted if the transplant is grown in some type of plantable container for setting out in your garden. Make sure to wait until the soil warms to above 50 degrees before setting out the plants.

When seeding, use three or four seed per foot of row and cover them to a depth of 1 to 1½ inches. Next, firm the soil over the seed with the flat side of your garden hoe to help conserve soil moisture and improve germination and emergence. The seedlings should emerge within seven to 10 days, again depending upon soil temperature. Once your stand is established, make absolutely sure that you thin the seedlings to 10 to 12 inches apart. Failure to provide adequate space between the plants will result in low yields at harvesttime.

During the next two to three weeks, make certain that the young sweet corn seedlings do not suffer from lack of water. Adequate soil moisture during this period will result in the development of a strong root system and vigorous plants. When the plants are about 12 inches tall, they should be dirted by covering the base of the plants with soil. Dirting the plants will help keep them from "lodging" or falling over when it's windy.

After dirting the plants, apply a sidedress application of nitrogen fertilizer. For each 35 feet of row, use about ½ cup of ammonium sulfate (21-0-0) or ⅓ cup of ammonium nitrate (33-0-0). Apply half the fertilizer to each side of the row 6 inches from the plants, lightly work it into the soil and water. When the plants are about half-grown, side-dress again as just described, using the same rates.

Downy mildew (left) and mosaic virus (top right) are foliage diseases that occasionally attack corn. The corn earworm (bottom right) is the most serious insect problem you'll encounter in growing corn. It can be controlled chemically with Sevin or organically with mineral oil.

As mentioned before, sweet corn has the genetic characteristic of producing suckers, or secondary shoots, from the base of the plants. Considerable controversy exists as to whether or not they should be removed. However, the answer is simple—don't waste your time removing them. These secondary shoots, if you provide an in-row spacing of at least 12 inches and 30 inches between rows, actually will carry on photosynthesis and benefit the main corn plant, resulting in higher yields of larger ears. As a bonus, they often will produce an edible, but usually smaller, ear for your enjoyment.

As your sweet corn plants grow, make absolutely certain that they do not suffer from lack of adequate soil moisture, especially during the period from tasseling to harvest. If moisture stress results during this critical time in the development of the ears, they often will be small and poorly filled. It may be necessary to water weekly or perhaps more often, especially during hot, dry periods.

Rolling of the leaves may occur during high temperatures and bright sunlight conditions, even though adequate moisture is available to the plants. During these conditions, the plants are simply transpiring, or losing water, through their leaves faster than they can absorb it through their roots. However, if the leaves remain rolled during the early morning hours, check the soil for adequate moisture and water if necessary. If the soil is fairly moist and the leaves remain rolled, other conditions may be the cause, such as excessive fertilizer, soilborne insects or diseases, or too much soil moisture.

Weed control is important if maximum yields and quality are your goal. Due to sweet corn's limited root system, weeds and grasses pose serious competition for soil moisture and nutrients. Remove young weeds and grasses by hand pulling. If cultivation is a must, work the soil no deeper than 1 inch to avoid damage to the corn roots. As with any vegetable, mulching around the corn plants will help control weeds and grasses and retain soil moisture.

Corn Earworms Are The Enemy

You'll be faced with several problems growing sweet corn in Texas, but none is more common and predictable than the corn earworm. Many gardeners are convinced that earworms come with the seed. The simple truth is they have a great affinity for sweet corn and will find your patch no matter where you garden in our great state.

The adult moth of the corn earworm initiates the problem by laying its eggs on the silks of the developing ears. The eggs hatch and the resulting larvae burrow into the tip of the ear and begin feeding on the kernels. With heavy infestations late in the season, the larvae may burrow directly into the side of the ears. Complete control is almost impossible. However, adequate control can be obtained by applying Sevin at the first indication of silk formation and repeating the applications every three days until the corn is mature. The treatments should be directed toward the ears to make certain that good coverage of the silks occurs.

If you prefer not to use pesticides and desire as little earworm damage as possible, a few drops of mineral oil applied to the silks of each ear will effectively prevent entry of the larvae into the ears. Apply the mineral oil when the silks first appear and repeat applications every three to four days until the ears are ready to be harvested.

Occasionally, other insects and various foliage diseases may become a problem during the season. Applications of a general purpose insecticide and/or fungicide usually will result in satisfactory control.

Sweet corn will be ready to harvest about 18 to 24 days after the silks first appear, depending upon the temperature as the ears mature. When your sweet corn is mature, the silks will become dark and dry. If you feel your corn is about ready, test a likely ear by opening the husk and pressing your thumbnail against a kernel. If gentle pressure causes a spurt of milky, white juice, it's ready for your dinner table.

Harvest your sweet corn by grasping the base of the ear and pulling downward with a twisting motion. This will cause the ear to snap from the stalk with no damage to the plant or tender ear.

Remember that sweet corn is best if harvested during the cool of the morning and consumed as soon as possible—the sooner the better. If you need to store some of your crop, put unhusked ears in a plastic bag and place them in the crisper of your refrigerator.

One last bit of advice to the cook. There's another reason for poor tasting sweet corn—overcooking! For corn-on-the-cob, bring the water to a rolling boil and drop in the ears. Bring the water back to a boil and cook the corn for only 3 to 4 minutes. Of course, your sweet corn also can be roasted in the oven or on the grill, steamed or used in a number of tasty dishes.

Quick Problem Solver: Sweet Corn

Problem	Causes	Solutions
Poor germination and emergence.	Old seed.	Always use current season seed.
	Planted too deep.	Plant seed at a depth of 1 to 1½ inches. Use greater depth on sandy soils.
	Low moisture.	Plant when soil has good subsoil moisture. Water is necessary to cause germination and emergence.
	Cold soils.	Never plant until soil is above 50 degrees. For extra sweet varieties, wait until soil temperature is over 60 degrees.
Plants yellow, stunted.	Cold soils.	As above.
	Low soil pH.	If soil pH is below 6.0, add lime.
	Low fertility.	Lightly fertilize plants with nitrogen.
Leaves ragged, have holes.	Armyworms, corn earworms.	Treat foliage with Sevin or *Bacillus thuringiensis*.

Plants small, stunted, unproductive.	Planted too early.	As above. Wait until soil temperature is above 50 degrees, 60 degrees for extra sweet varieties.
	Low soil moisture.	Maintain adequate soil moisture during early stage of plant growth.
Leaves "rolled."	Low moisture.	Check soil, water if necessary.
	Excess fertility (salts).	Avoid additional fertilizer. At next watering, apply additional water to help leach salts from soil.
	High temperatures, bright sunlight.	Normal reaction of corn plants.
Ears small.	Crowded growing conditions.	Thin plants to 10 to 12 inches between plants. Use 30 inch row spacing.
	Low soil moisture.	Maintain adequate soil moisture from tasseling to maturity.
	Low fertility.	Side-dress plants with nitrogen fertilizer.
Ears poorly filled.	Row rather than block planting.	Do not plant sweet corn in long rows, plant several shorter rows.
	Low fertility.	Side-dress plants with nitrogen fertilizer.
	Low soil moisture.	Maintain adequate soil moisture from tasseling to maturity.
	High temperatures.	Plant so that pollination and maturity will occur before average temperatures exceed 90 degrees.
Bi-colored kernels on ears.	Variety.	Some of the new varieties have yellow and white kernels.
	Cross-pollination.	White corn if pollinated by yellow corn will produce bicolored ears.
Worms in ears.	Corn earworms.	Treat with Sevin at first sign of silks and repeat at three-day intervals until corn is mature.
Poor flavor.	Overmature.	Corn will be mature about 18 to 24 days after silking. Harvest when kernels contain white, milky juice.
	High temperatures.	Plant so that maturity occurs when temperatures average 68 to 75 degrees.
	Storage length, conditions.	Use sweet corn as soon as possible after harvesting. If necessary, store for short periods in crisper in refrigerator.
	Overcooking.	Never overcook!

SWEET POTATO

Scientific Name: *Ipomoea batatas*
Family: *Convolvulaceae*
Perennial, grown as an annual
Warm Season
Varieties: Jewel, Centennial, Cordner
Expected Harvest: 2 to 3 pounds of roots per plant

SWEET POTATOES

Sweet potatoes are among the most challenging, rewarding and exciting vegetables to grow, especially at harvesttime. Digging for sweet potatoes is a lot like looking for buried treasure in your garden—you never know what you'll find.

Columbus discovered the sweet potato on one of his voyages to the West Indies and was so impressed with its taste that he gave some to Queen Isabella upon his return to Spain. Later explorers found sweet potatoes growing in much of Central and South America. Their culture soon spread to tropical, subtropical and warmer temperate areas throughout the world. Most historians think the sweet potato arrived in the United States after Columbus, as a result of trading between the early American settlers and West Indians.

Today, some confusion exists as to what is a sweet potato and what is a yam. Many supermarkets carry vegetables that are labeled both as yams and sweet potatoes, but the two appear to be exactly the same. Well, they are. There is a true yam but it's of African origin, is in no way related to the sweet potato, and is almost never sold at American markets. The confusion started when early slaves mistook the sweet potato for a yam because the two crops were grown and used in a similar manner. It wasn't long before sweet potatoes commonly were referred to as yams, especially in the South.

Our good neighbor state to the east, Louisiana, produces a large percentage of the sweet potatoes consumed in the United States. In an attempt to identify their sweet potatoes as superior and to increase demand for their crop, Louisiana sweet potato farmers decided a few years ago to trademark their sweet potatoes as "Louisiana Yams." The rest of us, though, grow plain old sweet potatoes.

Sweet potatoes can be grown in all areas of the state, but nearly all the commercial acreage is found in East Texas, for several reasons. First, that's where most of the good sweet potato soils are found and where the rainfall is adequate. And, most important, the sweet potato weevil is almost non-existant in East Texas.

Since the sweet potato is a root crop, the soil and how it's managed greatly influences the sweet potato's yield, shape and overall quality. Sweet potatoes can be grown successfully in a wide variety of soils if they're well-drained. They do best, however, on sandy loams. Poor, sandy soils have a tendency to produce low yields of smooth, high-quality roots, whereas rich, heavy soils produce high yields of rough, poor-quality roots. Poor or rich, soils having poor drainage will produce sweet potatoes that are misshapen, cracked and rough-skinned.

The ideal soil pH for sweet potatoes is between 5.5 and 6.5. If you're gardening in an area of Texas where acid soils are common and you have had trouble growing sweet potatoes in the past, consider having your soil pH tested. If it's below 5.5, lime should be added to bring the pH up to an acceptable level. Information on adjusting the pH of your soil can be found on page 394.

Preparing The Soil

Unlike most vegetable crops, sweet potatoes do not do better if high levels of organic matter are added to the soil. If you've been growing vegetables in your garden for a long time and have added organic matter on a regular basis, you probably don't need to add any more for sweet potatoes. They will do quite well in loose soils and are fairly drought tolerant once they're established. Sweet potatoes will grow in heavy soils if they're planted in high raised beds that provide adequate drainage. However, if you grow sweet potatoes on "new ground," working 1 to 2 inches of well-decomposed organic matter into the soil should be beneficial.

Two or three weeks before planting time, scatter lime, if needed, and a small amount of fertilizer over the planting area. Too much soil fertility will cause sweet potatoes to have small, stringy roots, rather than large, fleshy roots. That's the most common problem folks have with raising sweet potatoes.

The amount and type of preplant fertilizer you should use depends upon soil type, fertility and rainfall. If your soil is on the heavy side and fairly fertile, use about ½ pound of fertilizer with a 1-2-2 ratio, such as 10-20-20, for each 35-foot row. If the soil is sandy and poor, use about ¾ pound of the same fertilizer for each 35 feet. Apply the fertilizer in a 2-foot-wide band wherever you intend to plant sweet potatoes. Regardless of your soil type, use the higher amount of fertilizer if you garden in a high rainfall area or intend to irrigate your sweet potatoes. You can work the fertilizer, lime and organic matter into the soil at the same time, tilling it in to a depth of 8 to 10 inches.

Sweet potatoes will do best if planted on raised beds, especially if your soil is a little heavy. Use your shovel or a tiller with a bedder to form ridges and furrows, making the ridges at least 3 feet apart and 12 to 15 inches high. Use the flat side of your rake to form the ridges into rather peaked planting beds with a width across the top of 10 to 12 inches. Next, use your rake or something similar to tamp the beds firm. This will consolidate the soil particles, thereby aiding lateral movement of moisture within the beds. If you have a sandy-type soil, the finished beds should be about 8 inches high. For heavier soils, 10- to 12-inch-high beds are needed.

When your soil is ready for planting, the weather may not be. Sweet potatoes demand warm growing conditions and should not be set out until all possible chance of frosty weather has passed and the soil temperature 2 inches below the surface is at least 60 degrees. As soon as these conditions occur, you need to plant. Planting later will result in lower yields.

Planting sweet potatoes always refers to setting out slips, which are sprouts produced from mature sweet potato roots. An ideal slip is 8 to 10 inches tall, has at least five leaves, a stocky stem and a healthy root system. Good plants of the better varieties usually are available from several mail-order firms or from garden centers and nurseries. If, however, you do want to grow your own, a hotbed or cold frame is ideal for growing slips. About 40 days before the anticipated planting day, place disease- and insect-free sweet potato seed roots on their side in a bed of moist sand. Cover the roots with another 2 inches of moist sand. Maintain the temperature as close to 80 degrees as possible and water as needed to keep the sand moist. After the slips appear, add another inch or two of sand to produce a stronger root system. When the slips reach a height of 6 inches above the sand (total height of the slips will be 8 to 10 inches), they should be pulled up with a gentle twisting tug. For best results, the slips should be set out in your garden soon after they're pulled. A cool, cloudy, windless day or late afternoon is the ideal time for planting the slips.

Planting And Culture

When planting, use a trowel to make holes for the slips every 12 inches down the center of the beds. Set the slips deep, with at least three nodes (joints where leaves attach) below ground. Firm the slips in, leaving a depression around each one to hold moisture. Water thoroughly immediately after planting.

Within a few days, the slips should begin to grow vigorously. During the early growth of the plants, pull up any weeds or grasses that might compete with the sweet potato plants for nutrients and moisture. Soon, though, the dense foliage will cover the ground completely and effectively shade out any unwanted plants.

About four weeks after planting, side-dress the plants with the same amount and type of fertilizer you used prior to planting. Apply the fertilizer in a band to either side of the plants just at the base of the raised beds. Work the fertilizer into the surface of the soil and water lightly.

Once established, sweet potatoes are fairly tolerant of dry soils and often can make a decent crop with only naturally occurring rainfall. However, for maximum yields of quality roots, supplemental watering usually is necessary. Frequency of watering will vary with soil type, rainfall and the plants' stages of growth. The soil should be kept slightly moist, which may require you to water every five to seven days during dry spells. Wilting of sweet potato foliage during the heat of the day is common and is not necessarily a sign of dry soils. However, if the plants do not revive by

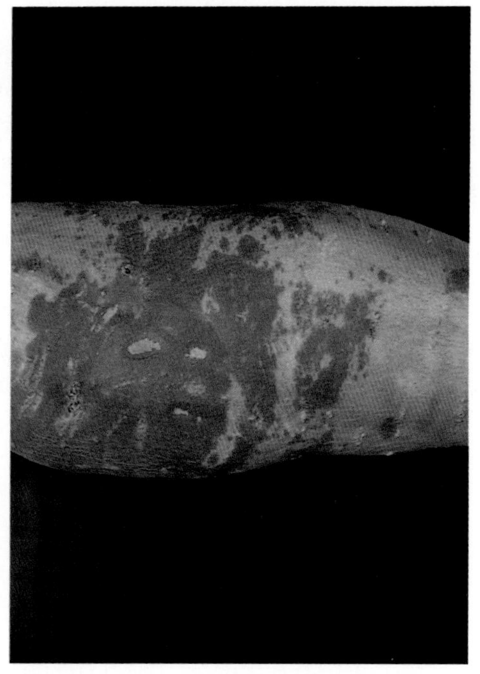

The sweet potato weevil will do serious damage to your crop. Scurf (right) is a disease that attacks sweet potato roots and is best controlled through good cultural practices.

early evening, you should water. Once the roots start to size, make an effort to avoid fluctuations in soil moisture or else cracking of the roots will occur. Overly wet soils also should be avoided or the result will be rough, misshapen roots at harvesttime. About a week before harvest is anticipated, allow the soil to dry to facilitate digging.

Mulching around the plants with a layer of well-decomposed organic matter will conserve soil moisture and help control weeds. It also offers another advantage when growing sweet potatoes: it will prevent the vines from rooting. As the vines extend outward and come in contact with moist soil, they will take root. If this is allowed to occur, they may also form sweet potatoes, which will reduce the size of the primary crop. If you don't mulch with organic matter, gently move the vines every seven to 10 days until the vines cover the beds to prevent secondary rooting.

About 110 days or so after planting, it's a good idea to check on the status of your crop of sweet potatoes. Sweet potatoes do not ripen or mature, rather they are ready when they reach a usable size. Carefully dig away the soil from around a couple of plants. If you find a number of good size roots, your sweet potatoes are ready for harvesting. Your crop of sweet potatoes can be left in the ground to continue sizing or until needed. However, you should dig up all potatoes before the soil temperature drops below 50 degrees to prevent chill injury to the roots.

Dig your crop when the soil is dry. A shovel is generally preferable over a spading fork for digging sweet poatotes, as it results in less damage to the tender roots. Gently lift the roots from the soil and place them in some type of container. While digging, separate out any roots that may have been damaged while harvesting and eat them first. After digging, handle your sweet potatoes like eggs. Do not wash or brush soil from the roots. Any damage to the tender skin most likely will cause the potatoes to decay while in storage. Next, spread your sweet potatoes out on newspaper in a protected area and allow them to dry for three to four hours. After drying, gently place the sweet potatoes in newspaper-lined containers and cure them in a warm and humid, but well-ventilated, area for about two weeks. In Texas our temperatures are such at harvesttime that you often can cure sweet potatoes satisfactorily by placing the containers in your garage and keeping them covered with wet burlap. After curing, store them in a place where temperatures are close to 55 degrees. Avoid temperatures below 50 degrees or chill injury to the sweet potatoes will occur, causing spoilage. When properly cured and stored, sweet potatoes will keep for about three months.

Insects And Diseases

Sweet potatoes are not bothered by a great number of insects and diseases, but those that are troublesome are real *humdingers*. By far, the most serious and devastating problem you'll face is the sweet potato weevil. Adult weevils are 1/4-inch long, reddish, ant-like beetles with dark heads. The adults seldom cause damage but their whitish larvae, or grubs, do extensive damage by tunneling through the roots and vines. Damage occurs both while the potatoes are in the garden and after they're harvested—if infested roots are placed in storage. Sweet potato weevils must be prevented culturally and by sanitary measures, rather than controlled chemically. Use only weevil-free slips (or seed potatoes) and weevil-resistant varieties, practice long-term rotations, destroy all residue from the crop immediately after harvest, and thoroughly clean the storage area. The insecticide Imidan can be used during slip production and to treat the sweet potatoes in storage. Consult the label for more specific information.

Parts of Texas, primarily in the northeast, are designated as "weevil free," although they are found there to a limited degree. If you garden outside this area, you are prohibited from transporting sweet potatoes into the free area in an effort to prevent the weevil population from increasing. Information on the status and boundaries of this area can be obtained from the Texas Department of Agriculture.

Nematodes cause sweet potato plants to become stunted and nonproductive. Heavy infestations will cause cracking and pitting of the roots, along with other surface blemishes. Control involves use of nematode-free slips (roots), resistant varieties, long-term rotations with non-susceptible vegetables such as onions and corn, and treating the soil. The soil fumigant Vapam, when used according to label directions, will result in good control of nematodes. (See page 408 for more information on nematode control.)

Diseases that attack the sweet potatoes' roots, including scruf, black rot and various types of soft rots are most common in Texas. Each of these diseases has its own particular characteristics but all have one thing in common—they rot sweet potatoes. Control is best achieved culturally by using disease-free slips, practicing long-term rotation, planting on well-drained soils or raised beds, following good watering practices, and curing and storing your sweet potatoes properly. In addition, if rotting has been a problem in the past, consider treating the slips with a fungicide before setting them out in your garden. Dipping the slips in a solution of Thiram or Mertek, according to label directions, just before planting will help prevent losses due to soilborne rots.

Quick Problem Solver: Sweet Potatoes

Problem	Causes	Solutions
Slips die shortly after setting out.	Damping-off (fungus).	Treat slips with fungicide dip before setting out. Avoid overly wet soils as well as cold soils.
	Cutworms.	Check soil at base of healthy plants for dark worms. If present, treat with appropriate insecticide.
	Dry soils.	Soil should be moist at planting time. Irrigate immediately after setting the slips out.
Plants sluggish, lack good color.	Cold soils.	Do not set out slips until soil temperature is above 60 degrees.
	Wet soils.	Plant on raised beds and avoid overwatering.
	Acid soils.	Sweet potatoes grow poorly if soil pH is below 5.5 Adjust pH by adding lime.
Plants lack vigor, grow slowly.	Low fertility.	Side-dress plants with small amount of fertilizer.
	Wet soils.	As above.
	Tight soils.	Add organic matter.
Roots stringy, lack good size.	Excess fertility.	Avoid overfertilizing at planting and when side-dressing. Plants produce vines rather than sweet potatoes.
	Secondary rooting.	Do not allow vines to root. Move the vines around during cultivating, etc. to avoid them rooting when they touch moist soil. Mulch with organic matter.
Roots rough, misshapen.	Tight, heavy soils.	Add organic matter to soil and plant on high raised beds.
	Excessive soil moisture.	Avoid overly wet soils, especially near maturity. Plant on raised beds.
Tunnels in roots, larvae present.	Sweet potato weevils.	Practice sanitation and use only weevil-free slips or seed roots. Use long-term rotations.
Roots cracked, surface pitted.	Nematodes.	Long term rotation and use of nematode-free slip will help. Soil can also be treated with a fumigant or nematicide.
Sweet potatoes rot in storage.	Improperly cured.	Cure in warm humid area for about 2 weeks. Consume any roots that show damage as the result of harvesting.
	Storage rot (fungi).	Use disease-free slips and practice good culture: raised beds, proper watering etc.

TOMATO

Scientific Name: *Lycopersicon esculentum*
Family: *Solanaceae*
Perennial, grown as an annual
Warm Season
Varieties: Bigset, Spring Giant, Celebrity, Jackpot, Floramerica, Better Boy; (canning) Chico, Roma; (cherry) Small Fry, Cherry Grande
Expected Harvest: 5 to 20 pounds per plant

TOMATOES

If Texans had to choose only one vegetable to grow in their gardens, without a doubt it would be the tomato, and the reason is quite simple. Once you've become accustomed to the great flavor of vine-ripened, home-grown tomatoes, those purchased at local grocery stores and supermarkets seem to be dull, tasteless imitations—at best!

Primarily for this single reason, the tomato is the most popular of all the garden vegetables. The most conservative of estimates indicate that tomatoes are grown in 92 percent of the home gardens in Texas. Even many of the good folks who refuse to call themselves gardeners have a tomato plant or two growing in a flower bed or in a container on their porch or patio.

However, popularity didn't come easy to the tomato—its road to the top has been long and difficult. The tomato originated along the slopes of the Andes mountains in South America. From there, migratory tribes of Indians took their *tomatl* with them as they moved northward. Early European explorers of this region discovered the curiously fruited plant and took it home with them. Settlers then brought the tomato to America, but we don't know when. Believe it or not, the first recorded instance of the tomato being grown in the United States was by Thomas Jefferson in 1781. However, there is no record of it being consumed until the early 1800s. Until that time, the tomato, which most Americans called the "love apple," was considered highly poisonous. It took the influence and popularity of the French cuisine of South Louisana to start the tomato on its way to becoming the most popular of all garden vegetables.

Today most Texans not only want to grow and eat their own tomatoes, they want to grow and eat as many as possible. Unfortunately, being popular doesn't mean "easy to grow." As most vegetable gardeners know, there are several obstacles to growing a really good crop of tomatoes in Texas. However, if you'll follow a little advice and adhere to proven cultural practices, your dreams of a bumper crop of delicious, vine-ripe tomatoes can become a reality.

Variety Selection Important

To have a chance at maximum yields of quality fruit, you must grow the right varieties! Using the right variety is vitally important when growing any vegetable in Texas, but absolutely imperative when growing tomatoes. Look high and low for transplants of the right varieties. Bigset, Spring Giant, Jackpot, Celebrity, Better Boy and Floramerica have consistently proven themselves as outstanding large-fruited varieties in all areas of our state. For canning varieties, you can't beat Chico and Roma. And don't fail to plant a few cherry tomatoes, such as Small Fry or Cherry Grande. If you haven't seen these "superstars" at your local nurseries and garden centers, complain to the managers. If it doesn't do any good, order seed and grow your own transplants as detailed on page 396. Whatever you do, get started on the right foot by growing the right varieties!

Notice the emphasis on transplants. Never seed tomatoes directly in your garden, and the reason is simple. For maximum fruit set and high yields, tomatoes must bloom before nighttime temperatures exceed 75 degrees and daytime temperatures reach above 92 degrees. In most areas of Texas, these temperatures occur fairly quickly after the last spring frost. If you plant seed in your garden when soil and air temperatures are favorable, your plants will bloom during unfavorable conditions. However, by setting out transplants, the plants will bloom at the right time, making fruit set and a large harvest possible.

These same environmental conditions also must be taken into account when planting tomatoes during middle to late summer for a fall harvest. Once our hot summertime temperatures drop into the favorable range, fruit set will occur. However, the first freeze often occurs about the time the first few tomatoes begin to ripen. Consequently, counting on a big harvest of ripe tomatoes in the fall is, at best, risky. But there are some ways, which we'll discuss later, to get around this problem.

Soil Preparation

To encourage vigorous plant growth and ensure the possibility of good yields, tomato transplants must be set out in a soil that has been well-prepared and properly fertilized. Regardless of your soil type, it can be improved by working in about 4 inches of compost, peat moss, grass clippings or any other suitable organic matter.

In addition, tomatoes respond extremely well to the addition of barnyard manure to the soil. Incorporating about 1 pound per square foot of area to be grown in tomatoes should be adequate. Generally, the manure alone will not supply all the nutrient needs of tomatoes. Therefore, the addition of commercial fertilizer usually proves beneficial come harvesttime.

If you garden in East Texas or along the upper coast, a fertilizer with a 1-2-2 ratio, such as 10-20-20, is satisfactory. In the other areas of the state, a fertilizer with a 1-2-1 ratio, such as 10-20-10 or 12-24-12, is adequate. Use 2 to 3 pounds per 100 square feet or 2 to 3 teaspoons per square foot of area to be planted in tomatoes. Use the lower rate if you incorporated barnyard manure or if your soil is on the sandy side.

You also should be concerned about the pH of your garden soil. Tomatoes grow poorly on soils having a pH lower than 6.0. If you garden in areas of Texas having acid soils, you should have your soil's pH checked. If it's too acid, add limestone, preferably dolomitic limestone, to raise the pH. Dolomitic limestone contains magnesium which oftentimes is available in insufficient amounts for tomatoes in most acid soils in Texas. Information on adjusting your soil's pH can be found on page 394.

After adding the organic matter, barnyard manure, dolomitic limestone (if needed) and fertilizer, till or spade them all into the soil 8 to 10 inches deep. Ideally, the job of preparing the soil should take place several weeks prior to transplanting.

Tomatoes don't like "wet feet," so unless your soil has a loose, friable texture, planting on raised beds to improve drainage is advisable. Use your tiller with a bedder or a shovel to form ridges and furrows that measure at least 3 to 4 feet apart, with the greater spacing being more desirable. Next, use your rake to form and shape the ridges into raised beds measuring about 20 inches wide and 6 to 8 inches tall. Use the flat side of your rake or something similar to tamp the beds firm to consolidate the soil particles, which will help water move laterally within the beds.

To encourage maximum plant growth, you should consider covering the beds with black plastic sheeting prior to transplanting in the spring. The black plastic will warm the soil, encouraging vigorous plant growth. This sheeting also will help conserve moisture and control weeds. Using black plastic as a mulch when setting out a fall crop is not recommended, due to the high temperatures that occur around and under the plastic during our hot Texas summers. However, a light colored plastic mulch that reflects the heat will work well. Information on using plastic sheeting as a mulch can be found on page 397.

Planting Time

Transplanting should occur as soon as possible in the spring, but hopefully after the last killing frost has occurred. However, do not delay setting out your plants. (Remember the concern about high temperatures during bloom.) If cold weather is predicted after you set the tomatoes out, protect them as shown on page 400. If the transplants are killed or damaged by the cold, replant as soon as possible. Do not try to salvage cold-damaged plants, as they seldom fully recover.

You also should be aware of the fact that tomatoes will shed their blooms if maximum daily temperatures remain below 55 degrees for very long. Obviously, this could be a problem if temperatures remain cool for an extended period of time in the spring. However, the benefit of early transplanting is still valid, because a greater number of blooms will still occur during favorable conditions. If early bloom drop, resulting from low temperatures is a problem, treat the blooms with a fruit-setting hormone that is available from most retail garden outlets.

Fall Crops

For a fall crop of tomatoes, set out transplants about 100 days before the first killing frost is likely to occur in your area. When setting out the plants, protection from high temperatures and dry soils is a must, as we'll discuss shortly.

The ideal tomato transplant should be dark green, about 6 to 8 inches tall, have six to eight true leaves and be about as wide as it is tall. It should not be excessively lush and tender, but it also should not have a "woody," tough stem. When purchasing transplants, carefully inspect the foliage and avoid those that show leaf burn or scorch, indicating some type of root problem or stressful growing conditions. Also, avoid transplants that have obvious spots or lesions on the leaves, indicating the presence of some type of disease.

Although tomato transplants usually are abundant in the spring, it's a good idea to start shopping early to make sure you can find the right varieties. If you find some a little too early to set out, take them home, plant them into larger containers and hold them until the proper planting time. However, avoid keeping them in the house or in any area that's too warm. Grow them outdoors but be ready to move them into a protected area if temperatures near freezing are predicted. As with all potted plants, be sure to water and fertilize lightly if needed.

When it's time to set out your transplants, the soil should be relatively moist, but not wet. If your garden soil is on the dry side, water

Tomatoes may well be the most popular garden vegetable in Texas and even people who don't have garden space often grow them in containers such as the whiskey barrel shown above. You also can grow tomatoes staked or in cages and can plant varieties that range in size from the small cherry tomatoes to the much larger varieties.

several days in advance of transplanting to supply the desirable soil moisture. Try to do the transplanting on a cloudy, overcast day or at least late in the afternoon. This is of special importance when setting out transplants for a fall crop.

Most tomato plants available for purchase, and probably those you grow at home, are grown in some type of plantable container, such as a peat pot or pellet. Peat, once it becomes dry, is very difficult to re-wet. As a result, the tomato roots will have a difficult time penetrating the peat and growing out into the soil. An excellent method of making absolutely certain the peat is thoroughly wet at planting time is to set the plants in a pan of water for a few minutes prior to transplanting. This easy technique will ensure thorough wetting of the peat, thereby encouraging early root growth and development.

Dig transplant holes two to three times wider than the plantable container, 3 to 4 inches deep and at least 3 feet apart. Apply about a cup of starter solution in each hole just prior to setting out the transplants. Starter solutions can be purchased at most retail outlets or a suitable one can be made by dissolving 2 level tablespoons of a complete garden fertilizer, such as 10-20-10, in one gallon of water. After applying the starter solution, allow it to soak into the soil before setting the plant in the hole. Set the transplant in the center of the hole and backfill with soil. Contrary to popular belief, deep planting is not always advantageous, especially on heavy soils in the spring. Heavy soils will remain cold longer and deep planting often will result in slow plant growth. If your soil is on the heavy side, the plantable container should be no deeper than about 2 inches beneath the soil surface. For transplants that are tall and leggy, lay them on their side instead of deep planting, again leaving the plantable container only a few inches beneath the soil surface. If your soil has a sandy nature, allowing good drainage and quick warming, deeper planting is satisfactory. After transplanting, firm the plants in, leaving a slight dish-shaped depression around each one to hold water.

If you're setting out plants that you've repotted into larger, nonplantable containers, handle them like eggs. Avoid disturbing or damaging the root system in any way. Dig a hole large enough to accommodate the root system, remove the plant from the container and set it just slightly deeper than it was growing in the larger pot. Handled right, chances are your first tomatoes will be harvested from these larger plants.

After transplanting, thoroughly water each plant. Allow the water to soak into the soil. About 30 minutes later, check to make sure the soil has not settled and exposed the top of the container to drying air. If this occurs, apply soil around the plant and water again.

It's a good idea to protect recently set-out tomato plants from excessive cold or heat by utilizing wooden shingles, plastic milk jugs, hotcaps, shade cloth or tomato cages wrapped with paper or plastic. Once the weather moderates or the plants become well-established, the protective devices should be removed. Information on protecting plants from elements can be found on page 400.

In the early stages of growth, especially if setting out plants for a fall crop, you'll need to water frequently until a strong root system is established. However, avoid keeping the ground puddled and soggy.

Caging Tomatoes

Shortly after planting you should decide if you intend to allow the plants to sprawl over the ground or provide support for them in some manner. It's an absolute certainty that yields and quality will be increased if the plants are grown upright, either staked, caged or utilizing some other

An excellent way to fertilize your tomato plants is with the Texas Pot Method. Simply place a pot between each tomato plant in the row. Put fertilizer in the pot and fill with water. Repeat several times until the soil is saturated.

Fertilize your tomato plants when they first begin to set fruit.

technique. Experience has proven without a doubt that growing your tomatoes in cages will result in greater yields of high quality fruit, while requiring a whole lot less work than any other method of providing support. Simply place a cage over each plant shortly after planting and wait for harvesttime! No pruning, suckering or tying is necessary. Additional information on using cages can be found on page 398. When setting out plants for a fall harvest, grow two plants in each cage. The result will be a larger number of early ripening fruit before the occurrence of the first killing freeze.

If you do not use the black plastic sheeting as a mulch, about three weeks after setting out the transplants is a good time to apply 3 to 4 inches of organic matter around the base of the plants. This will help conserve soil moisture and control weeds. Avoid applying the organic matter too soon in the spring or it will act as an insulator and keep the soil cool for a longer period of time. The result will be slow growth and delayed flowering

Water and mulch your tomato plants adequately to ensure a bountiful harvest.

which, as indicated earlier, will decrease yields greatly. For a fall crop, apply the organic matter immediately after transplanting.

For high yields, it will be absolutely necessary to fertilize the plants periodically during their growth. Once the plants start to set fruit, apply about 1 tablespoon of ammonium sulfate (21-0-0) or ⅔ tablespoon of ammonium nitrate (33-0-0) in a circle about 12 to 15 inches from each plant. After applying the fertilizer, lightly work it into the soil surface and then water thoroughly. Repeat this procedure every seven to 14 days.

The Texas Pot Method

If you're interested in the best crop ever, fertilize your tomato plants by what I call the "Texas Pot Method." After transplanting, bury a planting pot, coffee can, gallon milk jug or similar container midway between each plant (down the row). Make sure the lip of the container is aboveground and that there are sufficient holes in its bottom so that it will drain well. As soon as your plants set their first fruit, apply one level tablespoon of ammonium sulfate or ⅔ tablespoon of ammonium nitrate in each container and then fill it with water. Allow the water to drain and fill the container with water again. Keep adding water until the soil is saturated as indicated by the container remaining full of water. Depending upon soil type, you may need to fill the container with water several times. Fertilize as just described about once every seven days on loose, sandy type soils and every 10 days on heavier type soils.

What you're basically doing is nothing more than side-dressing the plants. However, rather than applying the fertilizer to the soil surface, working it in and then watering, you're dissolving the fertilizer in water and placing it 6 to 8 inches beneath the soil surface—where the roots are. This method of side-dressing tomatoes will maintain good fruit size and quality throughout the harvest season.

Watering Tomatoes Properly

One of the real secrets to successfully growing tomatoes is proper watering. Some of the most common problems you'll encounter when growing tomatoes in Texas, such as blossom-end rot and fruit cracking, are directly related to soil moisture.

Blossom-end rot causes the bottom of the fruit to turn black and shrivel. Although its cause can be related to calcium deficiency in the soil, it most commonly is associated with soil moisture, either too much or too little. As far as plants are concerned either one causes the same problems. If the soil is too wet or too dry, the plant is not able to absorb enough moisture through it's roots to compensate for that lost into the atmosphere through its leaves (transpiration). As a result, moisture is drawn from the fruit, causing the tissue at the bottom of the fruit to dessicate and turn dark. The result, blossom-end rot.

Fruit cracking occurs in two forms, concentric and radial. Concentric cracks circle the stem end of the fruit while radial cracks extend down the fruit, originating at the stem end. The tendency to crack is varietal, with some varieties much more prone to cracking than others. In general, varieties that produce large, flat fruit are more likely to crack than those that produce smaller, rounder fruit. However, regardless of variety, fluctuations in soil moisture will increase the frequency of fruit cracking. A sudden surge of water, applied by you or Mother Nature, when soil moisture is deficient can cause the fruit to swell, rupturing its skin and resulting in cracked fruit.

Losses from both blossom-end rot and fruit cracking can be lessened greatly by maintaining the soil in a uniformly moist condition, allowing it to neither get too dry or too wet. Mulching around the plants to conserve soil moisture, planting on raised beds to improve internal drainage and watering when needed will go a long way toward helping reduce both of these common occurrences.

By far the best method to water tomatoes is by using a drip or trickle system. Such a system uses a plastic tube or hose to apply a controlled amount of water, drip by drip, to the soil on a frequent and regular basis. Frequency of watering and length of application will vary with your soil type, plant size and the system used. In general, though, watering two to three hours every other day is sufficient. Follow the manufacturer's instructions for specific directions. For even more control of soil moisture, place the drip line beneath the black plastic mulch. The results—high yields of large fruit while conserving valuable water.

If you water your tomatoes more conventionally, such as by furrow irrigating or with a sprinkler, apply enough water each time to wet the soil to a depth of 6 to 8 inches. Apply the water before the top inch of soil becomes dry. If you use a sprinkler, water early enough in the day to allow the foliage to dry before nighttime or else diseases may become a problem.

Insects And Diseases

One thing you can count on when growing tomatoes in Texas is the occurrence of insects and diseases. By far the most troublesome "insect" is the spider mite, which really isn't an insect but a chigger-like spider. These almost microscopic pests are primarily a hot weather problem, but can become a serious problem anytime during the growth of tomatoes. They occur in large numbers on the underside of the leaves and suck the juices from the plants. The leaves develop yellowish spots on their upper surface that enlarge, reducing their ability to manufacture food for the plants. Severe infestations result in webbing on the leaf surfaces and, if the mites are not controlled, death of the plants. If you suspect a spider mite problem, shake the leaves over a piece of white paper and watch to see if any small "spots" fall on the paper and begin to move. If mites are present, treat immediately with Kelthane, applied three times at three- to four-day intervals. Multiple treatments will control the adult mites as well as those that hatch from eggs after the first application. Follow the label directions for the amount to apply and number of days from application to harvest.

A number of worms pose a threat to your tomato crop including tomato hornworms, fruitworms and cutworms. Hornworms are aptly named in that they possess a "horn" on their posterior. These ravenous feeders literally can strip tomato plants of their foliage overnight. Tomato fruitworms, which on sweet corn are called corn earworms, feed on foliage but do most of their damage by boring into the fruit. Fortunately, both of these pests can be controlled easily by applications of the biological insecticide *Bacillus thuringiensis*. Cutworms are nocturnal feeding and do their damage by cutting the plants off near ground level. Information on controlling cutworms can be found on page 404.

Unfortunately, pinworms are not easily controlled and are becoming more of a problem each year. Very small larvae of gnat-like insects, pinworms damage both the foliage and fruit of tomatoes. Pinworms often function much like leaf miners, boring between the leaf surfaces and rolling up the margins of the leaves over them, much like a cocoon. They also bore into the fruit, usually adjacent to the stem of the fruit. If uncontrolled, they can completely defoliate the plants and literally destroy any hopes of a bumper crop of tomatoes. Begin applications of diazinon or thiodan at the very first sign of a possible infestation of pinworms and remove any leaves showing symptoms of pinworms.

Aphids and leafminers are commonly a problem in Texas, but can be controlled easily if applications of malathion or diazinon are begun at the first sign of their presence.

Disease control begins with variety selection. If at all possible, grow only those tomato varieties that are listed as being VFN, which means they are resistant to verticillum wilt, fusarium wilt and nematodes. However, other diseases, such as early blight and southern blight, may still pose a serious threat to your tomatoes.

Early blight is by far the most common foliage disease of tomatoes. Symptoms include yellowing of the leaves of the plant from the bottom up. The infected leaves usually have dark, brown spots exhibiting "target spot" concentric rings. Early blight most commonly begins about the time the first tomatoes start to ripen and is especially likely to be a problem if wet weather occurs about this time. If uncontrolled, early blight can defoliate and eventually kill tomato plants. Spraying your plants with a combination of Benlate and Bravo, begun when your first fruit are about 50 percent their expected size and continued at seven- to 10-day intervals, will provide good protection and control of early blight. In addition, this combination of fungicides will control most of the other foliage diseases that commonly plague Texas grown tomatoes. Mix each of the fungicides according to its own label directions.

Occasionally, tomato plants just seem to wilt and die almost overnight. If upon examining the stem near the ground line, you find a brown rotted area covered with whitish cottony mold, the problem is southern blight. Southern blight is caused by a soilborne fungus and its development is enhanced by warm temperatures, high humidity and wet soils. Control is by prevention and includes rotation, proper watering

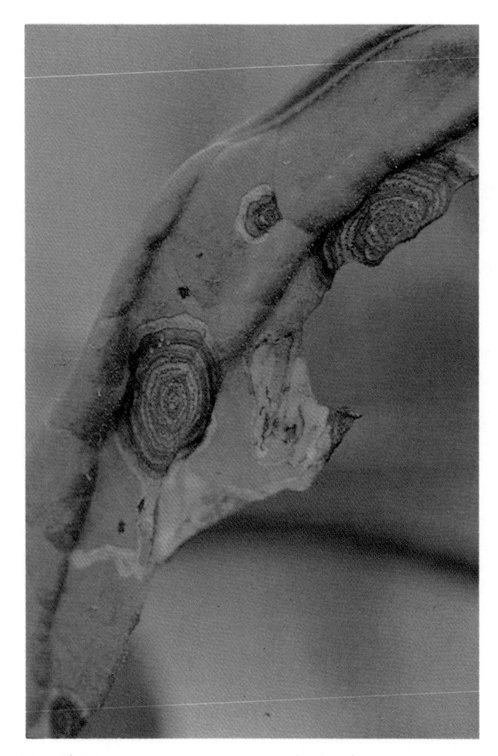

Early blight (left) and blossom-end rot (right) are two common threats to tomato crops in Texas and must be controlled.

practices and planting on raised beds for improved soil drainage. Plants exhibiting symptoms of southern blight should be removed from the garden and discarded in the trash, not composted!

Nematodes can still pose a threat to your tomato crop, even if you plant resistant varieties. They may be resistant but they're not immune! Information on controlling nematodes can be found on page 408.

Although not insects or diseases, birds certainly qualify as troublesome pests of tomatoes. And they wouldn't be such a bother if they would just go ahead and eat a tomato or two, rather than pecking holes in nearly every one that's ripe. Try hanging red Christmas tree balls on your tomato plants about seven to 10 days before you expect your fruit to begin ripening. The birds will be attracted to the "fake tomatoes" and will quickly determine that they are not at all edible. When your tomatoes start to ripen, most of your bird problems will be non-existant.

About 65 to 80 days after transplanting, the first ripe tomato should be ready for harvest. But don't take it in the house—eat it in the garden, right off the vine! You deserve the privilege and honor of enjoying the first of many delicious, vine-ripe tomatoes.

Quick Problem Solver: Tomatoes

Problem	Causes	Solutions
Transplants die shortly after setting out.	Cutworms.	Check for presence of worms beneath soil near healthy plant. If found, treat soil with appropriate insecticide.
	Damping-off (fungus).	Plant on raised beds for improved drainage. Avoid overwatering and mulching too early.
Plants grow slowly, lack vigor.	Cold soils.	Use black plastic as a mulch to help warm the soil. Avoid using organic mulches early in season and overwatering. Plant on raised beds.
	Low soil pH.	Add lime to raise the soil pH above 6.0. See page 394 for additional information.
	Low fertility.	Side-dress plants with light application of nitrogen fertilizer.
Blooms fail to set fruit.	Wrong variety.	Always use recommended tomato varieties.
	Cold temperatures.	Blooms will fail to set if temperatures remain below 55 degrees. Treat blooms with hormone.
	Insects.	Check blooms for presence of small, active insects (thrips). If present, treat entire plant with thiodan or malathion.
	High temperatures.	Plant early maturing varieties at the right time to encourage flowering during favorable temperatures. Tomatoes will shed their blooms if daytime temperatures exceed 92 degrees in combination with nighttime temperatures above 75 degrees.
	Minor element deficiency.	Treat foliage with foliar nutrient containing trace elements, such as iron, zinc and manganese.
Trails in leaves.	Leaf miners.	Treat foliage with diazinon or malathion.

Leaves exhibiting yellowish spots, mottling.	Spider mites.	Check underside of leaves for presence of microscopic mites. If found, treat with Kelthane multiple times.
Plants yellowing from bottom up, dark spots on leaves.	Early blight (fungus).	Treat foliage with both Benlate and Bravo at 7 to 10 day intervals.
Leaves curled, twisted; plants stunted.	Virus.	Remove infected plants and discard in trash. Chemical control ineffective.
Worms on foliage, in fruit.	Various worms.	Treat foliage with *Bacillus thuringiensis.*
Small larvae in fruit near stem end.	Pinworms.	Begin immediate applications of diazinon or thiodan.
Plants wilt suddenly, die.	Southern blight (fungus).	Discard plants. Rotation, water management and planting on raised beds will help prevent this soilborne disease.
Fruits crack around stem end.	Concentric or radial fruit cracks.	Plant on raised beds, mulch, water properly and avoid use of large, flat fruited varieties.
Bottom of fruits turn black.	Blossom-end-rot.	Plant on raised beds, avoid overwatering as well as allowing soil to become too dry. Remove affected fruit.
Fruits rough, "catfaced."	Cold temperatures during bloom.	Fruit that set when temperatures are below 55 degrees will often be mis-shapened, rough - but edible!
Large holes in fruit.	Bird damage. Hail damage.	See information on page 405. Be thankful it wasn't worse!
Whitish, water-soaked areas on fruit.	Sun scald.	Caging your plants will help prevent sun scald. Consider covering exposed fruit in some manner.

TURNIP/ RUTABAGA

Scientific Name:
(turnip) *Brassica rapa*
(rutabaga) *Brassica napus*
Family: *Cruciferae*
Biennial, grown as an annual
Cool Season
Varieties:
(turnip) Royal Globe, White Lady, All-Top
(rutabaga) American Purple Top
Expected Harvest: ¼ to 4 pounds per root; turnip greens, 4 to 10 pounds per 10 feet of row.

TURNIP/RUTABEGA

If you have difficulty distinguishing between turnips and rutabagas, you're not alone—most folks do! They're quite similar in appearance, so similar that the rutabaga seems like nothing more than a special type of turnip. Not true! Turnips and rutabagas are closely related, but distinctly different, species. Most turnips are white-fleshed and have rough, coarse, rather prickly leaves. Rutabagas generally have yellowish flesh and smooth, cabbage-like leaves.

Historically, the origin of the turnip can be traced back to before the time of the ancient Greeks, whereas the rutabaga dates back only to the 16th century. The rutabaga actually is believed to be a hybrid offspring of the turnip, probably the result of a genetic cross between the turnip and some type of cabbage. The turnip first was brought to America by Cartier in 1541. Just how or when rutabagas first were introduced is unknown, but they were being grown in the New World during the early 1800s. Their common name, Swedes, suggests they may have had a Scandinavian origin.

Not only are turnips and rutabagas similar in appearance, but cultural requirements are basically the same for both. Therefore, for ease of discussion—and since turnips are far more commonly grown in Texas than rutabagas—we'll concentrate on growing turnips, with reference given to rutabagas whenever appropriate.

The entire turnip plant can be eaten and most Texas gardeners raise turnips for both their enlarged roots and their tops. However, some folks raise them only for "greens" and there are several varieties of leaf turnips that don't form enlarged roots and are grown for their tops only. Therefore, when selecting varieties for your garden, be sure to select ones that meet your needs and taste. (Rutabaga tops generally are not eaten because they often are fibrous and, more importantly, because most connoisseurs of greens claim they have an off flavor.)

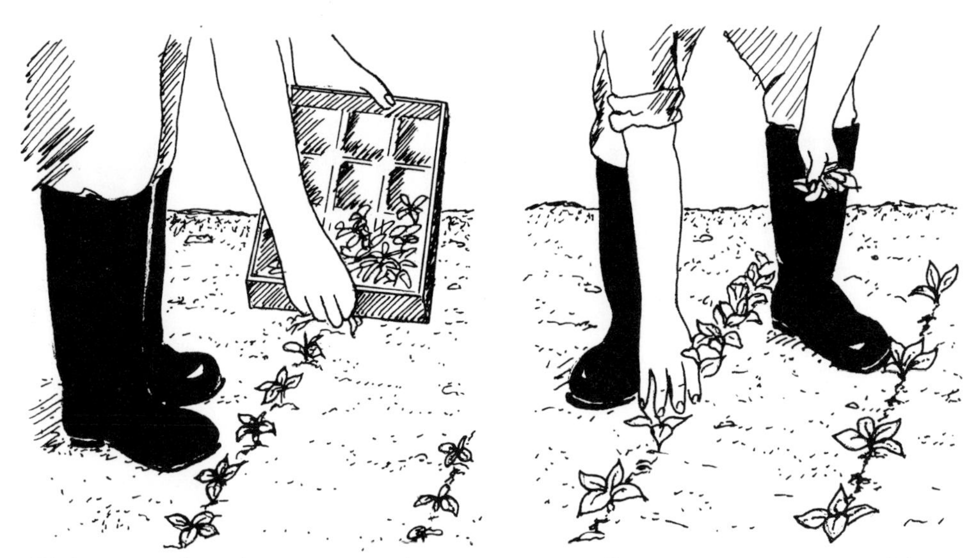

Within seven days after emergence, thin your turnip seedlings to an in-row spacing of about 2 inches. Thin again a little later to a final in-row spacing of 4 inches.

A Cool-Season Vegetable

Turnips are a cool-season vegetable and will grow best when temperatures range between 40 and 80 degrees. Therefore, for highest quality, begin planting as soon as the soil can be worked in the early spring and continue until about six weeks before maximum daytime temperatures are expected to exceed 80 degrees. (Rutabagas should not be planted in the spring except in the northernmost areas of Texas since they take about six weeks longer than turnips to mature and, consequently, would develop during unfavorably warm temperatures.) When maximum daytime temperatures fall below the magical 80 degrees, begin planting turnips (and rutabagas) again for fall and winter harvest. Although cold hardy, turnips can be damaged by temperatures below 20 degrees. To avoid the chance of injury, planting should cease in time to allow the plants to mature before temperatures get too low.

Obviously, in many areas of Texas planting can begin in late summer and continue right through winter and well into late spring. However, it's important to remember that turnips are biennials, meaning they normally take two years (one cold-induced dormancy) after planting to send up a seedstem or to flower. However, if planting occurs at a time to expose 4- to 6-week-old plants to prolonged temperatures of 45 degrees or below, dormancy will be induced. When the occurrence of warmer temperatures causes them to start growing again, your turnips will *think* they are into their second year of growth and flowering will occur.

Therefore, time your plantings to avoid exposing your plants to dormancy-inducing temperatures.

After deciding when to plant, you'll need to spend some time getting your soil ready. Turnips are not too particular about the soil they're grown in, but will do best on those that are loamy, well-drained and enriched with liberal amounts of organic matter. If your soil is on the heavy side, you'll find turnips can be grown and harvested somewhat later into the summer due to the soil's greater moisture-holding ability and tendency to stay cooler.

You should be concerned about your soil's pH, especially if you garden in an area of Texas where acid soils are common. Turnips will do very poorly on soils having a pH of 5.5 or lower. Therefore, if you've had problems growing turnips in the past and suspect your soil might be too acid, contact your local county Extension agent for information on having your soil tested. Additional information on adjusting the pH of your soil can be found on page 394.

Getting Your Soil Ready

When preparing your soil, spread 2 to 3 inches of well-decomposed leaves, grass clippings, hay or compost over the area to be planted and till or spade it into the soil. In addition, your turnips probably will respond to the application of some barnyard manure, but don't add too much. High levels of barnyard manure added to the soil just before planting may cause your turnips to develop rough, misshapen roots and should be avoided. Therefore, if you do add barnyard manure to your soil, it should be turned under several months prior to planting. Use well-aged manure at the rate of about ½ pound per square foot or 40 to 50 pounds per 35 feet of row.

The primary benefit of adding barnyard manure is soil improvement, although it also adds nitrogen that will help plant growth. Unless your soil already is fertile, you also should add commercial fertilizer to the soil. Depending upon your soil's fertility level and type, use about 1 to 2 pounds of a complete fertilizer per 100 square feet or per 35 feet of row. Use the lower amount if you used barnyard manure or if your soil is sandy. In East Texas and along the upper Gulf Coast, fertilizers with a 1-2-2 ratio, such as 10-20-20, work well. In most other areas, a fertilizer with a 1-2-1 ratio, like 10-20-10, is satisfactory. Scatter the fertilizer evenly over the area to be planted and work it into the soil 8 to 10 inches deep. All fertilizer, organic matter and lime, if needed, can be worked in at the same time.

Planting turnips on raised beds generally is a good idea, especially if your soil is on the heavy side and has less than ideal drainage. Use your

Your turnip plants should be spaced far enough apart to allow for proper development of the root.

shovel or tiller with a bedder to form ridges and furrows that measure at least 30 to 36 inches apart from the top of one ridge to the top of an adjacent ridge. Next, use your garden rake to form and smooth the ridges into raised beds, which should be 16 to 20 inches wide and about 6 inches high. The remaining lower areas will be furrows to facilitate watering and provide good drainage.

Due to the small size of the turnip seed, a well-pulverized and smooth planting bed is ideal. Rough, cloddy soils can easily result in the seed being planted too deeply. Use your garden rake to smooth and shape the planting area. Next, use the flat side of your rake to tamp the surface of the planting bed firm. This will consolidate the soil particles, which will help conserve moisture and aid the lateral movement of moisture within the planting beds.

When it's time to plant, your garden soil should be moist enough to initiate germination and emergence without having to water again until after the seedlings are up, which may take only three or four days. If your soil is on the dry side, water several days prior to the anticipated planting date.

Turnips can be planted in double rows on top of the beds, or the seeds can be broadcast over the bed surface. When planting in rows, use the edge of your hoe, a stick or your hand to make the seed furrows. The 16- to 20-inch-wide beds easily will accommodate two rows of turnips spaced about 10 to 12 inches apart. If you feel your soil is a little on the dry side, apply water directly in the seed furrow and allow it to soak in before seeding. Sow the seeds at the rate of about 10 to 12 seeds per foot of row (six to eight per foot for rutabagas) and cover about 1/4- to 1/2-inch deep. Use the deeper planting depth only if you have a loose, light-textured soil or when planting during hot, dry conditions.

If you opt to broadcast plant, scatter the seeds evenly over the bed and lightly rake the surface to help cover the seeds. Always rake down the row and not across or all the seedlings that emerge will be on the edges of the bed. If a number of seeds are still visible after raking, use soil from outside the bed to lightly cover them.

Whether you plant your turnips in rows or broadcast, use the flat side of your hoe to firm the soil over the seed. This will encourage water transfer from the soil to the seed and conserve the moisture in the seeding zone. If you're planting turnips during hot, dry conditions you can improve germination and emergence by scattering a thin layer of organic matter over the newly seeded area. This will help conserve valuable soil moisture and prevent the soil from crusting.

If the soil temperature at the seeding depth is between 60 and 100 degrees, and you haven't planted too deeply, the turnip seedlings should emerge from the soil in three to five days, sometimes more quickly! Under ideal conditions, turnips often will emerge within 24 hours after planting.

Once your stand of turnip seedlings is established, thinning usually is necessary. Within about seven days after emergence, thin the seedlings to about 2 inches apart. Remove the unwanted plants by gently pulling them from the soil. If you're growing turnips for greens only, additional thinning is not necessary. However, if you want to use both the greens and roots, thin the seedlings again about seven days later to a final in-row spacing of at least 4 inches apart. This will provide room for the enlarged root to develop. (The final in-row spacing for rutabagas should be 6 to 9 inches.) If you used the broadcast planting method, you need to thin the plants to 4 inches apart in all directions. Remember that turnip greens are edible at any stage and although the thinnings probably aren't large enough for cooking, they are great in salads. After thinning, water lightly to settle any disturbed soil around the remaining plants.

Protecting Your Plants

From this point on there are only two items you need to be concerned with: one, making certain adequate soil moisture is available to the plants; and two, protecting the plants from damaging insects and diseases.

To grow high quality turnips, it's important to maintain a rapid, unchecked state of growth. This can be achieved only if adequate soil moisture is available to the plants, especially when the plants are near maturity. Moisture stress during this time can cause the tops to be tough and pungent and the roots to be small, fibrous and misshapen. Therefore, during the last two to three weeks of growth, maintain the soil in a slightly moist condition. This may require watering weekly or more often, depending upon your soil type and Mother Nature. Apply enough water each time to wet the soil to a depth of at least 6 inches. By the same token, avoid over-watering because excessively wet soils can cause the roots and the foliage to deteriorate and rot.

Mulching around the plants, especially during hot, dry conditions, will help conserve valuable soil moisture, stabilize the soil temperature and help control weeds. After the final thinning, apply 1 to 2 inches of organic matter around the base of the plants.

Side-dressing with fertilizer generally is not necessary when raising turnips because they grow and mature so rapidly. However, if you plant one of the leaf varieties and plan to harvest by the cut-and-come-again method, apply a small amount of fertilizer after the first harvest to encourage foliage growth. Use ⅔ cup of ammonium sulfate (21-0-0) or ½ cup of ammonium nitrate (33-0-0) for each 35 feet of row. Regardless of whether you plant in rows or broadcast, apply the fertilizer in a band to each side of the row or bed of turnips about 6 inches from the plants, work it lightly into the soil and then water. (Since rutabagas take considerably longer to mature, they should be fertilized as just described about 50 to 60 days after planting.)

Insect and Disease Problems

As you might suspect, soilborne insects such as grubworms and wireworms can pose a serious threat to your hopes of a good crop of high quality turnips. If during soil preparation, you uncover numerous white, ½ to 1-inch long grubs with dark posteriors, or worms that are whitish to golden-colored, 1-inch long, slender and resemble a jointed wire, preventive control measures are needed. Diazinon, applied according to label directions, generally provides good control. Remember, if control

Turnips can be harvested by pulling up the entire plant or by the "cut-and-come-again" method.

measures are not taken prior to planting, it's too late come harvesttime.

Several foliage-feeding insects also frequently cause problems. Aphids, or plant lice, generally appear during cool weather and do their damage by sucking the plant's juices. Flea beetles, which get their name by their appearance and jumping ability, eat small holes in the leaves giving a "shotgun hole" look to the foliage. Malathion applied at the first sign of either of these pests will result in good control. Occasionally, cabbage loopers and various other types of foliage-feeding worms can be a problem, but are controlled easily by applications of *Bacillus thuringiensis* which is sold under numerous trade names including Dipel, Thuricide, Biological Worm Killer and others.

Turnip tops are often the target of foliage diseases, the most common being white rust and downy mildew. White rust often develops during warm, humid weather and is characterized by the appearance of white pustules on the lower leaf surfaces that usually develop in a circular pattern. The corresponding upper leaf surface commonly develops a yellowish color. Downy mildew prefers cool, wet weather to grow and develop, which it does very rapidly if uncontrolled. Symptoms are yellowish areas on the upper surface of the leaves followed by the

Turnips will become misshapen and of poor quality if you apply barnyard manure to the soil too close to planting time. It should be added well in advance to allow time for it to decompose properly.

development of a gray- to violet-colored downy fungal growth on the corresponding lower leaf surface. Affected areas turn black and die. Individual leaves or the entire turnip plant may become infected. Death of the plant is rapid if control measures are not taken. Both of these foliage diseases can be controlled effectively by applications of a fungicide containing zineb—if begun at the first sign of problems. If the diseases are severe and have spread throughout your turnip patch, control measures often prove ineffective.

Depending upon season, variety and what part of the plant you're harvesting, turnips will be ready for harvest in 30 to 60 days (75 to 100 days for rutabagas). The greens usually will have enough body and consistency for use about four to five weeks after planting, whereas the development of the root usually takes several weeks longer. Like the tops, turnip roots are edible when immature but often lack full flavor if harvested early. Many Texans claim turnips, both the tops and roots, develop a milder, sweeter flavor after the occurrence of frosty weather.

Harvesting can be accomplished by simply pulling up the entire plant and enjoying both the roots and the tops. However, if you're interested in tops only, you can use the cut-and-come-again method, which simply describes the technique of removing the older leaves as they mature and leaving the plant intact to continue producing more leaves. This technique also can be used if you're interested in some greens before the roots are ready to harvest. However, leaves must be present if you expect the roots to develop to their full-size, so don't harvest too many leaves.

Turnip roots should be harvested when they're 1½ to 2½ inches in diameter (5 to 7 inches for rutabagas) and while still sweet and tender. If allowed to overmature, they will become tough, fibrous and best suited for livestock consumption. Turnip roots can be stored for about two weeks by removing the tops, leaving about 1 inch of stem above the crown, putting them in moisture-proof plastic bags and placing them in the refrigerator. They can be waxed for long-term storage but since we can grow them most of the year in Texas, this practice generally is not worth the effort—unless you've got a real hankering for lots of turnips. (Since rutabagas require a longer cool season for growth and, consequently, will be less available from your garden, you might consider waxing some for long-term storage.) Turnip greens can be stored for about five days by putting them in moisture-proof plastic bags and placing them in your refrigerator.

Turnips can be eaten for either their tops or roots. If you want only the greens, you can plant varieties that don't form an enlarged root.

Quick Problem Solver: Turnip/Rutabagas

Problem	Causes	Solutions
Seedlings fail to emerge.	Old seed.	Always use current season seed.
	Planted too deep.	Never plant turnip seed deeper than ½ inch, ¼ inch on heavy soils.
	Dry soils.	Soil should be moist enough at planting to cause germination and emergence.
Seedlings die soon after emergence.	Damping-off (fungus).	Always use treated seed. Avoid overly wet soils, especially during cool weather.
Plants sluggish, have poor color.	Acid soils.	Add lime if soil pH is 5.5 or lower.
	Wet soils.	Avoid overwatering, plant on raised beds if gardening on heavy soils.
	Low fertility.	Side-dress with small amount of nitrogen fertilizer.
Leaves have "shothole" appearance.	Flea beetles.	Control with applications of malathion.
Small green to yellowish insects on leaves.	Aphids (plant lice).	Control with applications of malathion.
Plants spindly, weak.	Too crowded.	Thin seedlings to correct in-row spacing.
Roots fail to enlarge.	Wrong variety.	Be sure and use root forming variety if enlarged roots are desired.
	Too crowded.	Thin to proper in-row spacing.
Plants flower prematurely.	Dormancy induced by cold weather.	Plant at right time of year to avoid having plants exposed to temperatures below 45 degrees.
Roots cracked, misshapened.	High levels of barnyard manure.	If manure is used, it should be worked into the soil several months prior to planting.
	Low soil moisture.	Maintain adequate levels of soil moisture as roots near maturity.

Roots and tops bitter, tough, poorly developed.	Overmature.	Harvest at right stage of maturity.
	High temperatures.	Best quality will occur when growth occurs at temperatures between 40 and 80 degrees.
Whitish pustules on lower leaf surface.	White rust (fungus).	Control with early applications of a fungicide containing maneb.
Yellow spots on upper leaf surface followed by "downy" fungus growth on lower surface.	Downy mildew (fungus).	Occurs during cool, wet weather. Control with fungicide containing maneb.
Worms on foliage.	Cabbage loopers, etc.	Control with *Bacillus thuringiensis*.

WATERMELON
Scientific Name: *Citrullus vulgaris*
Family: *Cucurbitaecea*
Annual
Warm Season
Varieties: Charleston Gray, Royal Charleston, Jubilee, Royal Peacock, Royal Jubilee, Crimson Sweet
Expected Harvest: 2 to 5 melons per hill

WATERMELON

What could be better on a hot summer day than a slice of ice-cold watermelon? According to most Texans, not much! We eat and grow more watermelons than any other state in the nation. And, if Texas ever adopts a state vegetable, it surely will be the watermelon. Our summer picnics, cookouts, family outings and the Fourth of July just wouldn't be the same without a delicious, juicy, vine-ripened watermelon.

In some parts of the world, though, the watermelon is more than just a great-tasting dessert or snack. In Russia, watermelon juice is used to make beer and also is boiled down to a heavy syrup and used like molasses. In various parts of Asia, the seeds are roasted, salted and eaten like peanuts. In Iraq, Egypt and parts of Africa, watermelon is considered a staple for man, an animal feed and, in drier regions, a valuable source of water for both man and animal. And of course, right here in the United States, watermelon rind preserves are considered a real treat by lots of folks.

Man's culture of the watermelon dates back some 4,000 years to the ancient Egyptians. Historians first believed it was brought to Egypt from China, but later rejected the theory since wild forms of watermelon were never found growing anywhere in the Orient. The true origin of the watermelon remained a mystery until the 1850s when the great missionary and explorer, David Livingston, found large tracts of watermelons growing wild in Central Africa. Apparently, culture of the watermelon had spread from this region into North Africa, then to Asia Minor and eventually to the Far East and Europe.

African slaves and European colonists introduced the watermelon to the New World and the first record of watermelons growing in the United States was in Massachusetts in 1629. By the mid-1600s, Indians in Florida were growing them and Father Marquette, one of the first explorers of the interior of the United States, reported its culture along the

Mississippi in 1673. Due to its great taste and wide adaptability, the watermelon soon became an American favorite from coast to coast.

When Watermelons Are Ripe

The easiest way to start a discussion about watermelons is to begin at the end. The reason is simple—the most commonly asked question about watermelons is how to tell when they're ripe. If you purchase a watermelon at a supermarket, the question loses some of its significance. Someone has done the harvesting for you and chances are the melon you select will be ripe. However, as a gardener, this is a very important question, especially since most watermelon plants produce only two or three fruits. If you have a relatively small garden and grow only a couple of watermelon plants, you certainly don't want to waste any of the fruit by harvesting them too soon.

You need to check several factors to determine whether a watermelon is ready for harvest. First of all, the size of the melon should be consistent with those normally produced by plants of its variety. If the variety you're growing is supposed to produce fruits weighing about 25 to 30 pounds, your melon should be approximately that size. However, just because it's the right size doesn't necessarily mean the melon's ripe. The second characteristic to check is the ground spot, or area of the melon that has been in contact with the ground. It should be a dull, creamy-yellowish color—perhaps even rough in appearance and to the touch. Third, check the tendril, or tail, on the stem nearest to where it is attached to the fruit. It should be dried and withered if the fruit is near full maturity. Fourth, to make your grandmother and all the other "thumpers" happy, thump the melon. An immature watermelon when thumped produces a ringing, sharp sound whereas a ripe one produces a hollow, dull sound. If the watermelon in question passes the first three tests and also thumps good, chances are excellent it's nice and ripe.

Now that you can tell when to harvest a garden-grown watermelon, let's outline the steps you'll need to take to ensure yourself of having something to harvest. First, make certain you have sufficient room in the garden to grow watermelons. One of the major problems in raising watermelons in a home garden is caused by not providing the plants with adequate room to encourage vigorous vine growth. A single hill of watermelons requires a minimum of 24 square feet of space to produce a satisfactory crop of fruit. Even the new bush varieties require at least 18 square feet. So, if your garden space is limited, devote your time and effort to growing other, less space-demanding vegetables.

Soil Requirements And Preparation

When growing watermelons, it's important to remember that all cucurbits have extensive root systems, but none more massive or deep growing than the watermelon. Given the opportunity, the roots of a watermelon plant may grow several inches each day, extend out as far as the vines grow and can be found at a depth of 4 or more feet beneath the soil surface. Consequently, watermelons will do best when grown on deep, loose soil, but they can be grown satisfactorily on most soils—if they are well-prepared. Obviously, a tight, compacted, heavy soil will restrict root growth and development. The results will be expressed above ground as poor plant growth, delayed maturity, increased susceptibility to disease and problems related to moisture stress, such as small, misshapen, poor quality fruit.

Watermelons are more tolerant of acid soils than most cucurbits and will grow well on soils having a pH as low as 5.5. However, if you garden in an area of Texas where extremely acid soils are common, you should have your soil tested to determine if lime should be added to raise its pH. For information on adjusting the pH of your soil, see page 394.

Get your garden soil ready several weeks prior to planting by working it at least 8 to 10 inches deep—the deeper, the better. If your soil is on the heavy side, 2 to 3 inches of organic matter, such as well-rotted

Does anything taste better than a slice of cold watermelon on a hot day? And the best ones are the ones you grow yourself.

leaves, grass clippings or compost, worked into the planting area will do wonders. The organic matter helps loosen the soil and provides better drainage and aeration, thereby encouraging the development of an extensive root system. If your soil has a tendency to be droughty, organic matter will help it hold moisture and nutrients, which is a definite plus during dry periods.

When you work the organic matter into the soil, you also should add a small amount of fertilizer, preferably both barnyard manure and commercial fertilizer. Be careful, though, not to over-fertilize watermelons. Doing so can cause an internal fruit disorder called white heart. Generally, about 1/4 pound of well-rotted barnyard manure, along with 1 teaspoon of a complete fertilizer, such as 10-20-10, evenly distributed over each square foot of area will be adequate for growing watermelons. For you folks with larger watermelon plantings, this figures out to be about 250 pounds of barnyard manure and 10 pounds of commercial fertilizer per 1,000 square feet of area. If your soil already is fertile, use only the barnyard manure—or perhaps none at all. (Additional fertilizer will be applied during the growth cycle.) Till or spade the soil thoroughly, incorporating all the added ingredients.

Some garden publications recommend preparing and fertilizing a 2- to 4-square-foot area and planting watermelons in its center. This may work in other states, but unless you have ideal soil conditions, this practice is not recommended for Texas. As previously pointed out, watermelons have an extensive, spreading root system. Consequently, their feeder roots will grow so rapidly and vigorously that they will extend well beyond the small prepared area within only three to four weeks after planting. Therefore, it's far better to work up and fertilize the entire area that the plant's roots are expected to occupy.

The watermelon is obviously a warm weather vegetable. Ideally, your first planting in the spring should occur after all danger of frost has passed and the soil temperature at the seeding depth is at least 70 degrees. Additional plantings can be made up until about four months prior to your first anticipated frost. However, plantings made during late summer or early fall generally prove disappointing because watermelons that mature when average daily temperatures are below 70 degrees often have a low sugar content and lack good flavor.

Early warming of the soil will result by using black plastic sheeting as a mulch and by seeding or transplanting through it. In addition to warming the soil, the plastic will conserve soil moisture and help control weeds. Additional information on mulching with black plastic can be found on page 397.

You can tell if a watermelon is ripe when the ground spot is a creamy color and the tendril or tail nearest the fruit is dry and withered.

Since watermelons have an extensive root system, you don't need to plant on raised beds unless your soil is extremely heavy and has poor drainage. Therefore, when it's time to plant, all you have to do is rake the soil smooth and level the area. Garden-grown watermelons usually are planted in hills, or groups of seeds, spaced 4 feet apart in rows that are at least 6 feet apart. An even wider spacing is more desirable if space is available. Use a trowel, hoe or your hand to dig holes at the desired spacing. If you're seeding through black plastic, use a bulb planter, sharp knife or razor blade to cut holes in the plastic at the desired spacing. Drop three or four seeds in each hole and cover them ¾ to 1 inch deep, using the greater depth on lighter soils. Lightly firm the soil over the seeds to consolidate the soil particles, thereby conserving moisture and ensuring good contact between the soil and seed. With ideal soil temperatures and sufficient moisture, the watermelon seedlings should emerge in about seven days.

Within two weeks after emergence, thin each hill to two of the stronger, more vigorous plants. Pinch the unwanted plants off near ground level rather than pull them up to avoid disturbing the roots of the remaining plants. Make certain you thin the seedlings—if it's necessary. As mentioned ealier, there is a tendency to provide insufficient space for garden-grown watermelon plants. Avoid crowded conditions, which will cause the plants to compete with each other for nutrients, moisture and sunlight. Also, excessive foliage, caused by overcrowding, will cause pollination problems.

If you set out transplants instead of planting seeds, you can harvest watermelons about 10 days earlier. However, good, healthy transplants of the right varieties often are impossible to purchase, especially at the right time for setting out. If you're interested in growing your own transplants, see page 396. The ideal watermelon transplant for setting out should be about 3 weeks old, have one or two true leaves and should be growing in some type of plantable container, such as a peat pot or pellet. Dig holes 2 to 3 inches wide and just deep enough so that after planting the peat pots or pellets will be just below the soil surface. Place one or two plants in the center of each hole and backfill with garden soil. Firm the soil around the plants, leaving a slight dish-shaped depression to hold water and water immediately.

When transplanting through black plastic, use exactly the same procedure as just described. However, make sure the tender stems of the watermelon plants are not touching the plastic sheeting, which can damage or actually cut through the tender stems as the plants are moved back and forth by the wind.

There's always a temptation to plant early and use gallon milk cartons, hotcaps, row covers or something similar to protect the plants from frosty weather. However, watermelons dislike "cold feet" and research has shown that little, if any, benefit is derived from planting early and then providing protection from unfavorable weather—unless the soil is also sufficiently warm. Devices to protect plants, in combination with black plastic mulch, will result in environmental conditions that are conducive to early seeding or transplanting.

If you're interested in planting early, apply the black plastic two to three weeks prior to the frost-free date for your area of Texas. Wait about 10 days, depending upon the weather, before planting. This will allow the sun to warm the black plastic and the underlying soil. Immediately after planting, place hotcaps, milk cartons or another covering over the transplants or the newly planted seeds. The warm soil and air temperatures, aided by the black plastic mulch and protective covers, will cause rapid germination and healthy, vigorous plant growth. You should remove the protective coverings when night temperatures average above 60 degrees for five consecutive nights or, if necessary, when the plants need more room for growth.

When the plants start to vine, apply a sidedress application of nitrogen fertilizer. Use 2 tablespoons of ammonium nitrate (33-0-0) or 3 tablespoons of ammonium sulfate (21-0-0) per hill. Apply the fertilizer in a circle around the plants or in a band on either side about 15 to 18 inches from the plants. Work the fertilizer very lightly into the soil and water. If you haven't used the black plastic as a mulch, apply an organic mulch around the plants after fertilizing to conserve moisture and help control weeds.

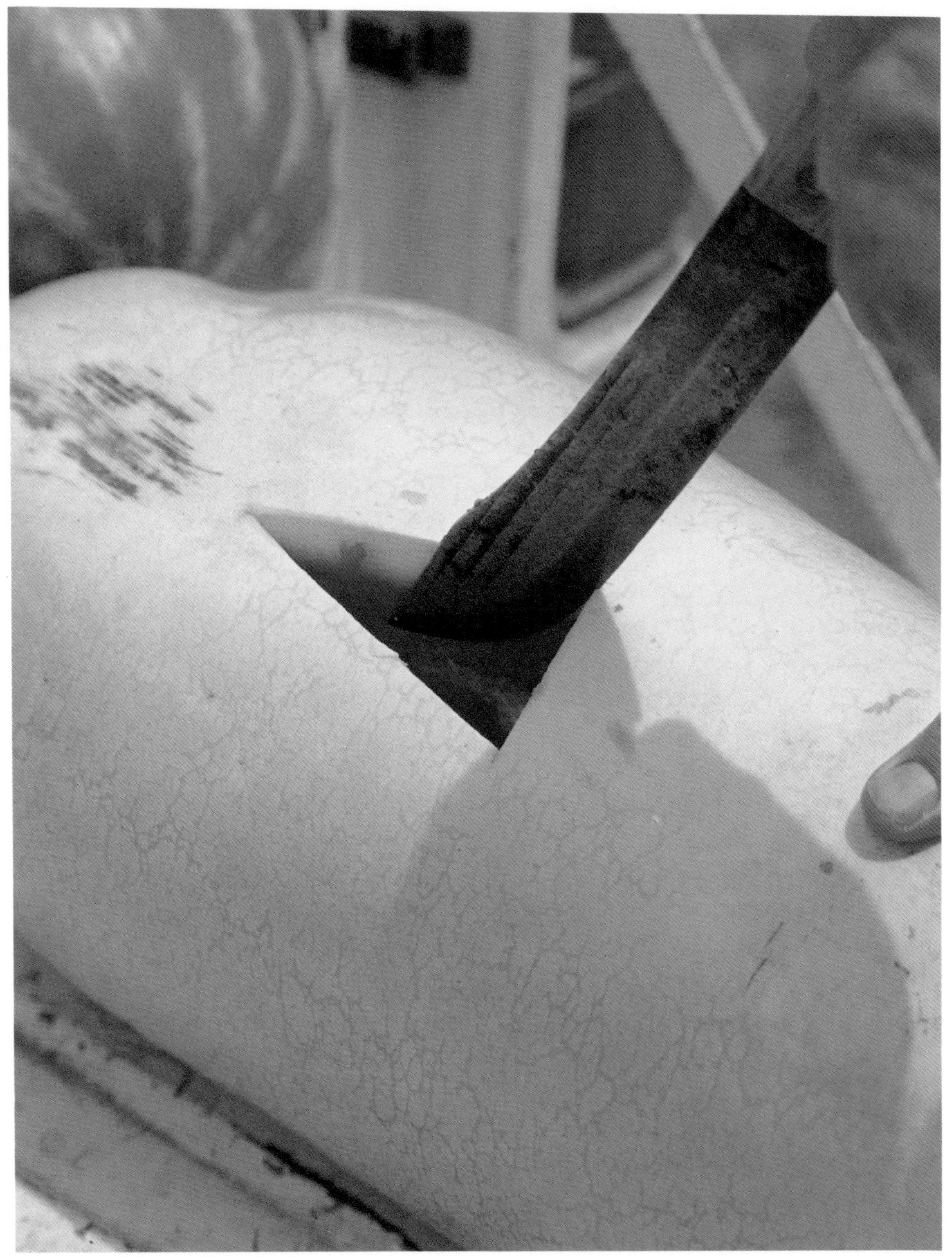

Many gardeners think the only sure way to tell if a melon is ripe is to "plug" it.

If growing watermelons on black plastic, the fertilizer should be applied at the edge of the plastic. Due to the vigorous growth of the roots, it will be only a short time before the plants benefit from the fertilizer. Unless the plants appear sluggish, additional side-dressings should not be needed.

Once daytime temperatures average above 70 degrees, you'll be amazed at how fast those small seedlings turn into large plants. If you have limited garden space, you will need to train the plants by positioning the vines so they grow down rather than across the rows. Due to the possibility of spreading diseases, avoid handling the vines when the foliage is wet.

Adequate Pollination A Must

Within about eight to 10 weeks after seeding or transplanting, your watermelon plants will begin to bloom and, hopefully, set fruit. Oftentimes, however, garden-grown watermelons fail to set fruit and the most common cause is lack of pollination. It's important to remember that watermelons, like the other cucurbits, produce both male and female flowers on the same plant. For fruit set to occur, pollen must be transferred from the male to the female flower. If you're not familiar with cucurbits, the female flowers are the ones with the small, immature fruit directly behind the petals. This pollen transfer is carried out primarily by honeybees.

When the plants are blooming, an absence of bees or the occurrence of any condition which limits or hinders honeybee activity, such as cloudy, wet weather, excess foliage or misuse of pesticides, will reduce fruit set significantly. This is especially true for watermelons as they produce far fewer female flowers than do some of the other cucurbits, such as cucumbers, cantaloupes and squash. Fewer blooms, along with poor conditions for pollination is a combination that's a sure bet for a disappointing harvest.

Cloudy, wet weather is a problem you'll just have to live with until conditions improve. Fortunately, most of the other factors that limit or hinder honeybee activity can be avoided or remedied. Excess foliage, which physically keeps the honeybees from the flowers, can be prevented by providing adequate space for the plants to grow and develop. The absence of honeybees can be overcome simply by placing a hive near your garden, if your neighbors don't object.

By far, the most common cause of poor pollination of watermelons (and other cucurbits) is misuse of pesticides. When treating your watermelon plants for control of insects and diseases, make absolutely certain you follow the label directions exactly and that you apply the pesticides during late afternoon when honeybee activity is at a minimum. This will lessen the chance of large numbers of honeybees being killed, or contaminated with the pesticide and causing damage to the hive when they return home.

If your neighbors violently oppose a beehive and, in spite of all your efforts and precautions, honeybees still consider your garden off limits, you can assure yourself a crop of watermelons by doing the pollinating yourself. Use a small brush to take pollen from the male flower and put it into the open female flower. It's important to note that the female blooms are only receptive to pollination for one day. As a result, you should make a pollinating visit as often as possible, ideally every day until several fruit are set on each vine. This technique works great, as long as you've only got a small planting of watermelons. If you've got a fair sized patch, smile at your neighbors and go get a hive of honeybees.

Because of the watermelon plant's extensive root system, it often can produce a crop with only the water Mother Nature provides. However, watering during dry periods is highly advisable. Moisture stress often will cause the occurrence of poor quality fruit and should be avoided if possible, especially from fruit set to maturity. Regardless of what kind of watering system you use, apply enough water to wet the soil to a depth of 6 to 8 inches.

As your crop of melons develop and enlarge, occasionally one of them will be misshapen and gourdy or otherwise of poor quality. These fruits should be removed as soon as you realize they are inferior. As mentioned earlier, the average watermelon plant will only produce two or three fruits. By practicing fruit pruning, you will make sure that the plants utilize the available sunlight, moisture and nutrients to produce only high-quality watermelons.

Roughly 45 days after a female flower is pollinated, the results will be a ripe watermelon. You avid gardeners can add this vital bit of information to the list of ways to determine when a watermelon is ripe. And it works, if you happen to be there when pollination occurs to begin the countdown.

Insect And Disease Problems

Since we've already discussed the technique of harvesting a ripe watermelon, it now seems most appropriate to identify the insects and diseases that, if uncontrolled, may prevent you from ever practicing what you've learned. Most of the insects that damage watermelons do so when the plants are relatively young. Aphids, or plant lice, usually appear on the undersides of theleaves and do their damage by sucking jucies from the plants, causing them to be weak and stunted. Another common pest, cucumber beetles, can be either striped or spotted and enjoy feeding on watermelon leaves, stems and flowers. Both of these insects also can transmit various types of viruses, which we'll discuss shortly. Adequate control of these pests can be achieved through early applications of malathion.

Generally in Texas, diseases pose a much more serious threat to your watermelon plants than do insects. Downy mildew is favored by moist conditions and usually first appears on the older leaves near the crown or center of the plant. Irregularly shaped, yellowish spots first appear on the leaves' upper surfaces and often are followed by a purplish, downy growth on the lower surfaces. Gummy stem blight also first occurs toward the center of the plant, causing brown to gray spots on the leaves, petioles and stems. The stem spots elongate and often cause the occurrence of a gummy exudate near the spots—hence its name. Both downy mildew and gummy stem blight can be controlled if applications of Bravo, or a

White heart (right) is a common disease of watermelons that is caused by excessive fertility.

Damping-off (left) causes seedlings or transplants to die suddenly and can be prevented through good cultural care. Downy mildew (right) is caused by moist conditions and first appears on the older leaves near the center of the plant.

fungicide containing maneb, are applied at the first sign of the diseases. Other leaf-spotting foliage diseases are often a problem on watermelons, but usually can be controlled adequately by either of the fungicides just mentioned.

Fusarium wilt is a very serious disease of watermelons, but usually is worse in commercial fields than in home gardens. Fusarium wilt is appropriately named as it simply causes the plants to suddenly wilt and die. This disease is primarily soilborne and control is best achieved by long-term rotations. Chemical control is ineffective.

Several virus diseases also pose a threat to your hopes of enjoying homegrown watermelons. Viruses must be prevented rather than controlled. Prevention begins by controlling insects, primarily cucumber beetles and aphids, which transmit the viruses during feeding.

Another serious threat to watermelons are soilborne nematodes. Nematodes cause knots, or galls, on the feeder roots and prevent them from being able to effectively absorb nutrients and water. The plants often turn yellowish and simply quit growing. Additional information on nematodes and their control can be found on page 408.

Another physiological disease is blossom-end rot, which causes the ends of the fruits to turn black and wither. Blossom-end rot of watermelons is very similar to the same problem that occurs on tomatoes and primarily is related to a soil moisture imbalance. Mulching and occasional watering to prevent moisture stress during dry periods will help prevent blossom-end rot. If the problem occurs, prune off all the affected fruits.

As mentioned during the discussion on fertilizing, white heart is an internal fruit disorder that is caused by excess soil fertility, primarily nitrogen. Consequently, white heart can be a serious problem when watermelons are grown in gardens having a high level of fertility. Unfortunately, this problem cannot be identified until after the fact. Therefore, if large, white, rather coarse-textured, tasteless areas occur within the heart of your garden-grown watermelons, reduce your rate of fertilizer significantly when growing your next patch of melons.

Quick Problem Solver: Watermelons

Problem	Causes	Solutions
Poor germination and emergence.	Old seed.	Always use current season seed.
	Cold soils.	Plant seed when soil temperature is above 70 degrees.
	Planted too deep.	Plant watermelon seed 1 to 1½ inches deep. Use the deeper planting depth on lighter soils.
	Lack of soil moisture.	Soil should be moist enough at planting to cause good germination and emergence.
Seedlings/transplants die suddenly.	Damping-off (fungus).	Use treated seed. Plant when soil temperature is satisfactory. Avoid wet soils.
	Cutworms.	Check beneath soil surface near healthy plant. If cutworms present, use appropriate insecticide for control.

Plants grow slowly, lack good color.	Cold soils.	Plant when soil temperature is above 70 degrees.
	Cold air temperature.	Use hotcaps. Wait until nighttime temperatures remain above 60 degrees before planting.
	Wet soils.	Plant on raised beds. Avoid overwatering.
	Low fertility.	Side-dress lightly with nitrogen fertilizer.
	Acid soils.	Soil pH should be above 5.5 for good plant growth. Adjust your soil's pH if needed.
	Nematodes.	Treat with nematicide.
Older leaves near crown of plant wither and die.	Downy mildew (fungus).	Treat foliage with Bravo or fungicide containing maneb.
Crown leaves die, exudate on stems.	Gummy stem blight (fungus).	Same as above.
Plants bloom, fail to set fruit.	Lack of pollination.	Bees necessary to transfer pollen from male to female flowers. Avoid spraying unless necessary and then only during late afternoon.
Fruits misshapen, gourdy.	Moisture stress.	Adequately prepare soil. Crowded growing conditions may cause shortage of soil moisture. Apply water if soil becomes dry, especially as fruits mature.
Plants stunted, leaves mottled.	Virus.	Control insects, remove severely infected plants.
Plants wilt suddenly, often die.	Fusarium wilt.	No control available. Practice long-term rotation.
Fruits lack flavor, good internal color.	Cool temperatures.	Fruits that mature when daytime temperatures average below 70 degrees will lack sugar and color. Avoid planting too late in the fall.
	Excess soil moisture.	Plant on raised beds and avoid overwatering.
Large, white, tasteless area found in fruit when cut.	White heart.	Excess fertility. Avoid applying too much nitrogen when preparing the soil and side-dressing.
End of fruit shriveled, often black.	Blossom-end rot.	Avoid moisture stress as fruit matures.

OTHER CROPS

There are many vegetables that will thrive in Texas gardens, but some aren't as well-known as others. In this chapter, we're going to look at some of those vegetables.

If you like lettuce, chances or good you'll like Chinese cabbage and endive. If you like onions, you're sure to like leeks. And if you like to cook, by all means try crops such as garlic, chives, parsley and horseradish that can enhance many recipes.

CELERIAC

Celeriac, also known as knob celery, celery root and turnip-rooted celery, is grown for its enlarged root, which usually is cooked rather than eaten raw. Its climatic and cultural requirements are similar to those described for celery, except that it is somewhat less sensitive to heat and drought and should not be side-dressed as frequently, perhaps only when about half mature. Celeriac is ready for harvest when the turnip-like root is about 2 inches or greater in diameter, but it does not develop its full flavor until exposed to frosty weather. In the milder winter areas of Texas, celeriac can be left in the garden and harvested as needed.

CHINESE CABBAGE

A quick, relatively easy-to-grow substitute for head lettuce is Chinese cabbage. In fact, Chinese cabbage just may be the easiest of all the crucifers to grow—if you pay attention to when and how it's planted and provide plenty of moisture and fertility.

There are many different types of Chinese cabbage, some with long pointed heads; some with short, squatly heads; and some that do not form heads at all. Regardless, they all have the same basic environmental requirements for successful culture—cool growing conditions. Consequently, in Texas they grow better when planted in the late summer or early fall.

Begin planting Chinese cabbage about three months before the first expected fall frost. Additional plantings can be made, but temperatures near 25 degrees may cause death or damage to the plants. In the southern areas of Texas, Chinese cabbage often can be overwintered. However, being a biennial Chinese cabbage probably will bolt or send up a seedstalk if it's first subjected to cold temperatures and then to warm weather and long days. This likelihood of bolting is the primary reason why planting in late winter or early spring is risky, although some of the new hybrids are better adapted to growth during unfavorable conditions.

Soil preparation, fertilization and seasonal cultural care is the same for Chinese cabbage as for cauliflower. However, Chinese cabbage should be seeded directly in your garden rather than transplanted—it simply does not like to be moved. The seedlings should be thinned to an in-row spacing of 10 to 14 inches within about seven to 10 days after emergence. Maintain the soil in a uniformly moist condition by frequent watering and mulching. Side-dress lightly with nitrogen every three weeks.

The disease and insect pests that are likely to attack Chinese cabbage are the same as those that attack other members of the cabbage family.

Most types of Chinese cabbage will be mature within 55 to 70 days after seeding. Like all leafy vegetables, Chinese cabbage can be consumed as soon as it reaches a usable size. You can either harvest the whole plant or use the "cut-and-come-again" technique. The heading types are mature when solid and it's best to harvest by using a sharp knife to cut through the stalk slightly below the crown of the plant.

CHIVES

Chives are perennials that belong to the onion family and in most gardening publications are classified as herbs, and rightly so. However they grow extremely well in all areas of Texas and deserve recognition as a garden "vegetable." Like most herbs, unless you're a real fan of chives, a small planting will go a long way.

Chives produce small, bulbous, onion-like plants that grow in clumps, producing attractive violet-colored flowers during late spring. Their leaves are usually about 6 inches long, tubular, hollow and uniquely flavorful.

Plant chives from early fall through spring in Texas, preparing and fertilizing the soil as you would for onions. You can plant either seed or sets (mature bulbs), but sets seem to become established more quickly and produce stronger, healthier plants. Plant the sets about 1 inch deep, spacing them about 5 to 6 inches apart. If you plant on raised beds, a 16- to 20-inch-wide bed will accommodate two or three rows of chives easily.

Growth of the plants will be rapid and actually enhanced by harvesting or cutting back the foliage about twice each year. Every three years, preferably in the fall, dig up and divide the clumps, replanting them to another part of your garden.

The young, tender leaves, possessing a delicate onion flavor, can be harvested at any time during the year and are best used fresh in salads, soups and stews. Harvest with a sharp knife or scissors, cutting the leaves back to within 2 inches of the soil. The bulbs are seldom used as they lack the desired flavor and aroma.

The foliage will die back in the winter and in the northern areas of the state the plants should be mulched to prevent the possibility of cold damage, although such damage is unlikely to occur most years.

ENDIVE

Endive is extremely popular in gardens across all of Europe, but is unknown to most Texans, even though it is much more tolerant of our weather extremes and less susceptible to insects and diseases than its close relatives, leaf and head lettuce.

Endive occurs in two distinct types, a narrow, curly-leafed type and a broad-leafed type that commonly is called escarole. The curly leafed type (endive) is more tolerant of high temperatures and should be planted for late spring or early fall harvest. The broad-leafed type (escarole) is hardier, much less likely to be damaged by cold temperatures and is best suited for late fall, winter and early spring harvests.

Seed three to four weeks before the last killing frost in the spring. Additional plantings can be made, but if endive is planted late and forced

Celeriac

Chinese Cabbage

Chives

Endive

to grow during high temperatures common in June, July and August, it will bolt or flower.

The initial planting of endive for a fall harvest should occur about 10 weeks prior to the first hard frost. Additional plantings can be made, but switch to escarole for its ability to withstand cold weather. Regardless of whether you plant endive or escarole, temperatures in the middle to low 20s often will kill the plants. If you garden in the milder winter areas of Texas, endive/escarole often can be harvested throughout the winter and into the spring. However, the onset of warm temperatures will almost always result in the plant's flowering.

Prepare and fertilize the soil as you would for lettuce. When seeding, plant single row due to the rather large size of the mature plants. Sow six to eight seeds per foot of row and cover 1/4 inch deep. During high temperatures, consider covering the seed with compost or something similar, as described on page 407. Shortly after emergence, thin the seedlings to an in-row spacing of 10 to 14 inches. The thinnings can be transplanted to other areas in your garden if desired.

About two weeks after thinning, side-dress lightly with nitrogen. During dry periods, maintain the soil in a moist condition and mulch around the plants to encourage vigorous plant growth.

Endive has a tendency toward a natural bitterness that is objectionable to most Texans. However, this off-flavor can be removed by blanching the plants. When the plants are about 10 weeks old and have developed good size, simply gather up the outside leaves and tie them together at the top with string or rubber bands, much like is done for cauliflower. If you're just interested in blanching the heart of the plants, place old plates or something similar over their centers. In the spring, blanching will take about three weeks whereas in the fall it may take twice as long. Make absolutely sure the foliage is completely dry before blanching or the leaves most likely will decay. Harvest immediately after blanching by using a sharp knife to cut through the stem of the plants near ground level. Endive is subject to the same diseases and insects as is lettuce, although not nearly as frequently.

GARLIC

Garlic is one of the most destinctive of all the seasonings and is closely related to the onion. Actually, it's little more than an onion that instead of forming a single bulb produces a compound bulb composed of cloves that are enclosed in a membranous "bag." As complex as this seems, garlic is relatively easy to grow in Texas. In fact, not long ago, Texas produced a large portion of the garlic consumed in the United States. Today, however, most of the garlic we use is grown in Mexico and California.

Garlic is grown almost exactly the same as bulb onions, with soil preparation, fertilization, time of planting, row and in-row spacing being identical, as are problems related to insects and diseases. However, garlic is planted from cloves, or sets, because it does not produce seeds. If given a choice, always plant the larger cloves as they invariably will produce larger garlic bulbs. Plant the cloves about 1 to 2 inches deep depending on soil type, using the shallower planting on heavier soils. Setting the cloves in an upright position in the planting furrow will ensure the production of good, straight-necked, high-yielding plants.

Garlic, like onions, is shallow rooted. Avoid cultivating close to the plants, remove competing weeds and grasses by hand and keep the soil relatively moist, especially during the early development of the bulbs. Mulching around the plants is highly advantageous and will increase yields. Water less frequently as the garlic nears maturity.

Garlic bulbs in reaction to day length and temperature. Long days and warm temperatures hasten bulbing and maturity. However, bulbing will not occur if neither the dormant cloves, nor the young growing plants, are exposed to temperatures between 32 to 50 degrees for at least 30 days. This need for exposure to low temperatures is the primary reason why garlic should be planted in the fall in most areas of the state or in late winter or early spring in the northern areas where the possibility of cold damage exists.

Elephant garlic is not a true garlic, but is more closely related to the leek. It's grown basically the same as garlic. Occasionally, elephant garlic fails to produce cloves, but instead produces what is called a "round." It appears to be similar to a leek or a giant green onion. Rounds generally result from planting the smaller elephant garlic cloves. The rounds can be consumed like garlic or can be saved for planting the following spring. Invariably, the result will be mammoth size garlic, rather than normal size elephant garlic.

When the tops begin to dry and fall over, your garlic is ready for harvesting. Use a spading fork to lift the soil and gently pull the plants from the ground. Place the bulbs in a partially shaded area for a few days to dry. Remove the tops, leaving about 1 inch attached to the bulbs, or tie or braid the tops together for hanging from a ceiling or wall. Properly matured garlic bulbs will store in a cool, dry area for an indefinite period of time. Be sure to set aside some of the larger cloves for your next planting of garlic.

Garlic

HORSERADISH

The horseradish is native to the area extending from the Caspian Sea to Finland and is known to have been in cultivation for more than 1,000 years. It was introduced into England in the mid-1500s and was first grown in the United States in 1806.

This cold-hardy perennial is a member of the *Cruciferae*, or cabbage, family that is grown for its pungent roots. It will grow in all areas of Texas, but does best in the cooler northern areas.

Prepare and fertilize the soil as for carrots, avoiding excessive fertility that may result in "all tops and no roots." If barnyard manure is to be used, it should be worked into the soil several months prior to planting or rough, misshapen roots may result. Planting is best performed in the very early spring, but also can take place in the early fall.

Propagation of horseradish is by vegetative means, utilizing side-root cuttings called "sets," which are removed from the main central root following harvest. All the small, slender roots between 6 and 14 inches long and about the size of a pencil are removed, trimmed and stored in a moist, cool place until time for planting.

It's best to plant horseradish in a bed to the side of your garden because of its tendency to become weed-like. Dig a furrow in the top of the bed about 5 inches deep. Plant the sets at an angle in the furrow, with their thick or top end about 2 inches below the surface of the soil. Space the sets about 12 to 14 inches apart.

Within 10 to 14 days the plants will emerge from the soil and grow slowly until late summer and fall when the plants will grow rapidly. During this period of time, all the care that's often needed is an occasional watering during exceptionally dry periods. Insects and diseases are seldom a problem, but are basically the same as those troubling cabbage.

Your highest quality horseradish will result from a late fall harvest, although being very cold hardy it can be harvested well into the winter and early spring. Simply dig up the roots with your spading fork, trim off the sets and save them for your next planting.

During harvest, be sure to remove all the roots (and pieces of roots) as completely as possible or they will sprout and you'll find yourself trying to control your horseradish, rather than enjoying it. For this reason, even though it is a perennial, horseradish should be grown as an annual by preparing a new planting area each spring.

JERUSALEM ARTICHOKE

The Jerusalem artichoke is really nothing more than a sunflower that's grown for its knobby, enlarged storage roots or tubers. And being a sunflower, it's easy to grow, requiring only a minimal amount of care and attention.

Jerusalem artichokes, or sunchokes, are not particular about the soils they're grown in as long as they drain well. Prepare and fertilize the soil as you would for potatoes. Plant in late spring or early summer, using tubers or pieces of tubers either purchased or saved from a previous harvest. Space them about 18 to 24 inches apart in rows that are at least 36 inches apart and cover to a depth of 2 to 3 inches. The tubers should sprout within two to three weeks.

Once the plants are up and about 8 inches tall, "dirt" them with 3 to 4 inches of soil just as you would potatoes. From this point on, all that you really need to do is keep the plants watered and free of competition from weeds and grasses. Mulching around the plants with 3 to 4 inches of organic matter will help accomplish both of these requirements. Within a suprisingly short period of time, the plants will be 6 to 8 feet tall and will produce small, sunflower-like blooms in late summer to add color to your garden. However, removing the blooms as soon as they appear will increase yields.

The potato-sized, irregular-shaped Jerusalem artichokes will be ready for harvesting 120 to 130 days after planting. However, for greater yields, wait until the tops have been killed by frost before digging up the tubers. After harvesting, the tubers can be stored for a month or more by putting them in plastic bags and placing them in your refrigerator.

In spite of the fact that the plants will be killed by freezing temperatures, the Jerusalem artichoke is a perennial and the tubers left in the ground will overwinter and sprout the following spring. Some Texans prefer to take advantage of this characteristic and harvest tubers from their original planting indefinitely. However, if the tubers or pieces of tubers are inadvertently spread around while preparing the soil, you'll soon find your garden full of artichoke "weeds." For this reason, it's generally best to "clean harvest" your planting of Jerusalem artichokes and replant them in a new area in your garden each year.

Jerusalem artichokes literally are free of insect and disease problems. Poorly drained, continually wet soils, however, will cause the tubers to rot in the ground.

LEEKS

Leeks are non-bulbing members of the onion family that, when mature, resemble giant green onions. Their stems are as much as 2 inches in diameter, they stand 18 inches tall and have flat leaves. They are very popular in Europe, but relatively unknown in the United States and Texas. However, they grow extremely well in all areas of our state and can add greatly to the flavor of soups, salads and numerous favorite recipes.

Prepare and fertilize the soil as you would for growing onions, adding liberal amounts of organic matter and barnyard manure. Seeding can begin three to four weeks prior to the last killing spring frost and the leeks will be ready for harvest during early summer, before temperatures become excessively hot. Leeks also can be planted in late summer for

Leeks

harvest during winter and early spring. However, being a biennial, leeks exposed to prolonged cold will go dormant and then bolt, or flower, when temperatures moderate and growth resumes in the spring. Therefore, time your planting so that they will be of usable size before the onset of cold temperatures.

Sow leek seeds at the rate of about eight to 10 per foot of row and cover ½ inch deep. If seeding during high temperature conditions, cover the seeds with compost or organic matter. In addition, it's a good idea to mulch over the seeded area with a layer of organic matter to conserve soil moisture and help control weeds.

The seedlings should emerge from the soil in two to three weeks. Thin the plants to an in-row spacing of 4 inches between plants about four to six weeks after emergence.

Leeks also do well when transplanted, but finding transplants in Texas is almost impossible. You can grow your own by following the directions for growing transplants found on page 396. Transplant leek seedlings as you would onions.

For optimum production and quality, keep the soil relatively moist during the early stages of the plant's growth and development, but allow the soil to remain on the dry side as the leeks near maturity.

New Zealand Spinach

Leeks commonly are blanched by "dirting" the plants about the time the stems are approximately 1 inch in diameter. The practice of blanching excludes light from the stems, causing them to become almost pure white and of extremely high quality. Connoisseurs of leeks often prefer not to use soil to blanch the plants. Instead, they tie heavy brown wrapping paper or black plastic around the stems to exclude light. A 5- to 6-inch-thick layer of organic matter also works well.

Leeks are harvested as needed, leaving the remaining plants in the garden. They are extremely cold hardy and will remain usable well into the spring. When harvesting, use a spading fork to lift the plants from the soil.

Texas-grown leeks are subject to the same problems encountered when growing onions, although usually not quite as often. Thrips and fungal diseases that attack the leaves are sometimes a problem, but usually can be controlled by timely applications of appropriate insecticides and fungicides.

NEW ZEALAND SPINACH

If you're looking for a vegetable that will produce lots of tasty greens, even during our hottest Texas summers, try New Zealand Spinach. Its flavor is similar to, but somewhat milder, than common spinach and it will produce excellent yields with only occasional attention.

New Zealand Spinach may taste like spinach, but the plant is very different. It will grow to a height of 2 feet, spreading 3 feet across. It is very sensitive to frost, so should not be planted in your garden until several weeks after the last spring frost, usually about the time you plant your okra.

Prepare the soil as you would for spinach but double the amount of commercial fertilizer. Plant single rows with the rows spaced 3 ½ to 4 feet apart. The seeds are very hard and, as a result, germinate slowly. Soak them prior to planting as detailed on page 403 (use warm water) for four to eight hours and then place the container in the refrigerator to chill the seed for about 24 hours.

Hill plant three to four seeds every 12 inches, covering them ½ to ¾ inch deep. The seedlings should emerge within seven to 10 days and each hill should be thinned to a single plant. Mulching around the plants following thinning will conserve soil moisture and control weeds. Once the plants become well-established, their dense foliage will shade out most weeds and grasses.

When New Zealand Spinach is about a foot tall, pinch out the growing tips of the plants to promote branching and leaf production. Side-dress afterwards with a small amount of nitrogen fertilizer to encourage continued foliage growth. Harvest by the cut-and-come-again method, removing the succulent, young leaves. Continue harvesting right through summer and up until the plants are killed by frost. If the spreading growth habit of the plants threatens to take over part of your garden, cut the plants back, but not too severely or they may not recover. New Zealand spinach is not usually troubled by insects and diseases. Slugs and aphids are occasionally a minor problem, but are easily controlled.

PARSLEY

It's certainly accurate to say that a little goes a long way when describing parsley. It's the most familar of all the herbs and widely used as a flavoring, but we'll consider it as a vegetable since it's commonly grown in many vegetable gardens across Texas.

There are two distinct types of leaf parsley—flat leafed and curly leafed—with the latter much more widely grown. In addition, there is a type grown for its parsnip-like edible root.

Prepare and fertilize the area to be planted as you would for carrots. Parsley is a long-term crop and although it can be planted in early spring in Texas, due to its dislike of our summer heat, it does best when planted in late summer or early fall for winter harvest. It is very cold hardy although severe, prolonged cold spells can cause damage or death of the plants. Most years, however, parsley can be harvested throughout the winter in all areas of Texas.

Even under ideal conditions, parsley seed germinates very slowly. Therefore, it's a good idea to initiate germination before planting by presoaking the seed for about 48 hours. Sow the presoaked seed in ½-inch deep seeding furrows using about six to eight seeds per foot of row. Rather than using soil, improve conditions for germination by covering the seeds with peat moss, compost or something similar.

Keep the planting area moist until the plants have emerged and the stand is established. When planting during high temperatures, cover the planted area with wet burlap or a board to cool the soil and encourage germination. Remove these covers as soon as the seedlings first begin to emerge. When the plants produce their first true leaves, thin them to an in-row spacing of 6 inches. The thinnings can be transplanted to other areas if desired.

After thinning is an ideal time to apply 2 to 3 inches of some type of organic mulch around the plants to conserve soil moisture and help control weeds. Although parsley is fairly drought tolerant, it will respond to adequate soil moisture.

About 60 to 70 days after seeding you can begin harvesting your parsley. Remove the outer leaves as needed, leaving the crown of the plant intact to produce new leaves for later harvest. After the first harvest, side-dress the plants with a light application of nitrogen fertilizer to stimulate foliage growth. The root-type parsley will be ready about 90 days after seeding and is harvested like carrots.

If you overwinter your parsley, it most likely will bolt or flower when temperatures moderate in the spring. This occurrence also is associated with the loss of foliage color and the development of a bitter, off flavor. If this occurs early in the spring (before it gets excessively hot), you can cut the plants back to near ground level, fertilize rather heavily and water thoroughly, which often will encourage the plants to produce new foliage. Parsley has been known to produce foliage growth suitable for use for several years when treated in this manner, especially in the cooler regions of the state.

Parsley is relatively free of insect and disease problems although occasionally foliage-feeding worms may require control.

Parsley

Parsnip

Salsify

PARSNIP

Parsnips were the potatoes of medieval and renaissance Europe and are still considered an important vegetable in many parts of the world. In Texas, however, parsnips are best described as an oddball, insignificant crop—that is until you learn to appreciate them. They're grown for their large, fleshy, white, 8- to 12-inch-long roots that have a distinctive, celery-like flavor and can be fried, boiled or used in soups and stews.

Parsnips do best when they mature during cool weather. Since they are a long-term, cold-hardy crop requiring 120 to 180 days to mature, they should be planted in mid-summer in most areas of Texas for late fall or winter harvest. Folks who appreciate parsnips claim they develop an even better taste when harvested after a hard freeze.

Work the soil deeply and fertilize exactly as you would for carrots, avoiding the use of too much fertilizer and manure, as excessive amounts will cause the roots to be forked and split. Realizing the need for a well-prepared, deep soil, planting on raised beds is encouraged. Two rows of parsnips, spaced 12 to 14 inches apart, can be planted easily on top of the beds.

Parsnip seeds germinate poorly and slowly, so use plenty of seed. Sow about one seed per inch of row or hill plant three to four seeds every 6 inches. Cover the seed about ½ to ¾ inch deep using compost or peat rather than soil. It's important to keep the soil fairly moist during germination and seedling emergence. Applying a thin layer of mulch over the seeded area will help conserve soil moisture and cool the soil.

It may require as long as three to four weeks before the seedlings emerge from the soil. During their early growth, the seedlings are weak and poor competitors for moisture and fertility, necessitating control of weeds and grasses. After the seedlings are at least 2 inches tall, thin them to an in-row spacing of 4 to 6 inches between the plants. As the plants develop, it's important that the soil never be allowed to get excessively dry or the roots will become tough, misshapen and lack good flavor.

Harvest the roots with a spading fork as needed, leaving the rest in the ground for storage. Parsnips are almost disease- and insect-free, although soilborne insects may feed on the roots occasionally.

RHUBARB

Rhubarb is a cold-hardy perennial that thrives in the northern states but simply will not grow well, if at all, in Texas. Rhubarb is grown primarily from root cuttings and requires two years from planting to first harvest. Unfortunately, it seldom lives long enough to become established, as the underground rhizomes (stems) that produce the desired leaf stalks grow poorly during even our mildest summers. It's just too hot during the summer in Texas for rhubarb to prosper, even in our most northern areas. Summertime temperatures that exceed 90 degrees will cause the rhizomes to produce a few thin, spindly leaf stalks having poor color. Eventually, the plants will wither and die.

Therefore, if you're a Yankee and have a real hankering for fresh rhubarb pie, it's often available, but not fresh from your garden. Depend on your local supermarket to supply the rhubarb and use your valuable garden space for other, more adapted and certainly more productive vegetables.

SALSIFY

Difficult as it is to imagine, the roots of salsify have a distinct oyster-like flavor and, in fact, it is commonly referred to as the oyster plant or vegetable oyster. Despite its association with the popular seafood delight, the oyster plant is almost an unknown commodity in Texas gardens.

Salsify is a biennial and belongs to the same family of plants as lettuce, endive/escarole and chicory. Soil preparation, fertilization and cultural care is similar to that for carrots. Since you're growing salsify for its long, slender roots, deep and thorough soil preparation is advisable.

Sow seed directly in your garden in early spring at the rate of six to eight seeds per foot of row. Shortly after emergence, thin the seedings to an in-row spacing of 6 inches. Mulch after thinning and keep the soil relatively moist, especially during the heat of summer, or the plants may send up a seedstem.

Salsify grows very slowly, producing long, slender, smooth, 1-inch-wide leaves that eventually will stand about 10 inches high. The salmon or brown-colored roots will reach a length of 12 to 14 inches in good, loose soil but will not be ready for harvest until late fall.

Harvest the roots as you would carrots. Salsify is very cold hardy and can be left in the garden and harvested as needed. If you cut the tops of some of the plants back to near ground level and cover them with about an inch of soil, you can enjoy a second harvest of greens in early spring. Harvest the tender sprouts, or chards as they're called in Europe, when they are 4 to 6 inches tall and prepare like asparagus, to which many claim they are at least equal in flavor.

Salsify has few insect and disease problems, although grubworms and wireworms can become a problem by feeding on the developing roots. If these pests are observed during soil preparation, treat the soil with an appropriate soil insecticide.

SHALLOTS

Shallots are nothing more than a mild type of bulbing onion that produces a number of small bulbs attached to each other at their base, rather than producing a single, larger bulb. They are much easier to grow than bulbing onions and considerably easier to keep. Consequently, shallots make an excellent choice for culture in your garden.

Shallots are grown basically the same as bulb onions, requiring the same soil preparation and fertilization. Planting is done in late fall in the southern half of Texas and in early spring in the northern areas. Mature bulbs, called sets, saved from the previous harvest or purchased at local garden centers or nurseries are planted instead of seed.

Plant the sets 6 inches apart. If you plant on raised beds, they will easily accommodate two rows per bed with the rows spaced 10 to 14 inches apart. Simply push the sets base first into the soil leaving their tip slightly exposed above ground. Water after planting to settle the soil around the sets.

Within a short period of time, the sets will begin producing a number of shoots, as many as eight to 10, each of which will produce bulbs (shallots) about the size of the one planted. If you desire, some of these shoots can be harvested and used as salad onions or scallions, leaving the rest to form bulbs.

As the plants grow and the bulbs develop, control weeds and grasses to prevent competition for water and nutrients. Shallots actually prefer somewhat dry soils, so don't water frequently or excessively. The bulbs may rot if wet conditions persist for prolonged periods.

During early to mid-summer the bulbs will mature, causing the foliage to turn yellow and whither. Lift the bulbs from the soil and place them in a warm, sheltered place to dry. They can be stored several months by placing them in a dry, airy place. Remember to save some of the healthier appearing bulbs for next years crop. Shallots are subject to the same insects and diseases as onions, but fortunately, not as frequently or as severely.

Shallots

SWISS CHARD

Swiss chard is really nothing more than "a beet without a bottom." Most historians think the beet, as we know it, was developed by the Romans, who selected Swiss chard plants for their enlarged roots. Today, Swiss chard is known by many names, including spinach beet, leaf beet and Swiss beet. Regardless of what it's called, Swiss chard deserves a prominate place in Texas gardens. It's easy to grow, nutritious and highly productive—almost beyond belief!

Swiss chard prefers cool temperatures, but also will do quite well during warm periods. In fact, Swiss chard, along with New Zealand spinach, can be an excellent source of tasty garden greens right through the heat of summer in most areas of our state. Seeding can begin three to four weeks before the last spring frost is expected and continued, if desired, up until about 60 days before temperatures near the mid-20s are expected.

Soil preparation, fertilization, planting and cultural care during the season is basically the same as for beets. However, Swiss chard should

Swiss Chard

be planted only in single rows, rather than double rows or broadcast. Once the seedlings are up, they should be thinned to an in-row spacing of 8 to 12 inches.

The soil should be kept moist to encourage the continued production of leaves. When the plants are 4 to 6 inches tall, a light side-dressing of nitrogen fertilizer will stimulate growth. After the first harvest, side-dress again to encourage continued succulent growth.

Swiss chard can be harvested once the outer leaves are about 4 to 5 inches long but will not reach their full texture and flavor until about 60 days after planting. To harvest, remove the older, but tender, outer leaves from the base of the plants with a sharp knife and leave the undisturbed inner leaves to continue growing for later harvest. Remove any old, discolored leaves as they will decrease production. By continuing to remove the outer leaves and keeping the plants well fertilized, watered, and disease- and insect-free, a single planting may continue to be productive for over a year.

This remarkable vegetable is relatively free of diseases and insects, although aphids and flea beetles will sometimes be a nuisance.

Mean Spring and Fall Freeze Dates

Mean dates of the last 32-degree spring freeze and the first 32-degree fall freeze at various stations throughout Texas are given below. These statistics were provided by the Office of State Climatologist, located at Texas A&M University, College Station, Texas.

Remember that these are mean dates and should be used only as guidelines in making your gardening plans. Freeze dates vary from season to season. You must also use your own judgment in deciding exactly when to set out transplants or sow seeds.

STATION	LAST SPRING FREEZE	FIRST FALL FREEZE	STATION	LAST SPRING FREEZE	FIRST FALL FREEZE
Abilene	Mar. 26	Nov. 12	Corsicana	Mar. 13	Nov. 20
Alice	Feb. 20	Dec. 4	Crockett	Mar. 16	Nov. 9
Alpine	Mar. 30	Nov. 10	Crosbyton	Apr. 11	Nov. 2
Amarillo	Apr. 20	Oct. 28	Crystal City	Mar. 2	Nov. 27
Angleton	Mar. 2	Nov. 30	Cuero	Mar. 8	Nov. 27
Austin	Mar. 7	Nov. 22	Dalhart	Apr. 25	Oct. 16
Ballinger	Mar. 30	Nov. 10	Dallas	Mar. 18	Nov. 12
Beaumont	Feb. 18	Nov. 24	Danevang	Feb. 23	Dec. 5
Beeville	Feb. 20	Dec. 5	Del Rio	Feb. 10	Dec. 10
Big Spring	Mar. 29	Nov. 11	Denison Dam	Mar. 26	Nov. 10
Boerne	Mar. 25	Nov. 9	Dilley	Feb. 25	Dec. 2
Bonham	Mar. 30	Nov. 7	Dublin	Mar. 26	Nov. 17
Borger	Apr. 17	Oct. 28	Eagle Pass	Feb. 20	Dec. 3
Brenham	Feb. 25	Dec. 2	Eastland	Mar. 29	Nov. 9
Bridgeport	Mar. 30	Nov. 5	Eden	Apr. 3	Nov. 7
Bronson	Mar. 24	Nov. 8	El Campo	Feb. 27	Dec. 2
Brownsville	Jan. 10	*	El Paso	Mar. 14	Nov. 12
Brownwood	Mar. 20	Nov. 18	Falfurrias	Feb. 10	Dec. 10
Cameron	Mar. 15	Nov. 21	Flatonia	Mar. 4	Dec. 4
Canadian	Apr. 9	Oct. 30	Follett	Apr. 20	Oct. 28
Carrizo Springs	Feb. 22	Nov. 26	Fort Stockton	Apr. 2	Nov. 10
Center	Mar. 17	Nov. 6	Fort Worth	Mar. 20	Nov. 15
Centerville	Mar. 14	Nov. 9	Fredericksburg	Mar. 27	Nov. 3
Childress	Apr. 1	Nov. 7	Gainesville	Mar. 29	Nov. 6
Clarksville	Mar. 26	Nov. 5	Galveston	Jan.25	Dec. 23
Cleburne	Mar. 26	Nov. 10	Gatesville	Mar. 24	Nov. 9
Coleman	Mar. 28	Nov. 5	Goliad	Feb. 22	Dec. 1
College Station	Mar. 6	Nov. 27	Graham	Apr. 3	Nov. 2
Colorado City	Apr. 5	Nov. 3	Greenville	Mar. 20	Nov. 12
Conroe	Mar. 6	Nov. 23	Hallettsville	Mar. 8	Nov. 15
Corpus Christi	Feb. 9	Dec. 12	Harlingen	Jan. 24	Dec. 26

Henderson	Mar. 11	Nov. 13
Hereford	Apr. 23	Oct. 24
Hico	Mar. 29	Nov. 2
Hondo	Mar. 3	Nov. 21
Houston	Feb. 4	Dec. 10
Huntsville	Mar. 9	Nov. 27
Iowa Park	Apr. 1	Nov. 2
Jacksboro	Apr. 2	Nov. 2
Junction	Apr. 2	Nov. 2
Karnack	Mar. 18	Nov. 4
Kaufman	Mar. 21	Nov. 15
Kenedy	Mar. 5	Nov. 26
Kerrville	Apr. 4	Nov. 6
Kirbyville	Mar. 22	Nov. 7
Knox City	Apr. 1	Nov. 9
Laredo	Jan. 1	Dec. 19
Levelland	Apr. 13	Oct. 30
Liberty	Mar. 1	Nov. 15
Lindale	Mar. 12	Nov. 11
Livingston	Mar. 14	Nov. 17
Llano	Mar. 27	Nov. 10
Longview	Mar. 15	Nov. 12
Lubbock	Apr. 11	Nov. 1
Lufkin	Mar. 18	Nov. 4
Luling	Mar. 3	Nov. 24
Madisonville	Mar. 9	Nov. 12
Marathon	Apr. 5	Nov. 1
Marshall	Mar. 14	Nov. 13
Matagorda	Feb. 13	Dec. 14
Maurbo	Feb. 23	Dec. 2
McAllen	Jan. 30	Dec. 10
McCook	Feb. 5	Dec. 8
McKinney	Apr. 1	Nov. 5
Mexia	Mar. 16	Nov. 21
Midland	Apr. 2	Nov. 6
Mineral Wells	Mar. 25	Nov. 6
Mission	Jan. 26	Dec. 18
Montague	Mar. 29	Nov. 6
Mount Locke	Apr. 23	Oct. 26
Mount Pleasant	Mar. 25	Nov. 9
Muleshoe	Apr. 20	Oct. 20
Nacagdoches	Mar. 16	Nov. 10
New Braunfels	Mar. 11	Nov. 26
Palacios	Feb. 12	Dec. 4
Palestine	Mar. 14	Nov. 15
Paris	Mar. 27	Nov. 10
Pecos	Mar. 31	Nov. 8
Pierce	Mar. 6	Nov. 27
Plainview	Apr. 11	Nov. 4
Port Isabel	Jan. 9	*
Port Lavaca	Feb. 18	Dec. 8
Port O'Connor	Feb. 6	Dec. 20
Poteet	Mar. 6	Nov. 19
Presidio	Mar. 18	Nov. 13
Quanah	Apr. 3	Nov. 4
Raymondville	Jan. 25	Dec. 22
Rising Star	Mar. 28	Nov. 6
Roscoe	Apr. 6	Nov. 6
Rusk	Mar. 16	Nov. 8
San Angelo	Mar. 25	Nov. 13
San Antonio	Mar. 3	Nov. 26
San Marcos	Mar. 13	Nov. 19
Sealy	Feb. 27	Dec. 2
Seymour	Apr. 4	Oct. 31
Sherman	Mar. 20	Nov. 7
Smithville	Mar. 11	Nov. 15
Snyder	Apr. 5	Nov. 4
Spearman	Apr. 22	Oct. 24
Spur	Apr. 17	Oct. 28
Sugar Land	Feb. 14	Nov. 29
Sulphur Springs	Mar. 24	Nov. 3
Tahoka	Apr. 6	Nov. 5
Taylor	Mar. 14	Nov. 18
Temple	Mar. 10	Nov. 24
Throckmorton	Apr. 4	Nov. 7
Uvalde	Mar. 9	Nov. 18
Van Horn	Mar. 31	Nov. 5
Vega	Apr. 21	Oct. 21
Victoria	Feb. 6	Dec. 8
Waco	Mar. 16	Nov. 18
Waxahachie	Mar. 25	Nov. 5
Weatherford	Mar. 28	Nov. 7
Weslaco	Jann.22	Dec. 13
Whitney Dam	Mar. 18	Nov. 10
Wichita Falls	Apr. 4	Nov. 6
Winter Haven	Feb. 24	Dec. 1

*occurred only once in ten years, or less

COMMON AND TRADE NAMES OF CHEMICALS

COMMON NAME*	TRADE NAME
benomyl	Benlate
chlorothalonil	Bravo, Daconil 2787
carbaryl	Sevin
copper hydroxide	Kocide 101
dimethoate	Cygon, Defend
diazinon	Diazinon, Spectracide
dicofol	Kelthane
Bacillus thuringiensis	Thuricide, Dipel, others
endosulfan	Thiodan
malathion	Cythion
maneb	Manzate, Diathane M22
meta-sodium	Vapam
phosmet	Imidan
sulfur	various trade names
thiram	Thylate, Arasan
thiabendzole	Arbotect, Mertect 340
zineb	Dithane Z-28

* Numerous companies market these products in Texas using their own trade name such as Ortho's Vegetable Garden Fungicide which contains chlorothalonil (Daconil 2787 or Bravo). When looking for a particular chemical for insect or disease control, check the label for the active ingredient which will usually be listed as either the common or trade name indicated above.
Common Name*Trade Name

HOW TO TAKE AN ACCURATE SOIL TEST

With a spade make a deep hole in the soil. Throw out a spade full of soil.

Cut a half to 1-inch slice of soil from the back of the hole.

Place this slice in a bucket.

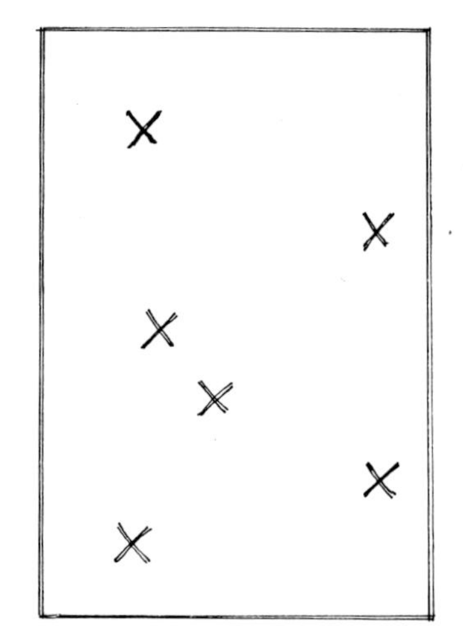

Repeat five or six times at different spots in your garden.

Thoroughly mix the six or seven slices you have in the bucket.

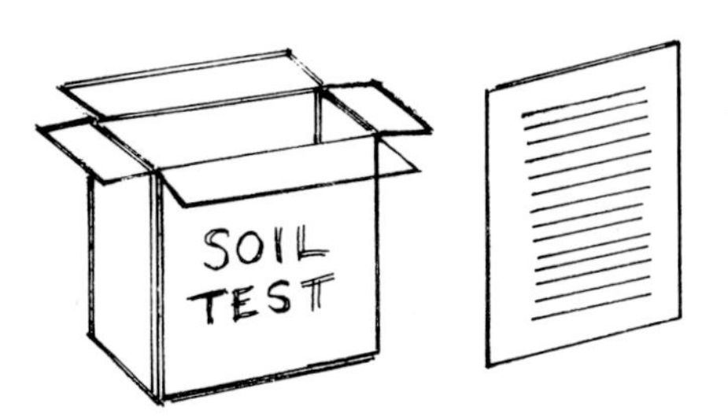

After thoroughly mixing, obtain a soil test kit from your local county Extension agent, fill out the form, place about 1 pint of the composite soil in the box, enclose payment and mail.

ADJUSTING THE pH OF YOUR SOIL

In growing plants, the term pH is used to express the degree of soil acidity or alkalinity. Vinegar and lemon juice are examples of weak acids, while milk of magnesia and household ammonia are alkaline products. Other terms often used by Texans to express the pH of soils are sweet and sour—a sweet soil being alkaline and having a high pH and a sour soil being acid with a low pH. Acid soils are fairly common in much of East Texas, while alkaline soils are predominant in most other areas of the state.

The pH of a soil is expressed as a number ranging between 0 and 14. Values below 7.0 are acid while those above 7.0 are alkaline. If a soil has a pH of 7.0, it is classified as neutral. Soils in Texas generally have a pH between 4.5 and 8.5, but exceptions do occur.

The significance of soil pH is that if your soil is too acid or alkaline, naturally occurring soil nutrients, or those that you add, are often not available to the plants. This is especially true of acid soils. You can generally garden successfully if your soil is too alkaline, but soils that are too acid need to be corrected.

The ideal pH for growing most vegetables lies between 6.0 and 6.8. If your soil pH is below 6.0, limestone should be applied to adjust the pH upward. In most instances, dolomitic limestone should be used if possible, as it supplies magnesium which is often deficient in many of our acid soils.

If you're gardening in an alkaline area of our state and the pH of your soil is near 8.0 adding sulphur will lower its pH and often correct chlorosis or iron deficiency symptoms which are especially common on beans and peas.

If you feel your soil pH is out of "kilter," contact your local county Extension agent and request information on testing your soil's pH. Commercial soil testing kits are available from garden centers and nurseries that will give you an indication of your soil's pH. Lime or sulphur should not be applied to your soil unless the need warrants their use.

If your soil's pH is known, the following tables can be used as a guideline for applying lime or sulphur to adjust its acidity or alkalinity.

Pounds of Limestone Needed to Raise Your Soil's pH

Change in	Pounds of limestone per 100 square feet		
pH desired	Sandy soil	Loamy soil	Clay soil
4.5 to 6.5	5.0	13.5	19.5
5.0 to 6.5	4.0	10.5	15.5
5.5 to 6.5	3.0	8.0	11.0
6.0 to 6.5	1.5	4.0	5.5
Above 6.0	Not necessary to add lime		

Pounds of Sulphur needed to Lower Your Soil's pH

Change in	Pounds of Sulphur Per 100 Square Feet	
pH desired	Sandy soils	Clay soils
8.5 to 6.5	4.5	7.0
8.0 to 6.5	3.0	4.5
7.5 to 6.5	1.0	2.0

Do not add sulphur if pH is 7.0 or below.

ROTO TILL YOUR GARDEN

Even though gardening is considered by many to be one of the best forms of exercise available, many Texans will be looking for an easy way to work up that stuff in the backyard that is loosely termed "soil." Many prefer the shovel or the spading fork and really enjoy getting out and working up the ground. But others look for simpler and easier ways to handle the same chore. Often this involves borrowing a rotary tiller from a neighbor or renting one for a couple of hours or the whole day. Buying one for a small garden is not economical.

The following tips on tilling a garden should make the job much easier:

•Leave a row untilled between passes. Two reasons for this are: Wide turns are much easier to negotiate with a tiller than "about faces," and the machine will not be pulling itself and you toward the next row (which it will do if you come close to the overlapping rows).

•In tilling heavy clay soil or breaking up ground for a new garden, reduce engine speed. The tiller digs better and bucks and bounces less.

•When tilling the garden the first time, don't try to work it to its maximum depth in the first pass. Set the brake stake for half the depth you desire. Then reset it to full depth and go over the ground a second time.

•Till only when the soil is slightly moist and friable. Tilling soil that is wet leaves large clods that harden as they dry. Also, clumps of mud clinging to the blades upset the tiller's balance, causing undue wear on you and the machine.

•Do not clean mud, roots or debris from the tines while the engine is running, even though it may not be in gear. To be extra safe, make certain the shift selector is in "neutral" and the spark plug wire is disconnected.

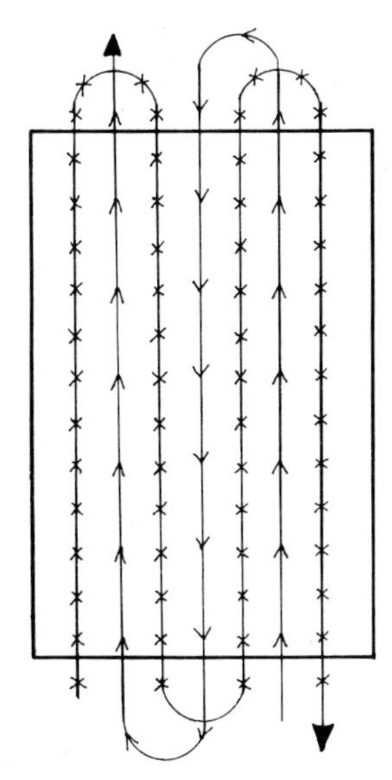

Leave a row untilled between passes to avoid "about faces" and the tiller pulling you into the next row.

Tilling or spading in organic matter is an important step in preparing your soil. When using a tiller, make several passes, each deeper than the previous one.

HOW TO GROW TRANSPLANTS

Sow seeds in shallow pan filled with sterile, moist potting soil. Cover seed about ¼ inch deep.

Place plants in protected area receiving full sun. Water as needed. When the plants are about 6″ tall, they are ready to be set out in your garden. Add water to soilless media only when moisture can no longer be squeezed out by pinching the medium between the thumb and forefinger.

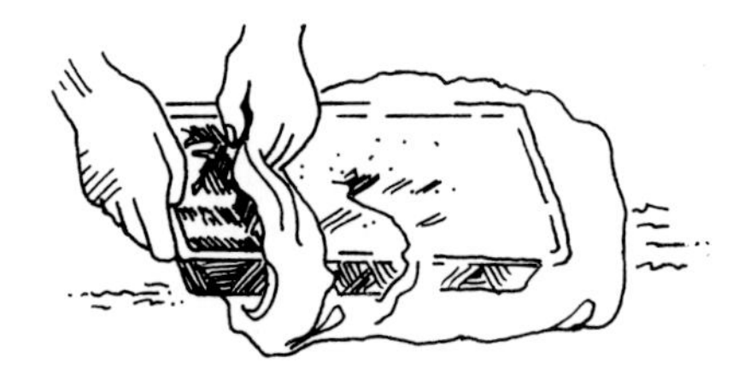

Water lightly and place pan in a plastic bag. Keep your "incubator" at about 75 degrees. Do not water again until seedlings emerge and then only lightly.

When first "true leaves" are formed, remove seedlings from flat and replant in peat pots or peat cubes. Firm in plants and water.

Kind of vegetable	Weeks needed to grow transplants	Seed planting depth	Optimum temperature for germination	Plant-growing temperatures	
				Day	Night
	(weeks)	(inches)	(°F)	(°F)	(°F)
Cabbage, broccoli and cauliflower	5 to 7	¼ to ½	85	60-70	50-60
Lettuce	4 to 6	¼ to ½	75	60-70	50-60
Onions	8 to 10	½	75	60-70	45-55
Tomatoes	5 to 6	¼ to ½	85	70-80	60-65
Peppers	7 to 8	¼ to ½	85	70-80	60-70
Eggplant	7 to 8	¼ to ½	85	70-80	65-70
Cucumber, squash, cantaloupe and watermelon	2 to 3	¾ to 1	85	70-90	60-70

HOW TO USE PLASTIC SHEETING AS A MULCH

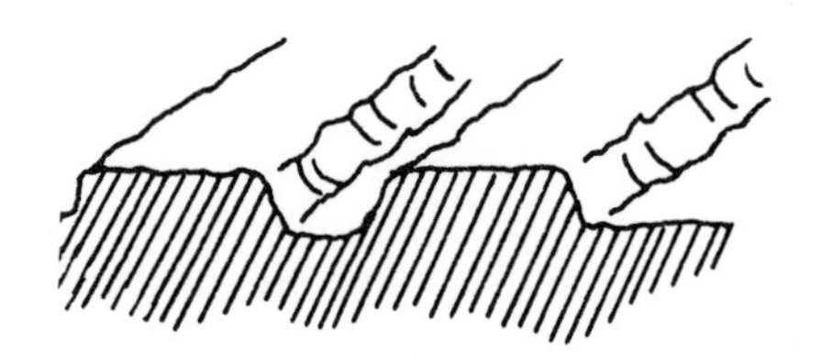

Form raised beds and flatten with garden rake or similar tool.

Cut slits or holes in plastic sheeting at desired spacing.

Cover raised beds with 1 and a half to 2 mil. plastic sheeting. If only small amounts are needed, plastic trash bags are ideal. Do not apply plastic sheeting to soils that are too dry.

Set transplants through the holes and firm in the plant.

After transplanting, water in the plant using a starter solution.

Cover edges of plastic sheeting with soil in order to hold in place.

HOW TO MAKE AND USE CAGES

Cages are nothing more than cylinders made of reinforcing wire, hog wire or a similar material used to support the plant and keep the fruit off the ground. The cylinder should be 18 to 20 inches in diameter and 2 to 5 feet tall. Concrete reinforcing wire is generally considered best and is available in rolls of varying lengths, but most commonly in 5-foot widths. It takes a length of about 5 and a half feet to make a tomato cage 18 inches in diameter. The cages are held together by bending and crimping the ends of the wire around one of the vertical wires.

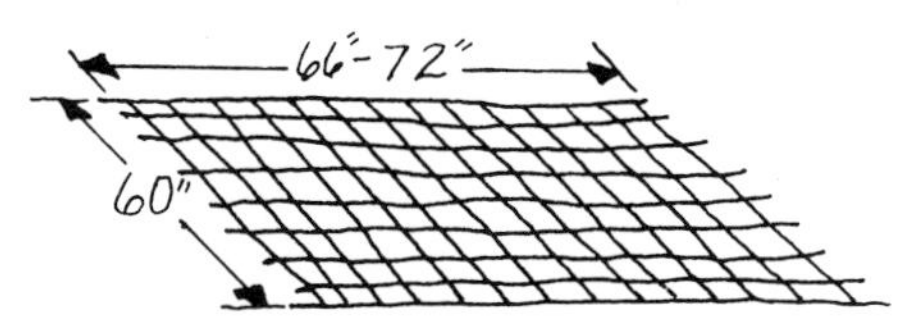

Use a section of concrete reinforcing wire or similar material that is about 60 inches in width and 66 to 72 inches long.

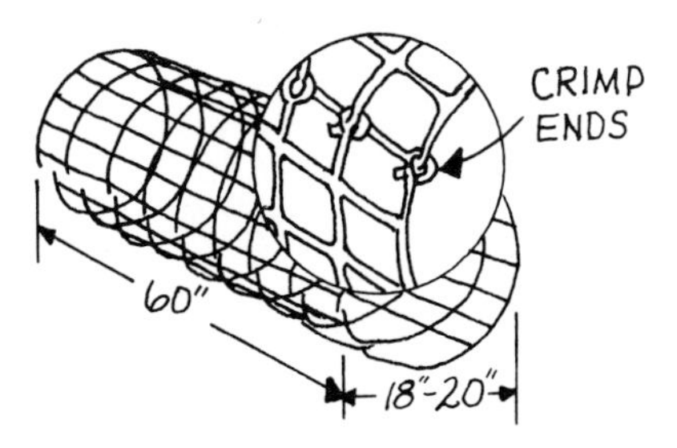

Crimp the ends together to form a cylinder that's about 18 to 20 inches in diameter.

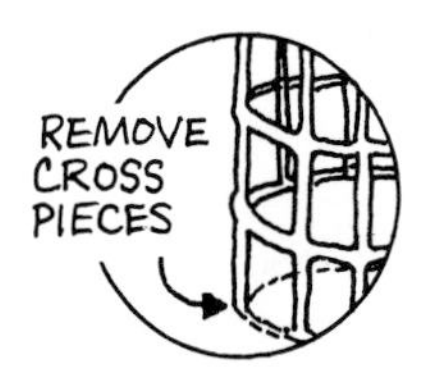

Remove the bottom rung to provide support for the cage and tomato plants.

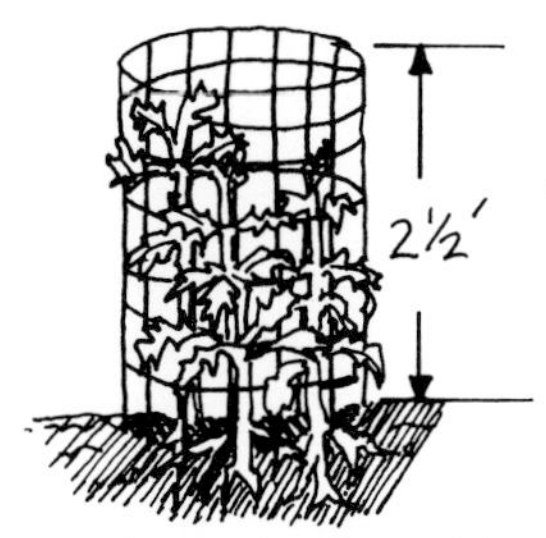

Half cages work great for some of the new bush or determinate type tomatoes.

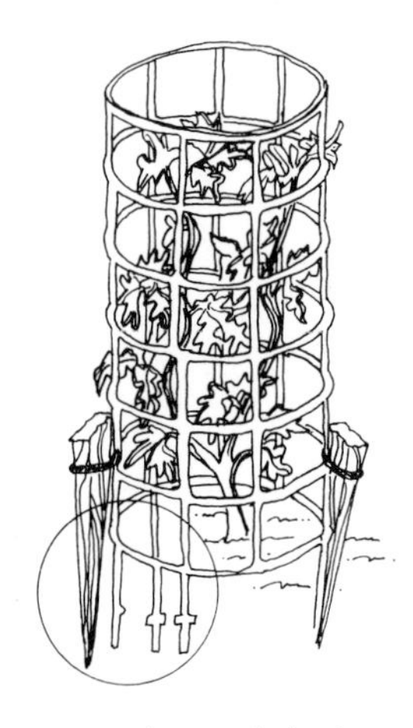

Extra support may be needed to keep taller cages from falling over.

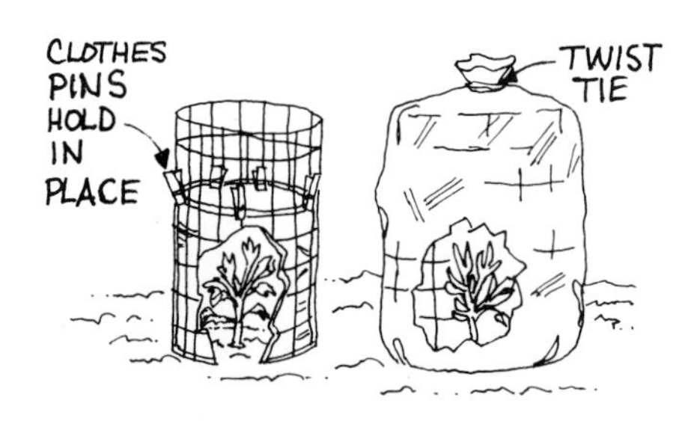

For protection from wind or late cold snap, cover cage with plastic.

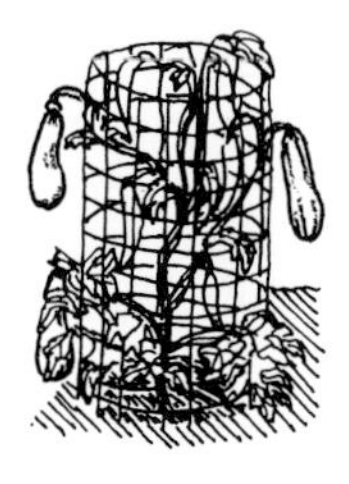

Cucumbers, beans and even cantaloupes can be grown extremely well in cages.

POLLINATING VINE CROPS

The members of the cucumber family—cucumbers, squash, pumpkins, watermelons and cantaloupes—all produce male and female flowers. Pollination is therefore necessary and is usually carried out by bees. Lack of bees; cloudy, wet weather; or improper use of insecticides will result in poor fruit set. You can ensure yourself a good harvest by pollinating the blooms yourself.

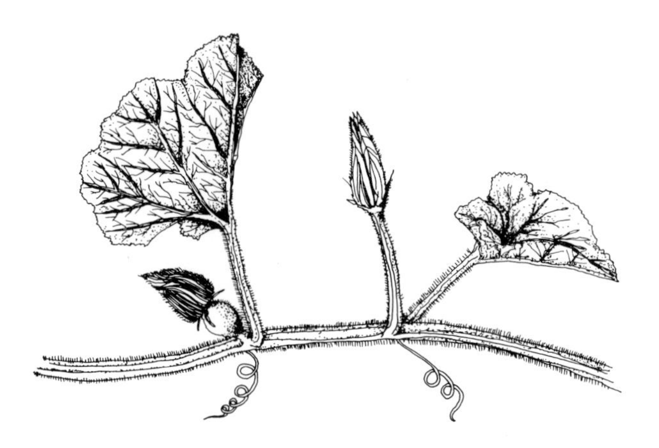

This drawing shows the difference between the female flower, with its round structure called an ovary, and the male, with its longer, thin stem. The male and female blooms are usually open and receptive to pollination for only one day.

You can pollinate the blooms by pulling off a male bloom and dabbing it onto the female bloom, thereby transferring the pollen. One male bloom will pollinate five to eight female blooms.

You can also use a cotton swab or small brush to transfer the dust-like pollen from the male flower to the female flower. This bee-like procedure should occur before 10 a.m. for maximum success.

Within just a matter of days, three to five for squash, you'll be in the garden harvesting.

HOW TO PROTECT PLANTS USING ROW COVERS

For an extra early crop of tomatoes, peppers, eggplants or other vegetables, seed or transplant early and provide protection for the plants.

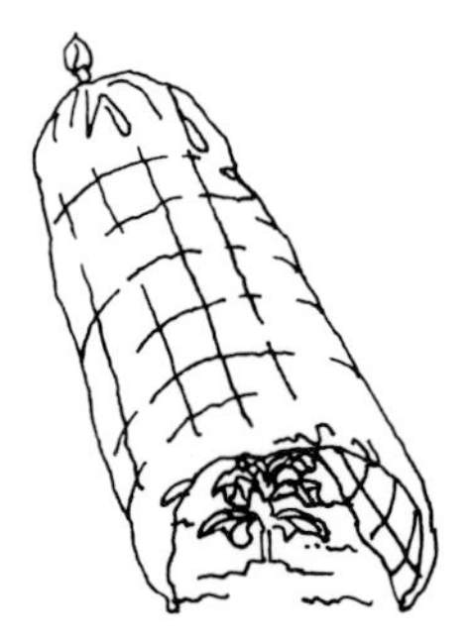

A row cover can be made from concrete reinforcing wire or similar material, covered with clear plastic and placed over the plants.

Fiberglass panels also can be used with great success.

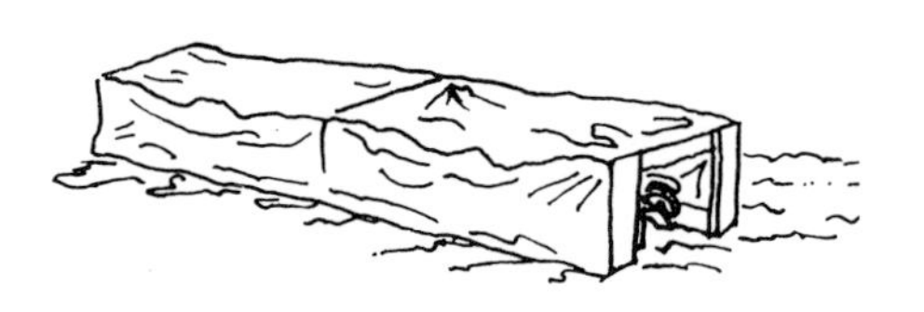

A wooden frame covered with plastic also works well and can be moved around the garden easily.

A crude but effective row cover can be made by simply draping clear plastic or newspapers over an A-frame.

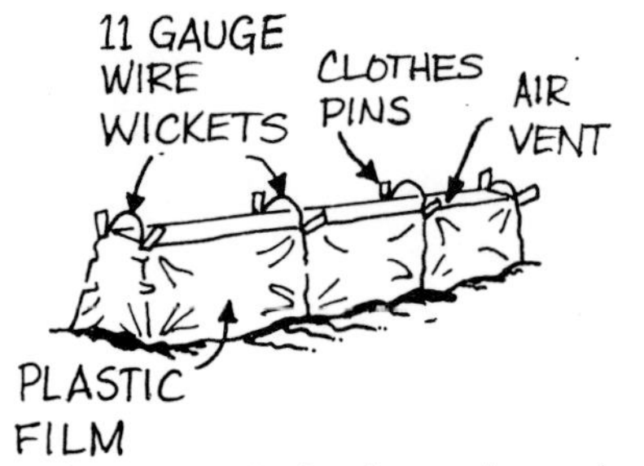

Wire hoops and plastic sheeting can be used for plant protection. Such a system allows the plastic to be lowered and raised, depending upon the weather.

HOW TO SAVE SEED FROM YEAR TO YEAR

To ensure proper identity after storage, leave seed in original packet or place in envelope or paper bag. Be sure and properly label as to variety name, source and date of purchase.

Place tissue containing powdered milk, along with the seed, in an airtight, dry glass jar and seal. Place in refrigerator.

Place 2 tablespoons of powdered milk in tissue paper. Roll and fold as needed to contain powder. Powdered milk will act as a desiccate and prevent moisture build-up in the jar.

Depending upon type of vegetable and viability of the seed, this type of storage conditions will maintain good germination for years.(see table)

REFRIGERATION STORAGE TIME FOR GARDEN SEED

Seed	Years	Seed	Years
Asparagus	3	Lettuce	5
Bean	3	Muskmelon (Cantaloupe)	5
Beet	4	Mustard	4
Broccoli	5	New Zealand spinach	5
Brussels sprouts	5	Okra	2
Cabbage	5	Onion	1 to 2
Carrot	3	Parsley	2
Cauliflower	5	Parsnip	1 to 2
Celeriac	5	Pea	3
Celery	5	Pepper	4
Chard, Swiss	4	Pumpkin	4
Chinese cabbage	5	Radish	5
Collard	5	Rutabaga	5
Corn	1 to 2	Salsify	2
Cucumber	5	Southern pea	3
Eggplant	5	Spinach	5
Endive	5	Squash	5
Kale	5	Tomato	4
Kohlrabi	5	Turnip	5
Leek	3	Watermelon	5

HOW TO BUILD A COLD FRAME

Excavate area for cold frame to a depth of about 6 inches and backfill with 2 inches of gravel and 4 inches of good topsoil or potting soil.

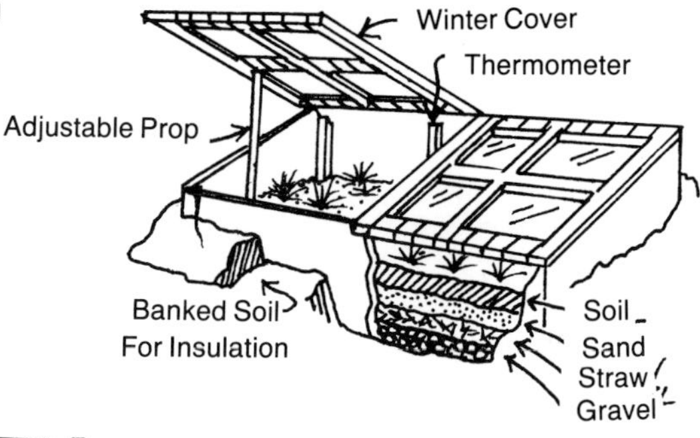

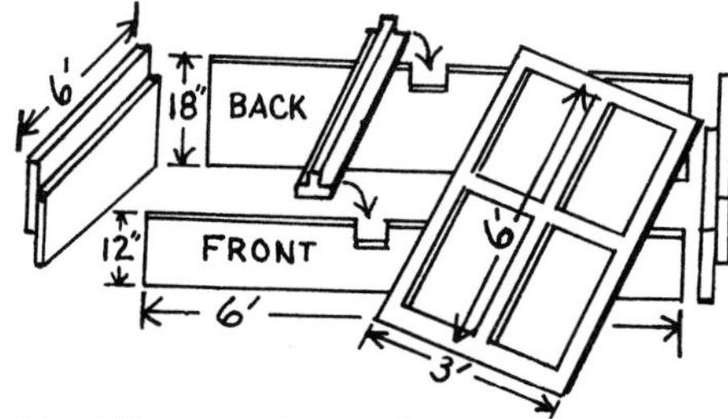

Build cold frame as shown using wood treated with a non-toxic preservative. Standard size 3-by-6-foot sash may be purchased from seed houses or greenhouse supply firms.

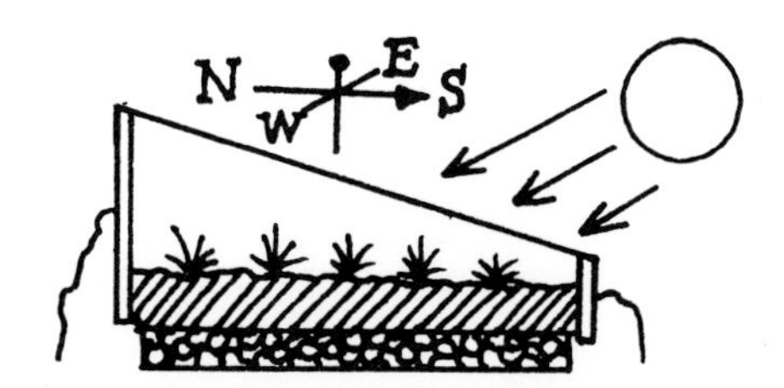

Be sure your cold frame is oriented to the south to take advantage of the warming rays of the sun.

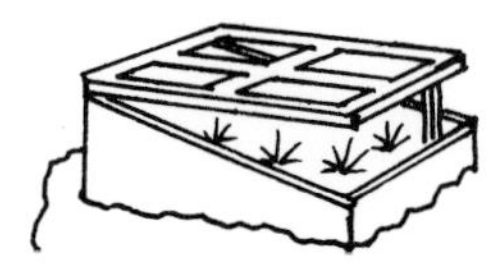

Maintain proper temperature conditions by adjusting the "sash" for ventilation.

HOW TO PREGERMINATE YOUR SEED

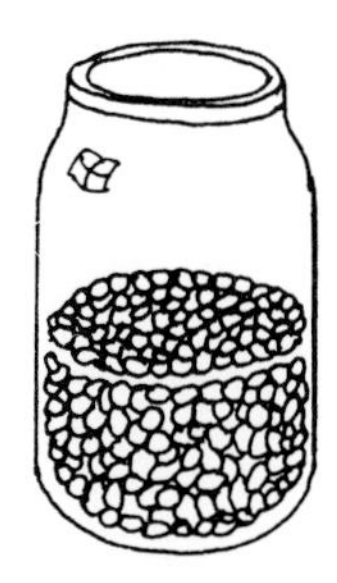

Place seed to be planted in container. Suitable seeds include bean, pea, vine crops, okra and most others.

Fill container with warm tap water, making certain the seed is covered with at least 1 inch of water.

Let soak overnight or perhaps for as long as 48 hours, depending upon the type of vegetable seed.

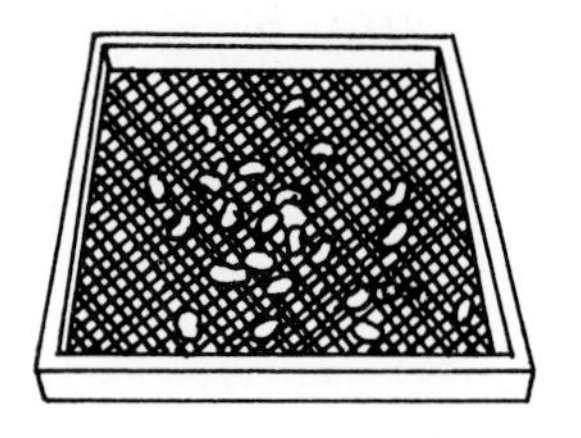

Place seeds on a drying screen or on absorbant towels to help remove excess water. If germination has started, avoid excessive drying and plant immediately.

Use care when planting, as pregerminated seeds are easily damaged.

HOW TO PREVENT CUTWORM DAMAGE

Before using any type methods for cutworm control, check around the plant for the pest. Cutworms are nocturnal and burrow beneath the soil during the day.

Coffee cans and other similar containers provide good control of cutworms.

A small stick placed in contact with the stem of plants and tied with a twist-tie provides excellent protection from cutworms.

If cutworms are found, treating the soil with diazinon, according to label directions, will give good control.

Gallon milk cartons have many uses including good control of cutworms. Bottom of gallon milk carton slit to form a collar for the prevention of cutworms.

Even the top can be used to prevent damage and to catch water.

Removing the bottom of a gallon milk carton and placing it over newly set out transplants provides both cold protection and cutworm prevention.

PREVENT BIRD DAMAGE TO TOMATOES

Various methods are used by home gardeners in an attempt to prevent bird damage to tomatoes. Scarecrows, aluminum pie plates, strings of brightly colored ribbons and various types of noise makers are used. Unfortunately, in a very short period of time, the birds are resting on the shoulders of the scarecrows, swinging on the strings of ribbons, ignoring the noise makers and looking at themselves in the reflective aluminum plates.

What can be done about bird damage? Well, one method that does work is to make use of old stockings or panty hose. This is done by cutting the nylon stockings or panty hose in about 15- to 20-inch lengths. Then one end should be tied shut. Next, the resulting tube should be slipped over a cluster of tomatoes. The open end is closed by using a twist tie or a short piece of string. If the tomatoes are not full size, the elastic nature of the panty hose or stocking will expand as the fruits enlarge. When the fruits ripen they can be easily harvested by untying the closed end and removing the red tomatoes. It's of utmost importance to place the hose or stocking tube over the cluster of tomatoes well before the tomatoes ever start to turn red. If the problem is not anticipated, the birds will get there before you do!

You can also "trick" the birds. When the tomatoes are about seven to 10 days from developing any color, hang several red Christmas tree balls in each of your plants. The birds will peck at the ornaments for a period of time and become frustrated. When your tomatoes do turn ripe, the birds won't be a problem! They will "remember" that the red balls are not tasty!

Another method of protecting tomatoes from bird damage is to harvest them when they are pink rather than full red. You may not believe it, but a tomato picked at the pink stage and ripened at room temperature has exactly the same taste and flavor as one fully ripened on the vine.

HOW TO TEST SEEDS

If you are concerned about the viability of your seed you can test them at home and avoid a lot of concern and at the same time assure yourself of a good stand once planting has occurred. "Germination tests" can be made indoors before the planting season, and thus avoid later problems.

If plenty of seeds are available, it is best to test 100 seeds at a time, although lesser amounts can be used. Place several sheets of paper towels on a flat metal surface (a cookie sheet is ideal) and dampen them. Make sure that the paper towels are thoroughly moistened, but not saturated. Place 100 seeds on the paper towels, spacing them rather than leaving them in a pile or clump. Cover the seeds with several more damp sheets of paper toweling. Keep the seeds at room temperature and sprouting should occur in a few days. Some seeds, such as radishes and mustard will germinate in as little as three days. But others, such as peppers, may take as long as 10 days and some, such as herbs, even longer.

After sufficient time, make a count to determine the number of seeds that have sprouted. If you used 100 seeds, this means that the number of seeds germinated is the percent of germination. If 90 seeds are found germinated, then the percentage of germination is 90. If another amount of seed is used, divide the number of seeds germinated by the total number of seeds tested, and the results will be the percentage of germination.

This simple test can be useful in determining whether or not your seeds are worth planting, and if they are, it gives you an indication of how thickly you should plant the seed. Seeds with a germination percentage of less than 75 percent should be planted thicker than those having a germination percentage of 85 or 90 percent. If the percentage of germination is too low, for example less than 50 percent, the seeds should probably be discarded and new seed purchased for planting.

Fold paper towel double (or use two sheets).

Place a known number of seeds on towel.

Roll towel over seeds. Secure with rubber band or string.

Place in cake pan, moisten or stand in glass containing about 1 inch of water.

Keep moist and check in about seven days. Determine percent of viable seed. Discard seed if percent of good seed is less than 50 percent.

HOW TO ESTABLISH VEGETABLES IN SUMMER HEAT

One problem faced by many Texas gardeners when starting a fall or summer garden is getting vegetable seeds to come up when planted during the heat of summer. This is expecially true for many cold-hardy vegetables, such as lettuce, carrots, broccoli and others that germinate poorly when the soil temperature is high.

It is important to provide a better environment for seeds to germinate and grow into healthy, vigorous seedlings. In most areas of Texas, bed the soil before planting. After the soil has been prepared and the rows marked off, use a hoe handle or stick to make a seed furrow. The seed furrow varies in depth but usually is about 1 inch deep.

Next comes a very important step. After the seed furrow has been made, use a watering can or water hose to apply water *directly* into the seed furrow. Apply sufficient water to wet the loosened soil to a depth of 4 to 6 inches. In some cases this may necessitate applying water several times.

After the water has soaked in, scatter the seeds evenly along the furrow. Always plant more seeds than needed. After planting, do not cover the seeds with garden soil; use a material such as compost, potting soil or peat moss for a covering. By using such a medium, a better environment is provided for seeds to germinate and grow. This eliminates problems associated with soil crusting and poor aeration. Use a light-colored material for a cooler seeding area. With a material like compost seeding depth is still important, but not critical. Small seeds planted a little too deep will still come up. In a few days, depending on the crop planted, seeds should germinate and begin to emerge. At this time do not allow the soil to dry out; apply additional water as needed.

Once plants have emerged, consider applying a protective shade or cover on the west side of the row to shield plants from intensive summer sun. This protection can be a board, cardboard or shade type cloth. Once the plants are 1 to 2 inches tall, thin them to the proper spacing. From this time on, most crops continue to grow and thrive and produce a highly productive crop of fall and winter vegetables.

Instead of covering the seeds with soil, use compost, potting soil, etc. Soil will not crust and the environment for germination is improved. If possible, use a light colored material to reflect heat.

Once the plants emerge, protect the seedlings from the intense sun for several days until they develop several true leaves.

HOW TO CONTROL NEMATODES

Nematodes are small, worm-like animals that live in the soil and feed on decaying organic material, insects, fungi, bacteria or other nematodes. Some forms, however, are plant parasites. Nematodes can be controlled by using several different nonchemical techniques.

(1) "Drying out" the soil, or summer fallowing, is one method. To do this, the garden must be free of any plants or plant roots. It should be spaded or rototilled regularly during the late summer months and kept dry. To live, nematodes require a layer of water around soil particles. When this layer is removed, the nematode dies. Rototilling or spading the soil helps remove soil moisture at a faster rate and also exposes the nematodes and their eggs to the sun's rays which decreases the number of nematodes.

(2) Plant rotation is another method of reducing nematode losses. The principal nematode in gardens is the root knot. This nematode is somewhat restricted in its host range. This characteristic is advantageous to the home gardener who can benefit by alternating non-host with root knot susceptible plants. The only non-host vegetables for use in your garden are onions and related family members, resistant tomato varieties and sweet corn. All other vegetables are susceptible to nematodes.

(3) You can also use cereal rye to control nematodes as shown below:

After first fall frost remove dead plants, apply a light application of complete fertilizer and till or spade area 8 to 10 inches deep.

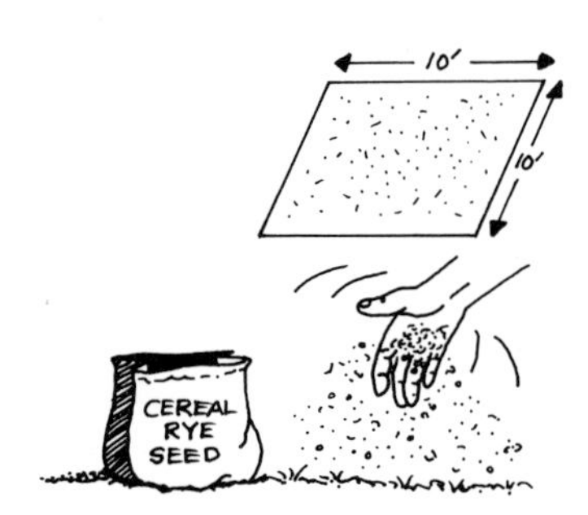

Broadcast 1 to 2 pounds of cereal rye (not annual rye) seeds per 100 square feet, rake lightly and water.

As cereal rye grows during the winter, water if necessary and lightly fertilize to encourage vigorous growth.

About two to six weeks before planting in the spring, shread and till in cereal rye residue. As it decomposes, chemicals are released that kill nematodes.

HOW TO RECOGNIZE NUTRIENT DEFICIENCY SYMPTOMS

Inorganic Elements	Deficiency Symptoms
Nitrogen (N)	Plants stunted, yellowing from bottom up and leaf tip back to petiole. Reduced size. Slow, stunted growth.
Phosphorus (P)	Plants stunted, short internodes, purple or dark green foliage; old leaves die back; flowers and fruit poor. Slow growth, delayed maturity.
Potassium (K)	Older leaves scorched on margin; weak stem; fruit shrivelled, uneven ripening.
Boron (B)	Tip of growing plant dies; bud becomes light green; roots are brown in center; flowers do not form.
Calcium (Ca)	Young leaves turn yellow then brown; growing tip bends; weak stem; short dark roots.
Iron (Fe)	Young leaves are yellow between veins first, top to bottom; veins, margins, and tips stay green.
Magnesium (Mg)	Leaves are thin, lose green color from between veins from bottom of plant up; tend to curve upward.
Manganese (Mn)	Tissue between veins turns white; leaves have dead spots; plant is dwarfed.
Zinc (Zn)	Terminal leaves are small; bud formation is poor; leaves have dead areas.

HOW TO STORE VEGETABLES

Storing vegetables at home is a good and inexpensive way to keep garden-grown vegetables. When stored properly, they keep most of their food value and original flavor. Successful storage depends on: proper choice of crops, careful harvesting and preparation, maintenance of a suitable temperature and humidity, and adequate care during the storage period.

Storage Requirements for Common Vegetables

Commodity	Ideal Temp. ° F	Relative Humidity	Average Storage Life
Asparagus	32	95%	2-3 weeks
Beets	32	95%	1-3 months
Broccoli	32	90-95%	10-14 days
Brussels sprouts	32	90-95%	3-5 weeks
Cabbage	32	90-95%	3-4 months
Cantaloupe	32	85-90%	5-14 days
Carrots	32	90-95%	4-6 months
Cauliflower	32	90-95%	2-4 weeks
Cucumbers	45-50	90-95%	10-14 days
Celery/Celeriac	32	90-95%	2-3 months
Collards/Kale	32	90-95%	10-14 days
Green beans	40-45	90-95%	7-10 days
Eggplant	45-50	90%	1 week
Endive/escarole	32	90-95%	2-3 weeks
Garlic	32	65-70%	6-7 months
Horseradish	30-32	90-95%	10-12 months
Jerusalem artichoke	31-32	90-95%	2-5 months
Kohlrabi	32	90-95%	2-4 weeks
Lettuce	34	95%	2-3 weeks
Leeks	32	90-95%	1-3 months
Okra	45-50	90-95%	7-10 days
Onions	32	65-70%	5-8 months
Parsnips	32	90-95%	2-6 months
Peas	32	90-95%	1-3 weeks
Peppers	45-50	90-95%	8-10 days
Potatoes	38-40	90%	5-8 months
Pumpkins	50-55	70-75%	2-3 months
Rutabaga	32	90-95%	2-4 months
Salsify	32	90-95%	2-4 months
Spinach	32	90-95%	10-14 days
Sweet Potato	55-60	85-90%	4-6 months
Sweet Corn	32	90-95%	4-8 days
Tomatoes	45-50	85-90%	4-7 days
Turnips/Rutabagas	32	90-95%	4-5 months
Radishes	32	90-95%	3-4 weeks
Summer Squash	32-50	90%	5-14 days
Watermelon	40-50	80-85%	2-3 weeks

GLOSSARY

Acclimate—Conditioned or becoming conditioned to a new climate or different growing conditions.

Acid (sour) soil—A soil with a pH below 7.0.

Aeration—The incorporation of air into the soil.

Alkaline (sweet) soil—A soil with a pH above 7.0.

Annual—A plant that completes its life cycle in one year or less and then dies.

Anther—Male part of the flower that contains the pollen grains. A part of the stamen.

Axil (leaf)—The angle or upper side where the leaf is attached to the stem.

Biennial—A plant that grows vegetatively during the first year and fruits and dies the second year.

Blanching—Excluding light to reduce the green color, or chlorophyll development, in plants as with celery, cauliflower and endive.

Blind—A seedling or mature plant that has lost its growing point and therefore ceases to grow.

Bolting—Premature flowering or seedstem formation.

Broadcast—Scattering seed or fertilizer uniformly over the soil surface rather than placing in rows or bands.

Bulb—Storage organ of a plant, composed of fleshy leaf bases wrapped around an embryo shoot or growing point, such as an onion.

Bulbil—A miniature bulb, which forms at the base of a mature bulb or on a stem in a flower head, as in some types of onions.

Buttoning—The formation of very small cauliflower heads, or curds, on small plants, caused by stress or late transplanting of overly mature seedlings.

Calyx—The outer series of modified leaves of a flower which are usually different in appearance from the petals.

Chlorosis—Lack of green color in leaves, caused by nutritional deficiencies, environmental conditions or disease.

Clone—A plant derived from another plant by vegetative propagation, such as grafting, cutting or divisions rather than from seed.

Clove—One of a group of small bulbs produced by garlic and shallots.

Cold frame—An enclosed, unheated but covered frame used to protect plants and extend the growing season. Usually covered with glass or plastic.

Complete fertilizer—One that contains all three of the major nutrients essential for plant growth; nitrogen, phosphorous and potassium.

Compost—Decomposed organic matter used for mulching as well as soil improvement and enrichment.

Corm—Enlarged base of a stem, bulb-like but solid, in which food is accumulated.

Crown—Growing point above the root where the leaves or tops develop as in lettuce, spinach, celery and carrots.

Cruciferae—The mustard or cabbage family of plants, commonly called crucifers.

Crust—A dense layer of surface soil that can form over seedbeds and inhibit emergence and growth of seedlings.

Cultivar—A scientific term for "cultivated variety."

Curd—The clustered flower buds that comprise the cauliflower head.

Cure—To prepare for storing by drying the outer skin, as with onions or sweet potatoes.

Cutting—Plant stem including a node that is cut or snapped from the plant and used to start a new plant.

Day length—Refers to the number of daylight hours needed to induce plants to flower. Most plants are classified as either short day, long day or day neutral.

Damping-off—A soilborne disease causing seedlings to die soon after germination, either before or after emergence from the soil.

Dioecious—Refers to plants that produce male and female flowers on separate individuals.

Direct seeding—Planting seed in the garden rather than setting out transplants.

Dirting—The practice of throwing soil on the plants for the purpose of blanching (celery), providing support (corn), or increasing depth of planting (potato).

Determinate (tomato)—Bush-type growth habit. Caused by stem growth ceasing due to the development of a terminal flower cluster.

Drip irrigation—An efficient watering method which uses plastic pipes or hose to apply small amounts of water, drop by drop, to the soil over a long period of time.

Dormant—Asleep. A dormant seed or plant is one that is in a temporary resting state, usually brought about by adverse climatic conditions.

Eye—Usually used to describe an undeveloped bud on a potato.

Fallow—Leaving a portion of garden unplanted during the growing season for purposes of soil improvement or pest control.

Family—A botanical term used to describe a group of related plants.

Fertilization—(1) Union of the pollen grain with the ovule to produce seeds. (2) Application of nutrients to the soil to encourage vigorous plant growth.

Fertilizer—A material that provides plants with nutrients. A fertilizer can be organic (i.e. derived from plant or animal matter), or inorganic (i.e. made by chemical methods).

Flat—A shallow container in which seeds are sown for later transplanting.

Friable (soil)—Crumbly, neither too moist nor to dry; easily worked.

Fumigation—The application of a chemical to the soil to control insects, diseases and weeds.

Fungicide—A pesticide used to control plant diseases caused by fungi, such as most leaf spots, molds and mildew.

Furrow—Shallow or deep "ditches" used for planting seed or for the application of irrigation water.

Furrow irrigation—The application of water in furrows between rows of vegetables.

Genus—Botanical name for a group of closely related species of plants.

Germination—The first stage in the growth of a plant from seed; sprouting.

Green manure—Plants worked into the soil while still green to provide fertility and to improve the condition of the soil.

Greens—Vegetables such as spinach, collards, kale, turnip and mustard tops.

Growing season—Period from planting to maturity of a particular crop. Also refers to the number of frost-free days per year.

Gynoeicious—A term used to describe plants that produce primarily all female flowers.

Hardy—Refers to plants that are able to withstand temperatures at or below freezing.

Hardening-off—The process of gradually acclimating plants that have been grown in protected areas to outdoor temperatures.

Herbicide—A pesticide used to kill or control weeds.

Hill—Refers to planting several plants or seeds in the same area, such as squash, cucumbers or watermelons.

Hotbed—The same type of structure as a cold frame, but supplied with artificial heat.

Hotcap—Waxpaper cones, sacks, cardboard boxes, plastic jugs, etc., placed over individual plants to provide protection from frost and wind.

Humus—Decomposed organic matter that improves the texture and productive quality of garden soils.

Hybrid—A plant produced by the cross-fertilization of two species or variants of a species.

Hydroponics—A method of growing plants without the use of soil.

Indeterminate (tomato)—Vine type growth habit. The terminal bud always remains vegetative rather than reproductive.

Inflorescence—The floral structure of a plant.

Inhibit—To suppress or inhibit plant growth or development.

Inoculation—Treatment of legume seed with nitrogen-fixing bacteria to stimulate growth.

Inorganic—Usually refers to chemical products (fertilizers); not composed of animal or plant materials.

Insecticide—A pesticide used to control insects.

Intercrop—The process of growing two crops in the same garden area.

Internode—Area of a plant stem between the nodes.

Interplant—The practice of planting an early maturing vegetable between a slower maturing one, such as radishes or lettuce between peppers.

Irrigation—Applying water to the soil by furrow, sprinkler or the use of a drip system.

Lateral—A branch or shoot arising from a larger stem.

Leaching—Loss of soluble minerals due to the result of water washing them out of reach of the plant roots. More of a problem on sandy soils than on heavy soils.

Leggy (plants)—Weak-stemmed and spindly plants with sparse foliage.

Legumes—Members of the *Leguminosae* family of plants, such as peas and beans.

Lifting—Digging a plant for consumption, replanting or storage.

Light soil—A soil having a sandy or course texture.

Lime (limestone)—A compound containing calcium and/or magnesium, applied to the soil to reduce acidity.

Loam—Soils that consist of sand, silt and clay, usually well- suited for vegetable culture.

Manure (barnyard)—Animal waste used as a source of fertility and as a soil conditioner.

Mildew—Refers to any number of plant diseases causing dusty or downy fungal growth on leaves, stems and fruit.

Mite (spider mite)—Very small sucking insects (spiders) that infest many garden vegetables. Commonly found on tomatoes, beans and eggplants during warm, dry weather.

Monoecious—Refers to plants having both male and female flowers on the same plant, such as squash and watermelons.

Mosaic—A collective term used to describe virus diseases of plants.

Mulch—Materials applied to the soil surface to conserve soil moisture, stabilize soil temperature, prevent erosion and control weeds.

Nematode—A microscopic, worm-like animal that attacks the root system of plants causing stunted and unhealthy growth.

Nitrogen—One of the nutrients essential for growth and green color of plants. Designated by the letter N.

Nitrogen fixation—Refers to the ability of certain root inhabiting bacteria to transform atmospheric nitrogen into a form usable by plants.

Node—That part of a stem that normally produces leaves or buds.

Nodules—Small, round swellings on the roots of legumes containing bacteria, which fix atmospheric nitrogen that can be used by the plant.

Nutrients—Mineral elements used by the plant in its growth and development.

Nymph An immature insect, resembling the adult stage, but usually without wings and reproductive organs.

Organic (fertilizer)—Materials composed of naturally occurring substances which when added to the soil provide nutrients for plant growth and development.

Ovary—The part of the flower in which the seeds are formed. Usually thought of as the immature fruit or seed pod.

Ovule—An unfertilized seed in an ovary.

Parasite—Plant or insect that attaches itself to another organism for the purpose of obtaining nourishment.

Parthenocarpic—Able to produce fruit without pollination. Such fruits are usually seedless.

Peat (moss)—Partially decomposed plant material taken from bogs and used as a rooting medium, soil conditioner or mulch.

Perennial—A plant which normally lives more than two years.

Perlite—White expanded volcanic rock in a ground form. Used in many potting soils.

Pesticide—General term for any chemical used to control pests.

pH—A numerical scale for measuring the acidity or alkalinity of the soil, ranging from 1 to 14. Acid soils have a pH of less than 7.0 while those greater than 7.0 are alkaline. A soil with a pH of 7.0 is neutral.

Phosphorous—One of the three major nutrients, designated by the letter P.

Pistil—The female organ of a flower consisting of the stigma, style and ovary.

Pollen—Reproductive material, usually dust-like which is produced by the male part of the flower.

Pollination—The transfer of pollen from the male to the female part of a flower.

Potassium—One of the three major nutrients, designated by the letter K.

Propagation—Increasing the number of plants by planting seed or by vegetative means from cuttings, divisions, grafting or layering.

Resistance—Ability to restrict disease or insect damage; can withstand severe climatic conditions.

Respiration—Chemical process involving absorption of oxygen from the air followed by the release of carbon dioxide.

Rhizome—A lateral growing stem possessing nodes that grow on or just below the soil surface. Sometimes a food storage organ of the plant.

Root—That part of the plant growing into the soil for the purpose of support and the absorption of moisture and nutrients.

Seedbed—Well-prepared area to be planted in seed or transplants.

Seedling—Young plant just following germination and emergence.

Side-dressing—Applying fertilizer on the soil surface to the side of plants so that light cultivation and/or watering will move it into the root zone.

Side-shoots—The smaller, secondary heads of broccoli that form after the central or main head has been harvested.

Silt—Soil particles that are between sand and clay in size.

Slips—Similar to a cutting. A method of propagating plants, such as the sweet potato.

Staking—Tying plants such as the tomato to a stake to provide support, keeping the fruit off the ground.

Starter solution—A fertilizer solution applied at the time of transplanting.

Stolon—A slender, prostrate underground stem. In potatoes, the tubers form at the end of stolons.

Stress (water)—Occurs when plants are unable to absorb enough water to replace that lost by transpiration. Causes wilting and, if severe, death of the plant.

Subsoil—The soil directly beneath the topsoil, from which it is usually derived. Usually infertile and of poor quality.

Succession planting—The practice of growing two or more vegetables per season in the same place.

Susceptible—Inability to restrict activities of insects or diseases; cannot withstand adverse environmental conditions.

Tamping—Lightly firming raised beds over the seed row or around newly set transplants to consolidate the soil particles.

Tendril—Highly modified leaf having the ability to grasp objects which results in some plants having the ability to climb.

Texture (soil)—Proportional amounts of sand, silt, clay and organic matter in a soil, i.e. sandy loam, silty clay, etc.

Thinning—Removing small plants to allow those remaining to have sufficient space to grow and develop.

Tilth—Refers to the physical condition of the soil. A soil having "good tilth" can be easily worked and cultivated.

Topsoil—The uppermost layer of soil, usually 2 to 24 inches deep.

Trace elements—Minerals essential for plant growth, but required only in small amounts. Also called "minor elements."

Training—Providing direction to the growth of plants such as cucumbers, watermelons and cantaloupes. Can also refer to "staking and training" tomatoes.

Transpiration—The loss of water into the atmosphere through openings called stomates found on the leaves of plants.

Transplanting—Moving a plant from one location and planting it in another.

Tuber—A swollen, underground stem used primarily for food storage. The edible portion of a potato is a tuber.

Tuberous roots—Thickened roots differing from tubers in that they lack nodes and internodes and buds are present only on the stem end. Sweet potatoes are tuberous roots.

Vernalization—The induction of flowering of plants as a result of exposure to cold temperatures.

Vermiculite—Heat expanded mica commonly used in synthetic potting soils.

Virus—An ultra-microscopic organism which invades cells, resulting in irreversible damage to the plants.

Weed—A plant growing out of place. A tomato plant in a cotton field would be a weed.

Wettable powder—A pesticide formulated with a filler and wetting agent to permit mixing with water.

Wetting agent—A material added to a pesticide to reduce surface tension and, thereby aid in its distribution and coverage of the plant.

INDEX